CHROMATIUS OF AQUILEIA

SERMONS AND TRACTATES ON MATTHEW

Ancient Christian Writers

THE WORKS OF THE FATHERS IN TRANSLATION

No. 75

CHROMATIUS OF AQUILEIA

SERMONS AND TRACTATES ON MATTHEW

TRANSLATED AND INTRODUCED
BY
THOMAS P. SCHECK

THE NEWMAN PRESS
New York / Mahwah, NJ

Book design by Lynn Else

Library of Congress Cataloging-in-Publication Data
Names: Chromatius, Saint, -407, author. | Scheck, Thomas P., 1964– translator.
Title: Sermons and tractates on Matthew / Chromatius of Aquileia ; translated and introduced by Thomas P. Scheck.
Description: New York ; Mahwah, NJ : Newman Press, 2018. | Series: Ancient Christian writers; 75 | Includes bibliographical references and index.
Identifiers: LCCN 2017044263 (print) | LCCN 2018020677 (ebook) | ISBN 9781587687228 (ebook) | ISBN 9780809106462 (hardcover : alk. paper)
Subjects: LCSH: Bible. Matthew—Sermons. | Bible—Sermons.
Classification: LCC BS2575.54 (ebook) | LCC BS2575.54 .C47 2018 (print) | DDC 226.2/06—dc23
LC record available at https://lccn.loc.gov/2017044263

ISBN 978-0-8091-0646-2 (hardcover)
ISBN 978-1-58768-722-8 (e-book)

Published by The Newman Press
an imprint of Paulist Press
997 Macarthur Boulevard
Mahwah, New Jersey 07430

www.paulistpress.com

PRINTED AND BOUND IN THE UNITED STATES OF AMERICA

To James I. McAuley, Esq., my Ukrainian Greek Catholic attorney friend from western New York, who first suggested that I translate saint Chromatius; and to Ladislav Sallai, professor of chemistry at Ave Maria University, who has been my very dear Slovak friend since 2008

In memory of my dear son Luke (1995–2017)

CONTENTS

ABBREVIATIONS

AA	Ad Antica Altoadriatoco
ACC	Ancient Christian Commentary on Scripture
ANF	Ante-Nicene Fathers
CCSL	Corpus Christianorum Series Latina (Turnhout: Brepols, 1953–)
CSEL	Corpus Scriptorum Ecclesiasticorum Latinorum (Vienna, 1866–1957)
CWE	Collected Works of Erasmus (Toronto: University of Toronto Press, 1974–)
DCB	*A Dictionary of Christian Biography*, ed. W. Smith and H. Wace, 4 vols. (London, 1877–87)
EEC	*Encyclopedia of the Early Church*, ed. A. Di Berardino, 2 vols. (New York: Oxford University Press, 1992)
Ep	Epistle
FOTC	Fathers of the Church (Washington, DC: Catholic University of America Press, 1947–)
GCS	Die Griechischen Christlichen Schriftsteller
HE	Eusebius's *Historia Ecclesiastica*
HThR	*Harvard Theological Review*
JECS	*Journal of Early Christian Studies*
JTS	*Journal of Theological Studies*
In Mt	Hilary's *Commentary on Matthew*
In Ps	Hilary's *Commentary on the Psalms*
L & S	*Lewis and Short's Latin Dictionary* (Oxford: Clarendon, 1879, 1993)
NPNF1	Nicene and Post-Nicene Fathers, first series

NPNF2	Nicene and Post-Nicene Fathers, second series
OCD	*The Oxford Classical Dictionary*, ed. S. Hornblower and A. Spawforth, 3rd ed. (New York: Oxford University Press, 1996)
PG	Patrologia graeca, ed. J. P. Migne (Paris, 1844–64)
PL	Patrologia latina, ed. J. P. Migne (Paris, 1844–64)
RSV	Revised Standard Version
SC	Sources Chrétiennes
Vir Ill	Jerome's *De viris illustribus*

INTRODUCTION

Saint Chromatius, bishop of Aquileia (345?–407?),[1] is an excellent witness to the faith of the church at the end of the fourth and beginning of the fifth centuries.[2] In spite of his relative obscurity (until recently) and the ill-fated way his writings were frequently attributed to others (to Jerome, Ambrose, John Chrysostom, and Augustine) for most of the church's history, his *Sermons* are edifying specimens of ancient Christian homilies on a variety of scriptural persons and themes; and his *Tractates on Matthew* amount to an impressive Christian commentary on the first eighteen chapters of Matthew's Gospel, with the most detailed coverage given to chapters 1—9. Both works reveal the formative influence of saints Ambrose of Milan (339–97) and Hilary of Poitiers (315–68). In spite of his simpler Latin style[3] in comparison with his more famous contemporaries, in my judgment Chromatius deserves to be ranked alongside the great Latin patristic gospel expositors Hilary, Ambrose, Jerome, and Augustine. Pope Benedict XVI's decision, in 2007, to include saint Chromatius in his Wednesday audiences in which he gave catechesis on the church fathers[4] was an auspicious one for Chromatius's reputation. I will summarize Pope Benedict XVI's sympathetic reception below. To my knowledge, the present volume contains the first complete English translation of saint Chromatius's *Sermons* and *Tractates on Matthew* to be published.[5]

Aquileia

Aquileia, obscure today perhaps but very well known in antiquity, is a city in Italy at the north end of the Adriatic Sea on the River Natiso, founded by the Romans circa 181 BC.[6] Its name was given to it from an omen that occurred at the time of its foundation in the form of an appearance of an eagle.[7] Aquileia had a safe harbor and was protected from the Adriatic by navigable lagoons. It quickly rose to prominence and attained great wealth and prosperity as the site of major commerce and trade. Its location was favorable: it was at the entrance of Italy and at the foot of the pass of Mount Ocra, which was the easiest passage from the northeast into the Italian plains. Aquileia became a trade center with the barbarian tribes of the mountains and on the Danube and its tributaries. After the provinces of Illyria and Pannonia had been permanently united to the Roman Empire, the increased involvement between the east and west added to Aquileia's commercial prosperity and importance. In imperial times it was a colony, sometimes dubbed *Roma secunda,* the second Rome. It was the capital of Venetia and Istria and grew into one of the world's largest cities, with an estimated population of one hundred thousand. This included a significant Jewish population. It was also strategically located from a military point of view. In AD 168, Marcus Aurelius made Aquileia the principal fortress of the empire against the barbarians of the north and east. Though situated in a plain, Aquileia was strongly fortified with walls and towers, and seems to have enjoyed the reputation of an impregnable fortress.

By the middle of the fourth century AD, Aquileia was ranked as the ninth of the great cities of the Roman Empire and was surpassed among those of Italy only by Milan and Capua. During the later years of the empire, it was the scene of several decisive events. In 340, the younger Constantine was defeated and slain on the banks of the river Alsa, almost beneath Aquileia's walls. In 388, it witnessed the defeat and death of the usurper Maximus by Theodosius the Great. A church council was held in Aquileia in 381 under the presidency of the Aquileian bishop Valerian and the leadership of Ambrose of Milan. Chromatius took part as Valerian's assistant. Eventually in 452, Aquileia was besieged by Attila, king of the Huns, and was finally taken by assault, plundered, and burned to the ground. It never again became a place of any importance.[8] Today Aquileia is a city of about five thousand inhabitants, filled with Roman ruins and also a beautiful and ancient basilica.

Life and Career of Saint Chromatius of Aquileia

Chromatius was probably a native of the city. Recent scholarship conjectures that he may have been born as early as 337 and may have studied in Rome between the ages of twelve and twenty.[9] He first appears in the historical record circa 369, when he is known to have baptized Rufinus of Aquileia, the most productive ancient Latin translator of Greek patristic works.[10] Chromatius resided there with his widowed mother, his brother Eusebius, and his unmarried sisters. This "protoascetic community" of which Jerome had been a part gathered at least from 369 to 372. Chromatius was the friend and correspondent of Ambrose, Jerome, Rufinus, and other leading ecclesiastics, and in later years was a firm supporter of John Chrysostom against his eastern assailants.[11] One of Jerome's early letters (374) is addressed to him.

> I salute your mother and mine with the respect which, as you know, I feel towards her. Associated with you as she is in a holy life, she has the start of you, her holy children, in that she is your mother. Her womb may thus be truly called golden. With her I salute your sisters, who ought all to be welcomed wherever they go, for they have triumphed over their sex and the world, and await the Bridegroom's coming, their lamps replenished with oil. O happy the house which is a home of a widowed Anna, of virgins that are prophetesses, and of twin Samuels bred in the Temple! Fortunate the roof which shelters the martyr-mother of the Maccabees, with her sons around her, each and all wearing the martyr's crown! For although you confess Christ every day by keeping His commandments, yet to this private glory you have added the public one of an open confession; for it was through you that the poison of the Arian heresy was formerly banished from your city.[12]

The reference to the suppression of the Arian heresy anticipates by seven years Chromatius's participation, while still a presbyter, in the council held at Aquileia, against the Arians Palladius and Secundianus in September 381. This council was called by the Western emperor Gratian at the behest of Ambrose of Milan. The minutes of the council record Chromatius's interventions in the proceedings.[13] On the death of Valerian, Chromatius became bishop of his native city, circa 388. He occupied this office at least until 407, traditionally regarded as the date of his death.[14]

Chromatius was pastorally active with many of his more famous contemporaries. It was at Chromatius's request that saint Ambrose expounded the prophecy of Balaam in an epistolary form.[15] Several of Jerome's translations of Scripture (e.g., Tobit, Prov, Eccl, Song, and Chron) and commentaries on the books of OT (commentaries on Habakkuk and Jonah) are indebted to Chromatius's insistence and monetary support. A number of contemporary figures, including Augustine and Rufinus, were disturbed by Jerome's interest in Hebrew philology and his translation work based on the Hebrew text of the Old Testament. They tried to dissuade him from Hebrew studies and even accused him of Judaizing, of tampering with the Old Latin translation that was in use in the Christian churches, a translation that had been made from what they considered to be the divinely inspired and infallible Greek Septuagint. In striking contrast with these critics, Chromatius belonged to the limited circle of Jerome's friends who understood his motives, applauded his principles, and encouraged his efforts in translating and expounding the Hebrew text of the Old Testament.[16] Yet, simultaneously, the magnanimous and scholarly Chromatius was also a lifelong friend and supporter of Rufinus of Aquileia (345–411), whom he had baptized around 370.[17] Moreover, when the friendship between Rufinus and Jerome was ruptured upon the publication of Rufinus's translation of Origen's *De Principiis* in 398, Chromatius maintained his friendship with both men and did his best to reconcile them. It is noteworthy that a number of Chromatius's *Sermons* and *Tractates* emphasize the importance of fraternal charity and unanimity.[18] Additionally, Chromatius even commissioned Rufinus with the task of translating the *Ecclesiastical History* of Eusebius into Latin, together with Origen's *Homilies on Joshua,* and he became the dedicatee of these works. If Chromatius was interested in seeing the Greek Origen and the Greek Eusebius made accessible to Latin readers in this manner, then he must have been favorably disposed to these writers. This is confirmed by the theological parallels between Chromatius's expositions and Origen's *Homilies on Exodus, Leviticus,* and *Joshua,* which are documented in the endnotes. It is also confirmed by Rufinus's preface to Origen's *Homilies on Joshua,* where he says that Chromatius has enjoined him to offer something for the building and construction of the divine tabernacle from the wealth and riches of the Greeks. Rufinus says further that he defers entirely to Chromatius's judgment in assessing the quality of Origen's offering. Judging from the evident correspondence between Origen and Chromatius's allegorical treatments of Leviticus, Joshua, and Judges, it appears that the Aquileian bishop assessed Origen's contributions favorably, in a manner similar to saint Ambrose's reception of Origen.[19] Here I might add that the critical edition used for the present translation omits mention of Origen's *Homilies and Commentary on the Song of Songs*, translated by Jerome and Rufinus respectively, but I believe that there is significant overlap between Origen's allegorical application of this wisdom book and Chromatius's exegesis. Moreover, there is evidence that Chromatius was influenced by Rufinus's translation of Origen's *Commentary on the Epistle to the Romans*, which was published in 406.[20] This too is left unmentioned in the CCSL critical edition. Hopefully future scholarship will explore all these connections in greater detail.

Finally, and in my judgment a matter of great importance, in the persecution of saint John Chrysostom (347–407) by Bishop Theophilus of Alexandria, which resulted in Chrysostom being deposed from his See of Constantinople in 404 on the trumped-up charge of Origenism, Chromatius warmly embraced John's cause and defended him in the West. The stature of Chromatius in the West is indicated by Chrysostom's mention of his name along with those of Innocent, bishop of Rome, and Venerius, bishop of Milan, in his protest addressed to the Western church.[21] In response Chromatius sent Chrysostom a letter of sympathy by the hands of the Western deputation, and in 406, he received from John a letter of grateful thanks.[22] Chromatius also wrote on Chrysostom's behalf to Emperor Honorius, who forwarded his letter to his brother Arcadius as an evidence of the sentiments of the Western church.[23] This involvement seems to confirm Chromatius's stature as one of the highest ranking ecclesiastics in his day, who was consulted for leadership in times of crisis. It is rather disconcerting to realize that in this same Chrysostom controversy, saint Jerome of Stridon was deeply entrenched on the side opposite Chromatius. Jerome was a radically loyal supporter of Bishop Theophilus of Alexandria, Chrysostom's (and Origen's) great enemy. In 404, after driving Chrysostom into exile, Theophilus composed an invective "of hysterical violence," denouncing Chrysostom as a "foul murderer, an enemy of the human race, a godless priest who made sacrilegious offerings, a blasphemer of Christ who should share the fate of Judas."[24] On his own initiative Jerome translated Theophilus's letter into Latin and thus made it available to the West.[25] I cannot imagine that Chromatius would have approved of such an action by

Jerome, but Jerome is known to have ignored Chromatius's advice on other occasions.[26]

Traditionally Chromatius's death is placed in 407, shortly after the Gothic invasion under Alaric and his brother-in-law Athaulfus, but on this date see below.

Surviving Writings of Chromatius

Neither Jerome nor Gennadius mentions any literary activity of Chromatius in their respective surveys of Christian authors. Jerome's work *De viris illustribus* dates to 392, and yet even by 398, Jerome fails to mention Chromatius in the preface to his *Commentary on Matthew* when he records his literary predecessors. This is not necessarily decisive evidence, since Jerome sometimes ignores his predecessors. But it does lead some scholars tentatively to infer that Chromatius's *Tractates on Matthew* may have been published after Jerome's *Commentary on Matthew* (398). Thus a date between 398 and 400 for Chromatius's *Tractates on Matthew* seems plausible. On the other hand, in Jerome's *Commentary on Matthew* there are a number of disparaging references to interpretations that Jerome rejects, interpretations that resemble Chromatius's own thoughts found in the *Tractates.*[27] Could this imply Jerome's direct familiarity with Chromatius's work?

Until quite recently, the bulk of Chromatius's surviving corpus remained unknown. Since 1960 however, thanks to the diligence of two priests, R. Étaix and J. Lemarié, Chromatius's *Sermons* and *Tractates on Matthew* have been brought to light. A French translation of the *Sermons* by H. Tardif appeared in 1969 and 1971 in SC 154, 164, edited by Lemarié, a French Benedictine who spent countless hours studying manuscripts and recognized similarities between a group of sermons in the manuscript *Paris Biblithèque Nationale Latin 742* and *5132.*[28] These two groups of sermons contained the beginning of a sermon on the martyrs Felix and Fortunatianus and made a reference to Aquileia. Lemarié then compared the sermons in terms of language, style, and content to the extant versions of Chromatius's *Tractates on Matthew.* He identified and published the first seventeen sermons as Chromatius's. The collection grew to the relatively stable collection of forty-one sermons. In his magisterial introduction, Lemarié discusses the points of theological importance in Chromatius's expositions.

Saint Athanasius (296–373) had lived in Aquileia in 345 and wielded influence there. Certainly Chromatius perpetuates the Nicene orthodoxy for which Athanasius had battled and suffered.[29] Even more so, Chromatius was a disciple of saint Ambrose of Milan, who had consecrated him to the episcopacy and whose writings loom large in the marginalia of the present edition. Generally Chromatius adopts Ambrose's interpretations and theological perspective. Lemarié emphasizes the simple yet elegant style of Chromatius's sermons. His Latin betrays a classical training, yet he never rises to classical heights. He is never abstract; his language lacks affectation and is spontaneous and clear. His sermons make use of analogies drawn from common life and connect with the listeners. Lemarié identifies the following passages (in Latin) as examples of Chromatius's moving and well-balanced mode of expression:

S 3.6: "The salvation of believers is the food [*esca*] of the saints."

S 3.6: "For Peter hungered not in order to set his thoughts on earthly food, but he was hungry to save the souls of those who believe in Christ."

S 5.4: "In respect to the world those who are like this seem poor, but they are rich in God. They do not have earthly means, but they have heavenly blessing."

S 9.1: "The very reason they accept death on Christ's behalf is so that they may remain forever in the church of Christ. For the death of martyrs is the beautiful adornment of the church, and the crown of virtue."

S 13.1: "The stoning of the prophets is an injury to Christ, and the death of the prophets is his death."

S 15.2: "The victory of the cross consists in faith in the Trinity."

S 15.4: "But he took off the tunic of his flesh, in order to cover our nakedness. Ultimately, the one tunic of the body of Christ has clothed the entire world."

S 15.5: "[Peter] did not refuse Christ's service, in order to have fellowship with Christ."

S 17.2: "For death, which was used to winning, was defeated by the death of the victor."

S 18.3: "Therefore the fleshly birth is from man; the spiritual birth is from God."

S 20.1: "For when we believe in Christ, we become foreigners to the world, so that we may be deemed members of God's household. Foreigners to the earth, citizens of heaven; last in the world, neighbors of Christ."

S 27.2: "Therefore the Lord's tears are the world's joys, since the reason he shed tears was so that we might merit the joys."

S 29.2: "He rescued Peter from death who vanquished death itself."

S 30.2: "For the death of one became the life of all."

S 31.2: "For the wounds of the Lord's passion have become the medicine of human salvation."

These simple but rhetorically effective expressions deserve mention simply by virtue of the fact that they were compiled by Chromatius's great modern rescuer from oblivion. I might add a memorable passage from S 3.2 that has a touch of sarcasm: "But perhaps some say that they cannot fast because of their stomachs. Is it because of your stomach that you don't give alms?"

Simonetti describes as the most obvious characteristic of Chromatius's exegesis the constant tendency to connect the scriptural text under interpretation with Old Testament passages. "He does this not so much to derive an allegorical interpretation from this juxtaposition as to underscore the unity of revelation, demonstrating how much of the Gospel message had been presaged and anticipated by the prophets and other figures of the Old Testament."[30] Chromatius is the source of the maxim, "Spiritual meanings are multiple."[31] He explains the biblical texts literally, allegorically, and morally, exhorting his hearers to virtue and to the avoidance of sin. Even when he engages doctrinal matters and opposes heresy, he does so more with ecclesial interests than with a speculatively christological and philosophical focus. His discussion of the Christian life features more prominently than interest in the sacraments, though there is a prominent focus on the sacrament of baptism in a number of sermons.[32]

Lemarié indicates that the sermon on the dedication of the new basilica in Concordia reflects the intense devotion to the saints and the manner in which their relics acted as connecting points of the local people to the broader reality.[33] This must have mirrored what Ambrose had done in Milan in 386–87, which shows the liturgical connection between Milan and Aquileia. Lizzi confirms this connection as follows:

> Chromatius's episcopal policy was, in fact, broadly inspired by Ambrose's directives, as is shown by the very large number of churches and martyria consecrated by Chromatius in Aquileia;[34] in terms of magnificence and numbers they can only be compared to those erected in Milan by Ambrose. This is also confirmed by Chromatius's sermons (some of which were formerly attributed to Ambrose), a very important source for the students of Christianization in and around Aquileia.[35]

Yves-Marie Duval also supports this scholarly motif by emphasizing Aquileia's Eastern orientation.[36] He argues that the threat of the resurgence of Arianism was real during Chromatius's tenure as bishop, and therefore his antiheresy polemic emerged from sincere concerns.[37]

One recent writer and translator of Chromatius is convinced that Arianism had already become extinct in Aquileia when Chromatius assumed the episcopacy in 388, and therefore his sermonizing against this perceived heretical threat was contrived. According to Robert McEachnie, Chromatius deploys his ecclesiastical power in order to demonize his opponents, "even just the memory of these opponents." Chromatius "constructed orthodoxy not simply by drawing a line in the sand, but by moving the goalposts."[38] Chromatius "intentionally forgot the past in order to frame the present."[39] He "constructed orthodoxy as a preexistent state."[40] McEachnie concludes his study:

> Chromatius's sermons reflected the growing size and power of an institutional church in his attempts to dominate the urban religious space. His rhetoric is indicative of shift from private, pluralistic religious arena to the monolithic, highly public medieval one. Chromatius created a power structure with the bishop at the head, battling perceived threats by drawing on his interpretation of Christian history, not unlike an Eusebius of Rufinus [*sic*].[41]

Although it does not seem strictly accurate to speak of Chromatius "creating a power structure with the bishop at the head," still there may be more than a grain of truth in McEachnie's last clause. Philip Amidon has recently observed that Rufinus of Aquileia made alterations to Eusebius when he translated his *History of the Church* into Latin (having been commissioned to translate this work by Chromatius). Whereas Eusebius does speak of a church united in doctrine and practice throughout its generations in the variety of its circumstances, Rufinus tries to accentuate the unity by muffling any hint of alteration in faith and order throughout the Christian centuries among those in communion with reputable bishops.

> For him [Rufinus] the one faith of Christianity is that declared by the Council of Nicaea of 325, whose creed and canons are the final documents he cites in his history. Their crowning place at the beginning of his continuation suggest their sufficiency as the constitution of the church. All passages of even the mildest subordinationist flavor in the original version of Eusebius's history are overwritten with a broad pro-Nicene nib.[42]

Amidon then very helpfully documents numerous examples of Rufinus "overwriting" Eusebius's words by his sometimes paraphrastic mode of translation. In my judgment this does not undermine the essential continuity between Rufinus and Eusebius's Christianity.

Granting this tendency on Rufinus's part, which I am quite certain he shared with many of his Latin contemporaries, it is not necessarily entirely helpful to read ancient Christian sermons solely in terms of orthodoxy's will to dominate, as McEachnie seems to do. This may oversimplify things and misunderstand why Chromatius actually wrote and delivered his sermons. To Chromatius, communion among churches is important, and schism and heresy affect the entire church. It is revealing that McEachnie admits that Chromatius's conception of heresy is faithful to the teaching of the New Testament Book of Acts, "which Chromatius used precisely to that end."[43] This suggests that despite a possible tendency to oversimplify doctrinal matters, Chromatius is still being essentially faithful to the Christianity he inherited from New Testament times. One might confidently add that the conception of heresy as a deviation from orthodoxy, and therefore as something from which Christians need protection, is represented not just in Acts but in the entire New Testament and early church period, the reconstructions of Walter Bauer and his modern disciples notwithstanding.[44]

The Date of Chromatius's Death and His Relation to Pelagius

In May 2008, an international conference was held in Aquileia to commemorate the sixteenth centenary of the death of Chromatius. The proceedings have been published, and most of the contributors have identified the actual year of the bishop's death as 407.[45] However, Pier Franco Beatrice, one the organizers of the conference, has recently challenged the traditional dating of Chromatius's demise, principally by identifying him as the Chromatius who is listed by Augustine as one of the fourteen Eastern bishops who acquitted Pelagius at the Synod of Diospolis in 415.[46] Beatrice speculates that in spite of the firmly entrenched historical tradition that Chromatius was bishop of Aquileia for eighteen years, from 388 to 407, there is actually only very late evidence for this tradition. He conjectures that Chromatius moved to Palestine in about 408, together with his friend and colleague Jovinus, the bishop of Padua, because of the new invasion of Alaric. (In Augustine's listing, Jovinus is also mentioned next to Chromatius as a bishop who was present at the Synod of Diospolis). Beatrice posits that Chromatius had joined the exodus of those fleeing from Italy.[47] Thus the year 407–8, which is traditionally considered the year of Chromatius's death, may simply be the date of his departure from Aquileia. Beatrice hypothesizes that he lived on to participate in the previously mentioned synod and died shortly thereafter.

Beatrice's reconstruction of the final years of Chromatius's life strikes me as very plausible. Years ago, C. P. Hammond had offered a similar challenge to the standard chronology of Rufinus of Aquileia's final years, and her research became the new reference point.[48] From the perspective of the current introduction, the most important and interesting aspect of Beatrice's research is the affinity he shows between Chromatius's doctrine of grace, merit, and free will, that of Pelagius, and that of saint John Chrysostom. This more balanced mode of explaining the operation of divine grace stands in tension with the predestinarian views that Augustine (d. 430) developed in his opposition to Pelagius, especially during the final decade of his life. It also may anticipate Catholic reactions to Augustine's doctrine that occurred in Gaul under John Cassian (360–435). I believe that the isolation of Augustine in his doctrine of grace and predestination may be even starker than Beatrice realizes, at least in this article, since Jerome himself, in spite of his polemical ad hominem attacks on Pelagius and on certain aspects of Pelagius's thought, adheres generally in his exegetical writings and even in his *Dialogue against the Pelagians* to an understanding of grace and free will that more closely resembles Chromatius, John Chrysostom, and the Greek exegetes like Origen (together with Pelagius), than it does Augustine's later views.[49]

To illustrate this point, Beatrice specifically cites Chromatius's treatment of the centurion Cornelius, the first pagan converted and baptized by Peter, according to Acts 10:1–48.[50] According to Chromatius, Cornelius was already leading an honest and praiseworthy life as a pagan before his conversion, following the dictates of natural law. For that reason, in some sense he *merited* to receive the faith and the Spirit in baptism. According to this point of view, faith is granted as a reward to those who are judged worthy of it because they have merited it (in some sense) by their good works. Chromatius is no innovator in such exegesis. His interpretation is shared by all Greek and Latin Christian writers of the first four centuries, above all by John Chrysostom, but including Jerome himself in the latter's *Commentary on Galatians.*[51] It is not surprising that Pelagius would have supported this exegesis. Here I would add to Beatrice's evidence that in *Tractate* 45.1 Chromatius takes a similar interpretive approach to the case of Jesus's calling of Matthew the tax collector. Chromatius says that in Matthew the gift of God's condescension and the example for our salvation excelled,

> so that we would know that every sinner must be chosen by God and can arrive at the grace of eternal salvation, *if a religious spirit and a devout mind are not lacking.* After all, Matthew is freely chosen by God, even though he was tangled up in worldly obligations and secular activities, yet *because of the religious devotion of his mind,* he *merits* <being appointed> by the Lord: "Follow me," surely by him who by virtue of his divine nature knows the hidden recesses of the heart. From what follows, ultimately, we know that this Matthew was chosen by the Lord not by the Lord's partiality but *by the merit of his faith and devotion.*

As Chromatius sees it, if I understand him correctly, Matthew, like Cornelius, was not chosen arbitrarily but he exhibited a meritorious disposition of receptivity that was rewarded with the bestowal of elective grace. Being chosen by God in these cases was conditioned upon being open and receptive to him. A biblical basis for such an understanding might be found in Matthew 10:11–13, where Jesus instructs his disciples whom he is sending on their mission to stay with those whom they find to be *worthy*. This condition of worthiness, which did not nullify the necessity of receiving baptismal grace, would have been prior to their hearing and acceptance of the gospel. Likewise, in Luke 8:5–8, Jesus speaks of the word of the gospel being sown on "good" soil in contrast with other types. Does that not imply a natural disposition of receptivity?

According to Beatrice, the man who introduced a radical innovation in the interpretation of the figure of Cornelius was Augustine of Hippo. Beginning with his *Ad Simplicianum* (396), Augustine shifted his thought on the question of the beginning of faith (*initium fidei*) and of the relationship between grace, faith, and good works. Augustine originated the interpretation that Cornelius, far from deserving faith with his works, had been able to do good works only because he had in some way been anticipated by the prevenient grace of God that had led him to faith, even though he still needed to be brought into the church through baptism. So it was faith, the arbitrary gift of the prevenient grace of God that resulted in his good works, and not vice versa.[52] Augustine claimed that the good works done by Cornelius as a pagan before his baptism were made possible by the help of the Spirit, not without some form of faith, albeit still imperfect and needing baptism.[53]

In other words, for Augustine God's arbitrary predestination precedes and underlies his calling to salvation of Cornelius and Matthew. God does not respond to their worthiness in any way by giving his grace. Rather, his arbitrary decision to give them prevenient grace is the sole cause of their faith and worthiness. To this Beatrice responds,

> No stronger contrast than this could be imagined: Chromatius's theology of merit, so distant from the theology of grace that Augustine was working on in those years, brings him closer instead to the characteristic positions of Greek orthodoxy and of Pelagius. It may therefore be concluded that the presence of Chromatius at Diospolis seems to be not only sufficiently documented on the chronological and prosopographical level, but also quite compatible with that circumstance, which required the authoritative

> intervention of the great Italian friend of Chrysostom in favor of Pelagius and his doctrine.[54]

John Chrysostom's doctrine of grace is in fact strikingly similar to Chromatius's.[55] Chrysostom, like Jerome, does not support the paradox for which Augustine later became famous, that when God rewards human merits, he is really rewarding his own gifts to humans.[56] Does the apparent theological affinity between Chromatius and Pelagius bode ill for Chromatius's orthodoxy? If one answers in the affirmative, then Chrysostom will have to be condemned together with them.[57] To begin with, it is noteworthy that Augustine himself did not judge the Council of Diospolis unfavorably.[58] Since Diospolis acquitted Pelagius's language of merit (to Augustine's chagrin), it seems that Augustine's predestination theory had made no headway in the East. The Eastern Bishops were not concerned to define precisely the role of grace in salvation, provided that the equally necessary synergism of free will was acknowledged. The conclusion I reached in my first discussion of the subject is one that I still find to be reasonable: Pelagius's one-sided emphasis on actual sin as the sole cause of the human predicament, his apparent exclusion of any inherited effects of the fall, and his early radical separation of the action of grace from the action of free will—these theses are outside the mainstream of the ancient Catholic theological tradition and are heretical.[59] But these issues were not on trial at the Synod of Diospolis. On the other hand, Pelagius's robust doctrine of free will; his interpretation of predestination as divine foreknowledge of faith and merit, and therefore as something that is not arbitrary but conditional; and his clear conception of the resistibility of divine grace—these doctrines are very much in line with the antecedent and contemporary Greek and Latin mainstream. It is Augustine who developed positions that seem to stand in tension with that consensus.[60]

Pope Benedict XVI's Wednesday Audience on Saint Chromatius

Beginning on March 7, 2007, Pope Benedict XVI devoted most of his catecheses at his Wednesday audiences to the fathers of the church from Clement of Rome to Augustine of Hippo. He treated saint Chromatius of Aquileia on December 5, 2007. It is first of all noteworthy that Pope Benedict describes Chromatius as a *peritus* (a theological "expert") of Bishop Valerian at the Council of Aquileia in 381. Joseph Ratzinger himself had been a *peritus* of the German archbishop of Cologne, Cardinal Frings, at the Second Vatican Council.[61] We tend to admire those in whom we see our own image. Pope Benedict extolls Chromatius as a wise teacher and a zealous pastor who gave priority to listening to the word of God and proclaiming it. The trinitarian mystery was a particularly dear subject to him, with an emphasis on the Holy Spirit, his presence and action in the life of the church. Chromatius also stresses the importance of the mystery of Christ, the incarnate Word and true man. From the *Tractates on Matthew*, Pope Benedict notes these recurring concepts: the church is one; she is born from the blood of Christ; she is a precious garment woven by the Holy Spirit; the church is where the fact that Christ is born of a virgin is proclaimed, where brotherhood and harmony flourish. "One image of which Chromatius is especially fond is that of the ship in a storm—and his were stormy times, as we have heard: 'There is no doubt...that the ship represents the Church.'"[62] Benedict concludes his catechesis on Chromatius with a lengthy citation from the conclusion to *Sermon* 16.4:

> Let us pray to the Lord with our whole heart, with complete faith, that he may deem it fitting to deliver us from every attack of the enemy, from all fear of the enemy. May he not consider our merits but his own mercy, he who thought it fitting long ago to deliver even the children of Israel, not in view of their merits but in view of his mercy. May he protect us with his accustomed pity, may he drive back the barbarian nations, may he do among us what holy Moses said to the children of Israel: "The Lord will fight for you and you shall be silent" [Exod 14:14]. He fights, he conquers, if he shows pity, if he forgives sins, if he does not look at our merits but his own clemency, since he is accustomed to be merciful even to those who are unworthy. We ought to pray as much as we can that he may consent to do this. For he says through the prophet, "Call upon me in the day of tribulation, I will rescue you and you will glorify me" [Ps 50:15].

The pope adds his own signature to these words: "God knows us, he knows me, he knows each one of us, he loves me, he will not abandon me."[63]

Text and Translation

I have translated the Latin text found in *Chromatii Aquileiensis Opera*, ed. R. Étaix and J. Lemarié, CCSL, 9A (Turnhout: Brepols, 1974). Since that date, R. Étaix continued to publish new discoveries of Chromatius's *Sermons* and *Tractates*, but I have not looked at these.[64] For the lemma of New Testament texts, I have used either the online (www.drbo.org) or printed version of the Douay-Rheims English translation of the Latin Vulgate as my base translation, but have also paid attention to the wording of the RSV Catholic edition. When Chromatius cites at length from the Old Testament, either in the lemmata or in the body of his *Sermons* and *Tractates*, I have consulted either the online (www.ecmarsh.com/lxx/) or printed version of Sir Lancelot Brenton's nineteenth-century English translation of the Septuagint. Chromatius's Old Testament is clearly the Old Latin, which was a translation of the Greek Septuagint, but, unlike Jerome, he is loose and inexact in his citations from Scripture.[65] Thus I have not used either of these modern versions slavishly but have followed Chromatius's wording carefully, and have always updated the archaic English. For most of the names of persons and places, I have endeavored to use those of the RSV Catholic edition. Scripture citations are given solely according to their locations in the RSV, even in cases when the LXX and the Hebrew have a different versification from the RSV.

SERMONS[1]

SERMON 1

On [the Passage in][2] *the Acts of the Apostles Where the Apostles Healed the Lame Man*

1. The law and the prophets not only predicted the coming of our Lord and Savior in humility by their words but they showed it by mystical examples. After all, among the other mysteries of the truth to come, it is even said in the law that if a traveler making a journey finds a bird with her chicks, he could take the chicks but leave the bird [see Deut 22:6].[3] It seems that this was justly observed for a time even according to the letter, so that when the chicks were taken, the mother was left to be able again to bear other chicks. But in this kind of precept according to the allegorical meaning, a future mystery was instead being shown, which we plainly recognize as having been fulfilled in the coming of Christ.[4]

2. For in that traveler of whom the law spoke, the Lord was signified because, in order to enter upon the journey of human life, he assumed a body from a virgin. This noble traveler then, when he had undertaken this journey of the world in the body of our flesh, and had found a bird with the chicks in the nest, that is, the synagogue with its children sitting in the nest of the law, he took the chicks and left the mother. For he separated the apostles from the synagogue, so that he might bring them from the nest of the law to the home of his church. This is why we read the statement in the Psalm: "For indeed the sparrow has found itself a home, and the turtle-dove a nest, where she may lay her chicks" [Ps 84:3]. The home refers to the church; the nest is the synagogue, since a nest is a temporary thing, just as the synagogue had grace for a time, as long as it also had chicks with it in the nest, that is, the prophets and apostles. But when they were removed from

it by Christ and given to their own master, that is, to his church, the synagogue remained like an abandoned nest.

3. Now the reason we have said this is because, though the multitude of Jewish people was countless, when Christ came in the flesh, very few believed. That this very thing would happen, Isaiah also clearly showed when he said, "And though the number of the sons of Israel be as the sand of the sea, a remnant is saved" [Isa 10:22]. He was indicating the remnant of the apostles themselves, and the others who believed during the time of the apostles from the Jewish people. Your love has heard[5] about them in today's[6] reading.[7] For when saints Peter and John had demonstrated the manifest sign of divine power on that lame man, it says, "On that day five thousand men believed" [Acts 4:4]. Through the prophet the Lord himself had predicted these miraculous signs, these five thousand men, when he said, "Behold I, and my children that God has given me. And they shall be [for] wonders in the house of Israel from the Lord Sabaoth on mount Zion" [Isa 8:18]. And this same prophet showed in what follows that these were the signs that would occur, when he said, "Then shall the eyes of the blind be opened, and the ears of the deaf shall hear, and the lame man will leap as a deer" [Isa 35:5–6]. We recognize that this was fulfilled in this very lame man, who had never walked from his mother's womb [see Acts 3:2].

4. If we reflect, we can recognize in the lame man hidden mysteries as well that are shown forth in advance. For when this lame man was at the beautiful gate of the temple [see Acts 3:2], he looked up at Peter and John and received healing [see Acts 3:7]. For a long time before we came to the knowledge of Christ, we were truly lame as well, for we limped on the way of justice. But we limped not in our physical steps but in the gait of our internal mind. For the one who is estranged from the way of justice, from the way of truth, even if he has straight feet, is completely lame because he limps in mind and soul. For he enters upon the journey of faith and truth not with physical steps but with the steps of the internal mind. Hence doubtless we limped for a long time on the way of justice, when we did not know Christ the Lord, the true way of salvation and life [see John 14:6]. But after we came to the beautiful gate of the temple and looked at the apostles of Christ with faith, then the steps of our mind were made strong so that we no longer limped upon the way of iniquity, but with straight steps we walk down the road of justice. For we came, or rather, were brought by Christ to the beautiful gate of the temple,

where lame people were accustomed to be healed. The beautiful gate of the temple is the gospel preaching, by which the temple of God, that is, the church, is adorned with spiritual beauty, in which those who are weak in mind and lame in spirit receive the healing of salvation. Finally, that beautiful gate of the temple received the lame man, but it returned him whole, just as the gospel preaching has received lame people and the weak who are brought to it, but it has restored them whole and healthy.

5. Do you want to know what kind of beautiful gate it is? Listen to David speaking in the psalm, as he says, "Open to me the gates of justice, and I will go into them, and give praise to the Lord" [Ps 118:19]. And he added, saying, "This is the gate of the Lord, the just shall enter through it" [Ps 118:20]. Many are the gates, he says, in the law and prophets; but these different gates lead to the one gate, that is, to the gospel preaching, which truly is the gate of Christ, because one arrives through the law and the prophets to the <gospel> preaching, which for that reason is properly called "the gate of the Lord," because through it there is an entrance for us to the kingdom of heaven. Listen to the patriarch Jacob pointing to this very thing in Genesis. For when Jacob saw the ladder fixed from the earth to the heaven, and God leaning upon it, he said, "This is the house of God, and this is the gate of heaven" [Gen 28:17; cf. 28:12–13]. For the gospel preaching is the gate of heaven, since through it there is an ascent for us to the kingdom of heaven. Our Lord and Savior first opened this gate for us by the key of his resurrection. For the reason he arose in his body, and with his body he ascended to heaven, was so that by <his own> ascent he might open the gate of heaven, which was indeed closed and bolted shut for everyone up to the time of the Lord's resurrection.

6. Therefore the way is opened by Christ's resurrection. Hence it is not without reason that the patriarch Jacob related that he saw a ladder in that place [see Gen 28:16] whose top reached to heaven, and the Lord was leaning upon it. The ladder fixed from earth to the heaven [see Gen 28:13 LXX] is the cross of Christ by which there is a place for us in heaven that truly reaches up to heaven.[8] On this ladder many steps of virtues have been inserted by means of which the stages of our ascent to heaven consist: faith, justice, modesty, holiness, patience, piety, and the other goods of the virtues [see Gal 5:22–23]—these are the rungs of this ladder. If we faithfully ascend by means of them, doubtless we shall reach heaven. Now it is right for us to recognize that the ladder signifies the cross of Christ, since just as a

ladder is held together by two beams, so too the cross of Christ is held together by the two testaments, containing between them the rungs of the heavenly precepts by which ascent is made to heaven.

7. But in the present reading, your love has heard how great was the love and unanimity of the believers during the time of the apostles.[9] It says, "And there was one heart and one soul of the believers. No one called anything his own, but they held everything in common" [Acts 4:32]. This is what it means truly to believe in God; this is what it means to live faithfully in the sight of the Lord. For why should those for whom heavenly goods are undivided have held their earthly goods divided up? So when we see people in need [see 1 John 3:17], especially Christians, we should freely share as if it were in common [see Gal 6:10; 1 Tim 4:10], as a sharing with the saints and elect of God, of whom the divine scripture testifies and says <...>[10], so that we may be able to have a share in the heavenly kingdom.

Sermon 2

Here Begins the Reading from the Acts of the Apostles Where It Speaks of Simon the Magician

1. In the gospel our Savior says many things to instruct us in our faith. Among other things he says the following: "The kingdom of heaven is like a householder (*paterfamilias*) who sowed good seed in his field. But when the men slept, someone came and over sowed weeds and went away" [Matt 13:24–25], and so on. And so, here our Lord and Savior calls himself a householder. But by this term he shows the great affection of his pious devotion toward us, when he shows that he is not only lord but father (*patrem*) of his family (*familiae*). For by this name of householder (*patremfamiliae*), he is referring to himself. In the name Lord there is the emotion of fear; but in the name of father there is the feeling of love. The Lord clearly shows this very thing through the prophet when he says, "If I am Lord, where is my fear? If I am father, where is my honor?" [Mal 1:6]. He calls himself Lord in order to be feared; but father, in order to be loved.

2. This householder then sows good seed in us, that is, the word of faith and truth, which he pours into the furrows of our soul with the plow of his cross, so that when justice takes root within us, we may

bear fruit worthy of faith. But on the other hand, the enemy over sows weeds, that is, the seed of faithlessness and iniquity. But it is clearly shown how the enemy can over sow seed of this sort. "When the men slept," it says, that is when the enemy over sows the weeds, those whom he finds sleeping, that is, overcome by the sleep of infidelity. But he cannot pilfer from those who are awake in faith. After all, if Adam long ago, in whose heart the Lord first sowed good seed, had stayed awake in respect to the precepts of the Lord, that enemy would never have been able to <overcome>[11] him. But when he found him asleep, that is, <overcome> with the slumber of negligence, at once he over sowed his weeds, so that instead of the fruit of life, he brought forth the fruit of death.

3. Now we have brought forth this comparison on account of the present reading because, when the Lord through his apostles was sowing the word of truth and faith everywhere, the devil, in opposition, over sows weeds upon the vessels that are worthy of him. Finally, your love has heard in the present reading how Simon the magician, after the word of God <was> sown in him, received the devil's seed [see Acts 8:9–18]. Indeed, as the text of today's reading has shown, through the preaching of Philip he believed and was baptized in the name of Christ [see Acts 8:4–13]; but at once, the devil made him a vessel of destruction [see Rom 9:22]. For as you have heard, dearly beloved, when he saw the Holy Spirit being given to those who had been baptized through the laying on of the apostles' hands, it says, "He brought a lot of money and said, Give me this ability so that anyone I lay my hands on may receive the Holy Spirit. Then Peter said to him, Your money perish with you, for you thought you could obtain grace by means of money" [Acts 8:19–20].

4. For the apostles were not carrying the grace of God to sell it, men who were buying back the entire world by the blood of Christ. Nor was it allowed to the apostles to receive earthly money for the grace of Christ, by means of which grace they freely gave heavenly treasures to those who believed. To them it had been said in the gospel, "Freely you have received, freely give" [Matt 10:8]. For if those who seek worldly honors and offices become distinguished [...], how could the apostles sell the honor of heavenly grace, which they themselves had received freely? Therefore it is not undeservedly that he says to Simon, "May your money perish with you since you thought you could obtain the grace of God by means of money. You have no share or lot in this word" [Acts 8:20–21]. And although this same Simon had

become [unworthy] of heavenly grace, and guilty of a most serious sin, saint Peter[12] still showed him the way to be restored to salvation. For he went on to say, “Repent from this wickedness of yours, and pray to the Lord, in the hope that the recollection of your heart may be forgiven you. For I see that you are in the bond of iniquity and the bitterness of gall” [Acts 8:22–23]. For indeed as far as it pertained to the holy apostle, who wanted no one to perish [see 2 Pet 3:9], he showed him the path to salvation. But that man was so blinded by the mindset of his faithlessness that he not only did not repent for such a terrible crime, but even committed many other sins later against the apostles and the church of Christ, as his actions show clearly.[13]

5. As a type of this Simon we clearly recognize the raven of long ago that was let out from Noah’s ark into the ruin [see Gen 8:7]. The former, to be sure, had been received into Noah’s ark, that is, into the church of Christ, when he believed and was baptized [see Acts 8:13]. But since, <after> he was baptized, he was unwilling to be changed by the grace of Christ, as one who was unworthy, he was cast out to ruin. For this Noah’s ark, that is, the church, is not able to keep people of this sort within it. In fact, this ark had received even Judas Iscariot into it; but because he did not deserve to be changed, or rather, because he remained like a raven in the blackness of his sins, he was cast out of the boat (*cymba*) of the apostles, as if from Noah’s ark, and met with the deluge of eternal death.

Therefore let us ask the Lord Jesus that none of us be found to be a raven in the Lord’s church, and utterly perish when cast outside. For the raven is every unclean person, every profane person, every heretic, who does not deserve to be in the church of Christ. Surely, if any of us is still a raven in his mind, which I do not think to be the case, let him pray to the Lord, that he may be changed from a raven into a dove, that is, go from being unclean to clean, from profane to faithful, from unchaste to chaste, from heretic to catholic. For God can make a dove out of a raven, who turned water into wine [see John 2:1–11], and who, as it is written, raised up sons to Abraham from stones [see Matt 3:9]. For only by becoming a spiritual dove and in no other way can we remain in the church of Christ. In fact, long ago, the dove that was sent out from the ark immediately returned <to> the same ark [see Gen 8:10–11]. For the one who is a spiritual dove does not withdraw from the church of Christ.

6. Would you like to know a raven whom the Lord turned into a dove? Consider that thief who was crucified with the Lord [see Luke

23:39–43]. He was a raven in the blackness of his sins. But after he confessed Christ on the very cross [he was changed from a raven into a dove], that is, from unclean to clean, from a blasphemer to a confessor, from the devil's thief to a martyr of the church. Therefore, do you want to be a dove, O human? Be in the Lord's church without the gall of wickedness [see Acts 8:23]. Be without the bitterness of sin, and you will rightly be called the Lord's dove.[14] For by nature a dove has no gall or bitterness. But if like a raven you abide in the uncleanness of the flesh and in the blackness of sins, even if you lie hidden within the church, you are outside of it. You may indeed seem to be within, according to humanity, but according to God, from whom nothing lies hidden, you are found to be outside. Therefore let us cast off all blackness of sin from our hearts, all uncleanness of the flesh, all bitterness of wickedness, so that we may truly deserve to be ever in Noah's ark, that is, in the church of Christ, and the following might be said of us that is written: "Who are these that fly like the clouds and come to me <as> doves with their chicks?" [Isa 60:8].

7. Finally, that eunuch too was found to be one of these doves of whom your love has heard in the present reading [see Acts 8:26–40]. For when he had come to Jerusalem <and> was on the return journey, he sat in his chariot reading the prophet Isaiah, and "the Spirit spoke to Philip and said, Go up and join yourself to that chariot" [Acts 8:29]. And he went up and stood there, and Philip said to him, "Do you think you understand what you are reading?" [Acts 8:30]. And he said to him, "How can I understand if no one explains these scriptures to me?" [Acts 8:31]. And when Philip sat down with him, he explained to him the prophetic Scripture that he was reading, showing and indicating the Lord Jesus Christ. And when Philip explained it to him, at once that eunuch believed and said to Philip, "Behold, water; what is there to hinder me from being baptized?" [Acts 8:37]. Philip said to him, "If you believe, it is permitted. And he said, I believe in the Lord Jesus Christ. And the two of them went down into the water and Philip baptized him" [Acts 8:37–38].[15]

8. Therefore this eunuch was chosen as a dove; but Simon the magician is rejected as a raven, since the former believed with his whole heart and with complete faith, whereas the latter approached with a doubting mind that was completely full of treachery. And therefore the former was received, the latter cast out; the former approved, the latter condemned. Since then we have been called to the divine knowledge too, to the grace of Christ, we ought to believe with our

whole heart and with complete faith, so that we may not be rejected with doubt-ridden and profane minds [see Rev 21:8], but may merit to be received with the saints and chosen ones of God into the future glory by Christ the Lord. Amen.

Sermon 3

Concerning the Centurion Cornelius and Concerning Simon Peter

1. Your love has heard how great was the pious devotion of Cornelius the centurion toward God. For although he was still a pagan he applied himself to fasting and prayers [see Acts 10:1–2]. For that reason it was not undeservedly that he merited to see an angel of the Lord in his home, who said to him, as <the present> reading reported, "Cornelius, your prayers have been heard, and your alms have ascended in remembrance before God" [Acts 10:4]. But I do not know whether any of us deserves to hear this from the angel, we who are devoted neither to fasting, prayers, nor almsgiving.[16] Recently, a fast was publicly announced, but few fasted. People come to church and pass the time telling stories or conducting worldly business rather than saying prayers. Poor people complain about their lack and their need, but no one gives alms. And we are surprised if we endure various trials, though we have minds so hardened in every respect. Therefore let us correct our negligence, and let us return to the Lord with our whole heart. Let us devote ourselves to fasting, prayer, and almsgiving, so that we also may deserve to hear what was said to Cornelius by the angel: "Your prayers have been heard, and your alms have ascended in remembrance before God" [Acts 10:4].

2. But perhaps some say that they cannot fast because of their stomachs [see 1 Tim 5:23]. Is it because of your stomach that you don't give alms? Give alms, and you will make up for the fasting. Devote yourself to prayer, purify your mind, this will be the equivalent of your fasting. But if you do none of these things, how do you think that you will be without sin, or how do you believe that you will be commended by the Lord, when you yourself do not listen to the Lord's command? Therefore it is said to Cornelius by the angel, "Your prayers have been heard, and your alms have ascended in remembrance before

God" [Acts 10:4]. If then we want our prayers to be heard by the Lord, we ought to commend them by good works and alms, just as saint Cornelius did, who deserved to be heard by the Lord. And actually saint Cornelius was still a pagan when he devoted himself to his prayers; for he had not yet believed in Christ. Truly this Cornelius is shown to be blessed in all things who fulfilled Christ's precepts even before he believed in Christ! For it was fitting that such a man as he was <the first> to believe from the Gentiles.

3. Yet already in the gospel the Lord had shown a type of this Cornelius to saint Peter when he says to him, "Go to the sea, and cast in a hook, and take the fish which comes up first, and when you open its mouth you will find a stater there" [see Matt 17:6]. We recognize that this was clearly fulfilled in this Cornelius. For on the hook of Peter he came up from the sea as the first fish; for he was the first to believe from the Gentiles at the preaching of Peter. For in the hook the preaching of the divine word is signified. Saint Peter is ordered to cast it among the people of the Gentiles as it were into the sea, from which this Cornelius happily was the first one caught. For as I have said, he was the first to believe from the Gentiles as Peter was catechizing. Finally, a stater was found in his mouth, before he was caught by Peter. For he was keeping the justice of God in the natural law even before he believed, and was serving God with fasting, prayers, and alms.

4. Well then, this saint Cornelius was serving God so faithfully even before he came to the knowledge of faith. Peter, it says, was in Joppa, staying with Simon the tanner [see Acts 10:5–6]. "And about the sixth hour, he went up to the higher parts to pray. And while he was praying, suddenly he began to be hungry" [Acts 10:9–10]. It says, "Fear came down upon him. And he saw a certain vessel descending from heaven, as it were a bright linen sheet tied at the four corners, wherein were all manner of four-footed beasts, reptiles, wild beasts, and birds of the sky" [Acts 10:10–12]. It says, "And there came a voice to him: Arise, Peter; kill and eat. And he said, By no means, Lord; for never has anything that is common and unclean entered my mouth. And the voice came to him saying, That which God has cleansed, you shall not call common" [Acts 10:13–15]. It says, "This happened three times; and the vessel was taken back into heaven" [Acts 10:16]. It says, "And behold the men who were sent from Cornelius stood before Simon's house asking if Peter was lodging there. But the Spirit said to Peter, Go down and go with these men, doubting nothing, for

I have sent them" [see Acts 10:17–20]. Now the reason this revelation was shown by the Lord to Peter was because Christ was about to invite all the Gentiles to his grace, <and to keep> him [Peter] from regarding believing Gentiles as unclean and unworthy. For there were more Jews who, though they had the law, stood forth as transgressors, than there were diverse nations who had sinned without the law [see Rom 2:12–14]. For it was plainly not right that the coming of Christ should benefit the Jews alone with salvation, since the reason he willed to suffer, he who was Creator of the world and Lord of the universe, was to save the whole human race leading to life, since the death of Christ became the redemption of the entire world.

5. But now let us consider both the timing and mystery of this revelation. Not without reason is Peter related to have gone up on the roof to pray at the sixth hour [see Acts 10:9]. Was there nowhere in the house where saint Peter could pray?[17] Or was he who kept constant fasts impatient for a meal, so that he grew hungry at the sixth hour of prayer? There is a mystical and spiritual meaning in actions of this sort. But let us look at the details. For the sake of prayer, saint Peter went up to the higher parts of the house. The higher parts, clearly, because by his faith he was seeking the things above [see Col 3:1]. He whose conversation was in heaven could not stay in the lower places, since the apostle says, "But our conversation is in heaven" [Phil 3:20]. Listen to the Lord showing this same thing in the gospel when he says, "And let him who is on the roof not come down to take anything from his house" [Matt 24:17]. He is on the roof whose life is situated high up, and who is far removed from earthly conversation. The Lord says to one like this then not to go down from the roof to the house; that is, do not forsake the higher life and go back to an earthly manner of life, that is, to the desires of the earthly house, to the lust of the flesh, to the desire of the world.

6. While Peter was in the higher places, at the sixth hour he began to be hungry [see Acts 10:10].[18] Obviously Peter, as the reading itself makes clear, was not hungry for earthly food (*cibum*), but for the food of human salvation. For the salvation of believers is the food (*esca*) of the saints [see John 4:31–38]. Finally, it was the sixth hour when he was hungry, and Peter obviously could not have been hungry at another time but at the sixth hour. For at the sixth hour, the Lord was crucified [see Matt 27:45; Mark 15:33; Luke 23:44; John 19:14]. By means of him the apostles began to hunger for human salvation. For Peter hungered not in order to set his thoughts on earthly food,

but he was hungry to save the souls of those who believe in Christ. The arrangement of the reading itself makes clear that this is the case. For he "immediately sees a vessel being let down from heaven, like bright linen, tied at its four corners, in which were all kinds of four-footed creatures, reptiles, wild beasts <and birds>" [Acts 10:11–12]. Then it is said to him, "Arise, Peter, kill and eat" [Acts 10:13]. In the vessel that he saw let down from heaven, a figure of the church was shown, which in fact comes down from heaven, as John says in Revelation: "And I saw the new Jerusalem descending from heaven" [Rev 21:2]. The reason a vessel of this sort is being held together by its four corners is because the preaching of the gospel on which the church relies is fourfold. Its outward form is shown to be like a bright linen because the church of Christ is gleaming and bright, having the radiance of heavenly life and the whiteness of saving baptism. He reported that he saw within such a vessel different kinds of animals, namely four-footed creatures, wild beasts, serpents, and birds of the sky, [for] Christ's church receives into itself people who believe from every race of men.[19] For a short time ago we were four-footed creatures, since we lived in this world as four-footed creatures without any notion of our salvation, and we looked forward not to heaven but to the earth. We were wild beasts, since we seized the property of others and raged against the blood of the innocent like wild beasts, biting with evil and injurious teeth. And we were serpents, when we brought forth deceit and venom with our tongue. And we were birds, when we ranged in different directions with a fickle mind.

7. But what was said to Peter? "Rise, kill and eat" [Acts 10:14]. Therefore we cannot be allotted the food of salvation unless we die to our former life. Otherwise, it is folly and completely pointless to believe that the Lord commanded Peter to eat serpents and wild beasts. Or did Peter actually have an earthly sword with him at the time of prayer? [see Luke 22:38; John 18:10]. Clearly saint Peter had a sword with him, but it was a divine one, that is, the Holy Spirit [see Eph 6:17], with which we are commanded to kill. For this sword, that is, the Holy Spirit, will kill with its sharp edge the ferocity of evil within us, the desires of the flesh and of blood [see Gal 5:16–17; 1 Cor 15:50; Matt 16:17], but only if we deserve to be killed to the world by such a great sword, so that we may be able to live to God!

8. Finally, when Peter said, "May it not be, Lord, for never has a common or unclean thing entered my mouth" [Acts 10:14], a voice from heaven says to him, "What God has cleansed, you should not

call common" [Acts 10:15]. For we are cleansed from all uncleanness when we come to the church of Christ by faith through his grace, through his mercy.[20] And he has related that this vessel was let down from heaven <three times> and then was taken back [see Acts 10:16]. For we cannot be cleansed or purified from sins except through the mystery of the Trinity. The grace of baptism is given in the name of the Father and of the Son and of the Holy Spirit [see Matt 28:19–20], so that we may be made clean from every defilement of sin. Since therefore we recognize such great mercy toward us, that we who are unworthy have been called to his grace that is so great, we ought to live and behave devoutly and justly in his sight, so that at the advent of his glory we may obtain not the punishments, with the unclean and the impious [see Rev 21:27], but the promises of the heavenly kingdom and the remuneration of everlasting life, with his saints and elect [see Titus 2:12–13]. Amen.

Sermon 4

On the Merchants Expelled from the Temple

1. When our Lord and Savior entered into the temple of the Jews and saw the illicit business being carried out, namely the selling of sheep, oxen, and doves, and money changers sitting there, as your love has heard in today's reading [see Matt 21:12–13; John 2:13–15], he made a whip out of cords[21] and expelled them all, and he overturned the chairs of those selling, saying to them, "My house shall be called a house of prayer; but you have made it a house of merchandise" [Matt 21:13; John 2:16]. The Jews were unmindful of the divine religion and faith. They made the temple of God a house of merchandise, and that is why they were all expelled. But they were expelled with a whip made of cords. Solomon plainly shows what is signified in the whip made of cords when he says, "And a threefold rope is not easily broken" [Eccl 4:12]. Doubtless in the threefold rope the Trinity is shown, which cannot be broken apart, since faith in the Trinity is incorruptible.[22] Frequently the heretics have attempted to corrupt this faith, as far as lies within them; but they have corrupted only themselves. But the faith in the Trinity necessarily should abide

incorrupt. And on that account Solomon says well, "A threefold rope will not be corrupted" [Eccl 4:12].

2. All then who act contrary to law are expelled from the temple with a whip of this sort made of cords because all who conduct themselves illicitly are condemned by no other judgment than that of the Trinity. And this is why the chairs of those selling doves are overturned, who seemed to be teaching the people while sitting on chairs, as if occupying the priestly rank. The chairs of the synagogue were overturned so that the chairs of the church would be sanctified in Christ. For the priestly office was taken away from the synagogue and given to the church. For the synagogue no longer deserved to possess the priestly office because it did not receive the chief priest himself, Christ the Lord. But let us see, or rather, beware lest any among us be found to be like this, who distributes sheep or oxen or doves in the Lord's temple. He sells sheep, who judges innocent one who pays coin. He sells oxen, who disperses the grace of God for an accepted price, though it is written, "Freely you have received, freely give" [Matt 10:8]. Whence even now money changers, namely those who reckon that God's work must be done for a wage, are shown to be overturned in the temple.

3. The church indeed is called a "house of merchandise," but of spiritual merchandise, where not earthly but heavenly money is lent on interest; it is not the interest of earthly coin that is acquired but interest of the heavenly kingdom. After all, we read the statement of the Lord in the gospel: "And why did you not give the money to the table of the money changers and I would have come and surely collected it back with interest" [Matt 25:27]. Daily therefore the money of the divine word, heavenly doctrine, is lent to us on interest in the Lord's church, and we do business with it well if we return it to the Lord with the profit of salvation and faith. In fact the apostles traded solely with this money, so that they gained the entire world for God.[23]

4. Therefore when our Lord and Savior had expelled from the temple all those who were acting illicitly, the Jews said to him, as your love has heard, "What sign do you show that you do these things? Answering them he said, Destroy this temple, and in three days I will rebuild it. And they said to him, This temple was built over the course of forty six years, and you shall raise it up in three days?" [John 2:18–20]. And the evangelist added, "But he was speaking of the temple of his body" [John 2:21]. What unbelief, or rather, faithlessness of the

Jews! They saw heavenly signs and divine miracles being done, and they demanded a sign from the Lord. Was it a small sign that a virgin gave birth [see Isa 7:14],

A

that shepherds...ran [...] angels...at the birth of the Lord [...]

R

that shepherds heard the voices of columns of heavenly singers at the birth of the Lord, and worshiped the Lord as a little child in the manger,[24]

than that a new star was shown from heaven [see Luke 2:8–10; Matt 2:1–11]? But still the Lord points to the sign of his own resurrection when he says, "Destroy this temple of God and I will raise it in three days" [John 2:19: Matt 26:61]. But though the Lord had said this about the temple of his body, the Jews thought that the statement pertained to the stone temple. It is not surprising of course if the Jews understood this statement of the Lord of the stone temple, who had a stony heart at all times. But the Lord said this not <of> the stone temple but of the temple of his body. For the proper temple of God is the body of Christ in which the Lord of majesty himself deigns to reside. In fact that temple is said to have been built over forty six years, since according to the Greek letters the name of Adam tallies up to the number forty-six. That temple was destroyed at the passion: the Lord arose on the third day, since on the third day the victor over death arose in his body.

Sermon 5

Concerning the Words of the Lord: Blessed Are the Poor in Spirit

1. In order to give his disciples a heavenly blessing, the Lord went up on the mountain with them. For today's reading from the gospel has related this. It says, "And Jesus went up on the mountain with his disciples, and stretching forth his hand over them, he said, Blessed are the poor in spirit, for theirs is the kingdom of heaven"

[Matt 5:3], and so on. Not without reason did our Lord and Savior give his disciples a blessing on the mountain. Surely it was not on earth, but on the mountain; not in the lower places, but in the higher places. And so, if you too want to receive heavenly blessings from the Lord, go up on the mountain, that is, seek the life above [see Col 3:1], and justly and deservedly you will obtain the desired blessing. But if you are involved in earthly actions, in earthly conversation, you will not be able to receive a blessing from the Lord; and therefore it is not without reason that it is written, "For he is the God of the mountains and not of the valleys" [1 Kgs 20:28].

2. To be sure God is the God of every location and of every created thing, since he is the Creator and Maker of all things [see Col 1:16]. But this is a profound and spiritual statement of the prophet, that "he is the God of the mountains and not of the valleys" [1 Kgs 20:28]. For God deigns to be the God of those who like mountains, that is, like all the saints, are raised toward the heights and toward things situated high up, by the faith of their merits. The patriarchs are mountains, the prophets are mountains, the apostles too are mountains, and the martyrs are mountains.[25] Our God is shown to be the God of all these saints. This is why we read the Lord's statement: "I am the God of Abraham, and the God of Isaac and the God of Jacob." And he added, "He is not the God of the dead, but of the living" [Matt 22:32]. But scarcely does he deign to be the God of the valleys, that is, of sinners and unbelieving men, who like valleys are submerged in the lowest places. For the impious and sinners do not deserve that our God be called their God, the faith and knowledge of whom they either despise or do not acknowledge. By the power of his divinity he is the God of all creation, since he is the Creator of all; but by his worthy regard and grace, he is shown to be the God of those who keep his precepts and faith.

3. Finally, that mountain on which the Lord gave blessings to his disciples presented a type of the church, which is compared with a mountain because its manner of life is on high [see Phil 3:20], and as a great mountain it will press down upon the earth, that is, the earthly way of life, not with the burden of a stone but with the weight of holiness. Do you want to know that the mountain properly signifies the church? Listen to the divine Scripture that says, "Who will ascend the mountain of the Lord, or who will stand on his holy place?" [Ps 24:3]. Surely this would not have been said of any earthly mountain: "Who will ascend the mountain of the Lord?" For not

only people but also wild beasts customarily climb up such earthly mountains. But he is properly speaking of the Lord's mountain, of the heavenly mountain, namely holy church, to whose faith and supernal life none but the blessed ascend. But one climbs this kind of mountain not by the exertion of the body but with the faith of the inner mind.[26]

4. And so let us always remain on this mountain with lofty faith, with spiritual actions, in order that we may deserve to receive these gospel blessings from the Lord, we to whom it is said, "Blessed are the poor in spirit, for yours is the kingdom of heaven" [Matt 5:3; cf. Luke 6:20.],[27] and so forth. They are "poor in spirit" because they are not puffed up with the devil's pride nor with any swelling of evil, but they maintain humility of spirit with faith. And certainly they are "poor in spirit" because they keep themselves away from worldly riches, from the desire of the world, from all earthly flesh. The Lord shows that these people are blessed in this manner when he says, "Blessed are the poor in spirit, for yours is the kingdom of heaven." In respect to the world those who are like this seem poor, but they are rich in God. They do not have earthly means, but they have heavenly blessing. They do not enjoy the riches of this world, but they receive the wealth of the heavenly kingdom and the treasures of eternal immortality. Finally, the Lord shows [that] theirs is the kingdom of heaven when he says, "Blessed are the poor in spirit, for yours is the kingdom of God." It is a blessed poverty that accumulates a gift as great as this! The first apostles boasted in this poverty, they who possessed the riches of heaven [see 2 Cor 6:10].

5. Therefore, if we are poor in this world, we should not grieve, since even the holy apostles were poor in this world. Do you want to go from being poor to becoming rich, or rather, to be rich in your very <poverty>? Be just, be devout, be godly, be merciful, and in God <you will have> great wealth, which no imperial treasury, no thief, not death itself is able to snatch from you. Therefore we have much wealth stored up in heaven, if we keep the commands of the Lord, if we remain faithful to Christ. These are eternal riches. Finally, listen to what the prophet Tobit says to his son: "We endure a poor man's life, son, to be sure; but you have great wealth if you fear God" [Tob 4:23]. Therefore let us fear God with our whole heart, that we may deserve to have great wealth.

Sermon 6

On the Gospel according to Matthew, Where It Says, Your Eye Is the Lamp of Your Body, and so on

1. After much heavenly doctrine, whereby our Lord and Savior instructed his disciples, in today's reading, as your love has heard, he says, "Your eye is the lamp of your body; if your eye is simple, your whole body will be clear. If your eye is evil, your whole body will be full of wickedness" [Matt 6:22–23]. The lamp of the body is understood as the sense of the mind and the faith of the heart. If this is bright and clear in us, doubtless it illumines our whole body. But the reason the lamp is recorded as a symbol of faith is because as a lamp illuminates the steps of those who walk at night, lest those walking either fall into a ditch or strike against any stumbling stones, so in the night of this world, the brightness of faith lights up the steps of our life, as the light of truth goes before us, lest we fall into the ditches of sins or strike against the stumbling stones of the devil. After all, Judas Iscariot, who did not have the lamp of faith in his heart [see Luke 22:53; John 13:30], at once fell into the pit of eternal death, so that he received the reward of death for the Lord of life.

2. And that is why he went on to say, "If your eye is evil, your whole body is darkened" [Matt 6:23]. An evil eye belongs to those whose mind is depraved, or whose faith is perverted—who walk not in the light but in darkness. John says of them in his epistle, "He who hates his brother is in darkness, and he walks in darkness, since darkness has blinded his eyes, and he does not know where he is walking. But he who loves his brother remains in the light, as he himself is in the light" [1 John 2:10–11; see 1:7]. But we can also apply the meaning of eye of the body, which is more precious among all the members, to the principal leader (*rectorem*) of the church.[28] If his faith is clear and his manner of life bright, doubtless he illumines the entire body of the church. But if he is a perverse teacher and heretic, clearly a doctor of that sort can cause the whole body to become darkened by the example of his life and faithlessness. For the light of truth and faith cannot shine forth in such people, where the darkness of error has established a night of faithlessness.

3. And fittingly the Lord added in the present reading, "No one can serve two masters. Either he will hate the one and love the other,

or he will stick to the one and despise the other." And he went on to say, "You cannot serve both God and Mammon" [Matt 6:24]. Here he shows two masters, God and the devil. But God is the true Lord; the devil is a false lord. The distance between true and false equals the distance between the Lord and the lord. The true Lord is the Creator of nature; the false one, the devil, is the changer of nature. The former is the author of salvation; the latter the author of perdition. The former leads humankind to heaven; the latter plunges humans into hell. The one draws humans into death; the other redeems them unto life.

4. And indeed God, although he is Lord of all, since all things were created by him, and he himself has dominion over all things, by the right of authority and by the power of his nature, nevertheless deigns to be Lord especially over those who faithfully serve the precepts of the Lord and God, and keep them; but the devil is understood as the lord only of those whom he has seduced away from their God and father, and subjected to the most wicked service of sin, and to whom he will dominate by a perverse justice through the domination of his own iniquity.

For this reason, then, the devil is called lord in a perverse sense,[29] whence not without reason he is also called a partridge in the prophet. For this is written: "The partridge will cry out, and gather things which were not its own; but in the last days they shall leave him, and at his end he will be a fool" [Jer 17:11]. But we ought to know why the devil is called a partridge. This partridge, that is, the earthly bird, entices the chicks of other birds with an alluring voice, and boasts over the chicks of others, as if they were its own chicks. But when these same seduced chicks have recognized the voice of the true parent, at once they leave the false parent and follow the true parent. So too we a short time ago had been seduced by the devil as by a false parent, by his alluring voice. But when we recognized the voice of the true parent, God, through the gospel preaching, then we leave the false parent, the devil, in order to follow the true and eternal parent, God.

5. There is another reason why the devil is called a partridge. When a partridge sees a man from afar, it covers itself with leaves in order not to be seen. So too the devil conceals the cunning of his malice, as it were with leaves, lest his deceit be understood so easily by man. And this is why the apostle said the following: "For we are not unaware of his wickedness" [2 Cor 2:11]. Therefore just as the devil is shown to be a false parent, so too is he a false master, since in both respects he is recognized as one who leads astray. But wretched is that

soul that follows such a parent, or such a master. But the one who follows such a master is not worthy of having God as its true Lord. And that is why the Lord says in the gospel, "You cannot serve God and mammon" [Matt 6:24]. Therefore if we serve works of justice, if we obey the divine precepts, doubtless we have God as our Lord, whose will we serve. But if we are enslaved to works of injustice, luxury, greed, impurity, and fornication [see Gal 5:19–21], we subject ourselves to diabolical domination, and we make disagreeable the passion of Christ, who delivered us from the unjust lordship of the devil. But may the Lord keep us from transferring from Christ's dominion to the devil's dominion. For the reason the Son of God deemed it fitting to suffer and be crucified for us was to rescue us from the profane dominion of the devil. This is why in all things we ought to serve the author of life and of our salvation faithfully, so that we may be able to reach that dominion of the heavenly kingdom. Amen.

Sermon 7 (fragment)[30]

Here Begins a Sermon for the Feast Day of Saints Felix and Fortunatus

Today is the [heavenly] birthday of the holy martyrs Felix and Fortunatus, who adorned our city by their glorious martyrdom....

Sermon 8

On the Lord's Ascension

1. The solemnity of this day bears no small festive grace. For on this fortieth day after the resurrection, as your love has heard in today's reading, our Lord and Savior ascended with his body to heaven in the presence of his onlooking disciples [see Acts 1:9–10]. He was received into a cloud, with the eyes of his disciples gazing, as the present reading has reported, and thus he ascended to heaven. A cloud comes to obey Christ, not to help him, but to offer its obedience to Christ and to display the service due to its Lord and Creator. But

when Christ ascended to heaven, he could not have been in need of help from a cloud, he who had created the very clouds along with the world. Thus he speaks through Solomon under the persona of Wisdom, saying, "When he prepared the heavens, I was there, and when he made the clouds firm above, I was joining things together before him" [Prov 8:27–30].

2. Indeed the Son of God now ascends on a cloud into heaven, while the apostles stand in awe and amazement, as today's reading reported, but now is not the first time he ascended. For from the beginning of the world he himself had both come down often from heaven and ascended. But now is the first time he ascends to heaven with a body.[31] And that is what the apostles marveled at, that Christ ascended to heaven with flesh, from where he had descended without flesh. But what is surprising if the apostles wonder at this, since the heavenly powers also marveled at this? For Isaiah makes this clear when he says the following under the persona of the heavenly citizens: "Who is this who comes out of Edom? The redness of his clothing [is] from Bosor. Beautiful [is] his robe, beautiful as a pool filled from a winepress" [Isa 63:1–2]. *Edom* means "earth," but *Bosor* means "flesh." This marvel then was seen by angels, that he who was born on earth from a virgin according to the flesh, this one who was seen to have suffered and been crucified in the flesh, ascended into heaven with the same flesh. Finally, mention is even made of the winepress, in order clearly to show the passion of the Lord's cross. For by the passion of the cross Christ was pressed as it were on the wood of a winepress, in order that he might shed his sacred blood for us. This is why there is talk of the "redness of his clothing from Bosor"; this is why his robe is shown to be beautiful. The "redness of his clothing" pertains to the shedding of his blood; but the outward beauty of his robe refers to the glory of his resurrection. For he arose glorious from the dead in the same flesh in which he shed his glorious blood for us. This is what is also said by the church about Christ in the Song of Songs: "My brother is resplendent and ruddy" [Song 5:10]. There is talk of his being "ruddy" because of the passion of the cross; "resplendent" is said because of the glory of his resurrection; because he who was seen as one rejected and humble in the passion appeared resplendent and glorious in the resurrection. Jeremiah likewise showed this mystery of his divinity and flesh in Christ when he says, "The breasts will fail [to flow] from a rock, or snow from Libanus" [Jer 18:14]. Thus in the "breast of the rock" he showed his incarnation from a virgin, but in

the "snow of Libanus" he showed the splendor of his divine brightness. Finally, when he was transfigured on the mountain, as we read in the gospel, his clothing became like snow, since it was resplendent with the glory of his brightness [see Matt 17:2; Mark 9:3; Luke 9:29]. Not without reason, however, is it said of Christ higher up, "The redness of his clothing [is] from Bosor." Not cloth, but clothing. For Christ is the prince of the martyrs; and that is why it is said of him, "The redness of his clothing [is] from Bosor," since he is surrounded by a crown of the martyrs like bright red clothing.

3. But let us return to the sequence. For the powers on high also marveled at the ascension of Christ to the heavens, when they said, "Who is this who comes from Edom? The redness of his clothing is from Bosor. Beautiful is his robe, beautiful as a pool full of the winepress." For the powers on high saw a new thing: the Son of God ascending to heaven with flesh. And therefore they said, "Who is this who comes from Edom?" It was a marvel to the angels, a marvel to the powers on high, that that flesh of which it was said to Adam, "You are earth and to the earth you will go" [Gen 3:19], was no longer on earth but flesh was ascending to heaven.[32] What profit did the devil's own malice bring him? Our earthly flesh (which he did not want to reign in paradise) reigns in heaven. For the Lord's ascension into heaven was indeed the wonder and exultation of angels, and the joy of the whole world; but it was the confounding of the devil and his true damnation. In the psalm, David also shows this admiration of the angels for the Lord's ascension to heaven, when he speaks in wonder in this way under the persona of angels and says, "Lift up your gates, O princes, and be lifted up, O eternal gates, and the Lord the king of glory shall enter in, strong and mighty in battle" [Ps 24:7–8]. For the powers on high were in awe, the angels marveled who were present at the Lord's resurrection, and therefore they cried out to one another to open the gate of heaven to Christ, the victor who was returning to heaven after the battle of his passion. For he had conquered the devil, he had conquered death, he had destroyed sin, he had waged war against legions of demons, and he had arisen victorious from death.

4. Christ therefore ascended with his body to heaven after the triumph of the cross, after the victory of his passion. Due service was rendered by angels. For some went before, others followed, when Christ ascended with his body to heaven. They exhibited fitting obedience to such a great king and such a great victor. For if everyone meets a human king after a victory with praises, how much more would all

the angels and powers on high have been obligated to meet Christ the eternal king, who ascended to heaven as a victor with his body, having triumphed over the devil and defeated death. And clearly it is not surprising if both angels and powers on high met Christ while he was returning to heaven, since even the Father himself is shown to have met him, just as the present psalm itself shows when it is said under the persona of the Son to the Father, "You have held my right hand, in your will you have guided me, and you have received me with glory" [Ps 73:23–24]. For with glory the Father received the Son returning to heaven, whom he placed at his right hand, as it says in another psalm: "The Lord said to my Lord, Sit at my right hand" [Ps 110:1]. For how could the Father's love be greater, or the glory of the Son more powerful, than to sit at the right hand of the Father? And therefore in the present psalm he well added from the persona of the Son, "For what remains in heaven, and what have I willed upon the earth besides you?" [Ps 73:25]. He willed to suffer on earth, and therefore he accepted the suffering of death for the sake of the salvation of the human race. He willed to ascend to heaven with his body. He sits at the right hand of the Father. Therefore there is one throne of majesty of the Father and of the Son, since there is no difference in honor between the Father and Son [see John 5:23], no distinction in dignity, but only the godly devotion of love.

Since therefore on this day the flesh of our nature ascended to heaven in the body of Christ, we ought to celebrate justly and deservedly the solemnity of this day, and so conduct ourselves in the present life that we deserve to become sharers of the glory of the Lord's body in the future life, in the heavenly kingdom [see Luke 20:35; Phil 3:21].

Sermon 9

Here Begins [the Sermon] on the Thirteenth Psalm, on Fools and the Unwise

1. In this psalm the prophet complains and says, "The fool said in his heart, There is no God. They are corrupt and have become abominable in their iniquities" [Ps 14:1]. We have found that there have been many fools in times past, people who either did not believe in God's existence or said that they did not. But the prophet's complaint

applies especially to the folly and unbelief of the Jewish people. After all the very number of the thirteenth psalm clearly shows to us the persona of the same Jewish people; for Ishmael, son of Abraham, who prefigured the Jewish people in all ways [see Gal 4:21–31], when he was thirteen years old received the sign of circumcision [see Gen 17:25]. Just as the persona of the people of the church is declared in the tenth psalm, because of the Decalogue of the law, since it fulfills the precepts of the law, so in this thirteenth psalm, a symbol of the Jewish people is shown, since Ishmael, as we said, received the sign of circumcision when he was thirteen years old.

Finally, since it is said in the tenth psalm, from the persona of the people of the church, "I trust in the Lord; how do you say to my soul, Move to the mountain like a sparrow" [Ps 11:1], in the sparrow the transgressor and apostate is signified, who has forsaken the house of God, the church, and moves to the mountains, that is, transfers to the worship of idols. This is just what the Jewish people did for a long time, who forsook God's temple that was in Jerusalem and sacrificed on the mountains, as the prophetic Scriptures make clear. But the people of the church who trust in the Lord make clear that they are unable to move to the mountains like that for any reason, since they say, "I trust in the Lord, how do you say to my soul, Move to the mountain like a sparrow." Moreover, for us there are the witnesses of so many martyrs who—during the times of persecution when they were compelled to move to mountains of this sort, that is, to the worship of idols—migrated more easily from their bodies than from their faith in Christ; they were more ready to move out of the world than from the church of God. For not even death itself can move martyrs from the church of Christ; or rather, the very reason they accept death on Christ's behalf is so that they may remain forever in the church of Christ. For the death of martyrs is the beautiful adornment of the church, and the crown of virtue.

2. These words of the prophet, then, concern the people of the church. But in today's reading your love has heard what he says about the Jewish people. "The fool said in his heart, There is no God" [Ps 14:1]. Let us see how this is so. As soon as the same Jewish people <came forth> from Egypt, they did not believe in the Lord in their hearts. And while Moses was delayed on the mountain, they made a calf for themselves that they worshiped, saying, "These <are> your gods, O Israel, which led you forth from the land of Egypt" [Exod 32:4]. Surely if they believed in God with their heart, after such great

veneration of God, they never would have knelt down before things made by the hands of men. The Jewish people therefore is shown to be foolish and unwise by all things, while they abandon the living and true God and seek the gods of the nations; while they despise the heavenly manna and long for cucumbers, melons, and Egyptian meats [see Num 11:5]; while they make more of slavery in Egypt than the freedom of faith; more of the prodigies of demons than of divine miracles.

3. But the same Jewish people betrayed their folly in this especially when they saw the wisdom of God, Christ [see 1 Cor 1:24], coming in the flesh [see 1 John 4:2; 2 John 7] <and> refused to recognize him; when they held in contempt his divine powers and unprecedented miracles. The blind were enlightened, the deaf heard, the lame were healed, paralytics were cured, lepers were cleansed, the dead were raised [see Matt 11:5; Luke 7:22], and the same Jewish people were in such great folly that they were not moved to faith in Christ even by these miracles, and not only were they <not> moved, but beyond that they rose up to condemn the Lord and Savior. Whence not undeservedly even in the sequence of this psalm <...> for he says this: "Their throat is an open grave; with their tongues they have used deceit; the poison of asps is under their lips" [Ps 5:9; 140:3]. If we reflect, we observe why it is said that their throat is an open grave. A grave contains within it nothing but corpses of the dead. The Jews then are rightly compared to graves because just as a grave contains nothing but corpses of the dead within it, so too <the Jews> <...> dead works of the flesh and spirit [see Heb 6:1; 9:14], they have made themselves a grave of their own life, containing within themselves the defilement and filth of sins. Do you want to understand plainly that the Jews are called graves? Listen to the Lord speaking in the gospel to the scribes and Pharisees: "Woe to you, for you are like whited sepulchers, which indeed appear to people beautiful on the outside, but within they are full of dead men's corpses and all filth. So too do you appear to people to be just, but within you are filled with greed and iniquity" [Matt 23:27].

4. And so it is manifest according to the Lord's testimony that for these reasons the Jews are called foolish of heart and an open grave. But we ought to consider the following, that not only is it said "throat," but "their throat is an open grave." Surely we note that this phrase was not spoken without a reason. For an "open grave" is spoken of a man who is awaiting his death there. The throat of the Jews then is rightly

called an open grave because they too open their mouth to receive the death of the Savior, saying to Pilate, "Crucify, crucify" [Luke 23:21; John 19:6]. Hence it is not without reason that the prophetic words have testified in the present psalm that they [are] likewise serpents: "with their tongues they have used deceit, the poison of asps is under their lips." Hence it is that John accuses them of such impiety in the gospel when he says, "Serpents, brood of vipers, who showed you how to flee from the coming wrath?" [Matt 3:7; cf. Matt 23:33]. They are not called serpents in a general way, but specifically "brood of vipers." For among serpents, the viper is the only species that is not born from an egg, but it bursts forth so to speak from its mother's womb.[33] But when it is born, it immediately kills its own mother. And so, with this <designation> the Jews are now called progeny of vipers because they destroyed their own mother, the synagogue, by the merit of their own impiety. Why do I speak of their mother? They have not even spared their own children, since they said, "His blood be upon us and our children" [Matt 27:25].

5. Since therefore the Jewish people was destined to commit such a great sacrilege, not without cause does the prophet cry out at the end of the psalm and say, "Who will bring the salvation of Israel out of Zion? The Lord, when he turns back the captivity of his people" [Ps 14:7]. In this he was clearly praying for the coming of our Lord and Savior. He knew that in no other way could the human race be delivered from the devil's captivity, except through the incarnation of Christ; and therefore he says, "Who will bring the salvation of Israel out of Zion?" For that one who deigned to be born of a virgin for the sake of the salvation of the human race not only brought salvation; for he delivered our captivity from the hand of the devil, having cast down the enemy and conquered death, so that he made us sons of God and coheirs of his glory.

6. And this is why the prophet added something at the end of the psalm not without cause and said, "Let Jacob be glad and let Israel exult" [Ps 14:7]. Surely he does not mean that carnal Jacob or Israel who rose up against its own Lord and Savior rebellious and impious, but spiritual Jacob, that is, the people of the church, which we are. For Jacob the patriarch acquired both names long ago by the merit of his faith. For long ago, Jacob the patriarch, who supplanted his brother when coming forth from his mother's womb, was called Jacob. But later on he was called Israel, since he received the rights of firstborn and the blessings [see Gen 25:26; 25:29–34; 27:1–41]. For reasons that

are clear, we recognize that each name fits us. For when we first come to believe, and are born from the womb of our mother the church, we become a Jacob, that is, those who supplant. For we supplant by our faith the faithlessness of our older brother, that is, of the Jews, and thus from being the younger we are made the older. And so, after this if we shall believe, we receive the brother's rights of firstborn, since we believe in the firstborn Son of God in whom the Jewish people was unwilling to believe; and so, later on we are called Israel, that is, those seeing God with the mind,[34] because with the eyes of faith we gaze upon the only begotten God [see John 1:18], who was born for our salvation. To whom be the honor and glory and power forever and ever. Amen [see 1 Pet 4:11].

Sermon 10

Here Begins [the Sermon] on the Gospel of Matthew Where It Speaks of the King Who Made a Marriage Feast for His Son

1. With many different parables our Lord and Savior convicted the Pharisees and the leaders of the Jews. Higher up he set forth the parable of the householder who rented out his vineyard to farmers [Matt 21:33–44]. But in today's reading it concerns a king who made a marriage feast for his son, as your love has heard. "And he sent his servants, to call them that were invited to the marriage. But they refused to come; but went away, some to their farm, others to their merchandise. But others laid hands on his servants, and having treated them contumeliously, put them to death" [Matt 22:3, 5–6].

2. In the present parable too, the king who made the marriage feast for his son is understood as signifying God the Father, who for the sake of human salvation celebrated the spiritual marriage feast of his only begotten Son. And how should this marriage feast be understood if not as when Christ the bridegroom joined the church to himself as his bride through the Holy Spirit? This marriage is spotless and inviolable because it consists not in fleshly love, but spiritual grace. After all the church is shown to be a married virgin when Paul says, "For I appointed you to one husband, to offer you as a chaste virgin to Christ" [2 Cor 11:2]. According to the worldly model, a married girl cannot be called a virgin. According to the heavenly mystery,

the church is shown to be married in such a way that she is a virgin. She is called married because through the Holy Spirit she is united with Christ; a virgin, because she remains unwedded and incorrupt in respect to sin. The author of this marriage is God the Father. The Holy Spirit is the witness. The attendants are angels. The invitation bearers are the apostles. And if you are looking for the spiritual pomp of this marriage, you will find it: it is the heavenly chamber of which it is written, "And he comes forth as a bridegroom out of his chamber" [Ps 19:5]. The choir of holy virgins occupies the first place in this marriage, of whom we read in the Scripture, "Virgins will be brought to the king behind her" [Ps 45:14]. <This> marriage has its harp, it has its musical instruments and cymbals. It is the harp of the law, the instrument of the prophets, <...> of which we read the in Scripture, "Praise him with strings and instrument; praise him with fine-sounding cymbals" [Ps 150:4–5].

3. And now let us look at the parable itself. The Father first invited the Jewish people to this marriage of his Son. For he sent just men to them, he sent prophets. But it says, "They refused to come" [Matt 22:3]. Again he sent other servants, more than before, namely the apostles and gospel preachers, saying to them, "Go, tell those who are invited, Behold, I have prepared my luncheon. The bulls and fatted beasts have been slaughtered. Come to the marriage" [Matt 22:9]. For in the luncheon <the mystery> of the Lord's passion is shown, in which <Christ> is the true food of life and meal of eternal salvation. For he is the living bread who comes down from heaven and gives life to this world [see John 6:33]. It is good that mention of the luncheon has been made; not of a supper, but of a luncheon (for a luncheon is normally held at the sixth hour) since it was the sixth hour when Christ was crucified for the salvation of the human race [see Matt 27:45], in order to show forth to us the heavenly meal and spiritual feast of his passion. He indicates just men and the prophets in the bulls that were slaughtered because of his Son's marriage. They were slaughtered by the Jews, since they predicted that the Son of God would come and suffer in the flesh. The just and the prophets are rightly called bulls because they brandished the horns of justice against the iniquity of the Jewish people. But the fatted beasts that were slaughtered point to those infants in Bethlehem who were slaughtered by Herod because they merited to die for the sake of Christ's name [see Matt 2:16].[35]

4. Since, then, the Jewish people refused to come to such a great marriage feast, that king sent his own servants to the exits of the

roads, saying, "Go and invite whomever you find to the wedding. They went out and gathered whomever they found, and the wedding feast was filled with guests" [Matt 22:9–10]. Therefore, because the Jews refused to come to this marriage feast, all the Gentiles were invited, from which we are, who come to the grace of Christ. For when the Jewish people excused themselves, such great preparation for the marriage feast could not perish. On that account we ought to give thanks for his mercy, that he invited us to such a great marriage feast as those who were unworthy. But we ought to be careful or afraid of this, that when the king enters and begins to look over the guests who are reclining there at the marriage feast, he may say to one of us what has been read in today's reading: "Friend, how have you come without a wedding garment?" [Matt 22:12]. And he commanded him to be removed by his hands and feet [see Matt 22:13]. The wedding garment is the grace of saving baptism, which shines not with the gleam of wool but with the splendor of faith. <...> for we obtain a snow-white garment from Christ, which we receive by the grace of baptism, since the apostle says, "You who were baptized into Christ have put on Christ" [Gal 3:27]. That man does not have a wedding robe of this sort, then, who either has not received the grace of baptism, or loses what he has received. When such a one is found, he is expelled from the wedding feast and is cast into the outer darkness [see Matt 22:13]. Therefore in every way we ought to preserve the wedding garment we have received through the grace of baptism, through the faith of Christ, whole and intact, so that we may be deemed worthy of the spiritual wedding feast in the church, and in the future may deserve to take part in the heavenly kingdom, with the saints and elect of God. Amen.

Sermon 11

On the Woman Who Anointed the Lord's Feet

1. Today's gospel reading reported that when the Lord was reclining at a feast with Lazarus, whom he raised from the dead, "Mary," the sister of Lazarus and Martha, "took a pound of pure ointment and anointed the feet of Jesus, and she wiped them with her hair and the whole house was filled with the fragrance of the ointment" [John 12:3]. As we read in many passages in the gospel, this saint Mary

pleased Christ by her great personal faith. Higher up when she was weeping for her dead brother, she even made the Lord weep [see John 11:33–35]; for she moved the author of piety to piety. And even though the Lord was about to raise Lazarus from death, nevertheless he wept as Mary wept, to show both his own piety and Mary's worthiness. But that the Lord wept for Lazarus shows his godliness; that he raised him from the dead shows his power. In the Lord's tears is shown a sign of the flesh he assumed; but in his raising of Lazarus is declared the power of his divinity. Higher up, then, Mary drew forth tears of piety from the Lord; but here she shows her emotion and devotion to the Lord. For she took a pound of pure ointment and anointed the Lord's feet and wiped them with her hair. Behold the religious devotion and faith of this holy woman. Others were reclining with the Lord; she anointed the Lord's feet. Others were exchanging conversation and words with the Lord; she with her silent faith wiped his feet with her hair. They seemed to be in the place of honor; she in that of obedient service. But Mary's obedience to Christ surpassed the honor of the reclining guests.

2. Finally, your love has heard in today's reading what the Lord said of her: "Truly I say to you, that wherever this gospel is preached in the whole world, even what she has done will be told in her memory" [Matt 26:13]. What then was the obedient service of this holy woman that is preached in the whole world and is preached daily? Consider the humility of this saintly woman. She did not immediately anoint the Lord's head, but his feet, though it is related that she anointed the Lord's head later on. Thus she anointed his feet first, and then his head. But she began with his feet, in order to become worthy of reaching up to his head. For as it is written, "He who humbles himself will be exalted, and he who exalts himself shall be humbled" [Matt 23:12]. And so, she humbled herself in order to be exalted. Finally, she wiped the Lord's anointed feet not with a towel but with her hair, to exhibit a greater service to the Lord. But in the fact that the woman wiped rather the Lord's feet with her hair, she sanctified her own head by his feet. For she sanctified the whole in herself of whatever was able to touch the body of Christ, who is the font of sanctity. For she rendered greater service in order to merit greater grace; just as one who is thirsty draws from a fountain's water that flows from on high, so this saintly woman took from the fount of sanctity the grace of delightfulness, in order to quench the thirst of her faith.[36]

3. But according to the allegorical and mystical reckoning, this woman has prefigured the church, which truly offered to Christ the complete devotion of its faith. And so she took a pound of precious ointment. In a pound there are twelve ounces. The church then has a measure of this precious ointment of this sort, which has accepted the teaching of the twelve apostles as a precious ointment. For what is more precious than apostolic doctrine that contains the faith of Christ and the glory of the heavenly kingdom? Finally, with the fragrance of this ointment the whole house is reported to be filled, since the whole world is filled with apostolic doctrine. For as it is written, "Their sound has gone forth into the entire earth, and their words to the ends of the world" [Ps 19:4]. But rightly the precious ointment contains within it different kinds of aromatic spices that give it its smell, since the apostolic doctrine also contains diverse spiritual graces by means of which it displays the fragrance of its odor. It is of course not surprising if the precious ointment signifies apostolic doctrine, since we read that the name of our Lord and Savior is also designated by a term of this sort. For thus we read the saying about him from Solomon under the persona of the church, which says, "Your name is ointment emptied out" [Song 1:2]. But not without reason is the name of the Lord called "ointment emptied out." For ointment, as your love knows, as long as it is contained within the vessel, retains the virtue of its odor within itself. But when it begins to be diffused and "emptied out," then the fragrance of its odor spreads far and wide.[37] So our Lord and Savior, when he was reigning with the Father in heaven, was ignored by the world; he was not known by the age. But when for the sake of our salvation he consented to "empty himself out" [see Phil 2:7] so that he came down from heaven and took a human body, at that time he diffused the sweetness and fragrance of his name into the whole world.[38] This is the ointment of which the prophet speaks in the psalm: "As ointment on the head that comes down to the beard, to the beard of that Aaron, which comes down to the fringe of his garment" [Ps 133:2]. This ointment then comes down from the head to the beard of Aaron and from there to the fringe of his garment, that is, to the entire body of the church.

4. But let us return to the subject. In that pound of ointment, then, that was pure or precious, the apostolic doctrine was shown that the church received. For the church had no other way of coming to Christ than by apostolic doctrine. But see the mystery of faith that is shown in advance in that woman. She did not immediately anoint the

Lord's head, but his feet. In the feet of Christ is shown the mystery of his incarnation whereby at the end of time he consented to be born from a virgin. But in the head is shown the glory of his divinity in which before all time he proceeded from the Father. Therefore the church first comes to the Lord's feet, and then to the head, since it never would have been able to recognize the glory of his divinity, which is from the Father, unless it had learned of Christ's incarnation from a virgin. And therefore we read the Scripture about the lamb that was offered in the law as a mystery of Christ: "You shall eat his head together with his feet" [Exod 12:9], that is, we should believe both concerning Christ, that he is God and man. God from the Father, man from the virgin. For in the head, as we said, his divinity is signified, which is from the Father; but in the feet is signified his incarnation, which is from the virgin. In no other way can we be saved except by believing both of Christ. Whence some heretics, such as Photinus, who confess only that Christ is a man, denying his divinity, hold on to his feet to be sure, but they do not have his head, since they have lost the head of faith.[39] But we rightly hold fast to both in Christ, since we confess both. We hold the feet, since we believe in his incarnation from a virgin. We also hold on to the head, since we confess his divinity from the Father.

5. Now in the hair with which the woman wiped the feet of the Lord is shown the people of the church, since they venerate the incarnation of Christ and apostolic doctrine. But these are the hairs of which we read that it is said to the church in the Song of Songs, "Your hair is as flocks of goats that have appeared from Gilead" [Song 6:4]. But rightly are the people of the church signified by hair, since just as hair is a great adornment for women, so the believing people adorn the church of Christ. But we can recognize likewise in the hair the soul's virtues being signified;[40] but in the precious ointment, the works of mercy. If then there be a work of mercy and piety in us, it is as if we are anointing the Lord's feet with precious ointment. Thus when we give alms to the poor, we anoint the Lord's feet, who said, "When you did it to one of my least ones, you did it to me" [Matt 25:40]. If the virtues of the soul are also in us, it is just as if we are wiping the Lord's feet with our hair. For Christ is refreshed and renewed in every virtue of our soul, in every pursuit of our faith, in every work of justice, mercy, and piety, since he himself is the author and founder of every good work.[41]

Sermon 12

On the Epistle to the Romans

1. As your love has heard, in the epistle that he wrote to the Romans the blessed apostle Paul discusses and demonstrates that the Son of God became incarnate from a virgin not only for the sake of the Jews, but also for the sake of the Gentiles [see Rom 1:3; 3:21–31; 15:7–12]. <The law> had predicted this, the prophets had foretold it too. For it would not have been right for the Son of God to descend from heaven, he who created all nations, for the sake of saving only one nation. To be sure, it was first offered to the Jews due to the merit of the patriarchs [see Rom 15:8] from whose race they descended. But because they repudiated the gift of such a great grace when it was offered to them, this salvation was given to various races and nations, as the apostle Paul says to the Jews: "It was necessary first to announce the word of God to you, but because you have judged yourselves unworthy of eternal life, behold we are turning to the Gentiles" [Acts 13:46].

2. Therefore the advent of Christ became the salvation of all nations, and the redemption of the whole human race. For it was the Creator who redeemed us. He who made us saved us. After all, it is not without a reason that are we said to have been redeemed by Christ rather than bought, since the apostle says of him, "Who redeemed us by his own blood" [see Rom 3:24; 5:9; Eph 1:7; Col 1:14].[42] He did not say "bought," but "redeemed," because what is redeemed is one's own, but what is bought belongs to someone else. For instance: If someone purchases a field or a slave, which he did not have before, he is said to buy it. But if he purchases one whom he had and lost, he is not said to buy but to redeem, since he is redeeming his own, and he is redeeming one whom he had possessed. This is why Romans who are set free from their captivity among the barbarians upon the payment of a price are said to be "redeemed" [see Rom 3:24], not "bought."

3. Therefore because humanity too was the work of Christ—for at the beginning of the world humanity was fashioned by him according to the will of the Father—humanity is rightly shown to be redeemed by Christ rather than bought, since he redeemed those who had been his own, and whom he himself had created. For long ago human beings had encountered the dominion of the devil as a barbarian captivity,

with the result that they withdrew from their original Lord and were captured by the enemy's deceit. But the reason we were redeemed by the blood of Christ, the reason we were liberated from the devil's captivity, was so that we might return to our original Lord. We should no longer withdraw from him, lest we again encounter the devil's captivity and by no means deserve to be liberated again [see Heb 6:6]. For the price was not small that the Son of God consented to offer for our redemption, namely his own sacred blood. If we make light of the grace of such a great redemption, we are deceiving ourselves. For the Son of God is not still to be crucified for us, that we might await another redemption. This then is the reason the apostle exhorts us by saying in today's reading that since we have the grace of such a great redemption before our eyes, we should faithfully obey the author of our redemption and salvation.

4. Now let us consider what the same apostle set forth with a profound spiritual meaning in the previous section, when he says, "There is one person who believes he can eat all things. But he who is weak eats vegetables" [Rom 14:2]. This is no trivial question among the apostle's statements. But let us see if with God's help we can give a partial explanation of it. The apostle is not speaking here of the weakness of the flesh and of bodily health, but of the weakness of the mind and the health of the soul. For true weakness is that kind when the mind is troubled by sins; and true health is that kind when the soul does not languish from any malady of sin. Desire, avarice: these <are> the illnesses of the soul. The lust of an illicit longing is a weakness of the mind. Fury, wrath, vanity, envy, and the other vices, these are illnesses of the soul and wounds to the mind, which lead the soul all the way to the endangerment of salvation and to the death of sin. And so, the one who lies sick in sins of this sort, even if he is sound in body, is sick all over. The one who is sick in his mind, is sick in his soul. But the one who is estranged from these vices, even if he is sick in body, is utterly healthy in mind, because God desires the health of the mind more than that of the body.

5. Do you want proof of this? That poor man Lazarus (*Eleazarus*), as we read in the gospel, was always weak in body until his death [see Luke 16:20–22]. For he was full of sores, but his mind was completely sound, since he was not sick with any malady of sin. After all, when he died he was taken by the angels and brought to Abraham's bosom. The rich man, on the other hand, at whose gate poor Lazarus was lying, was of sound body to be sure, but utterly infirm in his mind, since he

suffered from the malady of grave sin. He also had a fever of lustful desire, a fever of greed, and many wounds of sins. And therefore, as soon as he died, he was brought to the place of torments. O blessed sickness of Lazarus and wretched health of the rich man! The former is brought to the place of refreshment, the latter to punishment. The former to the eternal kingdom, the latter to everlasting punishment. Now the reason we have related these things is that we may know that the soul's health is more critical than the body's. For a bodily malady does not impede the soul's health; but a malady of soul, if it is not cured by good works, estranges it from salvation along with the body. Bodily health is good and desirable, but health of the mind is more potent, which procures salvation of the body as well; for health of the soul is the salvation of the body. The extent of the difference between the health of the body and the soul is shown in these matters. The body is cured by earthly medicine; the soul, by heavenly medicine. The body is cured by a compress of oil leading to health; the soul is restored by divine words leading to salvation.

6. But let us now return to the apostle's statement in which he says, "There is one person who believes he can eat all things; but the one who is weak eats vegetables" [Rom 14:2]. The one then who is sound in faith, sound <in> knowledge, sound in the heavenly precepts, sound in the works of justice, doubtless eats spiritually all things pertaining to the law and the faith. He hears the law, he eats the law, since the doctrine of the law is food to the soul. He hears the prophets, he eats from the prophets, since the preaching of the prophets is nourishment to the soul, and refreshment to the mind. He hears the gospel, he eats avidly from the gospel, since he hears Christ speaking there, the heavenly bread who came down to refresh the hearts of believers [see John 6:41]. He hears the apostle, he eats ravenously from the apostle, since he is rejuvenated by apostolic doctrine. And by this means the faithful soul eats from all things, since he is rejuvenated from every divine Scripture with the food of faith and the words of truth. Just as <if> someone eats according to the body <…> different foods at a great luxurious banquet, has received from all things, so the faithful soul that is rich in Christ feeds on all the words of God, and is refreshed and filled.[43]

7. He says, "But let the one who is weak eat vegetables" [Rom 14:2]. Everyone who is worn down by the malady of sin is weak. He cannot eat all things because his soul does not receive the divine mysteries. But let him accept the right precepts of the commandments

as vegetables, in order to be strengthened, and he can recover his health, and then he could be strong enough to eat all things. If then we are gripped by some malady of sin in the soul, we should hasten to the healing of salvation, that we may deserve to receive the more solid food of justice and faith, that having truly become spiritual athletes we may be able to conquer <and> overcome the adversary, strengthened by the food of justice, by the food of truth, by the food of salvation, as those who will receive the crown of life and the prize of eternal immortality [see Jas 1:12; 1 Cor 9:24–25]. But let us consider this very thing in greater detail. Suppose for instance that someone suffers in his soul from the malady of the lust of the flesh. The precept of chastity and modesty is essential to him because the modesty of his mind is the healing of his body, so that he can be healed from the infirmity of sin from which he suffers; for chastity of the mind is the healing of the body. If on the other hand someone is sick with avaricious greed, which weighs more heavily than any sickness of the soul, since "greed is the root of all evils" [1 Tim 6:10], as the apostle says, to such a person the precept concerning the works of mercy is critical, that he may know that he cannot be healed in any other way than by going from being greedy to becoming charitable, generous from being covetous. If on the other hand someone labors under the malady of fury and wrath, the precept about patience is critically important, so that he can be cured from the sickness of rage. If someone again suffers from the infirmity of resentment and hatred, to this one too the precept of charity and fraternal love needs to be instilled, so that his soul can be healed. For a man of this sort cannot be healed in any other way than by banishing hatred from his heart and receiving fraternal charity. For just as love is from God [see 1 John 4:7], so hatred is from the devil [see 1 John 3:15; John 8:44], for God is the author of charity but the devil is the inventor of hatred.

8. Evil and each of the vices of sins are sicknesses of the soul, for which the divine precepts are necessary, as vegetables, that people may be able to recover the health of salvation. For spiritual vegetables of this sort restore sick souls until they confer upon them a very complete healing. And this is what the apostle says: "But let the one who is weak eat vegetables." On that account perhaps we read this statement by the Lord: "All these things as vegetables <…>"[44] [Gen 9:3]. For he fell into a serious malady of sin and would not have been able to be healed in any other way but by eating the precepts of salvation. Therefore if we are gripped by any sickness of this sort, we ought willingly

to eat the precept of modesty, the precept of chastity, the precept of patience, the precept of love and charity, in order that we may be able to recover with complete health, and be capable of eating the more solid foods of justice and faith. For it pertains to the healthy and the strong to eat solid food; above all it pertains to spiritual athletes. If then we deserve to eat the more solid foods of justice and faith, doubtless we shall become spiritual athletes, so that we can conquer and overcome the adversary in this life. Amen.

Sermon 13 (fragment)

Here Begins [the Sermon] on the Gospel of Matthew Where It Says, Jerusalem, Jerusalem, You Who Kill the Prophets

1. As your love has heard in today's reading, after delivering many reproaches against the ungodliness of the scribes and Pharisees, our Lord and Savior says to Jerusalem, "Jerusalem, Jerusalem, you who kill the prophets and stone those who have been sent to you" [Matt 23:37].[45] Here they are convicted under the name of Jerusalem, not the walls of Jerusalem, <but the inhabitants> of the city, or rather, the synagogue of the Jews, which is very often called Jerusalem. For it is not the walls of the city that killed the prophets or stoned those sent to them, but the people of the synagogue. For they killed the prophets long ago, they stoned the just. But perhaps the Jews now say that they are clear of the blood of the prophets or from the killing of the just, since they were not in fact alive at that time. But since they do not believe in the statements of the just and of the prophets about Christ, it is just as if they are even now stoning the just and killing the prophets. For what greater violence can be committed against the just and the prophets than not to believe in Christ? Since the Jews do not believe in him, doubtless they stone the just, not with stones from the roads but with a blasphemous mouth; and they kill the prophets, not with an iron sword but with a faithless pen. For the blasphemy of the Jews against Christ <is> the stoning of the just and the killing of the prophets. But it pertains to a good soldier to accept death on behalf of one's own king. This ought to be understood of the just and the prophets, since they are both good soldiers and worthy servants of Christ. Hence, doubtless, the stoning

of the prophets is an injury to Christ, and the death of the prophets is his death.

2. The reason we have said this is because even today we see the Jews persecuting the just and killing the prophets, since they do not believe in the statements of the just and the prophets about Christ. After all, it is not said to the synagogue of the Jews, "Jerusalem, Jerusalem, you who *killed* the prophets," but "you who *kill* the prophets." And it is not said, "you who *stoned* those sent to you," but "you who *stone* those who have been sent to you." Thus all Jews should understand that they too are guilty of killing the just and for the blood of the prophets. Therefore it is said to the synagogue, "Jerusalem, you who kill the prophets and stone those who have been sent to you; how often have I wanted to gather your children, as a hen gathers her chicks under her wings, and you were unwilling" [Matt 23:37]. When he says, "How often have I wanted to gather your children," [he shows that] now is not the first time, but repeatedly....

Sermon 14

On the Healing of the Paralytic and on Baptism

1. When our Lord and Savior came to Jerusalem, as your love has heard in today's <reading>, there was a pool there that is called Bethsaida in Hebrew, and it had five porticoes [see John 5:1–2]. And so in all respects that pool offered an image of the coming baptism.[46] But the distance between the grace of that pool and the grace of saving baptism is as great as the distance between an image and the truth. That water was stirred once a year [see John 5:3–4], this water of the church's baptism is always ready to be stirred. That water was only stirred in one location, this water is stirred throughout the whole world. There an angel came down, here the Holy Spirit. There it was the grace of an angel, here the mystery of the Trinity. There the water healed only one person per year, here it saves people daily. That water cured only the body, this kind saves both soul and body. That [saves] from a malady, this delivers from sin. That delivered the body alone from a malady, this delivers body and soul from sin. Before that water a multitude of sick people were lying, since it healed only one person per year; but before this water no one lies but the one who refuses[47] to come and be healed. It is always ready to heal, if only they come to be

healed. After all the Gentiles came and were healed. The Jews refused to come, and therefore they have remained in a state of perpetual infirmity.

2. Through Solomon the Holy Spirit plainly shows how great the grace of the church's baptism is when he says the following to the church: "Your eyes are like doves washed with milk, sitting upon an abundance of waters" [Song 5:12]. Now the eyes of the church are understood as the apostles and the martyrs who are esteemed in the body of the church as eyes that are more precious, who are dipped with the milky baptism of the church, so that spiritually they have become as white as milk. Do you want to know how the apostles are washed with milk? Listen to Paul as he speaks: "I gave you milk to drink, not solid food" [1 Cor 3:2]. Fittingly he who has been washed with milk offers milk. However, we especially understand these eyes of the church washed with milk as those infants who were killed for the sake of Christ by Herod in Bethlehem [see Matt 2:16]. For they were truly washed in milk who, since they were still nursing, earned the right to die for Christ. They were washed in milk, then, who while sucking their mothers' breasts endured martyrdom on Christ's behalf. The Lord himself clarifies that baptism signifies martyrdom when he says the following to his disciples: "I still have a baptism to be baptized with" [Luke 12:50]. Surely he did not say this about water baptism in which he had already been baptized by John, but concerning the baptism of his passion in which the one who deserves to be dipped is sufficiently blessed. To be sure baptism in water is a good thing, but better still and best is the baptism of martyrdom. In the former, there is forgiveness, in the latter there is a prize. In the former there is remission of sins, in the latter a crown of virtues is earned.[48]

3. But well did Solomon relate that there is an "abundance of waters" in baptism, saying to the church, "Your eyes are like doves that are washed with milk, sitting upon an abundance of waters," since the grace of the church's baptism is abundant by the gift of which the entire world has been irrigated. The water of that pool of Bethsaida cured once a year, but the grace of the church's baptism flows daily, increases daily, overflows daily, throughout kingdoms, nations, countless peoples of nations who experience its gift. The Jewish people alone refused to recognize the gift of such great water. And therefore it is said by that infirm man, who was shown as a symbol of the Jewish people, "For while I am going, someone else goes down before me" [John 5:7]. For while the Jewish people seek and hesitate about

the coming of Christ, the Gentile people go ahead of them. Having received healing before them, they have become first in faith, those who were prior in respect to salvation.

4. But now we ought to consider what the Lord said in today's reading to him who was healed after thirty-eight years: "Behold, you have now been healed. Do not sin, lest something worse happen to you" [John 5:14].[49] Whatever sins you had have been forgiven you. You have been healed of every infirmity of sin, of sickness of the soul, of malady of the body, of the disease of illicit lustful desire; you have arisen as a new man from the bath of regeneration [see Rom 6:4; Titus 3:5]. Watch out that you do not return to your former sins and run into the danger of death, since the grace of baptism is given [only] once. If someone loses it by his own negligence, or rather, by infidelity, he becomes guilty of his own death, since he was unwilling to guard such a great grace. That is why before you came to baptism, you were asked whether you renounce the world and its pomp and its works.[50] And you answered that you renounce them. And thus did you come to the grace of eternal baptism. Your words are binding before God. Your response is written in heaven. You promised God your fidelity; you promised the angels who were present, since angels are at hand when faith is demanded of us. Consider what you are doing. If what is promised to a man is strong, what about what is promised to God? As it is written, "From your mouth" you will either "be justified" or "condemned" [Matt 12:37]. You will be justified if you fulfill what you promised to Christ; you will be condemned if you are unwilling to maintain fidelity to what you promised. Listen to what Solomon says: "For a man's own lips become a strong snare to him" [Prov 6:2].

5. Since therefore our affair is with a Strong One, we ought to keep faith with what we promised, to guard the grace that we received, lest we meet with very great confusion on the day of judgment, when it begins to be said to us, "Friend, how did you enter here without a wedding garment?" [Matt 22:12]. And we would begin to be taken away by our hands and feet, as it is written, and cast into the outer darkness. And that is why Solomon says to you, "At all times let your garments be white, and let not the oil be lacking on your head" [Eccl 9:8]. We have garments ever white, if we preserve the grace of baptism intact. And we always have oil on our head, if we guard the saving chrism that we received, and then we will not be confounded on the day of judgment, but rather we will deserve to rejoice together with all the saints and elect of God in the <heavenly> kingdom.

Sermon 15

On the Washing of the Feet

1. After receiving a body from a virgin, our Lord and Savior indeed showed many examples of humility. But the one that has been reported in today's reading surpasses them all, that he deigned to wash the disciples' feet. For it says this: "And getting up from dinner, he took off his tunic and girded himself, and began to wash the disciples' feet" [John 13:4]. And why he did this he shows subsequently when he says, "You call me Master and Lord, and you say well, for indeed I am. If I have washed your feet, the Master and Lord, you too ought to wash one another's feet. For I have given you an example that you yourselves should do" [John 13:13–15]. This humility of the Lord is astonishing and beyond compare. The Lord of eternal majesty washes the feet of his own slaves, and he to whom angels minister in heaven ministers to people on earth. He humbled himself on earth, to keep you from exalting yourself in anything. He washes the feet of his disciples, to prevent you from scorning to wash the feet of fellow slaves. You cannot flatter yourself about wealth, nor about birth, nor about rank, since it is the Lord of rank and authority who deigned to do this and carry it out. For he gave an example of humility that we ought to follow and imitate. Yet in that deed is contained a great mystery of our salvation. But one must speak of it in its own passage.

2. For now let us speak according to the letter. Surely Abraham washed the Lord's feet when he appeared to him at the oak tree of Mamre [see Gen 18:1–4]. But a slave washed for a master, for it was fitting that a slave washed the Lord's feet. And when Abraham washed the Lord's feet, he performed this not for the Lord but for himself, in order to receive a blessing. After all, on the occasion of this obedient act of service, he received a son in his old age from a sterile wife. For at that time, when the Lord appeared to him at the oak tree of Mamre at midday, Abraham saw the future mystery prefigured. For in that oak tree of Mamre the cross of the Lord was being shown. But in the midday hour, the time of the passion was shown, since, as we read in the gospel, the Lord was crucified at the sixth hour for the salvation of the world [see Matt 27:45]. And the reason it relates that Abraham was resting under an oak tree was because the faith of the patriarchs did not rest except under the cross of Christ; at midday, when the heat

was normally extreme, since nothing cools all the burning heat of sin in us but the cross of Christ, by the shade of his passion.[51] It was not of course without reason that the Lord appeared at midday to Abraham at an oak tree, since at that time especially Christ was manifested, when he undertook the cross of the blessed passion, at midday, for the sake of our salvation. Therefore Abraham washed the Lord's feet, but he washed the Lord's feet indeed for his own sake. But in that washing of feet, he laid aside all the defilements of sins, since the washing of the feet of our Lord purifies from sins.[52] Gideon also washed the Lord's feet, as we read in the Book of Judges, not in order to do a favor but to receive a gift.[53] After all on the occasion of doing this duty, he both received all that he asked for and saw in advance the mysteries of the salvation that was coming. He offered a sacrifice upon a rock; the Lord touched the rock with a rod; fire went out from the rock and consumed the burnt offering [see Judg 6:21]. In that rock, the incarnation of Christ was shown, from which that divine spiritual fire proceeded, that is, the Holy Spirit, who burns up the vices of sins. For we cannot become a sacrifice worthy of God unless we are illumined by that divine fire, that is, by the Holy Spirit, who burns up the vices of the flesh within us, so that he washes us from every defilement of sin. Then, when he went into battle against his enemies, he was ordered to select only three hundred men, by whom he brought back a celebrated victory over the enemy [see Judg 7:6, 16].[54] Obviously he could not have emerged as victor by any other number than by that one in which the mystery of the cross was signified. For in the number three hundred, according to Greek methods of calculation, the letter *tau* is signified, in which an obvious figure of the cross is shown. But he divided these three hundred into three parts, since the victory of the cross consists in faith in the Trinity.[55]

3. But let us return to the subject. Abraham washed the Lord's feet, Gideon too washed, but as slaves to their lord. Beyond all admiration is what is related in today's reading, that the Lord deigned to wash the feet of his own disciples. And let us speak first according to the letter. Behold how piously devout was that recompense. The apostles descended according to the flesh from the race of Abraham and from Gideon. Since therefore Christ repays, as one who is piously devout and good, he washed the feet of his disciples in order to render to the children in exchange for the gracious favor he had received from their parents. They had washed their Lord's feet; he washed the feet of his disciples, and paid back, only much more powerfully, in

exchange for the gracious gift. Back then they washed their Lord's feet in order to be sanctified; but the Lord washed the feet of his disciples, not in order to be sanctified but to sanctify them. They washed their Lord's feet in order to blot out their own sins; he washed the feet of his disciples in order to cleanse them from every defilement of sin. Back then Abraham offered to the Lord three ash-cakes [see Gen 18:6]; [the Lord] satisfied his children in the desert from five loaves [see Matt 14:17]. Back then Abraham made the Lord rest under an oak tree at midday; the Lord covered his children with the shade of his cross at midday, for it was at midday when the Lord was crucified [see Matt 27:45]. Back then Abraham killed a calf for the Lord; [the Lord] offered himself as a sacrifice for the salvation of his children.

4. But now let us look at the mystery of today's reading, although what we are speaking about is a mystery.[56] Well then, the Lord took off his tunic and girded himself with a towel. He put water in a bowl and began to wash the feet of his own disciples and wipe them with the towel with which he was girded. For not without reason is it said that the Lord took off his tunic and thus washed the feet of his disciples. And clearly it is at no other time that the feet of our souls are washed, and the footprints of our mind are cleansed, than when the Lord takes off his tunic;[57] at that time surely when on the cross he laid aside the tunic of the flesh he assumed, with which flesh he had clothed himself to be sure when he was born, but he took it off in his passion. But he took off the tunic of his flesh, in order to cover our nakedness. Ultimately, the one tunic of the body of Christ has clothed the entire world. And although the Lord took off the tunic of his flesh in the passion, yet he was not naked, since he had the clothing of the virtues. This then is what is understood by the tunic that was taken off.

5. But when he came to Peter to wash his feet, as today's reading has related, Peter said to him, "You shall never wash my feet. The Lord answered and said, If I do not wash your feet, you will have no part with me. But he answered and said, Lord, not only [my] feet, but [my] hands and head as well" [John 13:8–9]. At first, saint Peter refused the Lord's service, since he believed he was unworthy to have his feet washed by the Lord.[58] But after the Lord said to him, "If I do not wash your feet, you will have no part with me," he did not refuse Christ's service, in order to have fellowship with Christ. And therefore, since he knew that there was a great mystery concealed in the washing of the feet, for that reason he said, "Not only [my] feet, but [my] hands and head as well." He offered his feet, in order that the steps of his

life that had been made dirty in the defilement of sin in Adam would be washed by baptism. He offered his hands so that, since Adam had defiled his hands, which he had illicitly extended to the tree, our hands might be cleansed by the sacred baptism of Christ. He offered his head to be washed, lest the senses of his soul that are in the head should remain in the defilements of sinning Adam. And in this way he offered his entire self for baptism, he desired to be washed completely, so that through the washing of the head he might possess a clean heart; in the washing of the hands, he would carry out works of justice; but in the washing of the feet, he would walk with clean steps down the way of truth.

6. The Lord therefore washed the feet of his disciples to keep any traces of sin from Adam's defilement from remaining in us. For now the Lord is washing the feet of his servants whom he invites to the grace of saving baptism. And if it seems that this office is being carried out by humans, it is the work however of him who is the author of the gift, and he himself does what he himself has instituted. We exhibit the office, he bestows the gift. We do the duty, he the authoritative command.[59] But the gift is his, even if the service belongs to us. The grace is his, even if the duty is ours. We wash the feet of the body; but he washes the steps of our souls. We dip the body in water; he remits sins. We dip; he sanctifies. We on earth lay on our hands; he from heaven freely gives the Holy Spirit. For that reason, you catechumens, my sons and daughters, ought to hasten to the grace of baptism, so that by laying aside the filth of sins you may become entirely clean in the presence of our Lord and Savior, Jesus Christ....

Sermon 16

First Sermon for the Great Night

1. All the vigils that are celebrated to the honor of the Lord are indeed pleasing and acceptable to God, but this is the vigil beyond all vigils. After all, this night in particular is called "the vigil of the Lord." For we read that this is written: "This is the Lord's vigil for the watch to all the children of Israel" [Exod 12:42]. Now rightly this night is properly called the Lord's vigil because to this end he kept a vigil in life, so that we should not sleep in death. He indeed underwent the

sleep of death for us through the mystery of the passion; but that sleep of the Lord became a vigil (*vigilia*) for the whole world, since Christ's death banished from us the sleep of eternal death. For this is what he declares through the prophet when he says, "After I slept and woke up (*vigilavi*) and my sleep became sweet to me" [see Ps 3:5; Jer 31:26]. Clearly that sleep of Christ became sweet, who called us back to sweet life from bitter death. This night then is called the Lord's vigil because even in the very sleep of his passion he kept vigil, just as he himself demonstrates through Solomon when he says, "I sleep and my heart stays awake (*vigilat*)" [Song 5:2]; through which he clearly shows in himself the mystery of his divinity and of his flesh. For he slept in the flesh, he stayed awake in his divinity, because his divinity was not able to sleep. For we read this statement concerning the divinity of Christ: "Behold, he that guards Israel shall not slumber nor sleep" [Ps 121:4]. This is why he says, "I sleep and my heart stays awake," because in the very slumber of his passion he slept in his flesh, but his divinity illuminated the lower world, so that he rescued man who was being held in the underworld. For our Lord and Savior willed to illuminate all places in order to have mercy on all. He came down from heaven to earth in order to visit the world. He went down further to the lower world in order to illumine those who were being held in the lower world, in accordance with the statement of the prophet who said, "You who sit in darkness and in the shadow of death, a light has arisen for you" [Isa 9:2]. And so, fittingly, this night is called "the Lord's vigil" in which he not only illumined this world, but he also illumined those who were below (*apud inferos*).

2. Consequently, both the angels in heaven and humans on earth and the souls of the faithful in the underworld celebrate this vigil of the Lord. Angels in heaven celebrate this vigil of the Lord because by his death Christ destroyed death, trampled upon the underworld, saved the world and liberated humanity.[60] And they rightly celebrate because the world's salvation is the joy of angels. But if, as we read in the gospel, the repentance of one sinner is the joy of angels in heaven [see Luke 15:7, 10], how much more is the redemption of the whole world? Human beings on earth also celebrate because Christ undertook death for the salvation of the human race in order to conquer death by dying. And the souls of the faithful in the underworld celebrate because the reason Christ descended to the underworld was to keep death from reigning over them in the underworld. And what wonder is it if angels in heaven, humans on earth, souls below,

celebrate this vigil of the Lord, seeing that he who thought it fitting to die for us is the Creator of heaven, earth, and the lower world? We ought to say still more, that the Father himself celebrates this vigil of the Lord with the Son and the Holy Spirit, because according to the will of the Father, the Son underwent death, in order to give us life by dying. This vigil then is a feast not only for humans and angels but also for the Father, the Son, and the Holy Spirit because the world's salvation is joy to the Trinity. And therefore with all devotion we ought to celebrate the vigil of this great night, since on this night death was destroyed, the world was redeemed, the people were set free.

3. Rightly therefore this night is called "the Lord's vigil," since it is celebrated throughout the whole world to the honor of his name. The prayers of individual persons are as numerous as their longings; their lights are as numerous as the religious pledges springing from their merits. The darkness of the night is conquered by the light of devotion. The angels rejoice in heaven at the solemnity of this vigil. People on earth rejoice. The very powers of the lower world rejoice because the great solemnity of this night reached even to them. Although the Jews and Gentiles still seem to be alienated from this solemnity, yet they are not without joy, since they are overcome by a certain hidden grace and virtue of the name of Christ, who is lord over all. After all, a considerable number of pagans and Jews celebrate the solemnity of this vigil of ours as their own, even with glad hearts, if not through the religious ritual.

4. And since this is the night in which long ago the firstborn of the Egyptians were struck and the children of Israel were liberated [see Exod 12], let us pray to the Lord with our whole heart, with complete faith, that he may deem it fitting to deliver us from every attack of the enemy, from all fear of the enemy. May he not consider our merits but his own mercy, he who thought it fitting long ago to deliver even the children of Israel, not in view of their merits but in view of his mercy. May he protect us with his accustomed pity, may he drive back the barbarian nations,[61] may he do among us what holy Moses said to the children of Israel: "The Lord will fight for you and you shall be silent" [Exod 14:14]. He fights, he conquers, if he shows pity, if he forgives sins, if he does not look at our merits but his own clemency, since he is accustomed to be merciful even to those who are unworthy. We ought to pray as much as we can that he may consent to do this. For he says through the prophet, "Call upon me in the day of tribulation; I will rescue you and you will glorify me" [Ps 50:15].

SERMON 17

Second [Sermon] for the Great Night

1. The world itself is witness to how great a solemnity the present night is, during which vigils all night long are being celebrated; but not without reason, for on this night death was defeated, life lives, Christ rose from death. Surely he is that life of which Moses long ago had spoken to the people: "You will see your life hanging on the tree day and night, and you will not believe your life" [Deut 28:66]. This life then, that is, Christ the Lord, hung on a tree, when he was suspended on the cross for the salvation of the world. The Jewish people refused to believe in this life, and therefore incurred death, since the one who flees from life necessarily incurs death.

2. But it was not without reason that Moses predicted that this life would hang on a tree "day and night." As we read in the gospel, the body of the Lord was taken down from the cross on the very same day [see Matt 27:57; John 19:38]. But since it was still midday when the Lord was hanging on the cross, for three hours darkness came over the whole world [see Matt 27:45], and what is more, Christ hung on the cross throughout this day and night, seeing that night intervened in the middle of the day. For the sun could not bear the injury to its Creator, and therefore it was covered by darkness, lest it should be forced to take part in the crimes of the Jews. Even the sun shuddered at such a great crime of the Jews and that is why it received a veil of darkness, as a garment of mourning, to show that it was paying honor to the death of its Lord, as it were, with certain acts of obedient service. That "life" should be understood properly of Christ the Lord, he himself clarifies in the gospel, when he says, "I am the way, the truth, and the life" [John 14:6]. He is called the way because he leads to the Father; the truth, because he condemns falsehood; life, because he has dominion over death. Consequently, it is not without reason that the prophet says the following against death: "Where, O death, is your sting, where, O death, is your victory?" [1 Cor 15:55; cf. Hos 13:14]. For death, which was used to winning, was defeated by the death of the victor. And so life went down to death in order to put death itself to flight. Just as darkness is extinguished at the coming of the light, so death was destroyed by the coming of the original life. Although this life was not subject to death, yet it undertook death in the flesh, so that

it could destroy death itself by its hidden power. Just as if a lion should wear sheepskin in order to deceive the wolf, so Christ who is life took on flesh in order to deceive death, the devourer of human flesh. And so, since the Jews refused to believe in him, they incurred death, but we ought to believe in him, in order to be able to escape death.

3. This is the time of the Passover of which Moses long ago says to the people, "This will be the first month for you among the months of the year" [Exod 12:2].[62] So then, Moses declared the solemnity of this time the first month and the beginning of the year. For we ought to reckon this time as the beginning of the year. For it is befitting to call this month the first month, in which we have been saved from death. This is why the pagans are in great error when they consider January to be the first month. How then can January be understood as the first month of the year when in that month the whole world is found to be without grace as it were and arid? For at that time the earth has no grass, there are no flowers on trees, no buds on the vines. Therefore the first month is not January, when everything dies, but the season of Passover, when everything is made alive. For now the grass of the meadows rises from death, so to speak, now there are flowers on the trees, now there are buds on the vines, now the air itself is already joyous with the newness of the season, when sea captains undertake their voyages in safety. Therefore this time of the Passover is the first month and the New Year, when the very elements of the world are likewise being renewed. No wonder, of course, if the world is renewed at this time, since the human race itself has also been renewed today. After all, there are countless people throughout the whole world who have risen today in the newness of life through the water of baptism, having laid aside the oldness of sin [see Rom 6:4–6]. For at this time the sheep too are already safely bearing young, since they do not fear the cold of winter. In imitation of them, at this time the church of God produces for Christ as it were spiritual sheep, flocks of believers, as lambs, feeding them with the milk of life and with the drink of salvation. These are the spiritual sheep of which Solomon speaks: "Going up like sheep from the washing, all of them producing twins, and there is not a barren one among them" [Song 4:2; cf. 6:5]. These sheep then, that is, the sheep of the church, are shown to be bearing young by "the washing," since they produce children for God through the grace of baptism. They produce twin sons since they come to belief from the two peoples.

4. Hence the pagans err greatly in reckoning January to be the first month and the New Year, but it is not surprising that they err in respect to seasons since they err in respect to religion. But we who truly believe that this time of Passover is the New Year, we ought to celebrate the holy day with all delight and exultation and eagerness of soul, in order that we may be able fittingly to say that which we responded in today's psalm: "This is the day that the Lord has made, let us exult and be glad in it" [Ps 118:24]. We will be able to say this confidently, if we faithfully obey his commands in all things, so that we may be able to arrive at eternal life and perpetual rejoicing in the kingdom of heaven.

Sermon 17A

On the Passover

1. When our Lord and Savior came to the time of his passion, in order to show beforehand what great Paschal blessedness was before him, he said, "With desire I have desired to eat this Passover with you" [Luke 22:15]. We can recognize how great was the Feast of Passover from the fact that our Lord and Savior desired to fulfill it. The blessedness of this Passover was desired by angels, it was desired by the law, it was desired by the just, it was desired by the prophets, but its time had not yet arrived. And the Feast of this Passover had been contemplated long ago in the law, to be sure, but only in figure. What therefore the law contemplated in figure, Christ the Lord completed in truth. For Christ's suffering (*passio*) is the true Passover (*Pascha*), whence came the name of Passover.[63] The apostle's words clearly point to the same thing when he says, "For Christ our Passover has been sacrificed. And so," as the same apostle goes on to say, "let us celebrate the feast not with the old yeast nor with the yeast of malice and wickedness, but with the unleavened bread of sincerity and truth" [1 Cor 5:7–8]. Therefore, we must exclude from our hearts all yeast of malice and sin, so that we may become unleavened bread as it were, with a pure mind and upright conscience, in order that we may be able to celebrate Christ's Passover worthily.

2. But if we retain the yeast of sin and malice in our heart, we do not deserve to celebrate the Lord's Passover. And that is why the

apostle says, "Purge out the old yeast in order that you may be a new lump,[64] as you are unleavened" [1 Cor 5:7].[65] We are unleavened if we remain without the yeast of malice. We are unleavened if we are estranged from all sprinkling of sin. For as the apostle says, "a little yeast corrupts the whole mass" [1 Cor 5:6]. And therefore we ought to purge out and throw away from us all the yeast of sin, in order that we may deserve to enjoy the Passover feast, of which the Lord says to his disciples, "With desire I have desired to eat this Passover with you" [Luke 22:15]. Therefore we eat the Passover with Christ, since he feeds those whom he saves. For he is the author of the Passover, he is the author of the mystery, who fulfilled the Feast of this Passover for this reason, to refresh us with the food of his passion and restore us with his saving cup. Since therefore the Lord wanted to make us sharers in such a great feast, let us pray that we may receive his sacraments worthily in order that we may justly deserve to attain to the Lord's blessing. Amen.

Sermon 18

On Nicodemus and on Baptism

1. When our Lord and Savior was showing forth the power of his divinity with various signs and miracles, it says, "Nicodemus came to him, a ruler of the Jews, at night time, and he said to him, We know that you have come as a teacher from God. For no one does these signs that you do unless God is with him" [John 3:1–2]. This Nicodemus, ruler of the Jews, longed indeed to come to the Lord, but he feared offending the Jews, and therefore he came to the Lord not in the day but at night, since he was still in the grip of the night of ignorance and of the unbelief of the Jews. For Christ the sun of justice [see Mal 4:2] had not yet illumined his heart, since he had not yet recognized the light of truth. This is why the Lord said the following in the gospel: "He who walks in the day does not stumble. But he who walks at night stumbles, since the light of the world is not in him" [John 11:9–10]. The one who follows Christ, the eternal light, always walks in the day. The coming of night does not hinder such a person, since the light of truth is always in his heart. But the one who does not know the true light, even if he walks in the day, is always in the night.

Since therefore Nicodemus was still in the grip of the ignorance of the Jews, it is rightly said of him that he came to the Lord at night. But the very sentiment that is expressed makes clear that Nicodemus was at that time in the night of ignorance. For he says to the Lord, "We know that you have come as a teacher from God. For no one can do such signs that you do unless God is with him" [John 3:2]. He thought that the one who is the author of heavenly doctrine was one of the teachers. He marveled at the miraculous signs in one whom he ought to have recognized as the Lord of glory based on those signs, since no one but God could have worked such great miraculous signs. Therefore although Nicodemus came to the Lord at night time, yet since he had come to God, who is the true light, he did not depart without the grace of light.

2. And so the Lord said to him, "You must be born again" [John 3:3], in order to pour the light of the new birth into his heart. But since Nicodemus could not yet fully recognize the grace of such a great birth, he answers and says, "How shall this be? Can a man who is old enter into his mother's womb and be born again?" [John 3:4]. Then [Jesus] says plainly, "Unless someone is reborn from water and the Holy Spirit, he cannot enter into the kingdom of God. For that which is born of flesh is flesh; but what is born of Spirit is spirit" [John 3:5–6]. Here manifestly and clearly the Lord shows Nicodemus that there are two births: one earthly, the other heavenly; one of flesh, the other spiritual. But he shows that the spiritual is much more powerful than the fleshly when he says, "That which is born of flesh is flesh; but that which is born of Spirit is spirit."

3. Therefore the fleshly birth is from human beings; the spiritual birth is from God; the former is from humans, the latter from God; the former procreates a human being for the world; the latter gives birth for God. The former pours forth a birth for the earth; the latter transfers him to heaven. The former has temporary life, the latter eternal. Finally, the former makes children of humans; the latter children of God. For the latter spiritual birth is carried out completely invisibly, just as the former is carried out visibly. For the one who is baptized in the font is indeed seen to be dipped, he is indeed seen to come up out of the water; but what is accomplished in that bath is not seen, but the church of the faithful alone understand spiritually that a sinner goes down into the font, but one cleansed from all sin comes up. Blessed therefore and truly heavenly is that birth that makes children of God out of the children of human beings!

Since Nicodemus had not yet recognized this mystery, he says to the Lord, "Can someone, when he is old, enter again into his mother's womb again and be born again?" [John 3:4]. Nicodemus was still fleshly, therefore he spoke in fleshly terms. But the Lord, in order to lead his fleshly senses to the spiritual understanding, says, "Unless someone is reborn from water and the Spirit he will not enter the kingdom of heaven" [John 3:5], in order to show him with what birth it was necessary for each person to be reborn. For this spiritual birth makes infants out of old people. For those who are reborn in baptism are reborn into innocence, having laid aside the oldness of error and the evil of sin. For it is the spiritual womb of the church that conceives and gives birth to children for God.

4. Since therefore, you candidates for baptism (*competentes*), my sons and daughters, you have to be reborn in innocence through the grace of God; having laid aside all the oldness of sin, you ought to preserve intact and untainted the grace of your birth, so that you can truly be called and indeed be children of God [see 1 John 3:1], and be deemed worthy of entrance into the heavenly kingdom.

Sermon 18A (fragment)

On Baptism and on the Holy Spirit

...For this birth makes us worthy of the heavenly kingdom, since, as your love has heard, the Lord says, "Unless someone is reborn from water and the Holy Spirit, he will not enter into the kingdom of heaven." And he added, "That which is born of flesh is flesh," since it is born of flesh. "But that which is born of Spirit is spirit, <for God is spirit>" [John 3:5–6].[66] And how is it that the heretics have dared to deny that the Holy Spirit is God, when they see clearly that the Holy Spirit is called God by the Son of God? Therefore our spiritual birth is not without the Holy Spirit, and not unfittingly, since just as our first creation (*figuratio*) was by the Trinity [see Gen 1:26], so the second creation is by the Trinity. For there is no work of the Father without the Son, nor without the Holy Spirit, since the work of the Father is the work of the Son; the work of the Son is the work of the Holy Spirit. For the grace of the Trinity is one and the same. We are saved therefore now by the Trinity, since at the beginning we were made only by the Trinity.[67] In the creation of humanity there is one work of the Trinity;

there has been one loss for the Trinity, now long ago, in the perishing of humanity....

Sermon 19

On the Lord's Passion Where It Says, Then the Soldiers of the Governor Took Jesus into the Praetorium and Gathered an Entire Cohort around Him. They Stripped Him and Draped a Crimson Robe on Him [Matt 27:27–28]

1. Many readings have been introduced, to be sure, but from what source in particular ought we to speak than from the gospel, on which our salvation is uniquely based? The reading from the prophets is indeed good, but the gospel is better, since in the reading of the prophets there is prediction, but in the gospel, truth is revealed. The sayings of the prophets are obscured by the clouds of mysteries; but the sayings of the gospel are illumined by the brightness of the sun of justice [see Mal 4:2].

And so today's reading of the gospel has made known the injustices our Lord and Savior experienced from the Jews and the Gentiles for the sake of human salvation. For when our Lord and Savior was taken by the soldiers to be led to the cross, "they clothed him with a purple tunic and draped a crimson robe on him. And they placed a crown of thorns upon his head, and a staff in his right hand. And falling to their knees before him they worshiped him, saying, Hail, king of the Jews" [Matt 27:28–30].[68] Jews and Gentiles did these things indeed in mockery. But now, we recognize these very deeds as a heavenly mystery. Iniquity was at work in them; in the Gentiles the mystery of faith and the reckoning of truth [was at work]. As a king he is clothed with a purple tunic, but as the prince of martyrs with a crimson robe, since he shines as precious crimson with his sacred blood. But as a victor he received a crown, since a crown is conferred properly upon a victor. But as God he is adored on bended knee. Therefore as a king he is clothed with purple, as the prince of martyrs with crimson, as a victor he is crowned, as Lord he is greeted, as God he is adored.

2. But we can also recognize in the purple tunic the church being signified, which shines with royal splendor as it abides in Christ

the king. And this is why it is called a "royal race" by John in Revelation [Rev 1:6; cf. 1 Pet 2:9]. This is the purple of which we read the words in the Songs: "Its entire bed purple" [Song 3:10]. For Christ rests in the bed in which he will be able to find purple, that is, royal faith and a precious mind. For purple is truly shown to be a precious and royal thing, since although it is a natural product of the earth, yet it changes its nature when it is dyed, and it changes its outward appearance. It is one thing in its nature, another in its outward appearance. The nature in it is without value, but its change is precious. So too our flesh by nature is indeed without value, but it is made precious by the transformation of grace, since in the [purple] spiritual crimson, like purple it is dipped in three ways into the mystery of the Trinity. Whence if we want to be reckoned to be <in> the precious purple, we need to preserve the grace of our transformation, so that we can be deemed worthy of such a great king.

We can likewise apply the crimson robe to the glory signified in the martyrs, who have been dipped in their own blood and adorned with the blood of martyrdom, as they reflect precious red dye in Christ. This is the red dye that was long ago commanded to be offered to adorn the tabernacle of God [see Exod 26:31]. For the martyrs adorn the church of Christ. But that red dye that was commanded to be offered for the adornment of the tabernacle was twofold. For the martyrs of Christ have a twofold grace, since they hand over both body and soul to suffering. On the outside their flesh is stained with the blood of martyrdom, on the inside their soul is embellished with the confession of faith. And through this, martyrs offer a twofold red dye for the adornment of the tabernacle, since they become precious to the Lord in both their body and soul.

3. Now in the crown of thorns that the Lord received on his head [see Matt 27:29], our gathering was being shown, we who come to belief from the Gentiles.[69] Although we were once thorns, that is, sinners, yet by believing in Christ, we have been made into a crown of justice, since we no longer pierce or wound the Savior, but we surround his head with the confession of faith, as we confess the Father in the Son, since God is the head of Christ, as the apostle makes clear [see 1 Cor 11:3]. This is the crown that David once predicted in the psalm: "You set a crown of precious stone upon his head" [Ps 21:3]. Long ago, to be sure, we were thorns, but after we began to be counted in the crown of Christ, we became precious

stones. For he made precious stones out of thorns, he who raised up sons of Abraham from stones [see Matt 3:9].

4. And today's reading did not superfluously report that a reed (*arundinem*) was placed in the Lord's right hand [see Matt 27:29]. Listen to what David testifies about Christ in the psalm: "My tongue is a reed (*calamus*) of a swiftly writing scribe" [Ps 45:1]. Therefore, when he was about to undertake the passion, he took a reed (*calamum*) in his right hand, whether in order to grant pardon to our crimes with a heavenly annotation, or in order to inscribe his own law in our hearts with divine letters, as he himself says through the prophet: "I will write my laws in their hearts, and I will write them in their minds" [Jer 31:33]. But we can understand the reed (*arundine*) in another way, since the spiritual meanings are multiple. By reed, which is hollow and without marrow, the people of the Gentiles is demonstrably referred to, who long ago were without the marrow of divine law, empty of the faith, devoid of grace. A reed of this sort, then, that is, the Gentile people, is placed in the Lord's right hand, since the Jewish people who persecuted Christ were now esteemed to be in his left hand. But Isaiah shows that the people of the Gentiles are signified in the reed when he said the following about the Lord: "A bruised reed he will not break" [Isa 42:3; cf. Matt 12:18–21]. Although they seemed bruised by the devil, yet they were not broken by Christ but made solid.[70] But in the genuflecting of the worshipers [see Matt 27:29], the faith and salvation of the believing peoples was shown, who daily worship Christ the eternal king on bended knee.

5. Finally, today's reading related that when the Lord was led to his passion, "they found a certain man Simon of Cyrene. They compelled this man to carry his cross" [Matt 27:32]. In the cross of Christ there is the triumph of virtue and the trophy of victory. Hence blessed is this Simon who merited so much as to be the first to carry the signs of such a great triumph! To be sure, the Lord carried this cross first [see John 19:17], and then Simon was compelled to carry it in order that in his cross the Lord would clearly show the grace of the heavenly mystery, since he was God and man, Word and flesh, Son of God and Son of man. As man, then, he was crucified, but as God he triumphed in the very mystery of the cross. The passion pertains to his flesh, the triumph of victory pertains to his divinity.[71] For through his cross Christ triumphed over death and the devil. By the cross Christ ascended as on a triumphal chariot. And this is why

he chose four evangelists, as a choice heavenly four-horse chariot, to announce to all the world the champion of such a great victory. This Simon of Cyrene then carried on his shoulders the triumph of this victory; he became a companion of his passion in order to be a companion also of his resurrection, since the apostle says, "If we die together, we shall also live together. If we endure together, we shall also reign together" [2 Tim 2:11–12]. And therefore the Lord says in the gospel, "He who does not take up his cross and follow me cannot be my disciple" [Luke 14:27].

6. The cross of Christ is our victory, since the cross of Christ obtained the triumph of victory for us.[72] Who of us is so blessed as to deserve to carry Christ's cross in himself? He carries the cross of Christ in himself who dies to the world, who is nailed to Christ. Listen to the apostle showing this: "I have been crucified with Christ, but I live, no longer I, but Christ lives in me" [Gal 2:19–20]. Therefore the one who is estranged from the vices of the flesh, as the apostle says, estranged from the desire of the world, is nailed together with Christ. But the one who lives in the vices of the flesh, in the lust of the age, cannot say, "I am nailed together with Christ," for he does not live according to Christ, but according to the life of the world, according to the will of the devil.

Therefore the cross of Christ is the salvation of the world, and the triumph of heavenly victory. For even great kings long ago, when they won a celebrated victory over vanquished nations, made the trophy of victory in the shape of the cross, where they would hang the captured spoils of the enemy, as a sign for eternal remembrance. But the cross of Christ is a far different kind of victory. The victory of those kings came about by the destruction of nations, the overthrow of cities, the plundering of provinces.[73] But in this victory of the cross there is redemption of nations, salvation of cities, freedom of provinces, security for the whole world. Perhaps for the devil alone is there destruction, and captivity of demons, since the cross of Christ redeemed the world and took demons captive. After all, the captured spoils of demons hang down from the triumph of the cross of Christ. Even today the demons hang on the sign of the cross, they are tortured and burned, since they are held captive by the faith of the cross and by the sign of the passion.

7. Then when they came to Golgotha, it says, "They gave him vinegar mixed with gall. And when he tasted it, he was unwilling to drink it" [Matt 27:34]. This is what he himself had predicted through

David as coming in the future, when he said, "They gave [me] gall for my food and they gave me vinegar for my thirst" [Ps 69:21]. Consider the mystery. Long ago Adam tasted sweet fruit and obtained the bitterness of death for the human race. The Lord, on the other hand, accepted the bitterness of gall, in order to call us back from bitter death to sweet life. He accepted therefore the bitterness of the gall to extinguish in us the bitterness of sin; he accepted the sourness of the vinegar, but poured out the precious wine of his blood for us. And so, he endured evils, but paid back good things; he received death, but freely gave life. Not without reason was he crucified in this location, where it is claimed that the body of Adam was buried.[74] The reason Christ is crucified where Adam had been buried was so that life would work from that place where death had previously worked, so that life would rise out of death. Death through Adam, life through Christ, who thought it fitting even to be crucified for us, and to die, for this reason, to blot out the sin of the tree by the tree of the cross, and to absolve the penalty of death by the mystery of death.

Sermon 20 (fragment)

On the Passion

...Since then for the sake of our salvation our Lord and Savior deigned to undertake the passion of the cross too, we ought to have the grace of such a great redemption always before our eyes, and faithfully obey his precepts in all things. For we fell in Adam, but we have resurrected in Christ; we were broken by Adam's sin, but we have been put back together through the grace of Christ...

...Therefore in a potter's field of this sort, as the evangelist says, that is, in the church of Christ, there is a burial place for foreigners [see Matt 27:7]. For when we believe in Christ, we become foreigners to the world, so that we may be deemed members of God's household. Foreigners to the earth, citizens of heaven [see Eph 2:19]; last in the world, neighbors of Christ. Listen to the apostle Peter showing this same thing when he says, "As strangers and foreigners, keep yourselves from fleshly desires" [1 Pet 2:11]. And hear Paul saying something more: "You are dead, and your life is hidden with Christ in God. When Christ your life appears, then you too will appear with him in glory" [Col 3:3–4]. If then we are foreigners to the vices of the world, to the desires of the flesh, then we are buried in the potter's field, that is, in the church of Christ, but we are buried happily, because we are dead to this world in order that we may be alive to Christ. We are buried in respect to iniquity, we rise again to justice. We are buried to the vices so that we may rise again to the virtues. This is the very thing that the apostle Paul makes clear when he says, "For you were buried together with him through baptism into death, in order that just as Christ resurrected in life, so we too may walk in the newness of life..." [Rom 6:4].[75]

Sermon 21

<The First> Sermon on Saint John, Evangelist and Apostle[76]

1. Saint John the apostle and evangelist, whose [heavenly] birthday we celebrate today, had a uniquely great grace before the Lord, as we read in the gospel that he was singled out by Christ with a special affection. As we read in Revelation, after the Lord's passion, he was banished to the island of Patmos for the sake of Christ's name, and was chained up in shackles [see Rev 1:9–10]. But to that apostle the shackles were not a punishment but an honor. For it is an honor to endure injustice for Christ, and the greatest honor, that every injustice and punishment by humans that are inflicted for Christ's sake raise one up to glory. After all, John himself, when he was bound in shackles on the same island, was lifted up in spirit and testified that a door in heaven had been opened to him [see Rev 4:1]. Therefore to that holy man John, the shackles were not a heavy burden, but wings of virtue by which he was lifted up to heaven.[77]

But in Revelation, he himself has reported how great the glory of heaven was that he saw, when the door to heaven was opened for that reason. For he saw the throne of God in heaven [see Rev 4:2]; he saw the Son of God sitting at the right hand of the Father [see Rev 4:2]; he saw choirs of angels [see Rev 5:11]; he saw twenty-four elders and four living creatures full of eyes in front and behind, shouting in praise of the Lord with unceasing voices and saying, "Holy, holy, holy Lord God Sabaoth" [Rev 4:8; Isa 6:3]. "Heaven and earth are full of your glory." "Hosanna in the highest" [Matt 21:9; Mark 11:10]. In imitation of them the whole throng of the faithful call out daily in the church in praise of God. He saw as well many other secret mysteries he was commanded to keep silent about, as he himself attests [see Rev 10:4].[78]

2. Indeed, when he was on the island, as he himself relates, "a book was given to me, and I was told to eat it. And I ate it. And it was sweet in my mouth like honey; but in my stomach it was bitter. Then it was said to me, You must prophesy still to the nations" [Rev 10:9–11]. And this is what happened. For that book that he took to eat was the book of the Gospel that he wrote later. For when Domitian Caesar, who had banished him, was slain, he was released from the island, and then he wrote the Gospel book in his own name. He said that it was sweet in his mouth but bitter in his stomach: sweet because of the preaching, bitter because of the persecution, for while he preaches the sweetness of the faith, he experiences the bitterness of persecution.[79] Yet this bitterness of persecution has great sweetness, since through persecution one attains to the sweet glory of martyrdom. For even trees have bitter roots, but the fruits they are accustomed to bring forth are sweet. So too persecution: it seems bitter indeed, but it brings forth the sweet fruit of salvation, while it renders those whom it persecutes either into confessors or martyrs.

3. But what he has said can also be understood in another way, that the book of the Gospel that he received to eat was sweet in his mouth but bitter in his stomach [see Rev 10:9–11]. Those who understand John's statements with a faithful understanding attribute sweetness to his mouth, that is, to his preaching, because they understand his words about faith piously. But those who understand the statements of the same man with a perverse meaning, such as the heretics, stir up bitterness because they turn the sweetness of faith into the bitterness of faithlessness. And that is why the former are shown to be in his mouth, and <the latter> in the stomach. In the mouth, [the organ] from which God is blessed, are the Catholics; in the stomach, whence things are expelled into the drain, are the heretics. Catholics then provide sweetness to the blessed John from his Gospel; but the heretics provide him with bitterness. Photinus embittered John, he who refused to believe that Christ was God, whom John clearly showed to be God when he said, "In the beginning was the Word, and the Word was with God, and the Word was God" [John 1:1]. Arius embittered [John], who did not believe that the Son proceeded from

the Father, though it is believed that the Word of the Father, the Son, proceeded from the Father in no other manner than properly from the Father's heart.[80] All heretics embitter John, who either destroy or attack the faith of his preaching. Therefore saint John has sweetness from his preaching because of Catholics, bitterness because of heretics, and sweetness because of the church's faith, bitterness because of the faithlessness of the synagogue, which was unwilling to receive the preaching of John.

4. After he was sent from the island, then, saint John wrote the Gospel, which is proclaimed throughout the whole world. After many persecutions, which he endured for the name of Jesus, when he was already a very old man, he changed residence from this world to the Lord. Indeed the Lord had said about him, as we read in the Gospel, "Thus I want him to remain until I come" [John 21:22]. But the Lord had not said that because he was not going to die, but because he would experience a death without pain. For this is reported: "Jesus did not say that he would not die, but, Thus I want him to remain until I come" [John 21:23]. For the Lord comes to each of the saints when he leaves his body. John, then, when he was already burdened by extreme old age, said to his disciples, as the writing that reports his falling asleep shows, that they made a grave for him. The Lord had told him on which day he would depart. And so his disciples made his grave that was big enough for his body. Saint John cast himself in there, and without any pain, without movement, without strain, departed from his body so that he seemed to go out rather than be shut out of his body.[81] And the reason the Lord had said of him, "Thus I want him to remain, until I come," is because he received a blessed sleep without pain. In this location such great miracles and wonders take place that even unbelievers scarcely can believe it. And it is no wonder of course if his grace is at work there, where his body is laid, since it is likewise at work where a small portion of his ashes are found. For since our church as well has merited to possess his remains, we ought to celebrate with all faith and devotion the [heavenly] birthday of his falling asleep, so that we can receive our portion with him and with all the saints.[82]

Sermon 22

The Second Sermon on Saint John the Evangelist[83]

1. Many great and illustrious things are indeed reported in the Gospel about saint John, whose [heavenly] birthday is today; but since we cannot recount all of them, let us speak of a few from the many. For to say something about the merits of the saints is the merit of sanctity. Among all the disciples he was the youngest; youngest in age indeed but eldest in faith, who in the Gospel is recorded among the first ones. After all, whenever the Lord wanted to choose some of the apostles, he chose John too with them.

2. When he was about to enter the house of the synagogue ruler to raise up his daughter from death, he chose John along with Peter and James [see Mark 5:37; Luke 8:51]. For he wanted these three men to be witnesses, when he raised the dead girl. The Lord did this for two reasons: either because the divine law had predicted that "every matter stands <by the mouth> of two or three witnesses" [Deut 19:15], or because no one could be raised from the death of sin apart from the grace and faith of the Trinity. Therefore the Lord called in three disciples when he raised up the dead girl, in order to show the mystery of the Trinity.

Also, when he wanted to reveal his glory to the disciples on the mountain, he likewise took John with Peter and James [see Matt 17:1–8]. For he led these three disciples onto the mountain by themselves and was transfigured before them. And Moses and Elijah appeared to them: "And the Father's voice was heard from heaven: This is my beloved Son in whom I am well pleased. Listen to him" [Matt 17:5]. See this mystery too: the way the Son of God is shown to be the God of heaven, of earth, and of the lower world. From heaven the Father bore testimony to the Son; from earth three apostles are chosen; from the lower world Moses is summoned as witness, since Moses tasted death. And lest there be any location exempt from providing testimony to Christ, Elijah too, who had not yet tasted death, was led from paradise as a witness; so that the God of heaven, earth, paradise and of the lower world, would have witnesses from every location and place. Likewise here then saint John is chosen among the first of the apostles.

3. Likewise at the time of the passion, when the Son of God had been hung on the cross for the world's salvation, the Lord commended

Mary, his mother according to the flesh, to no one but John, saying to him, "Behold your mother." And to his mother: "Behold your son" [John 19:27, 26]; leaving his own holy mother Mary to John, not that he who protects everyone with his divine regard would abandon holy Mary, for he himself is the defender and protector of all, but in order to show the affection of his own piety toward Mary. For the Lord was obligated to show pious affection toward Mary, since he is the author of pious duty. Likewise here then John is preselected among the holy apostles, since he was loved by Christ with a unique affection in view of the merit of his grace [see John 13:23].

4. But after the passion, when the Lord was resurrected from death, Peter and John, hearing about the resurrection, ran to the tomb to see [see John 20:2–4]. And <John> reached the tomb first, though he was not the first to go in, since he reserved for Peter the right to enter first. Therefore, it was from the love that he had for Christ that John ran ahead to the tomb before saint Peter; but that he reserved the place for Peter shows his humility. That he ran ahead there stemmed from his love of Christ; that he kept back was derived from the dignity of his superior. And in this way he preserved humility <with respect to> Peter and faith with respect to Christ.

5. And the same saint John wrote the Gospel. There is no one who does not know how extraordinarily splendid it is. The Gospel according to John is particularly necessary to use against all heresies, since Christ's divinity is declared clearly in it, and because he is shown to be God [see John 1:1, 14]. Since therefore today is the [heavenly] birthday of this great apostle, let us celebrate his memory with appropriate honor, in order that aided by his prayers we may be able to reach that eternal glory that is prepared for the saints of God.

Sermon 23

Sermon on Cain and Abel

1. Divine Scripture has spoken of Cain and Abel, as your love has heard in today's reading. Abel was a shepherd of sheep, but Cain was a farmer. "And it came about that both offered gifts before the Lord. And Abel offered some of the firstborn of his sheep and his fatlings.

And God looked upon Abel's gifts; but he did not show regard for Cain's gifts. And Cain was exceedingly sorrowful and his countenance fell" [Gen 4:3–5]. And what do we say? Is God an accepter of persons [see Acts 10:34], so that he regarded the gifts of Abel, on the one hand, but did not regard the gifts of Cain? May no one ever believe that. But it is because nothing can lie hidden from God, who reveals the minds and hearts of all, since he is the judge of conscience. Therefore God regarded the gifts of Abel because he offered his gifts to the Lord with an honest heart and a pure mind. After all, the Lord tells the one who was thinking about murdering his brother, "For if you offer it rightly but do not divide it rightly, you have sinned, be still" [Gen 4:7]. Cain is being convicted by the Lord that he should not carry out in deed what he was thinking in his heart. But he was so blinded by hatred toward his brother in his mind that he thought neither of fraternal piety nor of the present judgment of God. Neither the pious duty toward his brother, nor brotherly love itself, nor the divine rebuke was able to call him back from his criminal purpose. And this is why not without reason the Lord says in the gospel, "If you offer your gift at the altar, and remember that you have something against your brother, leave your gift at the altar and go first to be reconciled with your brother, and then offer your gift" [Matt 5:23–24].[84] If then we want our gifts to be accepted by God, we ought to be reconciled with our sisters and brothers, after which, when hatred has been eradicated, <...> , lest we become like Cain.

2. With Cain and Abel then God saw the gifts of their sacrifices, but he took into consideration the conscience of their interior mind, so that the one who was pleasing in his heart would be pleasing in his gift; and the one who was displeasing in his heart would be displeasing in his gift.[85] The gift of Abel pleased God because he offered the gift to the Lord with a pure heart; Cain's gift displeased God because he offered the gift to the Lord not with a pure heart but with a wicked mind, since he was thinking about killing his brother. Indeed, according to the figurative reckoning, even the very gifts show the great difference between the offerers. Cain offered gifts from the fruits of the earth, since his thinking was earthly; but Abel offered gifts from the fruits of the sheep, to show a sign of his own innocence. And not only from the fruits of the sheep did Abel offer gifts, but the fatlings of the sheep, where the fat works of mercy are shown. Therefore the gift of our innocence is acceptable to God, when we add to it works of mercy, as it were the fatlings of the sheep.

Nor is the fact that Abel was a shepherd of sheep a superfluous point. For he prefigured in himself an example of the one who says in the gospel, "I am the good shepherd. The good shepherd lays his life down for his sheep" [John 10:11]. In Abel an image has gone <before> so that the truth may be manifested in Christ. The former was a shepherd from the earth, the latter a shepherd from heaven. The former a shepherd of animals, the latter of martyrs. The former a shepherd of irrational sheep, the latter of rational ones.

3. But let us notice the great mystery. Although our Savior is called a shepherd, yet he is also called sheep and lamb [see Isa 53:7; Jer 11:19]. Finally, not without a mysterious indication of the Lord's passion was it read in today's reading that Abel offered a gift to the Lord God from the offspring of his sheep. The holy patriarchs and prophets, deservedly innocent, are called sheep and rams. For we read a Scripture about them: "The rams of the sheep are clothed [with wool], and the valleys shall abound in corn" [Ps 65:13]. And again: "But we are your people and the sheep of your flock" [Ps 95:7]. From this flock of saints that untouched spotless sheep came forth, that is, saint Mary, who gave birth to that purple lamb contrary to nature, that is, Christ the king.[86] Rightly is Christ the Lord understood as a purple lamb, since he was not made a king but born one. No king is born a king from the start; but after he is born he becomes king, or he receives the royal purple as his clothing, or the regal office. But our Lord and Savior came forth from the virgin's womb with regal authority, since he was a king long before he was born of the virgin. For he stood forth as one born from God the Father as king and Son of God. Listen to the Lord declaring this very thing in the gospel. For when Pilate asked him, "Are you a king?" he responded, "For this I was born, and for this I have come into this world" [John 18:37]. Even those Magi in the east recognized the dignity of this king at the very moment of his bodily birth, when they said to the Jews, "Where is the one who has been born king of Jews? For we saw his star in the east, and have come to worship him" [Matt 2:2].

To the extent that Abel's faith was better, since he offered gifts to the Lord from the fruits of his sheep, so much the more religious is the devotion of the Christian people, which we are, who offer gifts of innocence and simplicity to the Lord, if only we merit <...> from the Lord. Therefore we offer a gift to the Lord from the fruit of our sheep, if we live simply and innocently in the sight of God. And we offer a gift to the Lord from the fatlings of the sheep, if we exhibit to God the works of mercy and piety, as the fat.

Sermon 24

Here Begins [a Sermon] on the Holy Patriarch Joseph

1. The divine Scripture impresses upon us a considerable number of things about the holy patriarch Joseph [see Gen 37—41]. And we too are attempting to say some things, as those who are offering crumbs from large loaves of bread. Hence we read that it is written in the gospel, "For even the little dogs eat of the crumbs that fall from their masters' table" [Matt 15:27]. Even if the crumbs from a great feast do not satisfy, yet they do feed. After all, as soon as we come to belief, we are fed with crumbs as it were from the apostles' precepts.[87] But when we make progress in the faith, then an abundance of heavenly bread is brought in, that we may be satisfied with the heavenly bread of him assuredly who says in the gospel, "I am the living bread who came down from heaven" [John 6:51]. Let us not reject the crumbs of doctrine, then, since the crumbs come from the bread; and the reason we should not suppress the crumbs is so that we may merit being refreshed with the bread loaf. But let us now come to saint Joseph, that we may be fed by the example of his chastity and modesty, as it were with some heavenly bread.

2. This saint Joseph, then, of whom your love has heard in today's reading, had a handsome body [see Gen 39:6], but he was more handsome in his mind, since he was both chaste in body and pure in mind. The outward beauty of his body shone in him, but the beauty of his soul shone more brightly. And though for many bodily beauty is often an obstacle to salvation, it was unable to harm the holy man, since the loveliness of his soul governed the outward beauty of his body. Therefore the soul ought to rule the flesh, not the flesh the soul, since the soul is lord of the flesh; but the flesh is handmaid of the soul.[88] This is why that soul is wretched in which the flesh holds sway, and which from being lord becomes a handmaid, since it loses the dominion of faith and takes up service to sin.

But the soul of the patriarch Joseph faithfully held fast to its own dominion. In him the flesh was not able to rule in any respect. Indeed, when he was asked by his own mistress, who was an unchaste woman, to sleep with her, he refused to give in, since not even in the state of slavery had he lost the soul's rule [see Gen 39:7–8]. Whence when he was attacked with a slanderous falsehood, he was put in prison [see Gen 39:20]. But the holy man reckoned that prison to be a palace, or rather, he himself was a palace in the prison, since where there is faith, chastity, and modesty, there is Christ's palace, there is God's temple, there is the dwelling place of the Holy Spirit.[89] If therefore any man is flattered by the outward beauty of his body, or if some woman boasts over the beauty of her flesh, let them follow the example of Joseph, let them follow the example of Susanna [see Dan 13]. Let them be chaste in body, let them be modest in mind; such people are beautiful not merely to humans but also to God. For there are three examples of chastity in the church that everyone ought to imitate: Joseph, Susanna, and Mary. Let men imitate Joseph; women, Susanna; and virgins, Mary.

3. But according to the mystical or allegorical reckoning, Joseph was a prefiguration and type of the Lord. After all, if we consider the deeds of Joseph, at least in some measure, we recognize a figure of the Lord in him, manifestly shown in advance. Joseph has a varied tunic [see Gen 37:3]; our Lord and Savior is known also to have had a varied tunic, since he received the church gathered from various nations as a garment of clothing. And there is another variety of this tunic, that is, of the church that Christ received. For the church has diverse and various graces: it has martyrs, it has confessors, it has priests, it has ministers, it has virgins, it has widows, it has workers of justice. But that variety of the church is not a variety of colors, but a variety of graces; for our Lord and Savior shines forth with this variety of his church, as with varied and precious clothing.

Joseph was forcibly separated from his brothers and was purchased by the Ishmaelites [see Gen 37:25–28]. Our Lord and Savior too was forcibly separated from the Jews and was purchased by the Gentiles.[90] Finally, the Ishmaelites who purchased Joseph were carrying various kinds of perfumes with them, so that from that it could be shown that the nations that were coming to faith would fill the whole world with the fragrance of different odors of justice.

4. But let us consider the great mystery. Twenty gold pieces were given for Joseph [see Gen 37:28 LXX];[91] thirty silver pieces for the

Lord [see Matt 26:15]. The slave is forcibly separated for a dearer price than the Lord. But human calculation is greatly deceived about the Lord because the one who was sold is priceless. But let us consider this mystery more carefully. The Jews offered thirty silver pieces for the Lord; the Ishmaelites, twenty gold pieces for Joseph. The Ishmaelites purchased the slave for a dearer price than that for which the Jews purchased the Lord. In Joseph they venerated an image of Christ; in Christ they held in contempt the truth itself. The Jews offered for the Lord a cheaper price, since they reckoned the passion of the Lord to be of less worth. But how cheap can the Lord's passion be deemed to be, at the price of which the entire world was redeemed? For Christ's passion redeemed the whole world and the entire human race from death. Listen to the apostle himself showing this when he says, "You were bought at a great price" [1 Cor 6:20]. Listen to the apostle Peter likewise testifying, "Not with earthly gold nor with perishable gold were you redeemed from your vain way of life, but with the most precious blood of the immaculate Son of God" [1 Pet 1:18–19]. If we had been purchased from death with gold or silver, our redemption would have been cheap, since a person is worth more than gold or silver; but now we have been redeemed at an inestimable price, since the one who redeemed us by his passion is of inestimable worth.

5. If we should consider the other deeds of Joseph, too, we shall recognize in all of them an image of the Lord prefigured. Joseph suffers a slander from an unchaste woman, and the Lord was often attacked by slanders from the synagogue. Joseph experienced the punishment of prison, and the Lord accepted the passion of death. The former is thrown into prison; the latter descended to the underworld. For divine Scripture frequently is accustomed to call the realm below a prison; whence the following is said by the prophet, "Bring my soul out of prison" [Ps 142:7]. For the holy prophet longed to be delivered from the lower world. But consider the mystery in this. After Joseph went forth from prison, he became lord of Egypt [see Gen 41:37–46]. And after our Lord and Savior went forth from prison, he obtained dominion over the whole world through the knowledge of his faith. For the name of Christ rules everywhere, he is lord everywhere; he is believed in by the world, he is manifested by the age [see 1 Tim 3:16]; he is honored by the nations, he is worshiped by kings.

SERMON 25

Here Begins a Sermon on Saint Elijah

1. The reading introduced us to saint Elijah [see 1 Kgs 17—18]. And fittingly we read about saint Elijah during this time of fasting, since Elijah too fasted forty days and forty nights [see 1 Kgs 19:8]. He did not seek the bread of the world, since he had the bread of life in himself, that is, the word of God, by whose food and power he was strengthened during those days. Thus he seemed stronger than he had been at any other time. Well then, many miracles are reported of this Elijah, as your love has heard in part in today's reading. But since it would take too long to explain each of them, since an hour's time, or even entire days, would not suffice to narrate them, so let us say a few things from the many, in order that we may understand many things in the few.

2. When saint Elijah was enduring the last persecution by King Ahab and by his wife Jezebel, the Lord said to him, "Go to the brook and I will command the ravens, and they will feed you there, and you will drink water from the brook. And daily they brought him loaves in the morning and meat in the evening" [1 Kgs 17:3, 6]. One understands the extent of the Lord's care for his saints from the fact that he deigns to feed <them> even by means of the ministry of ravens. David had already previously spoken well and truly in the psalm: "For God does not kill a just soul by famine" [Prov 10:3].[92] The prophet saint Elijah had a just soul that the Lord was unwilling to wear down with constant hunger, so that he fed him by the service of birds. And although for a just soul food is inner, that is, the word of God by which it is always refreshed, yet it is not deprived even of this bread by the mercy of God. And by the ministry of ravens it is supplied indeed to this saint Elijah in the desert. But to Daniel in the lions' den he commanded a meal to be brought by a ministering angel [see Dan 14:33–39]. For Daniel too had endured persecution for justice's sake at the hands of the Babylonian powers. But the injustice of persecutors does no harm to the souls of the just. Ravens feed Elijah, wild beasts do touch Daniel [see Dan 6:16–18; 14:31–32], and people lie in wait and pursue.[93]

3. But let us return to the subject. God then feeds his servant Elijah in the desert by the ministry of ravens, who brought loaves to him in the morning and meat in the evening. What do the Jews say,

who think that they are clean in this respect because they abstain from certain foods that are said mystically to be unclean in the law? Certainly a raven is an unclean animal according to the law [see Lev 11:15; Deut 14:14]. And in their interpretation, that which touches an unclean thing would necessarily be made unclean [see Lev 5:2; 7:19]. And how was saint Elijah able to have meat brought to him by ravens to use as food, if what a raven touches is unclean? But for Elijah, who possessed a clear conscience, not even food brought by ravens was able to be unclean. Clearly it is not food but conscience that defiles someone. And that is why the apostle rightly says, "To the clean all things are clean, but to the defiled nothing is clean" [Titus 1:15], even if they receive clean food. For clean food is defiled by an unclean conscience. After all, the Jews think that they are abstaining from unclean foods, but they are not clean because they are full of the uncleanness of sins [see Matt 23:25, 28]. Would that just as they think that they are abstaining from unclean foods, so they would abstain from the uncleanness of sins, so that they would become truly clean! But to eat clean food and not to have a clear conscience does not benefit at all for salvation. Therefore we ought always to have a clear conscience, so that all the food that we take in we may be able to have as clean; for food does not make someone unclean, but a bad conscience does [see Matt 15:17–20; Mark 7:19].

4. We have said this on account of the Jews, who think that no cleanness exists except in abstaining from certain foods, though saint Elijah, who was clean in all things, is shown to have received meat that unclean ravens carried to him; and he was never defiled by that meat, so that not only did he not offend, but he was transferred to paradise [see 2 Kgs 2:11]. But if we consider these deeds of Elijah in the spiritual sense and with the eyes of faith, we find mystical things and great mysteries. For in Elijah, who endured persecution from the very wicked woman Jezebel, a type of the Lord was shown, who endured persecution from the synagogue, a sacrilegious woman.[94] But in the ravens that brought food to Elijah, our calling was shown, we who came to belief from the unclean Gentiles, carrying the food of our devotion and faith to Christ the Lord. For the devotion and faith of believers is Christ's food [see Matt 25:35]. But let us consider the mystery of these ravens more carefully. For "ravens brought" to Elijah "loaves in the morning and meat in the evening" [1 Kgs 17:6]. They have brought loaves to the Lord in the morning who believed in Christ with all their heart, who carried the true food of faith in

their mouth. But the martyrs brought meat in the evening, who in the setting of their life handed over their own flesh in the evening, that is, their bodies for the sake of Christ's name; yet they carried this meat in their mouth, who for Christ's sake attracted martyrdom by the confession of their mouth.

5. Now let us consider the following point, that the same Elijah was sent to some widow woman who was in Zarephath of Sidon for her to feed him lest he die of famine [1 Kgs 17:8–16]. For as the reading has reported, she still had a small measure of meal and a small measure of oil. Elijah went to her and told her to make bread for him to eat. But she answered and said that she had nothing but a small measure of meal and a small measure of oil to make bread for herself and for her children, and then to die [see 1 Kgs 17:12]. Elijah said to her, "First make something to eat for me, for thus says the Lord: the flask (*capsaces*)[95] of meal shall not diminish, and the oil shall not diminish, nor will it fail from its vessel, until the day that the Lord gives rain upon the earth" [1 Kgs 17:13–14]. Great was the grace of the prophet, who promised so much to the woman; but the woman's faith helped the grace of the prophet.[96] For she believed with complete faith, so that she offered to Elijah what he requested. The facts themselves make clear that this woman believed with complete faith. From a small measure of meal, which was all that she had left, she offered bread to the prophet, before giving any of it to her children. For the prophet's merit weighed more than her love for her children. And this is why it is not undeservedly that this woman represents a figure of the church in all respects. Already back then she was venerating an image of Christ in Elijah. Love and grace shown to him takes precedence not only over her children but also her own life. This woman had not yet heard the Lord speaking in the gospel: "Whoever does not hate parents or children for my sake is not worthy of me" [Luke 14:26; Matt 10:37], and yet she fulfilled the gospel precept before hearing it. For at that time she saw the mystery of Christ at work in Elijah. This woman was a widow who had not yet believed in the man Christ, of whom John the Baptist says, "After me comes a man who came before me, since he was prior to me" [John 1:30]. To be sure this man came after John, since according to the flesh he deigned to be born from a virgin after John; but he was prior to John, since he was begotten from God the Father before all things.

6. But let us consider how this woman perfectly prefigures an image of the church. Before Elijah came to her, she was weary with

hunger along with her children, she was obviously weary and in the midst of an extremely severe famine, since Christ the bread of life had not yet descended from heaven [see John 6:41]; not yet had the Word of God been incarnated from the virgin. Listen to the prophet speaking: "I will send forth a famine on the land; not a famine of bread, nor a thirst for water, but a famine of hearing the word of God" [Amos 8:11]. For he is truly endangered by famine who is weary with a famine of the divine word. For a famine of earthly bread is far different than a famine of the divine word. A famine of earthly bread can only kill the body, but not the soul. But a famine of the divine word both kills the body and murders the soul. A famine of earthly bread shuts a man out from the present life; but the famine of the divine word casts a man out from eternal and perpetual life. The church was weary with danger of this sort before it received Christ; but after it received him, it escaped the danger of eternal death. This woman indeed had a small measure of meal and a small measure of oil before the coming of Christ, that is, the proclamation of the law and the prophets. But this was not able to suffice for life for her, without the grace of Christ fulfilling the law and the prophets. That is why the following words of the Lord were spoken in the gospel: "I have not come to destroy the law or the prophets, but to fulfill [them]" [Matt 5:17]. For the salvation of human life could not be in the law and the prophets, but only in the passion of Christ. After all, this is the reason the church later received Christ, and meal, oil, and wood began to abound. In the meal, the food of the word was shown; but in the oil, the gift of divine mercy; but in the wood, the mystery of the venerable cross by which heavenly rain is granted to us. For that is what Elijah says to the woman: "Meal and oil will not fail you, until the Lord brings rain upon the land" [1 Kgs 17:14]. Our Lord and Savior brought rain from heaven to us, that is the gospel preaching, by which he invigorated with life-giving waters the arid hearts of the human race, like thirsty ground.

Since therefore we are fed with heavenly food of this sort, we should not complain about the difficulty of fasting; or rather, we ought to say to the Lord the words that the prophet spoke in the psalm: "How sweet to my throat are your words, O Lord, beyond honey and the honeycomb to my mouth!" [Ps 119:103]. Thus, when the Lord sees our faithful devotion toward himself, he may repay us with heavenly grace and with all spiritual goods.

SERMON 26

For the Dedication of the Church of Concordia[97]

1. We ought to give unspeakable thanks to our God, who has deigned to adorn his church in all ways like this. The basilica has been completed to the honor of the saints, and it was completed quickly. Indeed, you were aroused by the example of other churches to an act of devotion of this sort; but we are pleased with your faith since you have surpassed their example. For you started later but finished earlier, since you previously earned the right to hold the relics of the saints. We have received the relics from you; you [have received] from us zealous devotion <and> emulation of faith. This sort of rivalry and religious competition is good, where one contends not from worldly greed but from the gift of thanks. With religious longing we have carried what had been brought to you from the gift of the saints; but based on this we stirred up your zeal, so that you even asked for a portion. It could not be denied, because what was being requested was just. The portion was given so that both you had the whole of it in the portion and we lost none of what had been given.[98] <This agrees with> what is written: "The one with more did not overflow, and the one with little did not suffer lack" [2 Cor 8:15]. And so, the church of Concordia has been adorned, by the gift of the saints, by the construction of the basilica, and by the ministry of the high priest.[99] For the holy man, my brother and fellow bishop, has earned the right to be honored with the high priesthood, he who through the gifts of saints of this sort has honored the church of Christ, who is the eternal priest [see Heb 5:6; 6:20; 7:3, 17, 21].

2. Numerous indeed are the merits of the holy apostles <whose> relics are kept here. But let us say at least a few things of the many that could be mentioned. For it is fitting that we preach something about the merits of those whose faith and glory shines throughout the entire world, whose virtue and grace is at work everywhere. For <as> the prophet says in the psalm about them, "Their sound <has gone forth> into all the earth, and their words to the ends of the world" [Ps 19:4]. Clearly the sound of the apostles has gone forth through every country, not only at that time when they physically preached Christ to the world, but even now it goes forth daily when <the virtue> of faith and spiritual grace works in relation to the diverse maladies of sins.

But we do not even expect less grace from the apostles just because we seem not to have the relics of them all. Where there are two or three, all are there, since the faith is in common and the grace is the same. Hear how the Lord himself makes this known <when> he says, "Where two or three are gathered in my name, there am I in their midst" [Matt 18:20]. If, then, Christ is with two or three, all the apostles are with Christ. It is necessary that where Christ is, there the whole choir of apostles is present. Whence we ought to believe and hold that all are there as it were in the few. But since we are not able to recount each of their merits, by treating these things somewhat briefly, we ought to tell whose relics we have in order that we may attain some progress in the faith.

3. The Gospels make clear how great saint John the Baptist was held by the Lord, how great likewise was John the evangelist, whose relics are kept here. The one John is the Baptist, the other the evangelist. The one recognized his Lord while he was still in his mother's womb [see Luke 1:41, 44]; the other found Christ while he was on the shore [see Matt 4:21–22]. The one baptized the Lord [see Matt 3:13–17]; the other reclined upon his Lord's breast [John 13:23]. The one is said to be the first among those born of women [see Matt 11:11; Luke 7:28]; the other is singled out with unique affection among the apostles [John 13:23]. The one is called an angel [see Matt 11:10; Mark 1:2]; the other is named a son of thunder [Luke 7:27; Mark 3:17]. The one showed Christ who was present to the people when he said, "Behold the lamb of God, behold him who takes away the sin of the world" [John 1:29]; the other made the Son of God known to the entire world through the preaching of his Gospel, when he said, "In the beginning was the Word, and the Word was with God, and the Word was God. This was in the beginning with God. All things were made through him, and without him nothing was made" [John 1:1–3]. Both men were eminent; both were very great. The one saw the Holy Spirit descending in the form of a dove upon the Lord [see Luke 3:22; John 1:32]; the other was seized in the Spirit and recognized the secrets of heaven [see Rev 4:1–2]. Finally, the one was cast in prison by King Herod on account of chastity [see Matt 14:3]; the other for the sake of Christ's name was banished to an island by Domitian Caesar [see Rev 1:9].

4. What should we say about the apostles Andrew and Thomas? What of Luke the evangelist? For their relics are held here as well. Andrew is the brother of saint Peter, who even himself took up the

cross for the sake of Christ, just as his brother Peter did. They were equals in suffering because they were equals in faith. For both were equal for Christ's sake; they took up his cross. And it was obviously fitting that those who were related by blood stood forth as brothers in the glory of suffering.

Now Thomas was also one of the apostles. This is the Thomas who had doubts after the Lord's resurrection. In order to strengthen his faith very fully, the Lord said to him, "Put your hand in my side and do not be unbelieving but believing" [John 20:27]. When he put it in and felt it, Thomas said to him, "My Lord and my God" [John 20:28]. The Lord said to him, "Because you have seen me, you have believed. Blessed are those who have not seen and have believed" [John 20:29]. To be sure, saint Thomas had doubts after the Lord's resurrection, but his doubting strengthened the faith of the church. And so Thomas touched the Lord's hands in order to recognize the prints of the nails; and he touched the Lord's side in order to feel signs of the body in the present wound. Otherwise enemies of the faith would claim that Christ had <not> resurrected from the dead in the same flesh.[100] After all, <though> saint Thomas both by the sight of his eyes and by the touch of his hand had proved that Christ had resurrected in his body, yet not even then did Marcion[101] and the Manicheans[102] want to believe that the Lord resurrected in the flesh. But what does Thomas say after he touched the hands of the Lord? "My Lord and my God" [John 20:28]. He only recognized Christ as his Lord by the power of his resurrection, since to conquer death and to raise flesh from death by one's own power pertains only to the divine power and the eternal majesty. And that is why he says to him, "My Lord and my God." When he had reached India, in accordance with the statement of the Lord, to preach Christ the Lord even in India, after many miracles and wonders that strengthened the faith of believers, he received his glorious death worthily.[103] Since, therefore, his body was kept buried in India, some merchant, a Christian man who was very devout, reached as far as India for the sake of doing business, in order that from there he might bring precious stones or Indian wages to the Romans from the desire of earthly gain. But instead of being a merchant of the world, he was found to be a merchant of God. For when he came to India, through revelation it was shown to him just where the body of saint Thomas was being kept, and he was warned to bring back his body to Edessa with him.[104] But that man in fact as a merchant of God showed contempt for worldly gain and began to think only about heavenly gain. For he discovered a better reward than Indian stones, which he had not <sought>....

Sermon 27

On the Resurrection of Lazarus

1. Christ Jesus, our Lord and Savior, made known the power of his divinity by many signs and miracles indeed, but especially in the death of Lazarus, as your love has heard in today's reading, when he showed that he was the one of whom it had been written, "The Lord of powers is with us, the God of Jacob our helper" [Ps 46:7]. Our Lord and Savior worked these miracles in two ways, bodily and spiritually, that is, visibly and invisibly, so that he showed the invisible power by the visible work. Higher up by means of a visible work, he illumined the man blind from birth with eyesight, so that by that invisible power he illumined the blindness of the Jews with the light of his knowledge [see John 9]. But in today's reading he gave life to the dead Lazarus, so that from the death of sin he raised up unto life the unbelieving hearts of the Jews [see John 11:1–44]. After all, because of Lazarus many of the Jews believed in Christ the Lord [see John 11:45]. For they recognized in the resurrection of Lazarus the manifest power of the Son of God, since to command the dead by one's own power does not pertain to the human condition but to the divine nature.

We read indeed that the apostles also raised the dead, but in order to raise them, they prayed to the Lord [see Acts 9:40; 20:9–12]; they did not raise them by their own power or authority, but by the invocation of Christ's name, who is lord of death and life. But the Son of God raised Lazarus by his own power. After all, when the Lord says, "Lazarus, come forth" [John 11:43], immediately that man came forth from the tomb, and death was unable to hold the one whom life was calling. The stench of the tomb was in the nostrils when Lazarus stood there alive. Death did not wait to hear the voice of the Savior repeat itself, since it could not bear the power of life, but solely at the Lord's voice, death released both the body of Lazarus from the tomb and his soul from the underworld; and the whole Lazarus proceeded alive from the tomb, who had not been entirely there.[105] One wakes from sleep more slowly than Lazarus was roused from death. The stench of the corpse was still in the nostrils of the Jews, and Lazarus stood there alive. But let us now consider the beginning of the reading.

2. The Lord says therefore to his disciples, as your love has heard in today's reading, "Our friend Lazarus is asleep; but I am going to rouse him from sleep" [John 11:11]. The Lord said well, "Our friend Lazarus is asleep," since he was truly about to raise him from death as if from sleep. But the disciples do not know why the Lord said this and say to him, "Lord, if he sleeps, he will get better" [John 11:12]. Then he answered and said to them plainly, "Lazarus is dead; but I am glad for your sake, so that you may believe, since I was not there" [John 11:14–15]. But if the Lord says here that he rejoices for the disciples' sake over the death of Lazarus, why is it that he is later reported to have wept over the death of Lazarus [John 11:35]? But let us consider the reason for the joy and the tears. The Lord rejoiced for the disciples' sake; he wept for the Jews' sake. For the disciples' sake he rejoiced, because through the resurrection of Lazarus their faith had the means of being strengthened in Christ. He wept because of the unbelief of the Jews, since not even by the raising of Lazarus would they believe in Christ the Lord. Or possibly the reason the Lord wept was so that by his tears he could blot out the sins of the world [see John 1:29]. If Peter could wipe away his own sins by the shedding of his tears [see Matt 26:75; Mark 14:72; Luke 22:62], why do we not believe that the sins of the world could be blotted out by the Lord's tears? Finally, after the Lord's tears, many from the Jewish people believed [see John 11:45]. The emotion of the Lord's piety partially overcame the unbelief of the Jews, and his pious outpouring of tears softened their discordant minds. And perhaps for that reason it is reported of the Lord in today's reading that he both rejoiced and wept, since as it is written, "He who sows in tears will reap in joy" [Ps 126:5]. Therefore the Lord's tears are the world's joys, since the reason he shed tears was so that we might merit the joys. But let us return to the subject.

He says therefore to his disciples, "Our friend Lazarus is dead; but I am glad for your sake, that you may know, for I was not there," [John 11:14–15]. Let us consider the mystery here as well. In what sense is the Lord saying that he was not there? For when he says plainly, "Lazarus is dead" [John 11:14], he clearly shows that he was present there. For the Lord could not have said this unless he had been present, since no one brought him news of it. For how was the Lord not present in the place where Lazarus died, since he contained all places of the entire world by his divine majesty? But here too our

Lord and Savior is showing in himself the mystery of his flesh and of his divinity. For he was not there in the flesh; but he was in his divinity, since God is everywhere.

3. So then, when the Lord came to Mary and Martha, the sister of Lazarus, upon seeing the crowd of Jews, he said, "Where have you laid him?" [John 11:34]. Was the Lord unaware of where Lazarus had been laid, who while absent had announced beforehand that Lazarus was dead, and who was everywhere by the majesty of his divinity?[106] But the Lord did this according to ancient custom. For he likewise said to Adam, "Where are you, Adam?" [Gen 3:9]. It is not that he did not know where Adam was, but he asked in order that Adam would confess his sin with his own mouth, so that he could earn pardon for the sin. And he asks Cain, "Where is your brother Abel?" [Gen 4:9]. And he said, "I do not know" [Gen 4:9]. It is not that he asked Cain because he was unaware of Abel's whereabouts, but that although Cain denied it, he was convicting him of the crime of murder, which he had committed against his brother. Finally, Adam was paid back with a pardon, since in response to the Lord's question, he confessed the sin he had committed; Cain, since he denied, was condemned with eternal punishment. So too here, when the Lord says, "Where have you laid him?" he is not asking because he does not know where Lazarus had been laid, but in order that the throng of Jews might follow him to the tomb of Lazarus, to see the divine power of Christ in the resurrection of Lazarus. They would then stand forth as witnesses against themselves, if they did not believe such a great miracle. For above the Lord had said to them, "If you do not believe me, at least believe the works, and know that the Father is in me and I am in him" [John 10:38].

Then when he came to the tomb, he said to the Jews who were standing around, "Take away the stone from here" [John 11:39]. What are we saying? Was the Lord unable to remove the stone from the tomb by a command, who removed the gates of the underworld by his own power? But he commanded men to do what could be done by men; but he showed by his own authority what pertained to the divine power. For it pertains to human power to recall a stone from a tomb; but to recall a soul from the underworld is of [divine] power. But it would have been easy, had he wanted to, to remove the stone from the tomb solely by the command of a word, since he created the world by a word.

4. Therefore when they removed the stone from the tomb, he said with a loud voice, "Lazarus, come forth" [John 11:43]. He was showing that he was the one of whom it had been written: "The voice of the

Lord is powerful, the voice of the Lord is magnificent" [Ps 29:4]; and again: "Behold he will add to his power a voice of power" [Ps 68:33]. This is clearly the voice of power and magnificence that immediately recalled Lazarus from death to life, and his soul was returned to his body, before he had uttered the sound of his voice. Although his body was in one place, his soul in another, nevertheless this voice of the Lord at once both returned the soul to the body and made the body present to the soul. For death was terrified when the voice of such power was heard. And it is no wonder of course if Lazarus could rise at a single word of the Lord, when he himself has declared in the gospel that all who are in their tombs will be resurrected at a single word alone, when he says, "The hour is coming, when all who are in their tombs will hear the voice of the Son of God, and shall rise" [John 5:25]. This is why it is beyond doubt that at that time when death heard the voice of the Lord, it would have released all the dead from its possession, had it not recognized that Lazarus alone had been summoned. And so, as the Lord says, "Lazarus, come forth, immediately he came out with his hands and feet bound, and his face was covered by a napkin" [John 11:44]. And what shall we say here? Could the Lord not have burst the bands with which Lazarus had been buried, he who shattered the chains of death?[107] But here our Lord and Savior shows in Lazarus a double miracle of his working, in order in this way to infuse the faith of belief into the unbelief of the Jews. For it is no smaller cause for astonishment that Lazarus was able to walk while his feet were bound, than to have risen from the dead....

Sermon 28

On the Words of the Apostle: Do You Not Know That Those Who Run in a Race

1. The blessed apostle Paul exhorts us to strive for the crown of heavenly glory not only by the teaching of the law but also by an example from this world. For as your love has heard, among other things he says the following: "Do you not know that those who run in a race indeed all run, but one receives the crown?" [1 Cor 9:24]. And he added, "Run in such a way that you take hold of it." According to the earthly example, many indeed, as the apostle says, run in the race,

but one receives the crown, that is, the one who runs better; so too in the race of the present life, many indeed run, but one receives the crown. The Jews run by means of the law, the philosophers by means of worthless wisdom [see Col 2:8]; the heretics too run by means of false preaching, Catholics run by means of the true preaching of the faith. But of all these, one receives the crown, namely, the Catholic people who head toward Christ on the right course of faith, to reach the palm and crown of immortality.

2. And the reason the Jews, the philosophers, and the heretics run in vain is because they do not go on the right path of faith.[108] For what benefit comes to the Jews to run by means of observance of the law, who do not know Christ, the Lord of the law? The philosophers also run by means of vain wisdom of the world, but their course is superfluous and vain, since they do not know the true wisdom of Christ. For Christ is the true wisdom of God [see 1 Cor 1:24], which is not decked out with words, nor with brilliant speech, but is known by the faith of the heart. And the heretics run by means of the poisonous claims of their faith, they run by means of fasts, they run by means of almsgiving, but they do not attain to the crown, since they do not believe in Christ faithfully. For their false faith does not deserve to receive the grace of true faith. The apostle makes this clear in another passage when he says, "And if I give away all my money to the poor and if I hand over my body to the fire to be burned, but have not love, it does not benefit me at all" [1 Cor 13:3]. For he who does not believe faithfully in Christ does not have the love of Christ. And therefore the apostle added rightly and said, "Run in such a way as to take hold." Therefore we ought to run by a faithful course in the faith of Christ, in the commands of God, in the works of justice, in order to be able to attain to the crown of eternal life.

3. Finally, the same apostle shows us in what follows how we must run, when he says, "Everyone who competes in a contest is self-controlled in all things; and indeed they [do this] in order to receive a perishable crown" [1 Cor 9:25]. See with what examples the apostle invites us to the crown of the promised immortality. In that earthly contest, those who want to win abstain from certain foods, they abstain from excessive drink, they abstain from all uncleanness, they practice such a degree of chastity that they do not even demand conjugal relations with their own wives. And in no other way do they hope to be able to win except by preserving the purity and chastity of their bodies. And after such great effort, what else do they receive

but a small, perishable, and insignificant crown? If then some people undertake such great effort for a perishable crown, how much more ought we to endure all effort, to whom a heavenly prize and crown of eternal glory is promised? It is therefore our task to strive in the contest with no light struggle, for we are contending against the spiritual forces of wickedness [see Eph 6:12], against the devil and his angels [see Matt 25:41]; we are contending against unrighteousness, against impiety, against evil, against unchastity, against the various enticements of sins. And if we struggle and win, we receive as many crowns as the vices we conquered.

4. And so, this struggle is great in which we exhibit a spectacle to the Lord [see 1 Cor 4:9].[109] When we engage in this contest, the Lord watches us, his angels watch us; we conquer on earth, but we receive a prize of virtue in heaven. Finally, when the holy martyrs were placed in the struggle of this contest, they not only conquered the vices of sins but death itself, and they received the prize of immortality. Our Lord and Savior was the first to contend and win in this struggle, in order to show us an example of combat and of victory.

By discussing these things with you, then, we are planting the seeds of good combat in your hearts, as those who find your hearts furrowed with the plow of justice. Therefore, cultivate the word we have sown in you in order that what has been sown may be able to germinate. But may God pour into you the moisture of his piety by his visitation, and may he grant increase to our seeds in order that you may be able to attain to the hundredfold harvest in the bundles of merits that are gathered in [see Matt 13:23; Mark 4:20].

Sermon 29 (fragment)

On Saint Peter and His Deliverance from Prison

1. Your love has heard in order how saint Peter was put in prison, bound with two chains, and handed over to four squads of four soldiers, and how he was delivered from there by an angel of the Lord [see Acts 12:1–17]. Saint Peter was put in prison, then, for the sake of Christ's name, but he was not able to dread the penalty of prison because he himself, even in prison, was a temple of God. He was bound with two chains, but in that very prison he tore off the chains of

crimes from believers. He was guarded by four squads of four soldiers, that is, by sixteen [for just as a centurion has a hundred soldiers under him, so a squad of four has four soldiers in it] but during that time of custody, he introduced the four Gospels to those who came to faith; and obviously he who was being kept under a divine guard would not have been able to be afraid of a human guard.[110]

2. Therefore when Peter was being carefully guarded in prison by four squads of four soldiers, bound with two chains, an angel of the Lord came to him, as your love has heard, and it opened the prison gates for him and said to him, "Get up and take your garment and cover yourself, and put on your sandals, and come, follow me" [Acts 12:8]. And he got up and followed him. And when he had come to the iron gate with the angel, at once the same gate by itself was opened for them. And it is not surprising, of course, if an iron gate was opened of its own accord for saint Peter, who had already received the gates of hell under his authority, when the Lord said to him, "You are Peter, and upon this rock I shall build my church; and the gates of hell shall not prevail against it. And whatever you bind upon earth shall be bound also in heaven, and whatever you loose upon earth shall be loosed also in heaven" [Matt 16:18–19]. Therefore, he opened the iron gate to saint Peter, who laid open the gates of hell; he rescued Peter from death who vanquished death itself.

3. But what was done with Peter then according to the letter, we also recognize is being done with us mystically, if we follow Peter's faith. For we, too, are placed in this world as in a prison. If then we merit being visited by God, an angel of God is sent to us and says to each one of us, "Gird yourself and put on your sandals, and cover yourself with your garment, and follow me" [Acts 12:8]. For we gird ourselves if we surround the loins of our body with the belt of chastity, since the apostle says, "Let your loins be girded in chastity" [Luke 12:35; cf. Eph 6:14; Isa 11:5; 59:17].[111] And we put shoes on our feet if we fortify the steps of our life with the gospel precepts and with the virtue of faith, so that we may tread safely upon the thorns of sins and the thistles of iniquity.[112] And we cover ourselves with our garment if we preserve that wedding garment, namely, the grace of baptism, unscathed within us. And so if we faithfully fulfill these things, at once the chains will fall from our hands, that is, the chains of sins with which we were held fast, bound up, and tied in our soul.

4. But the only way we can escape from prison, that is, from the error of this world, is by being visited by the Lord through his angel.

The iron gate will be opened to us, that is, the gate of death and punishment, which the Son of God shattered by the power of his passion. And then we come to the home of Mary, to the church of Christ, where Mary the mother of the Lord dwells [see Acts 12:12].[113] And there a girl meets us by the name of Rhoda [see Acts 12:13]. But the name Rhoda is a fitting one as a mystery of our salvation. For in the Greek language, *Rhoda* spells *rose*. Therefore when we come to Mary's house, no one but Rhoda meets us, that is, the congregation of the saints, which shines like a precious rose with the glorious blood of the martyrs....[114]

Sermon 30

On the Beginning of the Newborn Church

1. After our Lord and Savior Christ Jesus rose, having vanquished death, and ascended to heaven, his church gathered together in the number of a hundred men, as your love has heard in today's reading [see Acts 1:12–14]. Now it was gathered in the upper room with Mary, who was the mother of Jesus, and with his brothers. Therefore one cannot speak of the church unless Mary the mother of the Lord is there together with his brothers. For the church of Christ is where Christ's incarnation from the virgin is proclaimed. And the gospel is heard where the apostles, the Lord's brothers, preach. One cannot speak of the church where the synagogue of the Jews is, since it refuses to believe in the incarnation of Christ from a virgin or to listen to those who preach spiritually.

2. And at first, after the Lord's ascension to heaven, the church numbered only 120 men, but later it grew so large that it filled the entire world with countless people. But that this is what would happen the Lord makes clear in the gospel when he says to the apostles, "Unless a grain of wheat falls to the ground, it remains alone. But when it dies, it bears much fruit" [John 12:24–25]. The resurrection of the Lord's passion plainly bore "much fruit" for human salvation. For in the grain of wheat our Lord and Savior signifies his own body. For when it was buried in the ground, it bore great and countless fruit, since by the Lord's resurrection a harvest of virtues arose in the whole world and crops of believing peoples. For the death of one became the life of all. Rightly when elsewhere in the gospel he compares the

kingdom of heaven, he says the following: "The kingdom of heaven is like a grain of mustard seed cast into a garden which is the least of all seeds. But when it grows, it will become larger than all the garden plants, so that birds of the sky dwell in its branches" [Matt 13:31–32]. The Lord likened himself to a grain of mustard seed, and though he was the God of glory <and> eternal majesty, he became least, since he deigned to be born of a virgin with the body of an infant. Therefore he was sown into the ground when his body was handed over to burial. But after he rose from death through the glory of the resurrection, it grew on earth so that it became a tree, having branches on which the birds of the sky dwell.[115] The tree was a representation of the church that rose in glory through the death of Christ. Its branches are understood as none other than the apostles, since just as branches naturally adorn a tree, so the apostles adorn Christ's church with the beauty of their grace. The birds of the sky are known to inhabit these branches. Birds of the sky allegorically signify us, who come to the church of Christ, and rest in the teaching of the apostles, as it were, on branches.

3. But let us return to the subject. At first, then, after the Lord's ascension, the church was few in number. But later on it grew to such an extent that it filled the entire world, not only cities, but also the various nations. Faith is found among the Persians, among the Indians, in the entire world. It was not dread of the sword or fear of the emperor that rendered these nations obedient to Christ, but only faith in Christ made them peaceable. After all, when these nations were fighting against each other for earthly kingdoms, they laid claim to other countries and places, [but] when they came to faith and [confessed] the name of Christ, there is no more combat, since they all acknowledge one king of all, Jesus Christ. Among the nations there is no contention under this king; with equal consent they all worship him, adore him, and venerate him. For his sake they lay aside their savage dispositions and take pride in his grace and faith. And although diversity of kingdom causes them to quarrel over worldly empires, yet in terms of the kingdom of God and the unity of concord, they obey one emperor with the same faith, in terms of faith they all fight their campaign under Christ. From him they daily receive the soldier's pay of salvation and obtain the gifts of spiritual graces. And if necessity demands it, they are more readily prepared to lay down their lives for their king than to lose their faith; and <rightly> of course, since this king for whom we campaign offers his soldiers a reward even after death. A king of this world can provide nothing after death to a soldier

who is killed in his service, since he himself is subject to death; but Christ the king offers to soldiers who die in his service the reward of eternal immortality. A soldier of this world, if he is killed for his king, is conquered; but Christ's soldier conquers more at that time if he merits to be killed for Christ.[116]

Sermon 31

On the Apostles Healing the Sick

1. Your love has heard about the extent and diversity of the grace the apostles had before the Lord. Indeed first they spoke in different languages, so that they proclaimed to the whole world the only begotten Son of God as the Lord of all languages and Creator [see Acts 2:1–13]. For no language would have been able to believe the apostles while they were preaching in languages unless every language had heard them. For the apostles did not need men to interpret, since they had God and the Holy Spirit as their interpreter. For they did not need to be taught by men, since they had learned everything that they preached from Christ, the teacher of life. First, then, the apostles received this grace to speak in all languages; then they began to work these divine miracles: to restore sight to the blind, hearing to the deaf, walking to the lame, health to the infirm, life to the dead [see Acts 3:1–10; 5:15–16; 9:31–43]. This does not pertain to human power but to divine power. For the apostles were doing these miraculous signs not by human nature but by divine power. Iron of its own nature subdues everything and reduces everything to bits. Yet when a craftsman casts it into fire and sets it aflame, the iron works not in accordance with its nature but according to the power of the fire. So the apostles, who were set aflame by the divine fire, that is, by the Holy Spirit, began to work divine miracles not in accordance with their mortal nature but according to the power of God. For to command death does not pertain to mortal nature but to the divine power.

2. Now upon the sick the apostles worked a twofold grace, bodily and spiritually. For to be sure, they delivered their bodies from physical ailments, but they freed their souls from the maladies of sins. For infirmity of the soul is more serious than that of the body. David shows this very thing clearly in the psalm when he says, "Bless the Lord,

my soul, because he pardons all your iniquities, who heals all your diseases" [Ps 103:2–3]. "Your diseases" therefore are far more serious than the diseases of the body. Diseases of the body bring a person temporal death; but diseases of the soul obtain eternal death. In fact, long ago when Adam showed himself to be a transgressor of the divine command in paradise, he did not experience a bodily disease, but a sickness of the soul, through which he would have perished with eternal death had the grace of Christ not redeemed him from death. Finally, listen to the prophet showing this very thing when he says, "By his bruises we are all healed" [Isa 53:5]. For the wounds of the Lord's passion have become the medicine of human salvation. But diseases of the soul are cured not by human medicine, but only by the grace of Christ. Diseases of the soul are the fevers of sins and the wounds of transgressions, which creep into the body not from the outside but from within the soul. Wounds of the soul of this sort are cured not by human beings but by God; not by the lance of an earthly blade, but by the lance of the divine word that penetrates inside the soul. Listen to the prophet saying this very thing: "For it was not a mollifying plaster that restored them to health, but your word, O Lord, which heals all things" [Wis 16:12]. And this is why the following words of David were spoken: "He sent his word and healed them" [Ps 107:20]. Fittingly, when the prophet was praying to the Lord for the iniquity of the Jewish people, he speaks as follows: "And is there no balm in Gilead, or is there no physician there? Why has not the healing of the people gone up in you?" [Jer 8:22]. Here the prophet is not speaking about balm but about heavenly medicine, nor about a human physician, but about God the physician.

3. But we ought to consider carefully the following: since there are diverse infirmities in the human race, and diverse maladies of sins, how can the prophet here promise healing for all infirmities by a single medicine of balm? In accordance with the worldly example, diverse maladies demand different medicines; according to the heavenly mystery, all infirmities of sins are cured by the single medicine of balm, and they are cured every day. We know that balm originates nowhere else but from a tree. Therefore, since the prophet promises a cure by means of balm, doubtless the medicine of the Lord's cross is being proclaimed through which eternal healing has been given to the human race. This one medicine, then, has cured the diverse infirmities of the world and daily cures them, since the preaching of the cross of Christ is the medicine for sins, as your love has heard.[117]

And it heals not only maladies of the body but also maladies of the soul. For when they believe in Christ, they are delivered from every infirmity of sin.

For those who were sick on their beds were carried before the apostles, as today's reading has reported, but also those who were being harassed by unclean spirits, and they were all healed. And whoever was touched even by Peter's shadow immediately recovered his health [see Acts 5:15–16]. A marvelous grace was in the apostles. Even their shadow could cure infirmities. But perhaps this seems unbelievable to those who doubt or have little faith that the shadow of the apostles could have brought benefit to human infirmities.[118] Doubtful minds do not believe that the apostles could do this, if they do not see even now the same ones doing similar things. For the shadows of the apostles are at work upon the infirm and upon those in difficult straits, and upon those who are beset by unclean spirits, and they show forth a heavenly cure upon them by the merit of their faith. Therefore it cannot be doubted that long ago the shadow of the apostles could do so much, whose relics now we recognize as being capable of so much. And if they were doing this only in that location, where they seem to have suffered for Christ, it would have been miraculous; they bring this about now, even where they did not suffer, so that to the degree that works greater than these are demonstrated, to that extent merits greater than these are declared. The reason we have said this is because it was read in today's reading that the infirm were liberated from every malady in which they were held by Peter's shadow, or by that of the other apostles [see Acts 5:15–16].

4. Your love has heard about the extent of the love and unity of the believers during the time of the apostles. It says, "And there was [but] one heart for every soul, neither did anyone say that any of his goods was his own, but all things were common unto them" [Acts 4:32]. The reason they so pleased God was because they led a life like that. For why should they have possessed their <earthly> goods separately, whose heavenly goods are not separately divided up? Or why should they not have held all things in common, who were in common possession of the Lord of all things? What belonged to one belonged to all, and what belonged to all belonged to each individual. In this sharing they were already imitating the fellowship of the future glory, when the kingdom of the saints will be in common, when no one contends over property lines, possessions, houses. There everyone's

joy will be shared, and gladness is shared, since what belongs to one belongs to all, and what is for all is for each.

But I am apprehensive that the well-known unity and charity that characterized the believers in the apostolic era may spell our condemnation. In consideration of our avarice, it is clear that we preserve neither unity nor peace nor love. They reckoned their own things common, we want to make other people's property <our own>. We contend over property lines and possessions, as if we were never going to die. We expect everything from earth, nothing from heaven, everything from the present life, nothing from the future glory and uninterrupted immortality. We do not recall the words of our Lord and Savior: "What does it profit a man if he gains the whole world and forfeits his soul?" [Matt 16:26; Mark 8:36]. And again: "See and be on guard. For a man's life is not in the abundance of his possessions" [Luke 12:15]. For this reason we ought to be strangers to avarice and cupidity, strangers to envy, discord, and dissension. But we should strive for peace, concord, unity, so that we may be able to have communion of eternal life with so many people of such quality, of whom this is said, "And there was one heart and one soul in all the believers and for them all things were in common" [Acts 4:32]. And the reason we ought to help brothers and the poor who experience need, as if we share this in common with them, is because in common with us we have one God the Father and one Lord, the only begotten Son of God, and one Holy Spirit, and one faith, and the grace of one baptism [see Eph 4:4–6], through which we are reborn to God into eternal life.

Sermon 32

On the Lord's Birth

1. "And it came to pass in those days that there went out a decree from Caesar Augustus, that the whole world should be enrolled. This enrollment was first made when Quirinius[119] was the governor of Syria. And all went to be enrolled, every one into his own city" [Luke 2:1–3]. <If> we consider all these things in the spiritual sense, we find no small mysteries. Thus was the first complete census of the entire world set in motion at that time, when the Lord was born according to the flesh; for at no other time was it fitting that the first census of the entire world be set in motion, except when he was born to whom

the human race had to be enrolled in a census; nor under another emperor except under him who first received the name Augustus, since the true and eternal Augustus was he who was born from a virgin. The former Augustus Caesar was a man, the latter God; the former was emperor of the earth, the latter emperor of heaven; the former a king of men, the latter king of angels.[120]

For even the name of this governor, Quirinius, under whom the census was set in motion, corresponds to the heavenly mystery. For *Quirinius* translates from Greek into Latin as "ruler," a name that fits no one better than Christ the Lord, who is lord of human flesh and soul. For as we read it written about him, he is "Lord of lords" [Rev 17:14; 19:16; 1 Tim 6:15; Deut 10:17], who is lord not only of earth but of heaven. There are many dominions on earth and in heaven, to be sure, but he is the one Lord who is lord of them all. Fittingly, therefore, at the birth of the Lord a census of the entire world was set in motion, since he was the one for whom the whole world had to be enrolled in a census for salvation. Those who are enrolled by the earth's emperor are enrolled for this purpose, to weigh out the tribute that is owed and to pay the necessary poll tax.[121] And we are assessed by Christ the eternal king for this purpose, to weigh out the tribute of our poll tax and to pay the necessary poll tax of faith, which chiefly the martyrs have done, who offered their very <bodies> for the sake of Christ's name.[122]

At that time, then, when a census of the entire world was set in motion, the Lord was born according to the flesh. But he was born in Bethlehem [see Luke 2:4]. Clearly it was not fitting for the Lord to be born anywhere else than in Bethlehem. For *Bethlehem* means "house of bread." This location received its name long ago as a prophecy, since the one who was born from a virgin in Bethlehem was "the bread from heaven" [John 6:41]. If one praises so many cities that produced the greatest kings, what is loftier than this place, where the Lord deemed it fitting to be born as the king of heaven, the king of the earth, and of the entire world?

2. So then, when Joseph and Mary came to be enrolled in Bethlehem, as today's reading has related, "Mary gave birth to her firstborn son and wrapped him in swaddling clothes and placed him in a manger, since there was no room in the inn" [Luke 2:7]. Therefore he who <was> born from the virgin is shown to be the firstborn, and not only firstborn but only begotten; firstborn from the Father, firstborn from the virgin; firstborn from the Father because he was from the Father

before all things; only begotten from the Father because he alone is from the Father. Likewise, he is declared to be both from the virgin and firstborn and only begotten: firstborn because he was first from the virgin; only begotten because he alone is from the virgin. See to what great humility the Son of God debased himself for our sake: he who reigns with the Father in heaven is placed in a manger; he who dispenses the robes of immortality is wrapped in swaddling bands; he who is lofty and powerful appears in the body of an infant.

3. Yet even these doings of the Lord contain sacred mysteries. He was wrapped in swaddling bands because he himself took up our sins upon himself as cloth bands, as it is written, "He carries our sins and suffers pain for us" [Isa 53:4].[123] Therefore he was wrapped in swaddling bands in order to strip us of the cloth bands of our sins; he was wrapped in swaddling bands in order to weave together the precious tunic of his church with the Holy Spirit; or certainly the reason he was wrapped with swaddling bands was to invite the various peoples of those who believe in him. For we come to belief from diverse nations, and we surround Christ like cloth bands, we who once were cloth bands to be sure, but now we have already become Christ's precious tunic. But that our Lord and Savior was laid in a manger showed the following, that he would become food for believers. For a manger is where animals come together to get food. Since then we too <are> rational animals, we have a heavenly manger where we come together. For our manger is Christ's altar, where we daily gather to consume there the food of salvation from the body of Christ. Now the Lord was laid in the manger because "there was no room in the inn" [Luke 2:7]. In the inn the synagogue is signified, which did not deserve to receive Christ into itself, being preoccupied with the error of unbelief. But the inn is correctly understood as the synagogue, since just as different nations indeed drive to an inn, so the synagogue has become an inn of all unbelief and of total error, whence Christ was unable to find room there. And therefore he is found placed in a manger, that is, in the church of the Gentiles, which received our Lord and Savior unto itself with all faith and with complete devotion, since he is the true nourishment of all believers and the spiritual food of souls.

4. An angel declared this physical birth of the Lord at first to the shepherds watching over their flock. No one but shepherds ought to have been the first to know of the birth of the prince of shepherds. Spiritually the shepherds of flocks refer to the bishops of churches who guard the flocks entrusted to them by Christ, to prevent them

from being attacked by wolves. It reported this: "But there were shepherds in that region keeping watch at night and each one watching over his flock" [Luke 2:8]. If, then, we always stay awake in the faith of Christ and in the precepts of the Lord, rightly do we preserve those flocks entrusted to us by Christ, rightly we are called shepherds of the church. But if we are weighed down with the slumber of negligence and infidelity, not only will we not be able to guard the flocks entrusted to us but not even ourselves, just as the teachers of the Jews did long ago, being evil and worthless shepherds, who destroyed both themselves and the Lord's sheep. But may the Lord keep away from us destruction of this sort, so that we may never be overwhelmed by the slumber of infidelity; but may he grant his grace and mercy, so that we may always be able to stay awake in his faith. For our faith is able to stay awake in Christ. And may your devotion always stay awake, since just as the teaching of the priest stirs up the people to the works of justice, so the devotion of the people stirs up the priests, and thus it happens that the flock rejoices over the shepherd and the shepherd over the flock.

5. Therefore, as your love has heard in today's reading, the angel says to the shepherds, "I bring to you news of great joy, for today a Savior has been born to you, Christ the Lord, in the city of David" [Luke 2:10–11]. Obviously it is a great joy for the shepherds. The prince of shepherds has been born both to guard their sheep and to put the demonic wolves to flight. Whence the birth of Christ according to the flesh is gladness for the shepherds, safety for the flocks, flight for the wolves. Thus an angel says to the shepherds, "I bring to you news of great joy, for today a Savior has been born to you, Christ <the Lord> in the city of David." For what could have been a greater joy than that an angel brought news to shepherds that the king of glory, the Christ and Lord of eternal majesty, willed to be born of a virgin for the sake of human salvation? Yet today's reading has made known that not only shepherds but also angels were made glad over this birth of the Lord. For it says, "And there was with the angel a multitude of heavenly host, saying, Glory to God in the highest and peace on earth to men of good will" [Luke 2:13–14]. For it was fitting that at the birth of such a great king not only humans, but also angels rejoiced, since he was the Creator of humanity, Creator of angels, and God of all power. Since therefore on this day our Lord and Savior deigned to be born according to the flesh, let us too rejoice with the

angels with a heavenly exultation, and let us be glad with a spiritual gladness with faith, with devotion, and with holiness of heart.

Sermon 33

On the Hallelujah[124]

1. The very word *hallelujah* invites us to the praise of the Lord and to the whole confession of faith. For *hallelujah* translates from Hebrew into Latin in two ways, as "Sing to him who is," or surely, "Bless us O God together as one," both of which are necessary for our salvation and faith. For we ought to sing "to him who is," we who long ago sang to those who were not, namely, to the gods of the nations and to the images of idols. But we sang in vain then, since what we worshiped were vain things. Vainly did we sing, since we were speaking disgraceful things, when we praised the gods of the nations, when we constructed illicit and profane loves of the pagan gods of whom the prophet says, "Let the gods that have not made heaven and earth perish from under the earth and from under this sky" [Jer 10:11]. Listen also to David speaking in the psalm: "All the gods of the nations are demons; but the Lord made the heavens" [Ps 96:5]. And so for a long time we sang in vain, but after we came to belief and to divine knowledge, we began to sing "to him who is," namely, to God the Almighty Creator of heaven, the Founder of the earth, the Maker of the world, the very Maker of man, who says to Moses, "You shall say thus to the sons of Israel: He who is sent me to you" [Exod 3:14]. For he is the one who always was and who abides forever. We sing hallelujah to him fittingly and justly because the fact that we exist and that we are alive is not of our power nor of our capacity, but of his worthy regard and godliness. We ought to sing things that are worthy of such a great God who always existed and is, things that befit his praise and majesty, because he is eternal, omnipotent, immeasurable, the Creator of the ages and the Savior of the world, because he has such great love for human beings that he even gave up his own Son for the salvation of the world, since the Lord himself says in the gospel, "God so loved this world, that he gave his only begotten Son, that everyone who believes in him would not perish but have eternal life" [John 3:16].

2. So then, *hallelujah* means "Sing to him who is"; *hallelujah* means likewise "Bless us, O God, together as one." Upon consideration, we note that this latter translation agrees with our faith and salvation. Therefore when we say, "Hallelujah," we pray, "O God, bless us together as one." If then we are together as one by faith, peace, concord, unanimity, we are worthy, so that we deserve to be blessed by the Lord together as one. For this is written: "Behold, how good and how pleasant it is for brothers to dwell as one" [Ps 133:1].[125] And again: "God who makes those with the same character dwell in a house" [Ps 68:6]. And so we are blessed by God if we are found together as one, that is, abiding in the unity of faith, in the concord of peace, in the affection of love, according to what the apostle exhorts and admonishes when he says, "But I implore you all to think the same thing, and let there not be schisms among you. But that you be perfect in the same mind and in the same knowledge" [1 Cor 1:10]. Whence if there is discord, if there is division and dissension among us, we are not worthy of God's blessing. For how can we boldly answer with the paternal words "Hallelujah," that is, "Bless us, God, together as one," when we are not found as one? Therefore let us always be as one that we may deserve to be blessed together as one.

This response, "Hallelujah," is not befitting for heretics, schismatics, nor for any enemies of the church's unity. They are not together with the church as one, who do not gather with us as one. For even the Lord himself makes this clear in the gospel when he says, "He who is not with me is against me. But he who does not gather with me scatters" [Matt 12:30; Luke 11:23]. For it pertains to Christ to gather into one; but it belongs to the devil to scatter into different directions.[126] Therefore the one who loves the church's unity follows Christ; but the one who delights in scattering follows the devil, since the devil is the author of scattering. And that is why we read the statement from Solomon: "There is a time to scatter stones, and a time to gather" [Eccl 3:5]. For a long time it was the time when the devil scattered us in different directions; but the time came again when Christ gathered us into one. It follows that we ought to flee discord and avoid it, since we recognize the devil as its author, but to follow the church's peace and unity, so that we can worthily and deservedly respond "Hallelujah," that is, "God bless us together as one."

3. Consider how much grace is found in this interpretation of *hallelujah*. Each one of us responds, "Hallelujah," and we ask for a common blessing so that each of us may be blessed as one. For we

are one body in the church [see 1 Cor 10:17], and through what one prays for, he obtains for all, and what all pray for, it is given to all the people from which the church is gathered. We ought to understand that this is said to the people of the Gentiles and to the people of the Jews. After all, a distinction was made in what was said: "Who lifts up the helpless from the earth, and raises up the poor from the dung heap" [Ps 113:7]. A man is called "helpless" who has nothing; but he is "poor" who appears to have something. And so, in the "helpless," the people of the Gentiles are signified, who had absolutely nothing, because they had received neither the law nor the prophets. But the "poor" are the Jewish people, who seemed to have something from the law and the prophets, based upon the merits of the patriarchs, the grace of the just, but they lay in a dung heap because they lay in bodily vices, in the filth of sins, in the error of pagans. But the people of the Gentiles who are signified in the "helpless," lay on the earth because they worshiped earthly idols, because their hope was solely on earth, not in heaven. Both therefore are lifted up because both are saved. Both are raised up because both are set free: the former from the earth of vices, the latter from the dung heap of sins; the former from the worship of idols, the latter from transgression against justice. And they are lifted up in order to be placed "with princes" [Ps 113:8], that is, with the apostles and prophets who are the princes of God's church.

4. Nor is it a superfluous point that though two are recorded, one is shown to be placed with the princes, since out of the two peoples one people of the church was made and placed in honor of the princes of the people and was associated with the apostles and prophets. And so, from two callings one people was made, since the two began to be one, as the apostle says: "And he called those who are far off and those who are near; for he is our peace who made the two one" [Eph 2:17, 14]. Finally, in order to show that one church came from two callings, he made an addition at the end of the psalm and said, "Who places the barren woman in a house, a mother rejoicing over her sons" [Ps 113:9].[127] Before the coming of Christ, the church was barren, for it had not received the seed of justice, it had not given birth to any offspring of faith. It was barren with respect to faith, barren with respect to the production of justice. But after the coming of Christ, it received the seed of the divine word and was made fertile and fecund. Daily it bears and gives birth to countless children for God throughout the whole world, in all nations. Daily it conceives and

daily it bears children, since all who come to belief are generated by its spiritual womb. This is why the prophet cries out to her and says, "Rejoice, O barren one, you who do not give birth, break forth and shout, you who do not bring forth, for many more are the children of the desolate than of her who has the husband" [Isa 54:1]. For a long time the synagogue had a husband, namely, the law that lorded over it, but it could not give birth to any fruit of justice, and so it generated useless children; it procreated them not for God but for the world; not for salvation in God but for dominion. But the church, which was barren and infertile for a long time, has now been made fruitful. For daily she conceives a fetus of justice, she bears offspring of salvation, she generates countless children for God, since daily for God children are generated by the church. We are conceived by the church when we come to belief; we are regenerated in fact by the bath of water; we are born in baptism unto God.

5. Since therefore believers are being saved every day, it is as if children are being generated daily for the Lord by the church. The church is shown to be the mother of these children, so many and so great, when it is said, "He places the barren woman in the house, a mother rejoicing over his children" [Ps 113:9]. And so these are the children of which it was said in Genesis as a type of the church that "she is the mother of all the living" [Gen 3:20]. It does not say of the dead, but of the living, because the church produces only living children. For those she gives birth to truly live through faith in God. They are estranged from dead works. But the church does not deem it fitting to be the mother of the dead, that is, of infidels and sinners, for all unbelievers and unfaithful are reckoned as dead before God, even if they are physically alive. Hence we read the Lord's statement in the gospel: "Leave the dead to bury their own dead" [Matt 8:22]. But the just and the faithful, even if they depart from the body, are reckoned to be alive to God. Hence we read the Lord's statement in the gospel: "I am the God of Abraham and the God of Isaac and the God of Jacob." And he added, "He is not the God of the dead, but of the living" [Matt 22:32]. Assuredly, Abraham, Isaac, and Jacob are alive to him. According to the body, they had already died, and yet they are said to be living, since they were alive to God in view of the merit of their faith and justice.

And so, whoever lives in this world justly and faithfully is shown to be alive even after death, and to live with a better life, since in this life there is the opportunity to sin, in that one there is security in the kingdom. In this life there is death, in that one there is the immortality of the kingdom. In this one calamity, in that one happiness.

Therefore if we live justly and faithfully in the sight of the Lord, we are rightly called children of the church, for the church is shown to be the mother solely of the living. But if we behave unfaithfully and unjustly in this life, we do not deserve to be called children of the church. And therefore we ought to live and act in this world in such a way that we can be called children of the church, that we may deserve to reign rightly and justly with the church in future glory.

Sermon 34 (fragment)

On the Lord's Epiphany

1. On this day our Lord and Savior was baptized by John in the Jordan [as we have heard when the divine reading was read], and therefore this is no insignificant solemnity; on the contrary it is a great one, even very great. For when our Lord deigned to be baptized, the Holy Spirit came upon him in the form of a dove [see Luke 3:22], and the Father's voice was heard saying, "This is my beloved Son, in whom I am well pleased" [Matt 3:17; cf. 17:5].

2. O how great is the mystery in the heavenly baptism! The Father is heard from heaven, the Son was seen on earth, the Holy Spirit is shown in the form of a dove; since it is not a true baptism, and there is no true remission of sins, where the truth of the Trinity is not present, neither can the remission of sins be given when the perfect Trinity is not believed.[128] But the church's baptism is one and true, which is granted once when someone is dipped once, and is made new and clean: clean since a person lays aside the filth of transgressions; new since he rises up into a new life and lays aside the oldness of sin. For this baptismal bath makes a person whiter than snow, not the skin of his body, but in the brightness of his mind and in the purity of his soul.

Therefore the heavens were opened at the Lord's baptism, so that through the bath of regeneration [see Titus 3:5] the kingdom of heaven would be shown clearly to believers in accordance with that sentence of the Lord: "Unless someone is reborn from water and the Holy Spirit, he will not enter the kingdom of heaven" [John 3:5]. Therefore the one who is reborn has entered, and who does not neglect to guard his baptism; and thus likewise the one has not entered who has not been reborn.

3. Since, therefore, our Lord had come to give a new baptism for the salvation of the human race and remission of all sins, he himself first deigned to be baptized, not that he who had not committed sin laid aside his sins, but so as to sanctify the waters of baptism in order to blot out the sins of all believers through the baptism of those reborn. He therefore was baptized in water in order that we through baptism would be washed from all sins....[129]

Sermon 35 (fragment)

On Susanna

1. In today's reading that you have heard [dearly beloved], the story of the most noble woman Susanna was read to us, who has offered to us a model of chastity and an example of purity [see Dan 13].[130] To be sure, she was lovely in appearance, but lovelier in character. For with her the beauty of soul surpassed that of body; for the body's beauty is temporary, but the soul's beauty is eternal. For she was not adorned with bodily necklaces, nor did she have earrings on her body, nor rings, nor pearls, but she was filled within with every ornament of the virtues. For in place of earrings she had the divine words, in place of a ring she had comely faith, in place of pearls she had the precious works by which daily she beautified the appearance of her mind and soul.

2. Using this example among others, the blessed apostle Paul exhorts the women and says, "Finally, let women be holy, adorning themselves not with plaited hair, or gold, or pearls, or costly attire, but preserving chastity with good works" [1 Tim 2:9–10; cf. 1 Pet 3:3–5]. Whence refined women are wide of the mark who do not consider themselves to be beautiful unless they wear jewelry like this in contradiction to the apostle's statement. Truly such presumptuousness of theirs merits the Creator's indignation.[131] Why do you cover your face with white and red, as if making corrections to the image of God in you, who made your face the way he wanted? For the features you were born with are the work (*opus*) of the Creator God; but what you add on your own is evidence (*argumentum*) of the devil, who wants to defile

the work of God in you.[132] Why do you desire to adorn yourself with gold, or with costly raiment, when you ought to be adorned with faith and holy character? Therefore if you desire to please God, follow the example of Susanna: be chaste, be modest, be of virtuous character, be a worker of justice, and you will be sufficiently beautiful, and not only to God but also precious to men. For this beauty usually pleases faithful husbands as well, if he finds in his wife beautiful actions and comeliness of mind....

3. Susanna, then, for the sake of purity, even despised death. For she is denounced by two ruined elders, she is accused as if guilty and condemned as an adulteress [see Dan 13:41]. But the holy and admirable woman preferred to submit to death with her purity intact than to live with a bad conscience.

But when she was being led to death, God stirred up the holy spirit of the boy Daniel, who is called "desirable to God" [see Dan 9:23; 10:11], who both made known Susanna's innocence and revealed the false accusation of her accusers [see Dan 13:44–59]. Whence it came about that the innocent Susanna was set free before the just judgment of God and the elderly falsely accusing adulterers perished by a deserved death. The king of Babylon roasted them in fire on account of the iniquity that they committed in Israel, and because they were committing adultery with the wives of their own citizens [see Dan 13:62].

4. Therefore Susanna has prefigured the church, namely by the example of purity and modesty, since she remained in the paradise of Christ by faith and by the manner of her life [see Dan 13:4, 7], just as all the faithful in the church strive to please Christ, their God and head, by the purity of their character, the holiness of good works, right faith, firm hope, and perfect love. Finally, chastity and modesty are aided by fasting. For we fast to this end, not merely to abstain from food, but to separate ourselves from all the vices of the flesh, namely, from bodily lust, from concupiscence of soul, from depraved thoughts, from hatred and ill will, from detraction and murmuring, from fury and wrath, from all vices and sins together. But merely to abstain from food is not fasting. That is why, when we fast, we ought especially to abstain from vices, lest it be said to us by the Lord through the prophet, "That is not the sort of fast I have chosen, says the Lord..." [Isa 58:5].

SERMON 36 (FRAGMENT)[133]

On Praising God

...And therefore it is proper that we all praise God with one voice, one mind, that is, with one concord, one faith, one hope, one love. And so God deems it fitting to be praised by the just, he does not deem it fitting from sinners. He consents to be praised by Catholics, he does not consent to it by heretics. He deems it fitting from the faithful, not from the unfaithful. For this reason we ought to act in such a way and to live in such a way that we are considered worthy of praising God, and may the prophetic words be fittingly applied to us: "Praise the Lord, ye servants (*pueri*), praise the name of the Lord" [Ps 113:1]. We do this justly and deservedly if we faithfully obey his will and commandments in all things....

SERMON 37 (FRAGMENT)

On the Storm That Was Stilled

1. [Our Lord Jesus Christ ascended into a boat with his disciples, just as the gospel truth reports, to sail across the channel {see Matt 8:23–27}. And a great storm came upon the sea, so that the boat was covered by waves][134]...This boat in which Christ ascended can be understood in two ways. For this boat is understood as the cross on which Christ ascended for our redemption. Our Lord and Savior who steers the entire world is contained in the small wood of the boat. He who created the entire world saved it by the wood of his cross. He who consented to die for us on the cross, who even guards his people with an everlasting watch, slept in the boat. He who thought it fitting to free us from the danger of eternal death endured danger at sea. He who through holy preachers daily in the holy church rouses us from the sleep of unbelief and ignorance was roused by his disciples.

In another way as well this boat is understood as the holy church. To be sure, at first it was few in terms of the number of believers, but later on it grew into such great numbers of believers that it filled the entire world. And therefore it is no longer called a boat but a great ship.[135] Hence the sea signifies this world.

2. "And behold there came a great disturbance on the sea so that the boat was covered by waves" [Matt 8:24]. A great persecution arose against the church not long after the Lord's passion; and the cruelty of irreligious men instigated by demons fought against the church's faithful, so that the assembly of faithful people was nearly wiped out by the persecutions of the wicked [see Acts 8:1]. But as the disciples were sailing, Christ fell asleep [see Matt 8:24]. This means that for the sake of testing her faith he permits his church for a short time to be tested by afflictions and persecutions of this world.

"And the disciples went and woke him, saying, Lord, save us, we are perishing. Then he got up and commanded the winds and the sea, and a great calm occurred" [Matt 8:25–26]. When the faith of those who pray does not hesitate, however often the Lord is struck by the prayers of the faithful for their needs, he quickly gets up to show pity. But we ought to rouse our Lord and Savior to show his pity, with insistent prayers and with meritorious faith, however often we are overwhelmed by trials and distresses as by storms at sea, that he may deign to bring help and aid to those who hope for his mercy, as he himself says through the prophet: "Call upon me on the day of your affliction; I will rescue you and you will honor me" [Ps 50:15].

Therefore, let us call upon the Lord with all our heart, and with all our faith, that he may deign to set us free from all anguish, from famine, war, death, captivity, from every danger, that we may be able to glorify his name in everything, and laden with the worthy fruits of good works, we may be worthy to reach the port of our heavenly country.

Sermon 38 (fragment)

Here Begins a Sermon of Saint Augustine on the Passage, God Made Tunics of Skin for Adam and His Wife

When the divine reading was read, we heard of the extent of God's grace toward humanity, even after the violation of his command. It says, "And God made tunics of skin for Adam and his wife, and he clothed them" [Gen 3:21]. For they were both naked after sin, since they had lost the clothing of shame, in order to obey the devil speaking through the serpent rather than the Lord's command.[136]

Therefore they were naked, despoiled of the tunic of God's grace and the clothing of his godliness. For one who is not clothed with God's grace is naked in respect to every good, even if he has many tunics. Thus it is not without reason that God made tunics of skin for Adam and his wife and clothed them, in order to show the grace of Christ's passion. For in no other way could the human race have been clothed, since they had been stripped naked of the grace of God, except by the passion of Christ the Lord, from which source the whole world is redeemed and liberated from eternal damnation and death.

2. Scripture has added the following as well: "For God let Adam go out of paradise, lest he stretch forth his hand toward the tree of life and eat of it and live forever" [Gen 3:23, 22].[137] Not without a mystery did God forbid the man from living forever, who had despised the precepts of eternal salvation entrusted to him; but the reason God prohibited him from touching the tree of life was to keep him from living for eternal punishment. For if the man had not been redeemed from sin and had tasted from the tree of life, he would indeed have lived forever, not indeed for glory but for eternal punishment. Thus it was necessary that the humans first be punished with the penalty of death for their transgression of the commandment, and then to be summoned back to grace.[138] In fact, what the tree of life in paradise was unable to offer humanity at that time, the passion of Christ supplied; and he received the lost grace through the tree of the cross, which at that time he could not have recovered through the tree of life....

Sermon 39 (fragments)

On the Beatitudes

When our Lord and Savior was going around many cities and regions preaching and healing every sickness and every disease among the people, "seeing the crowds before him," as today's reading has related, "he went up on a mountain" [Matt 5:1]. Rightly the lofty God goes to a lofty place in order to preach lofty words to those who desire to ascend to the lofty heights of the virtues. And it is good that the new law is preached on a mountain, since the law of Moses was given on a mountain [see Exod 19, 20]. The latter consists in ten words, leading to education and instruction for the present life, the former in eight Beatitudes, since it leads those who follow them to eternal life and to the heavenly homeland....

"Blessed are the meek, for they shall possess the earth" [Matt 5:4].[139] The meek then ought to be peaceful in spirit, sincere in heart. The Lord clearly shows that their merit is not small when he says, "For they shall possess the earth." Surely this refers to that land of which it is written, "I believe that I will see the good things of the Lord in the land of the living" [Ps 27:13]. Therefore the inheritance of that earth is the body's immortality and the glory of the eternal resurrection. <...> For meekness does not know arrogance, it does not know boasting, it does not know ambition. Whence not without cause does the Lord exhort his disciples elsewhere, saying, "Learn from me, for I am meek and humble in heart, and you will find rest for your souls" [Matt 11:29]....

"Blessed are those who mourn, for they shall be consoled" [Matt 5:5]. Not those who mourn for the loss of dear ones, but who bewail their own sins, who wash away their transgressions with tears; or surely, those who mourn for the iniquity of this world, and who deplore the transgressions of others....

"Blessed are the peacemakers, for they will be called sons of God" [Matt 5:9]. Behold how great the merit of peacemakers is, when they are no longer called slaves but sons of God. This is not without reason, for the one who loves peace loves Christ, the author of peace, whom the apostle Paul named peace when he said, "For he is our peace" [Eph 2:14]. But he who does not love peace follows discord, since he loves the devil, who is the author of discord. For indeed he first created discord between God and humanity, since he made humanity a transgressor of God's command. But the reason the Son of God came down from heaven was to condemn the devil, the author of discord, and to make peace between God and humankind by reconciling humankind with God and by calling back God to humankind in grace. And the reason we ought to be peacemakers is to merit being called children of God. Since without peace not only do we lose the designation of sons and daughters, but even the very name of slaves, since the apostle says, "Love peace, with which none of us can please God" [see Heb 12:14; 11:6]....

SERMON 40

Preface to the Lord's Prayer

1. To his disciples who asked him how they ought to pray [see Luke 11:1], our Lord and Savior Jesus Christ gave to them, among his other salutary precepts, the same form of prayer that you as well know quite well even from today's reading.[140] Now let your love hear how he teaches his disciples to pray to God the Father Almighty: "But you, when you pray, enter into your room, shut the door, and pray to your Father" [Matt 6:6]. What he calls a room, he shows to be not a hidden house, but he is reminding us to reveal the secrets of our heart to no one but him. And to pray to God with the door closed means to close off our heart from evil thoughts with a mystical key and with closed lips to speak to God with an uncorrupted mind. But our God is a hearer of faith, not of voice. Therefore our heart is closed with the key of faith against the plots of the adversary and lies open to God alone, whose temple it is known to be, so that when he dwells in our hearts, he himself may be the advocate in our prayers. Therefore the word of God and the wisdom of God, Christ our Lord [see 1 Cor 1:24], has taught us this prayer, so that we may pray as follows:

2. "Our Father who art in heaven" [Matt 6:9a]. This is the voice of freedom and complete confidence. Therefore you must live with this kind of character, that you may be able to be sons of God and brothers of Christ. For by what temerity does he presume to call God his own Father, who deviates from his will? Hence you, dearly beloved, show yourselves worthy of the divine adoption, since it is written, "As many as believed in him he gave them power to become children of God" [John 1:12].

"Hallowed be thy name" [Matt 6:9b]. That is, not that God be hallowed by our prayers, since he is always holy, but we ask that his name be kept holy in us, so that we who have been sanctified in his baptism may persevere in that which we are beginning to be.

"Thy kingdom come" [Matt 6:10a]. When indeed does our God not reign, especially when we consider that his kingdom is immortal? But when we say, "Thy kingdom come," we are asking for our kingdom to come, promised to us from God, acquired by the blood and passion of Christ.

"Thy will be done on earth as it is in heaven" [Matt 6:10b]. That is, in that place [heaven] let your will be done, so that what you want done in heaven, this we would do without reproach while we are placed on earth.

"Give us this day our daily bread" [Matt 6:11]. We ought to understand spiritual bread here. For Christ is our bread, who said, "I am the living bread, who came down from heaven" [John 6:51]. We call it "daily" because we ought to ask always to be free from sin, so that we may be worthy of heavenly nourishment.

"And forgive us our debts as we also forgive our debtors" [Matt 6:12]. With this precept he signifies that we can earn pardon for sins in no other way than by first pardoning others who transgress against us, just as the Lord says in the gospel: "If you do not forgive people their sins, neither will your Father forgive you your sins" [Matt 6:15].

"And lead us not into temptation" [Matt 6:13a]. That is, do not allow us to be led by the one who tempts, the author of depravity. For Scripture says, "For God does not tempt to evil" [Jas 1:13]. But the devil is the tempter. To conquer him, the Lord says, "Watch and pray that you not enter into temptation" [Matt 26:41; Mark 14:38].

"But deliver us from evil" [Matt 6:13b]. The reason he says this is because the apostle said, "You do not know what you ought to pray for" [Rom 8:26]. Therefore we must pray to God Almighty in such a way that whatever human weakness is not able to be on guard against and avoid, this our Lord Jesus Christ may deign to grant to us mercifully, that we may be able. He lives and reigns as God in unity with the Holy Spirit through all the ages of ages. Amen.

Sermon 41

*A Sermon (*Declamatio*) of the Roman Bishop Chromatius on the Fifth Chapter of Matthew, or a Sermon on the Eight Beatitudes*

1. This assembly of people and the crowds that are here for the market day give us the opportunity, brothers and sisters, to set forth the words of the gospel. For worldly affairs customarily are examples of spiritual things, and earthly things offer an image of heavenly things. For even our Lord and Savior often admonishes us about heavenly things by means of earthly things when he says, "The kingdom of heaven is like a net cast into the sea" [Matt 13:47]. And surely,

"The kingdom of heaven is like a man doing business, looking for a fine pearl" [Matt 13:45]. If then the market has this sort of meaning, that each person either sells what he no longer needs or buys what he lacks, for his own advantage, it is not out of order that I too set forth the merchandise that the Lord has entrusted to me, the preaching that is assuredly heavenly, since indeed he has chosen me as well, even if I am unworthy, indeed the least of those servants to whom the Lord distributed talents to do business with and to make a profit [see Matt 25:15–16]. Nor of course will merchants be lacking when by God's grace there is an audience of this size and nature. But it is more necessary to strive after heavenly gain, where earthly profit is not being neglected.[141] I desire, dearest brethren, to set forth for you these precious pearls of the Beatitudes from the holy gospel; and so open the treasuries of your hearts, make a purchase, take hold of them with eagerness, possess them with joy.

Our Lord and God, the only begotten of the Most High Father, who deigned to become man from being God, teacher from being Lord, when great crowds were gathering from different regions, took his disciples, that is, his apostles, "went up on a mountain, opened his mouth and taught them, saying, Blessed are the poor in spirit, for theirs is the kingdom of heaven. Blessed are the meek, for they will possess the land" [Matt 5:1–4]. Using precious stones, the Lord and Savior paves the path, so to speak, with a number of very solid steps by which holy and faithful souls can crawl and climb their way up to that highest good, that is, the kingdom of heaven. Briefly, then, dearest brothers and sisters, I long to show you what these steps are. Only let your minds and souls be completely attentive, for the things of God are not of trivial importance.

2. "Blessed are the poor in spirit, for theirs is the kingdom of heaven" [Matt 5:3]. What a wonderful commencement to the heavenly doctrine, brothers and sisters! He begins not by inspiring fright but with a beatitude, not by causing terror but rather longing. For in the manner of a superintendent of the public games, or a referee at the gladiatorial exhibitions, he sets forth the great prize for the competitors in this spiritual stadium, so that when they see the prize, they would not be afraid of the effort required nor shrink back from the dangers involved. Therefore, "Blessed are the poor in spirit, for theirs is the kingdom of heaven." He did not call the poor blessed without qualification nor without precision, but he added, "poor in spirit." For not all poverty is happy, since it often arises out of necessity, sometimes

it comes about through evil habits, even as a result of divine wrath. Therefore blessed is that spiritual poverty of those who for God's sake make themselves poor in spirit and will by renouncing the goods of the world, by voluntarily dispersing their own money. He calls them blessed deservedly, since they are "poor in spirit, since theirs is the kingdom of heaven"; for by means of voluntary poverty, they pursue the wealth of the heavenly kingdom.

Then he says, "Blessed are the meek, for they will possess the land" [Matt 5:4]. Admirably, a second step is shown after the first: "Blessed are the meek, for they will possess the land." But just as it is impossible to stand on a second step out of order, without climbing onto the first, so a man will not be able to be meek unless he has first become poor in spirit. Well then, how can a spirit that is set amid riches, amid the cares and anxieties of the world, from which arise deals, lawsuits, provocations, anger, troubles without end, how, I say, can a soul be meek and mild amid these things, unless it first cuts itself off from all causes of wrath and renounces every occasion for quarreling? A sea does not become tranquil unless the winds cease; fire is not put out unless you remove the material to burn and the thorny brushwood; so a soul will not be meek and quiet if it does not renounce those things that provoke and inflame it. It is good, then, that a step is joined to the step, since the poor in spirit are already beginning to be meek.

3. And a third approaches: "Blessed are those who mourn, for they will be consoled" [Matt 5:4]. How ought we to understand this salutary mourning? Surely not that which arises from damaged goods, nor that which arises from the loss of dear ones, nor that which arises from the loss of secular offices. Surely none of these things will cause grief to one who is already poor in spirit.[142] Salutary mourning is that which is carried out because of sins, because of the recollection of divine judgment. For the soul formerly established amid countless occupations and bitter experiences in the world was not able to think of itself; it has already become secure and meek, and begins to look at itself more closely, to examine its actions day and night, and in this way the wounds of past crimes begin to appear, and then salutary mourning and tears follow, so salutary that soon a heavenly consolation takes place. For he is truthful who said, "Blessed are those who mourn, for they will be consoled."

4. Let us approach the fourth [step], brethren: "Blessed are those who hunger and thirst for justice, for they shall be satisfied"

[Matt 5:6]. For truly after repentance, after mourning and tears over our sins, what other form of hunger and thirst could arise than for justice? For just as the one who has traveled through the gloom of night is already eager for the approaching light, and the one who has digested bitter bile longs for food and drink, so too the mind of the Christian man, after he has digested his own sins by means of mourning and tears, now hungers and thirsts only for God's justice. And fittingly he will rejoice in being sated with that for which he longs.

5. And let the fifth step present itself: "Blessed are the merciful, for they shall obtain mercy" [Matt 5:7]. No one will be able to give to another unless he first gives to himself. After procuring mercy for himself, then, and after being sated with justice, he now begins to feel pain for the wretched, he now begins to plead for other sinners. Having become merciful even to those who are his enemies, he will prepare a larger reserve of mercy for himself, through religious action of this sort, at the coming of the Lord. That is why it is said, "Blessed are the merciful, for they will obtain mercy."

6. Behold, the sixth step is at hand: "Blessed are the pure in heart, for they shall see God" [Matt 5:8]. Obviously they will already have a pure heart, obviously they will already be able to see God, who are poor in spirit and meek, who lament their sins, who have been reinvigorated by justice, who are merciful, and in adversities too the eye of their heart is so sincere and bright that without any inflammation of malice, they look upon the unapproachable brightness of God without obstruction. For cleanness of heart and purity of conscience will allow no cloud to block the view of the Lord.

7. Brothers and sisters, it then follows, "Blessed are the peacemakers, for they will be called children of God" [Matt 5:9]. Great is the worth of those who strive after peace, when they are registered with the name of children of God. And this kind of peacemaking is good indeed, which occurs between those who are quarreling over worldly property, or over vain glory, or grudges. But this reward is small, since the Lord had said as an example to us, "Who appointed me judge or divider over you?" [Luke 12:14]. For he had already said before, "Do not seek to get back things that have been taken from you" [Luke 6:30]. And in another place, "How can you believe when you accept glory from one another?" [John 5:44]. We should understand peacemaking in a more powerful and lofty sense, then, as that kind, I would say, by which pagan people who are God's enemies are led to peace through constant instruction; that by which sinners are corrected and

reconciled with God through repentance; that by which rebellious heretics are set straight; that by which those who are in discord with the church are made disposed to unity and peace. For truly those who are peacemakers in this fashion are not only blessed, but will be worthy and deserving to be called sons of God. For by imitating the Son of God himself, Christ, who is proclaimed by the apostle as our peace and reconciliation [see Eph 2:14–16; 2 Cor 5:18–19], they are allotted fellowship in his name.

8. "Blessed are those who suffer persecution for the sake of justice, for theirs is the kingdom of heaven" [Matt 5:10]. There is no doubt, brothers and sisters, that envy is the constant companion of good deeds. For without speaking here of the cruelty of the persecutors, when you begin to hold to a strict justice, to strike back against insolence, to summon unbelievers to the Lord's peace; finally, when you begin to disagree with men of the world who are in error, at once persecutions arise; inevitably hatred arises, jealousy tears apart. Ultimately, it is in this way that Christ brings his audience to this last step, to the top summit, not only that they may hold up in the midst of suffering, but even rejoice together in dying.

9. "Blessed are you when they persecute you and reproach you and falsely speak all evil against you because of justice: Rejoice and exult, for your reward is great in heaven. For thus they persecuted the prophets who were before you" [Matt 5:11–12]. It is the perfection of virtue, brothers and sisters, after so many administrations of justice, to endure reproaches from people for the sake of truth, to be afflicted with torments, finally to be put to death, and not to be terrified, holding forth the example of the prophets before us, who, when torn apart in different ways for the sake of justice, merited to be conformed to the sufferings and to the reward of Christ. This is the higher step on which Paul, looking at Christ, said, "But there is one thing, forgetting what is behind and stretching out to what is before me, I follow after the prize of the upward call of God in Christ Jesus" [Phil 3:13–14]. And still more plainly to Timothy, "I have fought the good fight, I have completed the race" [2 Tim 4:7]. As one who had climbed all the steps, he added, "I have kept the faith. What remains is the crown of justice laid up for me" [2 Tim 4:8]. For truly this is what remained, once the whole race has been completed, for Paul to reach the higher step of martyrdom, rejoicing throughout his trials and sufferings. Therefore the Lord's words are a fitting exhortation: "Rejoice,

exult, for great is your reward in heaven." And he plainly shows that the rewards increase corresponding to the increase of persecutions.

10. Brothers and sisters, the eight steps of the gospel that have been shown are constructed out of costly stones, as I said. Jacob's ladder has been shown, whose top reached from the ground to heaven [Gen 28:12]. The one who climbs it finds the gate of heaven, and the one who enters through it shall stand rejoicing without end in the sight of the Lord, to praise the Lord forever with the holy angels.

This is our merchandise, this is our spiritual trade. Let us give what we have, O blessed ones, let us offer poverty of spirit, that we may receive the abundance of the heavenly kingdom according to his promise. Let us offer meekness, that we may possess the land and paradise. Let us weep over sins, both ours and those of others, that we may merit consolation from the goodness of the Lord. Let us hunger and thirst for justice, that we may be fattened up all the more abundantly; let us show mercy that we may obtain true mercy; let us live as peacemakers, that we may be called sons of God; let us offer a pure heart and a chaste body, that we may be able to see God with a lucid mind. Let us not fear persecutions for the sake of justice, that we may become heirs of the heavenly kingdom. With joy and gladness let us embrace reproaches, torture, finally death, if it comes about for the sake of God's truth, that an abundant reward may be given to us in heaven, with the prophets and apostles.

But that the conclusion of our words may agree with the introduction, if there is joy for merchants because of present and fleeting profits, let us rejoice all the more and be glad together that today we have found such pearls of the Lord to which no worldly goods can be compared. For us to merit purchasing, obtaining, and possessing them, we must ask for the Lord's help and grace, together with power, to whom be the glory in the ages of ages. Amen [see 1 Pet 4:11].

Sermon 42 (doubtful fragment)

On the Suffering of Saint Peter

...Hence the Lord says to him, as you heard in today's reading, "Simon son of John, do you love me? He answered and said, You know, Lord, that I love you. Again the Lord said to him, Simon, son of John, do you love me? He answered and said, You know, Lord, that I love you" [John 21:15–16]. What are we saying? Did not the Lord, who knew the secrets of hearts, know that he was loved by Peter? Or was a single answer from Peter not sufficient for the Lord, who knows all things before they are said? But the Lord questions Peter three times, in order that a threefold confession would condemn a threefold denial.

Then the Lord says to Peter, "When you were younger, you girded yourself and went where you wanted. But when you are old, another shall gird you and lead you whither you wouldst not. And this he said, signifying by what death he should glorify God" [John 21:18–19]. In the old age of his life, saint Peter took up the cross for Christ. For the Lord had said elsewhere in the gospel, "He who does not take up his own cross and follow me cannot be my disciple" [Luke 14:27]. The disciple of truth fulfilled the master's command. He took up the cross for Christ in order to glorify the Lord's cross.

But when he was led to the cross, he thought that he should be affixed to the cross with his feet upside down. He did not shrink from suffering but preserved humility, lest a servant should be judged the equal of his Lord. The punishment of suffering was the same, but the grace was not the same, since Peter was crucified for himself, but Christ was crucified for the salvation of the world. Peter was crucified so that he might obtain the glory of his own suffering. Christ was crucified in order to crown the whole world with the glory of his passion. Peter was nailed with his feet upward, so that he might hasten with the swiftest of steps to heaven; Christ is raised on the cross with his hands nailed, so that he could cover the entire world with the outstretching of his hands....

TRACTATES (*TRACTATUS*) ON [THE GOSPEL OF] MATTHEW[1]

PREFACE[2]

1. Although the mystery (*sacramentum*) of our salvation and faith is found in all the divine Scriptures, yet it is especially contained in the gospel proclamation, in which the secret of the heavenly mystery (*arcani*) is revealed to us as well as the entire mystery of the Lord's passion and resurrection. Now since the gospel is divided into four books, there are four writers: Matthew, Mark, Luke, and John. Long ago they were prefigured and predestined to the duty of this divine work by the Holy Spirit, as the blessed Luke has reported: "Since many have attempted to arrange a narrative of the things that have been fulfilled among us" [Luke 1:1]. For Matthew is shown to have written the first Gospel by divine authority and the grace of the Holy Spirit, then Mark and Luke, last of all John, after he came back from the island of Patmos [see Rev 1:9], after the death of Domitian Caesar by whom he had been banished.[3] After he had been set on this island and had written the Book of Revelation, it was disclosed to him that he too would write a Gospel on account of the different heresies that were already beginning to spring up by the devil's instigation.[4]

2. Matthew certainly and John too belong to the number of the twelve apostles, who not only were with the Lord before the passion but also kept company with him after the resurrection for forty days [see Acts 1:3]. They carefully narrate everything they saw and heard according to what John testified in his epistle, saying, "As we have heard and seen with our eyes, and our hands have examined concerning the Word of life, these things we declare to you" [1 John 1:1–3]. Now Mark was Peter's disciple and interpreter.[5] He did not see the Lord in the flesh but he wrote a Gospel while flooded with heavenly grace and full of the Holy Spirit. Luke also had not seen the Lord in

the flesh, but, because he had been very well educated in the law, since he was a companion of the apostle Paul in everything, having been instructed by the grace of God, he carefully set forth the Acts of the Apostles and he wrote a Gospel in his own name, narrating from the very beginning all the events in the order, just as he had learned them from his relations with the apostles, as he himself attests, saying, "Just as those who are of the age and who were ministers of the word handed down to us" [Luke 1:2].

3. Therefore, the authority of these four evangelists is firm and immutable because they wrote everything by one principle. Granted that by a sure accounting of them, various principles are taught, but they do not disagree among themselves on anything because the sense of the faith of all of them is one and the same, concerning the Lord's incarnation, birth, passion, resurrection, and also his two comings. And because we are endeavoring to say a few things about the Gospels, proper care and the cause of the matter itself warns us to test also the truth of the Gospels prefigured from the law of the Old Testament, since indeed the apostle says, "The law was a shadow of things to come" [Heb 10:1]. For neither can the new things stand without the old nor were the old things able to have any stability without the new. We will speak of all these things in more detail in their own place in a sermon on the two testaments.[6]

4. Thus, both the type and the number of the four Gospels was clearly shown in the law and the prophets, as in the four rivers that flowed from one source out of Eden [see Gen 2:10],[7] and in the four rows of stones that Aaron wore woven in the priestly garment on his chest [see Exod 28:15–21], and in the four rows of twelve oxen that Solomon set up in the temple under the bronze sea [see 1 Kgs 7:25; Jer 52:20]. In all of these, the expressed examples of the future truth cannot be doubted. This is also why Elijah the Tishbite, by the Holy Spirit, since he was not ignorant of the mysteries of the gospel preaching to come, when he freed the people from error and turned them from idols to God, poured out four jugs of water as a sacrifice that he offered, when he had put the burnt offering on the wood, and he did this three times [see 1 Kgs 18:34–38]. And fire came down from heaven, so that clearly even then he was declaring an image of the coming hope, that is, the mystery of the cross and the number of the Gospels and the grace of baptism and the faith in the Trinity, in which we are baptized. And he made a worthy sacrifice to God

himself, when the fire from heaven comes upon us, that is, when the Holy Spirit is given to us as his gift.[8]

5. But we find these Gospels depicted even more clearly and plainly by the prophet Ezekiel in the four living creatures whose face and form are both described.[9] He says, "Their likeness was the face of a man and the face of a lion and the face of a calf and the face of a flying eagle" [Ezek 1:10]. Surely this is a clear prefiguration of the evangelists.[10] Although they are shown with different faces in view of the variety of each one's principle, their proclamation is nonetheless not different. In fact, the same prophet, when he said that the faces are specific to each, related higher up that each of them had four faces, that is, that each living creature had four faces. The reason for this is not obscure, namely that each one of them is understood to have said all things, and all of them one thing. While a certain cause and rationale distinguishes and separates them in the faces and number, on the other hand the unity of their proclamation makes them indistinguishable and inseparable because you will find everything in each and the whole in all. But we ought to understand and recognize this very difference between the faces. He says, "The face of a man, and the face of a lion, and the face of a calf, and the face of a flying eagle." The face of a man is understood as the Gospel according to Matthew.[11] The reason it is "of a man" is because he began to make the introduction from the bodily birth of the Lord, saying, "The book of the generation of Jesus Christ, son of David, son of Abraham" [Matt 1:1], etcetera. In this way he announces the origin of his human birth. For that reason, then, he is thus shown with the face of a man. Now, the face of a lion is understood to be the Gospel according to John because, when the other evangelists had said that Christ our God was made human according to the assumption of flesh and was born of the virgin, he immediately in the introduction of his words revealed his timeless and divine birth, saying, "In the beginning was the Word and the Word was with God and the Word was God" [John 1:1], and so forth. With this voice, the preacher of such great divinity roared like a lion to frighten off the heresies.

6. Revelation also mentioned these living creatures, but we must carefully examine why, when the prophet had said that the first face was of a man, then of a lion, did Revelation put the face of the lion earlier in reversed order, saying, "The face of a lion and the face of a man" [Rev 4:7]. Indeed we need to take note that this is not fortuitous but for a firm reason. For the reason Matthew has been shown first in

order by the prophet with the face of a man is because he was the first to write a Gospel. But John is reported before him in Revelation for this reason, because by proclaiming the timeless and coeternal Son of the Father, he surpassed every beginning by the excellent arrangement of his preaching. Thus, he is placed later as to time or order, but he is regarded first as to faith, since he knew the secrets of the divine mystery from reclining on the Lord's bosom [see John 13:25]. But the fact that John is preferred for the sake of the faith does not detract from the other evangelists, since they all were watered by one and the same Spirit to the perfect instruction of the church and wrote about the Lord what was necessary and perfect. For, because many different heresies were to come, the Holy Spirit so governed the pen of each as to expound the complete and perfect mystery of the heavenly faith through all of them, by which he silenced all enemies of the truth. After all, through Matthew and Luke the Holy Spirit at once opposes those wretched people who deny that the Son of God was born of a virgin for our salvation, judging this as unworthy for God. Through them he clearly shows both the birth of the Lord according to the flesh and the conception and birth from the virgin [see Matt 1:23; Luke 1:26–30]. But those who dared blaspheme the true divinity of the Son of God and the unlimited nature of his eternity, denying in particular that he was born of the Father and is true God and had always been with the Father, saints John and Mark nonetheless oppose at once, condemning the infidelity of their blasphemy, testifying in the beginning of their Gospels that the only begotten Son of God is God [see Mark 1:1, 11; John 1:1].

7. But as we are carefully pursuing all these things, I seem to have gone on longer than I had intended to. Let us return to the subject. As has been summarized above, saint John is shown with the face of a lion.[12] The Gospel according to Luke, however, is recognized in the face of the calf because he writes according to the law. After all, he began with the priesthood of Zachariah, saying, "In the days of Herod the king of Judea, there was a certain priest by the name of Zachariah from the order of Abijah, and his wife of the daughters of Aaron" [Luke 1:5], and so on. Now the reason he has been represented in the persona of a calf is because the law according to which he is writing had decreed that among the other sacrifices a calf be offered for the sins of the people as a type of the future truth [see Lev 9:2]. Hence, not without cause was it only this evangelist who made mention of this fattened calf, which is killed for the salvation and return of the lost son

out of the exulting father's joy [see Luke 15:23]. For the reason saint Luke mentioned this was to declare that our Lord and Savior suffered for the sins of the human race in accordance with the prefiguration of the law. But the face of the flying eagle is understood as the Gospel according to Mark, who began with a prophetic testimony, saying, "The beginning of the gospel of Jesus Christ Son of God, as is written in Isaiah: Behold, I send my angel before your face. A voice of one crying in the wilderness: Prepare the ways of the Lord, make our God's paths straight" [Mark 1:1–3]. And because the eagle is often shown as a figure of the Holy Spirit, who has been spoken in the prophets [see Gen 1:2; Deut 32:11; Isa 40:31], he is thus depicted in the face of an eagle. For he is the only one who reported that our Lord and Savior flew away again to heaven [see Mark 16:19], that is, went back to the Father, as David had said, "He ascended upon the cherubim and flew; he flew upon the wings of the winds" [Ps 18:10].

8. Finally, that we should know that the reason for such a great mystery is ordained in each of the evangelists by the Holy Spirit, the same faces also fit the persona of our Lord and God.[13] For he is understood to be a man because of the flesh that he took on from the virgin, and as a calf because of what he himself offered as a sacrifice worthy of God for our sins, and as a lion in view of the power of the virtue that defeated death in triumph, allowing in himself no attack from external terror, and as an eagle because, when the mystery of the passion was completed, he flew like an eagle on high, taking the booty of his human flesh with him, which he snatched from our jaws.

9. For the same reason in the prophet Zechariah we also read the foretold number of the evangelists. It is reported by the prophet for the same purpose: "I saw four chariots going out of two mountains, and these mountains were mountains of bronze. In the first chariot were red horses, and in the second chariot were black horses, and in the third chariot were white horses, and in the fourth chariot were varied and dappled horses. And I said to the angel who was speaking in me, What are these, lord? He answered and said to me, Do you not know what these are? And I said, No, lord. And he told me, These are the four winds of the sky that stand with the Lord of the whole earth" [Zech 6:1–8].

And so this is the exact number of the chariots. Then, the following rationale, which was promulgated by prophetic reason, teaches us to perceive a type of the gospel truth in these very things. Hence we clearly notice that the Gospels have also been depicted in these chariots as well. But by depicting the four horses going in four directions, he made the following known, as we mentioned earlier, that each of the Gospels must be understood in the four and the four in each. Granted that the preaching of the evangelists seems rightly to be in four portions, yet in an inseparable manner they harmonize with each other as one through the unity of the faith. In fact, that we might know clearly that the Gospels were prefigured in these chariots, when the prophet asked the angel who was speaking to him about what these were and he was told this: "These are the four winds of the sky that stand with the Lord of all the earth," [winds] that he reported went around the whole earth by God's command.[14] And lest we should think that the saying was about those winds that blow through the lands and generate waves or produce storms, which would be a quite foolish interpretation, since nothing but heavenly things were shown to the prophet, who longed for divine and eternal things, the Lord fittingly added additionally, "These are the ones that circle the earth; they soften my fury" [Zech 6:8]. Thus we recognize clearly that the divine wrath, which came from the people's sins, could not otherwise be appeased except through the gospel preaching, which ran throughout the globe. Through it the remission of sins and salvation was given to the human race.

10. Even the arrangement of the world itself rests upon the reckoning of this evangelical number: for we recognize four seasons that the year revolves around and the four corners of the earth to which the four guardian angels have been assigned, as Revelation relates [see Rev 7:1].

11. And although there are said to be four Gospels because of the number of the evangelists, nevertheless among them all there is one gospel, since the Lord says, "And this gospel will be preached throughout the whole world" [Matt 24:14]. He did not say "Gospels" but "gospel." The apostle shows this too when he says, "If anyone preaches to you a gospel other than what you have received, let him be accursed" [Gal 1:9; cf. 2 Cor 11:4]. Hence, it is plain that there are indeed four books of the gospel, but the gospel is reckoned as one in these four books. And for that reason one must not pass judgment should we sometimes say "Gospels" because of the number of evangelists or as the custom established by the elders. For we are naming them "Gospels" in this way as the most important books, or we are designating the number of the evangelists. But on the authority of the Lord and of the apostle, we confess and believe that there is one gospel.

12. While wishing to establish the number of evangelists from a painstaking study of the various testimonies of the prophets, I have extended the sermon longer than I intended to. But we strive now to discuss the arrangement of the Gospel according to Matthew, even with little insight and mediocre speech.

Tractate 1 on Matthew 1:1–17

1. Well then, saint Matthew has begun to write a Gospel with an introduction of this sort: "The book of the generation of Jesus Christ, son of David, son of Abraham. Abraham begot Isaac, Isaac begot Jacob" [Matt 1:1–2]. And the rest that follows. As we said,[15] Matthew narrates the birth of the Lord according to the flesh, and for this reason he runs through his family line from Abraham, treating the tribe of Judah separately, until he reaches Joseph and Mary. But since the evangelist begins with Abraham by family succession and records the names of everyone in order, one must inquire diligently why he calls Christ our Lord son of David and son of Abraham only, when he says, "The book of the generation of Jesus Christ, son of David, son of Abraham." At any rate, we know that the evangelists do not say things like this without a reason for this arrangement. Each man, Abraham and David, in accordance with the promise of the Lord and the dignity of his race, stood out as worthy source for the generation of Christ according to the flesh.[16] For the Lord had promised to Abraham, who through circumcision is the prince of the Jewish race, that in his seed all nations would be blessed [see Gen 12:3; 17:10; Gal 3:8], that is, in Christ, who received his body from the race of Abraham, according to what the apostle interpreted to the Galatians, saying, "The promises were spoken to Abraham and to his seed. He did not say, 'and to seeds,' as to many; but, as to one, 'and to your seed, which is Christ'" [Gal 3:16]. Therefore, just as Abraham is the first in the Jewish race in respect to fleshly circumcision, so David is first in the tribe of Judah in his rank as king. For to him likewise God promised that from the fruit of his belly, the eternal king, Christ the Lord, would be born [see 2 Sam 7:11–16; 1 Chr 17:11–13]. For David was the first king from the tribe of Judah, from which the Son of God received flesh. Thus Matthew not without reason reckoned Christ our Lord as son of David and Abraham. For both Joseph and Mary are descended from the race of David, that is,

from the royal line. David too descended from Abraham, who stands forth according to his faith as the father of nations and according to the flesh as the prince of the Jewish race [see Rom 4:1–18]. But since our Lord and Savior is reckoned by the evangelists as son of David and Abraham according to the flesh, one must ask why David is put before Abraham, the prince of faith, in the arrangement. For this is what he says: “Son of David, son of Abraham.” We understand that he recorded it this way for the following reason: granted that the origin of the Lord’s incarnation pertains to both men, yet this very thing was promised through David even with a mysterious sign inserted. For it is written thus: “The Lord has sworn truth to David and he will not disappoint him,” for “from the fruit of your belly I will set [him] upon my throne” [Ps 132:11].

2. After the ordered listing of all the generations then, the evangelist again marked out this very number with a threefold arrangement, returning to the father of the race, Abraham, with whom he began. Thus he says, “All the generations from Abraham to David are fourteen generations. And from David to the transmigration of Babylon are fourteen generations, and from the transmigration of Babylon to Christ are fourteen generations” [Matt 1:17]. And since in this threefold arrangement, in terms of calculating the whole number, the evangelist could have recorded simply forty-two generations, one should ask why Matthew, the writer of the Gospel, divided it up using a threefold division into these three groups of fourteen generations.

[He marked off] the first division, then, in which he said, <“All the generations from Abraham to David are fourteen generations”>. I think that the same saint Abraham, as the prince of faith, himself earned in the first place both his intimacy with the divine discourses and he received the sign of circumcision as a sign of the truth to come. And likewise he earned the right to prefigure the mystery of the Lord’s passion for the salvation of the human race by his offering to God the dutiful sacrifice of his only beloved son [see Gen 22]. Saint David then is worthily associated with such a great patriarch, to conclude this number of fourteen generations, because he too according to his position was found to be a noble king and prophet, who prefigured Christ, the eternal king and true prophet, by the example of his kingship and prophecy.

3. [He marked off] a second division too, saying, “From David to the transmigration of Babylon are fourteen generations.” And [he distinguished] the number of this division too by commencing

with David and concluding with a fitting end at the transmigration of Babylon.[17] Thus we recognize the spiritual return of our redemption from the devil's captivity. But we need to traverse the following point not negligently, that though the evangelist reported that there were fourteen generations in this division, in the Book of Kingdoms, where the list of all the generations is recorded, seventeen generations are found written from David to the transmigration of Babylon. And since it is plain that the evangelist could hardly have been ignorant of this list of generations, since he spoke not by his own authority but through the Spirit of God, one must ask why he left out three generations in between and mentioned only fourteen generations. For the Books of Kingdoms, as I said earlier, show that there were seventeen generations. For we read the following in these same books after a considerable number of generations: "Josaphat begot Joram, and Joram begot Ochoziah, and Ochoziah begot Joash, and Joash begot Amasiah, and Amasiah begot Oziah" [1 Chr 3:10–12]. But in the division of generations that he composed, the evangelist recorded the following: "Joram begot Oziah" [Matt 1:8], keeping silent about three generations in between, namely those of Ochoziah, Joatham, and Amasiah, though according to the report of Kingdoms, Joram begot not Oziah but Ochoziah, and Ochoziah begot Joash, Joash Amasiah, and Amasias Oziah. But the evangelist records that this Oziah was born from Joram. We have proven by the steps of generation that he is actually in the fifth spot according to the Books of Kingdoms, as we said. The evangelist left out three names in between, as I said, and suppressed these names assuredly not through ignorance but for solid and essential reasons. For he did not want to associate unclean and accursed seed with the generation of Christ. For this Joram had married into the family of Ahab and Jezebel. He took a wife by the name of Gotholiah, a criminally depraved and profane woman, by whom he begot Ochoziah, Ochoziah [begot] Joash, Joash [begot] Amasiah, in whom the four generations of seed and of the iniquitous stock of Ahab and Jezebel are fulfilled [see 2 Kgs 8:26]. Concerning this seed, the Holy Spirit had borne witness, saying that he would eradicate every male from the house of Ahab [see 1 Kgs 21:21; 2 Kgs 9:8]. Jehu the son of Nimshi fulfilled this prophecy when he was anointed by the one whom Elisha the prophet sent [see 2 Kgs 9:1–10]. He received a promise that his seed would reign in Israel till the fourth generation [see 2 Kgs 10:30; 15:12]. Therefore, the blessing on Jehu for the one inflicting vengeance against the house of Ahab was as great as the cursing of the generation of Ahab and Jezebel. This agreed with what the Lord himself had said earlier to Moses, that he would pay back the sins of the fathers on the sons till the third and fourth offspring on those who hate him, and preserve the covenant for those who love him [see Deut 5:9–10]. And therefore when he made his enumeration, the evangelist rightly rejected the seed of Joram at the fourth generation, which came from Gotholiah, daughter of Ahab.

4. In fact the evangelist reports the third division as follows: "From the transmigration of Babylon to Christ fourteen generations" [Matt 1:17].[18] In this division too, in which the evangelist reported the number of fourteen generations, that is, "from the transmigration of Babylon to Christ," no more than thirteen are found. And since it is not proper that the evangelist by whom the Holy Spirit spoke either erred or could have been deceived, doubtless he has left to us the task of investigating the interpretation of this fourteenth generation, which he comprehended in the number. But if we understand the mystery of our salvation, that God became man and moreover that the Son of God wanted to become the Son of man, in these two generations as well, of the divine and the human, we find that the number comprehended by the evangelist has been fulfilled. For two generations are reckoned to the Lord: of Spirit and flesh, of God and man. For he who is the Spirit and the Word and God born of the Father before eternal times remained the only begotten Son of God. He is the same one too who was born in time from a virgin into a body for the mystery of human salvation. Whence not without cause the evangelist conjoined as a unity under two generations the nativity of the Word and the flesh, that is, of God and man.

5. For it is found to be not without reason that this number has been established and recorded by the evangelist. It is distinguished by sets of four and ten generations in a threefold division. For indeed in the Ten Commandments of the law and in the four books of the gospel, this number reveals to us the unity and concord of the law and the gospel. For the law, as we said, is contained and written down in ten words, but the gospel is deemed to be composed in four books. Hence not unfittingly this number is decreed by the evangelist by the generations, since Christ had already come as the fullness of the law, who joined the New Testament to the Old. Fittingly too, David in Psalm 14 shows the mystery of this perfect number. Throughout the entire text of this psalm the teaching of prophecy forms the blessed and perfect man [see Ps 15]. And lest he should seem to have passed

over anything without a spiritual interpretation, the very tripartite division [of Jesus's generations] shows us the mystery of the perfect Trinity.

6. But since our opinion about the reckoning of the gospel number has been explicated, no insignificant question arises at the very end, since indeed the sequence of another evangelist, namely Luke's, who runs back through the same Joseph up to David, appears to dissent from this arrangement of generations that saint Matthew traverses from David to Joseph [see Luke 3:23–31]. Matthew traces the family of Joseph, to whom the Virgin Mary was betrothed, by royal succession, that is, from David through Solomon his son, and then through the other kings. Luke, on the other hand, reverses this when he lists the generations. He shows that the line of the generation of the same Joseph runs down from David, to be sure, but through Nathan [see Luke 3:31], that is, through another line of David's family. For both Nathan and Solomon are sons of David [see 2 Sam 5:14; 1 Chr 14:4]. Therefore there are two lines of David's generation: one descending through King Solomon, another running through Nathan. And since it is clear that Joseph descends from the generation of one line, one must ask why a different series of generation is reported by the two evangelists. For Matthew says that Joseph was born of Jacob, according to the line that he traces [see Matt 1:16]. Luke, on the other hand, records that the same Joseph was the son of Heli according to his own line [see Luke 3:23]. And since there is no doubt that the evangelists are <not> contradicting each other or saying things that clash in any respect, whose sense assuredly agrees irrespective of these accounts, the rationale and cause of this problem needs to be sought.[19] Of this we may briefly introduce what differences they had in mind. For very many assert that this Joseph, according to the report of saint Matthew, was born of Jacob, but he is listed by Luke as a son of Heli according to the reckoning of the law, since the same Luke, as we mentioned earlier,[20] follows carefully the reckoning of the law, in which it had been written that if anyone should marry a wife and die without children, his brother should marry the wife to raise up seed for the dead man, so that what was born from him would be called by the name of the dead man [see Deut 25:5–6; Matt 22:24; Mark 12:19; Luke 20:28]. And since Heli is said to have died without children, it is said that Jacob took Heli's wife, since he was his near relative, and from her he begot Joseph. For this reason the same Joseph is reputed to be the son of two fathers: Jacob according to the flesh, as Matthew reports,

and Heli according to the law as Luke writes. Others thought that this problem ought to be interpreted no further than this: properly speaking, Joseph was born from the line of generation that Matthew lists; but from that line that Luke writes, the holy Virgin Mary descends, who was the Lord's mother according to the flesh. She was reputed to be Joseph's spouse according to the gospel faith, since the woman is a portion of the man according to the account of Genesis [see Gen 2:23], and according to the apostle, the man is called the head of the woman [see Eph 5:23]. Therefore Luke asserts that Mary's generation was transferred to Joseph, since indeed the family line customarily is reputed in the men, not in the women. Others think, on the other hand, that this diversity of lines ought to be understood in the following way.[21] They say that the royal race descends from that line of generations that Matthew lists, which we know is most excellent; but from that one that Luke runs through is shown a mixture of the priestly race, since both the authority of the law and the corroboration of the gospel make clear that the royal and priestly races are mixed together. For in the law it is written that Naason took the daughter of Aaron the priest [see Exod 6:23 (?)], but in the Gospel it is said to Mary by the angel concerning Elizabeth the wife of Zechariah the priest, "For behold your kinswoman Elizabeth" [Luke 1:36]. But since she was from the seed of Aaron the priest, Elizabeth would not have been called by the angel a kinswoman of Mary unless she were from the association of a mixed family. Thus it is clearly understood that Mary's stock descends from both tribes and it was plainly worthy and fitting for the heavenly mystery, that this same Mary, who merited to be mother of the Lord according to the flesh, was born both from the royal race and from the priestly stock. From her the Son of God, who is king and eternal priest, assumed the body of his human flesh. Let it suffice to have said this much about the preface of the Gospel and about the problem of the generations. Let us now attend to what follows.

Tractate 2 on Matthew 1:18–23

1. After listing the generations, blessed Matthew indeed added the following regarding the hope of our salvation, saying, "Now the birth of Christ was thus. When Jesus's mother Mary was betrothed to Joseph, before they came together, she was found to be pregnant

by the Holy Spirit" [Matt 1:18]. This then is the heavenly mystery, this is the mystery secret and hidden from the ages [see Eph 3:9; Col 1:26], that a virgin has conceived by the Holy Spirit [see Isa 7:14]. Luke reveals in greater detail the manner of the Lord's incarnation, for he recounts how an angel came to Mary and greeted her, saying, "Hail, full of grace" [Luke 1:28], and the rest that follows. And when she asked him how what he was announcing to her could take place, since she had not known a man, he said to her, "The Holy Spirit will come upon you, and the power of the Most High will overshadow you. And thus even the holy thing that will be born from you will be called the Son of God" [Luke 1:35]. It was fitting that saint Mary, who was about to conceive the Lord of glory in her womb, be illumined after this by the Holy Spirit and the power of the Most High, so that with a sanctified womb she received into herself the Creator of the world. Indeed, both Matthew and Luke began with the corporeal birth of the Lord. John, however, commenced with his divine birth, when he said, "In the beginning was the Word and the Word was with God, and the Word was God. This was with God in the beginning. All things were made through him, and without him nothing was made" [John 1:1–3]. Thus the evangelists help us to recognize the divine and corporeal birth of the Lord, which they describe as a twofold mystery and a kind of double path. To be sure, both births of the Lord are indescribable, but that from the Father vastly exceeds every mode of narration and wonder. The bodily birth of Christ is in time; his divine birth is before time. The former is in this world, the latter before the ages. The former from a virgin mother, the latter from God the Father. Angels and men stood as witnesses at the corporeal birth of the Lord; at his divine birth there was no witness except the Father and the Son, because nothing existed before the Father and the Son. But because God the Word could not be seen in the glory of his divinity, he assumed visible flesh to show his invisible divinity. He took from us what is ours, in order to lavish upon us what is his.

2. When therefore saint Mary had conceived by the Holy Spirit in accordance with the announcement of the angel and showed herself to be well along in her pregnancy, saint Joseph, to whom the same Virgin Mary had been betrothed, not knowing about the secret of such a great mystery, wanted to dismiss her secretly. For the evangelist added this: "Joseph, since he was a just man, and was unwilling to expose her, wanted to dismiss her quietly" [Matt 1:19]. He thought that she who even while pregnant remained a virgin was an adulteress;

he reckoned to be defiled she who was the mother of virginity; and he believed that she who had conceived the author of life was worthy of death. Yet consider the resolve of the just man. Although he thought saint Mary was an adulteress, yet he was not disposed to offer her up for condemnation, lest he should stain his own holy conscience with the blood of someone else. Some of our own people, when they are soaked in the uncleanness of their wicked acts, go after their own wives or innocent persons, or they consider them worthy of condemnation for a trivial suspicion, when perhaps they themselves are the one who should be subject to condemnation before God and should be held guilty by the divine judgment. And therefore the apostle says well, "But do you think, O man, that you who judge the other and do those things, that you shall escape the judgment of God?" [Rom 2:3]. We have said these things in passing on account of certain insolent people who are swift to accuse, ready to condemn. But it is practically pointless to say anything about adultery when Mary's virginity is being proclaimed.

3. While saint Joseph then was still unaware of so great a mystery and wanted to put Mary away secretly, he was warned in a vision by an angel, who said to him, "Joseph, son of David, do not be afraid to take Mary as your wife, for that which is born from her is of the Holy Spirit" [Matt 1:20]. Saint Joseph is made aware of the heavenly mystery, lest he think otherwise about Mary's virginity. For it would not have been right for a just man to be in error over such great virginity. He is also made aware of it for this purpose, to exclude the evil of suspicion and receive the good of the mystery. The following words were said to him: "Do not be afraid to take Mary as your wife, for that which will be born from her is of the Holy Spirit," so that he would recognize the integrity of his spouse and the virgin birth. Obviously, at first it was not appropriate for so great a mystery to be revealed to anyone other than Joseph, who was reckoned to be Mary's husband, and no reproach of sin was attached to his very name. For Joseph translates from Hebrew into Latin as "beyond reproach." Notice here too the order of a mystery. Long ago the devil spoke first to Eve the virgin [see Gen 3:1], then to the man, that he might pour into them the word of death. Here, a holy angel speaks first to Mary, then to Joseph, in order to reveal to them the Word of life. In the former case, a woman was chosen unto sin; in the latter case, she is chosen first unto salvation. In the former case, the man fell through the woman [see Gen 3:6]; in the latter case, he rose again through the virgin. The angel therefore

said to Joseph, "Joseph, son of David, do not be afraid to take Mary as your wife, for that which will be born from her is of the Holy Spirit."

4. And he added, "She shall bring forth a son, and you shall call his name Jesus. He shall save his people from their sins" [Matt 1:21].[22] But this name of the Lord by which Jesus is called from the virgin's womb is not new to him but old. For *Jesus* translates from Hebrew into Latin as "Savior." This name is uniquely fitting to God because he says through the prophet, "There is no just one and Savior besides me" [see Isa 43:11; Hos 13:4]. Lastly, when the Lord himself spoke through Isaiah about the bodily origin of this nativity, he said the following: "He called me by my name from the womb of my mother" [Isa 49:1]; by his own name, surely, not that of another, since he was called Jesus according to the flesh, that is, Savior, who was Savior according to his divinity.[23] For Jesus, as we said, is expressed as "Savior." This is what he says by the prophet: "He called me by my name from the womb of my mother." And that he might more fully show us the mystery of his incarnation, he went on to say, "He made my mouth like a sharp sword and as a choice arrow in his quiver he hid me" [Isa 49:2]. By the arrow he signified his divinity; by the quiver the body he assumed from the virgin in which his divinity was covered up with a veil of flesh. Even in the Book of Exodus the Lord shows that this name of his by which he is called Jesus is an old one to him, when he says the following to Moses about Jesus (*Iesu*) the son of Nun, who had received this same name as a type: "I am sending my angel before your face that you may obey him and not despise him. For he does not draw himself back, for my name is on him" [Exod 23:20–21]. For Hoshea (*Uses*), son of Nun, who was the leader after Moses, began to be called Jesus, as a type of the Lord who was going to come in the flesh [see Num 13:8, 16; Deut 32:44].[24] Therefore when the angel says of the Lord in the present passage, "She will bear a son and you will call his name Jesus," he shows the mystery of his incarnation, since Jesus is one, Word and flesh, Son of God and Son of Man, not two separate things (*non alius et alius*) but one and the same, he who was born of the Father and who was begotten from a virgin. Therefore, "he has saved," and daily "saves his people" whom he draws away from idols, the people he redeemed by his holy blood and to whom he promises eternal salvation.

5. And the evangelist added, "But all this happened in order that what was spoken by the Lord through the prophet Isaiah would be fulfilled: Behold the virgin" [and below, all the way to][25] "God with us" [Matt 1:22–23; cf. Isa 7:14]. And so, according to the preaching of

the prophet, a virgin conceives, a virgin gives birth, for the sake of the world's salvation. See here the mystery as well; see that salvation is restored to the world in the same manner by which long ago the ruin of sin had snuck in. Adam is fashioned out of virgin earth [see Gen 2:7]; the Son of God is born of the Virgin Mary.[26] There a virgin conceived death; here a virgin gave birth to life. There a man fell through a virgin; here a man stood through a virgin. There was the ruin of death, here the triumph of victory. But David also shows that the Son of God took flesh from a virgin, when he says, "A man shall say, mother Zion; and he was made a man in her; and the Most High himself has founded her" [Ps 87:5]. Here "mother Zion" signifies saint Mary, who is the mother of the Lord's flesh, in which the Son of God "was made a man," since "the Word became flesh" [John 1:14], as the evangelist attests. But he himself is the Founder of this very flesh, since he himself has stood forth as both the author and creator of his own physical birth. And that is why he added, "And the Most High himself has founded her." Solomon shows this too when he says, "Wisdom built a house for itself" [Prov 9:1], since Christ, who is the "wisdom of God" [see 1 Cor 1:24, 30], fashioned a body for himself in the womb of the virgin. And with good reason, when the Lord spoke through David in the psalm under the mystery of his incarnation, he says the following: "But I am a worm and not a man" [Ps 22:6]. Surely he does not mean that he is a worm, but he is showing the mystery of his physical birth. For just as a worm arises from the ground spontaneously and without seed, so the Lord came forth from the virgin's womb without a man's seed. And obviously it cannot be doubted that that psalm properly pertains to the Lord's person, since in the subsequent section of that psalm it is clearly said from the persona of the Lord, "They divided my garments between themselves and cast lots upon my garment" [Ps 22:18]. Elsewhere too the Holy Spirit makes clear through Isaiah that a virgin (*virginem*) will give birth, when he says, "And there shall come forth a rod (*virga*) out of the root of Jesse, and a blossom shall come up from his root" [Isa 11:1]. The rod (*virga*) from the root of Jesse signified the Virgin (*virgo*) Mary, who traces her origin from the stock of Jesse through David. For as the evangelist and apostle make clear, the Virgin Mary was from the tribe of David [see Luke 1:27; Rom 1:3; 15:12], from which the blossom of human flesh arose in Christ. This is the rod that without moisture from the earth sprouted into the fruit of a nut, when it was placed in the tabernacle of testimony, as a sign of eternal remembrance by a new and wonderful mystery [see Num 17].

By that sign the priesthood of Aaron was confirmed. And thus there in the rod of Aaron, Mary was shown, who truly without moisture from the earth sprouted the sweetest fruit, since without a man's seed she produced a son, who became the true fruit of human salvation, cleaving like a nut to the wood of the passion, and setting out his fruit via the fourfold proclamation of the gospel, through which the true and eternal priesthood of the church is confirmed. But the reason Mary is recognized in the unique rod is because she knew no union with a man. The reason the rod was inscribed with a priestly name is because saint Mary, as we showed earlier, descended not merely from the royal race but also from a priestly origin.[27]

6. In this a truly new and wonderful sign has been shown, that has never existed in the world: a birth from a virgin, the newness of the Savior, the infancy of the Creator. He who had previously stood forth as born of the Father is born from a virgin; he who had created angels and all things is created according to the flesh in the womb; he who is God appears as a man; he who is the Lord of glory is looked upon as a baby; he who is lofty in his majesty appears tiny in his body; he who bears the whole world and the age is borne by his mother's hands. Finally, then, the evangelist declares that he who was born of a virgin in accordance with the prophet's testimony is God, when he says, "And they shall call his name [this] Emmanuel, which means God with us" [Isa 7:14]. And so, let all impiety be silent, which either denies or does not know that the Son of God is God, since it is made known by both prophetic and gospel testimony that he who was born of a virgin is God. Indeed we could prove this by countless testimonies, but that discussion should be reserved for its own place. Let it suffice that our Lord and Savior has been plainly shown to be God, even in his physical birth, since the prophet says, "And they shall call his name Emmanuel, which means God with us." To him is the glory and praise in the ages of ages. Amen.

Tractate 3 on Matthew 1:24–25

1. Next the evangelist reported, "And Joseph rising up from his sleep" [and the rest up to] "and he called his name Jesus" [Matt 1:24–25]. Joseph therefore learns through the angel about the sign of the heavenly mystery and joyfully complies with the angel's warnings.

Rejoicing, he follows the divine commands and takes saint Mary and glories with exultant prayers that he is deemed worthy to hear that the virgin mother of such great majesty is called by the angel to be his wife. But concerning what the evangelist said, "And he did not know her till she brought forth a son" [Matt 1:25], several foolish people are accustomed to stir up a question, thinking that after the Lord's birth saint Mary *was* united with Joseph. But this is not admissible as an interpretation on the grounds either of the cause of the faith or the rational account of truth. For far be it that after the sign of so great a mystery, and after the birth of the Lord's condescension, one should believe that the Virgin Mary knew a man. For in the law of the Old Testament there is that Mary, the prophetess, the sister of Moses and Aaron [see Num 26:59; 1 Chr 5:29; Mic 6:4]. She remained a virgin who did not know a man, after she beheld the sight of heavenly signs in the plagues of Egypt, the parting of the Red Sea, and when the Lord's glory went before them and was seen in a pillar of fire and cloud [see Exod 15:19–21].[28] And thus it is not fitting to believe that the Mary of the gospel, a virgin who contained God, who beheld the God of glory not in a cloud but was worthy of carrying him in her virginal womb, should be believed to have known a man. Noah, who was made worthy to converse with God, declared that he would abstain henceforth from the conjugal need. After hearing God's voice speaking from the bush, Moses abstained from conjugal relations. And is it right to believe that Joseph, a just man, should be believed to have known saint Mary after the birth of the Lord's nativity?

2. But in what he says, "And he did not know her till she brought forth a son" [Matt 1:25], commonly Sacred Scripture is accustomed to designate an end point, as it were, for things that do not have an end point, and to attribute a definite time period for things that are not limited by time. Let us indeed record a few of the many examples of this. God says the following through Isaiah to the people: "I am who I am; and *until* you grow old, I am" [Isa 46:4].[29] When he says, "*Until* you grow old, I am," he appears to attribute a definite time limit on himself, but God should not on that account be understood to be limited by time, who has to be confessed as eternal. In another passage, too, in the same prophet, the Lord reproaches the Jews for their sins, and among other things he says the following: "I live, then, says the Lord, for this sin will not be forgiven you *until* you die" [Isa 22:14]. Yet the unjust who persevere in their sins are held liable to punishment all the more so after their death. <Likewise> it is said in the psalm under

the persona of the just ones, "As the eyes of a maidservant to the hands of her mistress" [and the rest up to] "he have mercy upon us" [Ps 123:2]. Here too it seems that there is a definite time limit, when it is said, "*Until* he have mercy on us," though we know that the eyes of the just ones are fixed on God all the more after they attain mercy. In the gospel too the Lord himself says the following to his disciples: "And I am with you all the days *until* the end of the age" [Matt 28:20]. In this statement too he appears to attribute a time limit, as though the Lord promises his disciples that he will be with them till the end of the age, when there is no doubt that after the end of the age the Lord will be with his disciples all the more. For once immortality has been granted, according to the apostle's statement, the Lord must be seen no longer "through a mirror and enigmatically, but face to face" [1 Cor 13:12]. If you look, you will find many other countless examples of this. Thus when it is said in the present passage, "He did not know her *till* she brought forth a son," you ought to notice that all time has been signified by means of an indication of a small amount of time.

Tractate 4 on Matthew 2:1–9

1. Next the evangelist reports, "When Jesus was born in Bethlehem of Judah" [and the rest up to] "and we have come to worship him" [Matt 2:1–2]. Earlier Isaiah had predicted that this would happen when he said, "They shall come from Saba bringing to the king gold, frankincense, and precious stone, and they shall announce the salvation of the Lord" [Isa 60:6]. Surely this refers to him whom the Magi announced when they saw the sign of the star, as the one born king of the Jews, Christ the Lord. And so, even beyond measure, all the news coincides with the human wonder at the birth of the Lord: The angel speaks to Zechariah in the temple; he promises that Elizabeth will have a son [see Luke 1:8–13]; when he does not believe the angel, the priest becomes mute [see Luke 1:18–20]; the barren one conceives [see Luke 1:24]; the virgin gives birth [see Luke 2:7]; John is inspired to exult in the womb of his mother [see Luke 1:44]; Christ the Lord is born and announced by an angel, and it is proclaimed to shepherds that he is the world's salvation [see Luke 2:10–11]; the angels rejoice, the shepherds exult [see Luke 2:20]. Great gladness

arises in heaven and on earth over this wonderful birth. The new sign of the star from heaven is shown all the more, through which the Lord of heaven and earth is recognized as the one born king of the Jews, namely he of whom it had been written, "A star shall rise out of Jacob, and a man shall spring out of Israel" [Num 24:17].[30] Thus the union of the divine and human nature in the Son of God was recognized by the indication of the star and the man. And this is why in Revelation the Lord himself testifies about himself as follows: "I am the root of Jesse and the race of David and the bright morning star" [Rev 22:16]. For by the appearance of his birth, once the night of ignorance was dispelled, he sprang forth as a resplendent star for the salvation of the world. The splendor of his light penetrated even the hearts of the Magi, and infused them with spiritual light, so that they recognized the king of the Jews, the Creator of the sky, by the sign of a newly rising star. For Magi are authors of a false religion and would not have been able to recognize Christ our Lord unless they had been illumined by the grace of divine condescension.

Again, therefore, God's mercy has superabounded through the coming of Christ, so that the knowledge of his truth spread itself to the entire human race. The reason it previously shone forth all the more was so that pious devotion to God might be known manifestly and no one would lose the hope that salvation could be given to the one who believes, since he has already seen that it was given all the more. But the reason the Magi were chosen first for salvation from the nations was so that through them the gate of salvation would be opened to all Gentiles.[31]

But perhaps someone is wondering how the Magi could have known about the Savior's birth based on the sign of the star. First, to be sure, we say that this was a gift of the divine graciousness. Second, we read in the books of Moses that there was a certain prophet from the Gentiles named Balaam who prophesied the coming of Christ and his incarnation from a virgin in clear words. For among other things, he says in the words of his prophecy (as we have already mentioned earlier), "A star shall arise out of Jacob and a man shall spring forth from Israel" [Num 24:17]. These Magi, then, who saw a new star in the east, are reported to have traced their lineage from the race of that Balaam, prophet of the Gentiles, who had said, "A star shall arise out of Jacob and a man shall spring forth from Israel."[32] And the reason they believed when they saw the sign of the new star was because they recognized that a prophecy of their own ancestor had been fulfilled.

Thus they showed themselves to be not only successors of his race but also heirs of his faith. Balaam the prophet saw their star in his spirit, they saw it with their eyes and believed. He predicted that Christ would come by a prophecy; they recognized that he had come by the vision of faith.

2. Finally, they proceeded at once to Herod and said, "Where is the one who has been born?" [and the rest up to] "to worship him" [Matt 2:2]. They sought among them the king of the Jews, the one born as Christ the Lord. They knew that he came from their race, since Balaam had prophesied this. But this faith of the Magi spells the condemnation of the Jews. The former believed a single prophet of their own; the latter refused to believe so many prophets. The former understood that the functions of the magical arts would cease at the coming of Christ; the latter refused to understand the mysteries of the divine law.[33] The former confess a foreigner; the latter fail to recognize one of their own. For "he came to his own [things], and his own [people] did not receive him" [John 1:11]. And this star was indeed seen by everyone, but it was not understood by everyone. Just as our Lord and Savior was indeed born for all, one was born for the sake of all, but he has not been received by all, he has not been understood by all. He was understood by the Gentiles; he was not understood by the Jews. He was recognized by the church; he was not recognized by the synagogue.

3. Since therefore the Magi had come to Jerusalem after the glorious effort of a long journey, seeking the king of the Jews, at once, it says, "Herod the king and all Jerusalem" [Matt 2:3] were troubled by the devotion of the Magi's faith. The chief priests and the scribes of the people are assembled [see Matt 2:2–4]. They ask them where the Christ was supposed to be born. They replied, "In Bethlehem of Judah" [Matt 2:5], in accordance with the prophetic proclamation. For thus it had been written: "And you, Bethlehem of Judah, are not least among the princes of Judah: for from you shall come forth a prince who will rule my people Israel" [Matt 2:6]. But Herod and the residents of Jerusalem were not ignorant of Christ our Lord, but they knew of him and showed contempt. For they seek from the testimony of the prophet <and> learn well that the Christ would be born in Bethlehem. Now this location, Bethlehem, where the Lord was born, had received its name as a prophecy.[34] For *Bethlehem* translates from Hebrew into Latin as "house of bread," since there it was befitting that the Son of God be born, who is the bread of life, according to

what he himself says in the gospel: "I am the living bread who came down from heaven" [John 6:41]. This <is> the location of which it is said elsewhere by a prophet, "God will come from Libanus, and that holy one from the dark shady mountain" [Hab 3:3]. By these words he indicates the location and loveliness of this place. In fact, this prophetic statement agrees with the earlier statement, where it was declared that the Lord would be born in Bethlehem. Here it is said, "God will come from Libanus"; there an addition is made after it was said, "A prince shall come forth from you, who will rule my people Israel; and his going forth was from the beginning of days" [Mic 5:2]. It should not be thought, based on these words, as Photinus claims,[35] that the Lord had a beginning, from the time when he was born of the virgin; for since the one who was born in Bethlehem is shown both to have existed from the beginning of days and to be Lord, let it be taught most manifestly.

4. Next the evangelist relates, "Then Herod summoned the Magi," [and the rest up to] "and it stood above the child" [Matt 2:7–9]. Thus Herod, the unjust king, plotted against the eternal king, since he feared for his own kingdom, which he held unjustly. For this Herod was not from the tribe of Judah nor from the race of David, but he seized control of the kingdom of the Jews surreptitiously with the patronage of the Romans favoring him, in the manner of a tyrant. And that is why he plotted against the Lord's birth, the one born king of the Jews, whom he had recognized from the Magi. And so he inquires from them the time of the star's appearance; he sent them to Bethlehem, as if he himself wanted to worship him. He feigned concern, in order to conceal his deceit. For he was thinking about killing the Lord, not worshiping him. The Magi meanwhile reach the place by the star's guidance, and they recognize the Creator of the sky, since a sign from the sky pointed him out. They did not seek human guidance, since they had received guidance from a star of the sky. But neither were they able to go astray, since they were looking for the true way, Christ the Lord, him assuredly who said, "I am the way and the truth and the life" [John 14:6]. With a new sense of wonder over the events, the star makes its journey in the sky, and throughout their entire journey the companion star does not abandon the Magi. And by the same course they come together all the way to Bethlehem, and there the star halts above our Lord and Savior and points to the only begotten Son of God, to whom is the glory in the ages of ages. Amen.

Tractate 5 on Matthew 2:10–12

1. Therefore the evangelist reports, "And behold, the star that they had seen in the east" [and the rest up to] "gold, frankincense, and myrrh" [Matt 2:10–11]. But now, after the service of the star, after the course of the Magi, let us see how glorious was the dignity that attended the king who had been born. For immediately the Magi fall down and worship the one born as Lord, and there in his very cradle they venerate the infancy of the crying child by offering him gifts. They perceive one thing with the eyes of the body, something else with the vision of their mind. The humbleness of the body he assumed is seen, but the glory of his divinity is not concealed. It is a child who is seen, but it is God who is adored. How inexpressible is this mystery of the divine condescension! For our sake that incomprehensible and eternal nature does not disdain taking on the infirmities of our flesh. The Son of God, who is God of the universe, is born as a human being in a body. He permits himself to be placed in a manger, within which are the heavens. He is confined to a cradle, one whom the world does not have room for. He is heard in the voice of a crying infant, at whose voice the whole world trembled in the time of his passion [see Matt 27:51]. And so, the Magi recognize this God of glory and Lord of majesty when they see him as a child. Isaiah likewise shows that this child was both God and the eternal king, when he said, "For a child has been born to you; a son has been given to you, whose empire has been made on his shoulders" [Isa 9:6].

The Magi offer him gifts, therefore, namely gold, frankincense, and myrrh, in accordance with what the Holy Spirit had earlier testified about these things through the prophet, when he said, "From Saba they shall come bearing gold, frankincense, and precious stone, and they shall announce the salvation of the Lord" [Isa 60:6]. Clearly we recognize that the Magi fulfilled this prophecy. They both "announced the salvation of the Lord," that the Christ was born as the Son of God, and in the gifts offered they confess that Christ is God, king, and man.[36] For in the gold the authority of his kingdom is shown, in the frankincense the honor due to God in the myrrh the burial of the body. And therefore they offered gold as to a king, frankincense as to God, and myrrh as to a man. David too testifies about this as follows: "The kings of Tharsis and the isles shall offer presents, the kings of the Arabians and Saba shall bring gifts" [Ps 72:10]. And in order to show very powerfully to whom these gifts were to be given, he adds in this same psalm, "And there shall be given him of the gold of Arabia" [Ps 72:15]. In another psalm as well, the same David does not keep silent about the myrrh, when he spoke of the passion of the Lord and said, "Myrrh and stacte and cassia [are exhaled] from your garments" [Ps 45:8]. Likewise Solomon speaks of this myrrh from Christ's persona as follows: "I have gathered my myrrh with my spices" [Song 5:1], and again: "I gave off a sweet smell like myrrh" [Sir 24:15]. Surely in this he clearly testifies to the burial of his body, which burned with the sweetest divine smell throughout the whole world. Finally, the same David is shown to indicate these Magi when he says, "Ambassadors shall come out of Egypt; Ethiopia shall hasten [to stretch out] her hands" [Ps 68:31]. For since Sacred Scripture often calls this world "Egypt," we rightly understand these Magi as the "ambassadors of Egypt," having been chosen, as it were, as ambassadors of the whole world. In the gifts that they offered, they consecrated the belief of all the Gentiles and the commencement of faith.

2. And so, after the offering of the gifts, the Magi are warned, "Do not go back to king Herod. And so they returned to their country by another way" [Matt 2:12].[37] This provides an example to us of virtue and faith, that once we have come to know and adore Christ as king, we should abandon the way of our former journey, which was the way of old error, and we should now go back by another way, on which Christ is our guide, heading for our country, namely, paradise, from which Adam was driven out. This country is mentioned in the psalm: "I will please the Lord in the country of the living" [Ps 116:9]. Thus the Magi, being warned, go back by another way. They frustrated the tyrant's cruel designs, and in this manner, through the Magi the boy who was born a king is identified, and the wiles of the tyrant Herod are defeated. But long ago Isaiah predicted that our Lord and Savior, as an infant, would be triumphant, even at his birth, at the very beginning of his bodily life. He said, "For before the child knows to call his father and mother, he will take the power (*virtutem*) of Damascus and the spoils of Samaria in opposition to the king of the Assyrians" [Isa 8:4]. By "power of Damascus," which the Son of God received when he was born as a child, is meant the gold that was offered by the Magi. But "the spoils of Samaria" mean those same Magi whom he drew away from the error of Samaria's superstition, that is, from the worship of idols. Those who previously were the spoils of the devil [see Luke 11:22] because of their false religion later became the spoils of

God through their recognition of Christ. The "king of the Assyrians" signifies Herod, and in fact the devil, against whom the Magi themselves rose up as adversaries, namely, by worshiping the Son of God, our Lord and Savior, who is blessed in the ages of ages. Amen [see Rom 1:25; 2 Cor 11:31].

Tractate 6 on Matthew 2:13–18

1. Then the evangelist reports, "Behold, an angel of the Lord appeared to Joseph" [and the rest up to] "out of Egypt I have called my son" [Matt 1:13–15]. Joseph therefore was commanded to accept this child, about whom Isaiah had said, "For a child has been born to you, a son has been given to you, whose empire has been made on his shoulder" [Isa 9:6]. Now he said, "a son has been given to you," because Christ the Lord was born as a child and was reputed to be a son of Joseph and Mary [see Luke 3:33]. As to his going down to Egypt, the same Isaiah had predicted that this would happen long ago when he said, "Behold, the Lord sits upon a light cloud and will come into Egypt" [Isa 19:1]. By this statement a manifest sign of the Lord's incarnation was shown. For since the Lord himself is called "the East from on high" [Luke 1:87; cf. Zech 3:8], "the sun of justice" [Mal 4:2], it is not unfitting that he predicted here that he would come on a "light cloud," that is, in a holy body, a body incapable of being weighed down by any sin, by which he covered the light of his own majesty with the veil of a bodily cloud. Hosea as well points to this same thing when he says, "The king of Israel has been cast off, on that account let Israel be small, and I loved him. And out of Egypt I called my son" [Hos 11:1].

After the grave transgression of Egypt long ago, and after many blows had been divinely inflicted upon it, God the Father Almighty, moved by godliness, sent his Son to Egypt, so that Egypt, which long ago under Moses had paid out the penalties owed to its wickedness, might now by accepting Christ receive the hope for salvation. How great is God's mercy shown by the advent of his Son! Egypt, which of old under Pharaoh stood stubborn and rebellious against God, now has become a receptacle and dwelling place of Christ. The Lord's mercy toward Egypt was like that shown toward those Magi, who merited recognizing Christ the Lord. For, although the Magi had for a long time dared resist the divine powers at the time of Moses [see Exod 7:11], now there are Magi who, having seen but a single sign in heaven, believed in the Son of God. And thus the former magicians were handed over to punishment for their lack of faith; but the latter were brought to glory through faith, since they believed that God had been born in a body, the one whom the former were unwilling to recognize in his divine powers. But in these things the wickedness of the Jews stands out as noteworthy: Egypt receives Christ our Lord, Magi offer him worship, but Herod and the Jews wickedly persecute him.

2. Let the sermon follow the order of the events. When Herod saw, therefore, that he had been outwitted by the Magi, after this he openly poured out the wrath that he had been concealing. For the evangelist relates the following: "Then Herod, when he saw that he had been deceived by the Magi, was exceedingly enraged" [and the rest up to] "and she refused to be consoled because they are not" [Matt 2:16–18]. For Herod, as we have said, wanting to destroy the Savior of the world, sent to Bethlehem and commanded that all children two years of age and under be killed, figuring the age according to the time that he had learned from the Magi. He thought that his edict would reach even to the Lord himself, the author of life. The Holy Spirit had already foreseen and accused his wickedness beforehand through Solomon, speaking under the persona of the church, who said, "Who will give to you my brother, the one who nurses at the breast of his mother?" [Song 8:1]. Now by saying, "Who will give to you?" he showed that Herod did not have power to oppose him who is the Lord and prince of all powers. Thus not without cause did the Lord likewise testify about himself through the same Solomon and say the following: "Evil men will seek and not find me. For they hated wisdom and did not adopt the Word of the Lord, and they did not want it" [Prov 1:28–30]. Indeed the Spirit also said through David, "For you are he that drew me out of the womb; my hope from my mother's breasts. I was cast on you from the womb; you are my protector from my mother's belly" [Ps 71:6; 22:9–10]. Saint Moses also testified that Christ the Lord, an infant, could not have been killed while still nursing, in these words, saying, "You shall not cook a lamb in the milk of its own mother" [Exod 23:19]. He is indicating the same thing, that Christ our Lord, who is the true Lamb of God, was to suffer only at the appointed time.

Well, then, all the babies were slain in Bethlehem. When these innocents died on Christ's behalf, they became the first martyrs of

Christ.[38] And David is shown to give an indication of them, when he says, "From the mouths of infants and nursing babies you have perfected praise because of your enemies, that you might bring ruin to the enemy and the avenger" [Ps 8:2]. For in this persecution even tiny infants and nursing babies are killed on Christ's behalf and attain to the martyrdom of perfected praise. The wicked King Herod is destroyed, he who had usurped the realm to avenge himself against the king of heaven. Thus it is that those infants not unfittingly have stood forth as blessed in all ways, who deserved to be the first to die for Christ, our Lord and Savior, to whom is the praise and glory in the ages of ages. Amen.

Tractate 7 on Matthew 2:19–23

1. Then it follows, "But when Herod died" [and the rest up to the passage where it says] "and immediately he took the child and its mother and went to the land of Israel" [Matt 2:19–21]. In that which the angel said to Joseph, "Those who were seeking the life (*animam*) of the child are dead" [Matt 2:20], he declares plainly that the Son of God, perfect God, took on perfect manhood, that is, not only a body but also a soul (*animam*). The reason we say this is because some have dared to claim by a foolish proclamation that the only begotten Son of God received only a [human] body.[39] But they are refuted both by the angel's testimony and also by the declaration of the Lord himself, who mentioned his soul in several passages, saying, "I have authority to lay down my life (*animam*) and I have authority to take it up again" [John 10:18]. And again, "My soul (*anima*) is grieved to the point of death" [Matt 26:38; Mark 14:34]. And again, "The Son of Man came to save what was lost" [see Matt 18:11; see RSV fn.; cf. Luke 19:10] and "to give his life (*animam*) as a redemption for many" [Mark 10:45]. Thus our Lord and Savior has clearly shown in himself the perfect nature of a human being. For since a long time ago because of sin the entire person incurred the sentence of death, both in body and in soul, necessarily the Lord received both in order to save both. Therefore the reliability and truth of the events according to the letter is uncovered. [That after Herod's death Joseph was warned by the angel to go back to the land of Israel with the child and its mother], but even in these events there is a spiritual understanding. Herod was a symbol (*typum*)

of Jewish unbelief, just as Egypt was a symbol of this world. After he visits it, he returns again to visit the children of Israel, "when Herod was dead" [Matt 2:19], that is, with a certain portion of the unbelief extinguished.

2. Then it follows that when Joseph had gone forth from Egypt [and the rest up to] "that he will be called a Nazarene" [Matt 2:21–23]. Now our Lord and Savior is called "a Nazarene" both because of the name of the place, that is, of the city of Nazareth, and because of the mystery of the law. For according to the law, those were called Nazarenes who made an extraordinary vow of chastity to God, preserving the hair of their heads [see Num 6]. A fixed law had commanded them to offer sacrifices [see Num 6:10–11]. Therefore, because the author and prince of all sanctity and purity is Christ the Lord, who said through the prophet, "Be holy, since I am holy, says the Lord" [Lev 11:44; 19:2; 20:7], it is not unfitting that he is called "a Nazarene," since it was he who, following truly what was prefigured in the law, offered the sacrifice of his own body for our salvation as a vow promised to God the Father. David spoke about this vow when he said of the Lord, "Just as he swore to the Lord, he vowed a vow to the God of Jacob" [Ps 132:2]. Moreover, in order that the same Lord would clearly show that he was to be called a Nazarene according to the flesh, he testified through Solomon and said the following: "For my head is filled with dew, and my locks with drops" [Song 5:2]. For the physical sign of the Nazarenes's sanctity was that he did not touch with a razor the locks and hair of his head.

Samson was also called a Nazarene, a man powerful in spirit and mighty in strength (*virtute*), but as a type [see Judg 13—16]. If we consider his exploits, in him too we shall recognize precedents of the Lord prefigured. He had seven locks [see Judg 16:13]. To this corresponds the sevenfold Spirit and the seven churches [see Rev 1:20; 5:6]. For him all his strength (*virtus*) was in his head. To this corresponds that all power (*virtus*) is in God, since "God is the head of Christ" [1 Cor 11:3; cf. 1:24], as the apostle makes clear. In the former his power was hidden; in the latter divinity was concealed. Samson took a journey and killed a lion with his hands [see Judg 14:6]. Our Lord and Savior by the mystery of the body he assumed killed a lion, the devil [see 1 Pet 5:8], with his hands outstretched on the cross [see Rom 10:21]. Samson drew forth a honeycomb from the mouth of the lion [see Judg 14:8–9]; the Lord rescued his own people from the jaws of the devil, who became sweet to him through their faith. Samson

<saved> the people by waging war against the enemy [see Judg 15:15]; the Lord delivered his own people from everlasting death by annihilating the demons. Samson is shut up in a city with locked gates [see Judg 16:2]; the Lord is shut up in a sealed tomb [see Matt 27:66]. Do not be shocked that the Lord's body is called "Lord." Listen to the angel speaking to the women concerning the Lord's body: "Come, see the place where the Lord has been laid" [Matt 28:6]. Samson escapes safely with the broken bolts and removed gates [see Judg 16:3]. The Lord comes forth free from death [see Matt 28:9] with the body he received, having destroyed the bars of hell's residence and having opened the grave. Lastly, Samson in his death enclosed his enemies in the collapse of the buildings he struck down [see Judg 16:29–30]. The Lord, at the time when he deigned to die, annihilated the devil with all his angels, striking not a single house but the whole world, that is to say, the only begotten Son of God, to whom is the praise and the glory in the ages of ages. Amen [see 1 Pet 4:11].

Tractate 8 on Matthew 3:1–3

Let us return therefore to the subject matter,[40] to prevent the exposition from containing digressions and confusing the sequence of the statements. For it indeed follows, "In those days John the Baptist came" [and the rest up to] "make straight his paths" [Matt 3:1–3]. It was predicted that saint John the Baptist would be the precursor of the Lord to prepare his ways, not only by this testimony of the prophet, but it was likewise spoken by a prophecy of David under the persona of the Father: "I have prepared a lamp for my Christ" [Ps 132:17]. But as for how these ways of the Lord were to be prepared, we ought to observe the understanding of heavenly things based upon a comparison with earthly things. Therefore, let us set before our eyes the coming of some earthly king, how with all care and all solicitude it is announced what route he will take on his journey. Thus all the roads on which the king will spend his journey are fortified with diligent zeal. Ditches are filled in, hills are leveled, and all stumbling blocks are removed lest they impede the journey of the traveler. Saint John, precursor and servant of the Lord, announced the coming of the heavenly king and prepared the journey for the Lord in the hearts of believers on the ways of salvation and of faith, so that when all the vices of sins had been cleansed by the confession of repentance, those things that were pressed down low by sin would be raised up to faith, and things that seemed raised by the swelling up of pride would be leveled to humility, and he would take delight in embarking on such a journey on which there would be no stumbling block of unbelief. But in a psalm containing his own prophecy David too shows these ways of the Lord, which saint John prepared in the Gospel, when he says, "Make known to me your ways, O Lord, and show me your paths" [Ps 25:4]. And he shows subsequently what these ways are when he says, "All the ways of the Lord are mercy and truth" [Ps 25:10]. Hence John prepared these ways of mercy and truth, faith and justice. Jeremiah also testifies about this as follows: "Stand in the ways of the Lord, look at the paths of the eternal God, and see what the way of the Lord is, and walk in it" [Jer 6:16]. Because therefore the heavenly kingdom is found in these ways, not without cause did saint John add, "For the kingdom of heaven has come near" [Matt 3:2]. So, do you want the kingdom of heaven to be near for you as well? Prepare these ways in your heart, in your mind, in your inner being. Pave within you the way of purity, the way of faith, the way of holiness. Build roads of justice. Remove from your heart every scandal of stumbling blocks. For it is written, "Remove the stones from the road" [Jer 50:26]. And then indeed Christ the king enters via the thoughts of your heart and the very movements of your soul, as if walking down paths. To him is the praise and the glory in the ages of ages. Amen [see 1 Pet 4:11].

Tractate 9 on Matthew 3:4

1. The evangelist has reported the kind of clothing and food John the Baptist had. He says, "But John had clothes of camels' wool" [and the rest up to] "and wild honey" [Matt 3:4]. And so, first, according to the letter the heavenly life and glorious humility of John are shown. He who had contempt for the world did not seek the world's costly clothing. And he who trampled upon worldly delights did not have any desire for succulent foods. What need was there of expensive worldly clothing for one who was wearing the garment of justice? Or what dainty earthly foods could one desire who was fed on divine discourses and whose true food was the law of Christ? [see 1 Cor 9:21; Gal 6:2]. He had to be this kind of precursor of the Lord, a prophet

and apostle of Christ, one who gave himself completely to the God of heaven and who had contempt for the things of the world. Hence it is not without reason that he is even called an angel from the Lord [see Matt 11:10; Mark 1:2; Luke 7:27], since while placed in this world, his angelic life trampled upon the world itself. But in this food and outward appearance it is shown not only that he despises the goods of the world, but that he mourns for the iniquity of this world. Thus he lamented the unbelief of the people whom he was exhorting to repentance, when he said, "Brood of vipers, who warned you to flee from the coming wrath? Produce fruit, therefore, worthy of repentance" [Matt 3:7–8]. But we recognize that this feeling for the people existed in the saints even in times past. Saint John showed himself to be their brother by this example. Moses is overwhelmed with grief due to a serious transgression of the people, and he was moved by such great love for the people that he asked to be blotted out from God's book if the people's sin is not blotted out [see Exod 32:31–32]. Jesus son of Nun, successor of Moses, lay prostrate before God for the sin of the people, from morning till evening [see Josh 7:6]. Samuel mourns for King Saul and all the people until the day of his own death [see 1 Sam 15:35]. Elijah afflicts himself with the starvation of a fast and with abstinence from food for the sake of the people's iniquity [see 1 Kgs 19]. Jeremiah does not cease weeping for the sins of the people, and says, "Who shall give water to my head and a fountain of tears to my eyes? Then I would weep for this people day and night" [Jer 9:1]. And in a similar fashion all the prophets mourned for the transgressions of the people.

2. And since we recognize the blessed humility of saint John in the way he dressed and ate, let us now see what can be understood spiritually. There is no doubt that in John's tunic the calling of the church is prefigured, which is composed out of diverse nations as if from the hairs of camels, by the Holy Spirit, through the prophetic and apostolic proclamation. For the nations from which the church has been plucked are being compared symbolically to camels. Now in the leather girdle that surrounds his loins, the honor of chastity and purity is shown, by which saint John was truly girded. For his extreme abstinence scoffed at his own flesh, as dead skin. Following the example of John, we ought to be girded with this girdle of chastity too, since the apostle says, "Let your loins be girded in chastity" [Eph 6:14]. This is why the Lord commands his disciples in the gospel to have their loins girded [see Luke 12:35], for in the law one could not

eat the Lord's Passover as a type unless one's loins were girded [see Exod 12:11], since only a pure soul and chaste flesh deserves to eat the divine mysteries. But in the locusts saint John had as food, he is signifying those who before they come to the knowledge of God are carried off in different directions by a wandering and inconstant mind, and who kick back against the faith [see Acts 26:14]. But when they are captured by the grace of God, they are refreshed by John's preaching and by the faith of the apostles and by their own readiness to believe, as if by some kind of heavenly food. This agrees with what the Lord says in the gospel: "My food is to do the will of him who sent me, the Father" [John 4:34]. But we also recognize in the locusts this calling of the Gentiles that is shown in the writings of Solomon, when among other comparisons he speaks of locusts. For he says the following: "And the locusts, who have no king and march in order at one command" [Prov 30:27]. That is to say, the Gentiles, who, when they did not have God as their king, they did not know the author of life and of human salvation. But when they heard the word of the gospel proclamation, they swarmed together to the grace of God with one mind and in concord in the unity of the faith. But another prophet also records that the locusts signify the Gentiles, when he says, "I looked and behold, a generation of locusts was coming" [Amos 7:1]. But in the wild (*silvestri*) honey we observe that the just and merciful are indicated, who live in the forest (*silva*) of this world, that is, in the error of the age. For wild honey, although it is gathered by no zeal and effort of human beings, nor even by any care of human diligence when a container is set there, nevertheless it is naturally sweet in and of itself. So the majority of the Gentiles, who have been educated by no utterance of heavenly doctrine, before they receive the knowledge of divine law, before they are gathered to the faith within the church, since their lives retain a charm in themselves by their natural goodness and honesty, are compared with the sweetness of wild honey. That saint Cornelius the centurion offers us a clear example of this reality in himself.[41] He was restrained by no bond of divine law, yet he lived in accordance with natural justice and carried out the precepts of the law. For this reason he is praised in the Acts of the Apostles through the Holy Spirit with such a testimony as this: "Cornelius was a just man and feared God and gave much alms to the people" [Acts 10:1–2]. And it was said to him by an angel, "Cornelius, your prayers have been heard and your alms have ascended in remembrance before God" [Acts 10:3–4]. Likewise, that eunuch of Queen Candace offers an example to us that is not dissimilar [see Acts 8:27–40]. Though he came from the Gentiles, because of his natural justice, he merited to have saint Philip the deacon sent by the Lord to baptize him. But the apostle Paul clearly declares these same things when he says, "Since the Gentiles, who do not have the law, are a law to themselves naturally, who show the work of the law written in their hearts" [Rom 2:14–15]. When therefore minds like this come to the knowledge of Christ, doubtless they stand out like honey for the apostolic and prophetic preaching, possessing a honey-sweet life, and thus from being wild honey they become domestic honey to our Lord and Savior, who is the author of their calling and of human salvation. To him is the praise and glory in the ages of ages. Amen [see 1 Pet 4:11].

Tractate 10 on Matthew 3:5–9

1. Next the evangelist says, "Then all Judea went out to him from Jerusalem" [and the rest up to] "for God is able to raise up sons of Abraham from these stones" [Matt 3:5–9]. Isaiah testified earlier to the grace of this time in which saint John was exhorting sinners to repentance and while set in the desert was baptizing those who confessed their sins. He said the following: "Be glad, O desert, let it flower as the lily, and let the desert places of the Jordan flourish and exult. Be strong, O relaxed hands, and be comforted, O weakened knees. You fainthearted, be strong and do not fear" [Isa 35:1–4; cf. Matt 11:4–6; Luke 7:18–25]. Thus did John exhort those who came to him to purge away by the confession of repentance the sins that they had committed by transgressing the precepts of the divine law. Then by doing things worthy of repentance they could earn sufficient pardon before God. God is the one who had said through the prophet, "I do not will the death of the one who dies up to the time that he turns back and lives" [Ezek 18:32; cf. 33:11]. And again, "When you shall turn and groan, then you shall be saved and you shall know where you were" [Isa 30:15]. And again, "Turn to me and I will turn to you, says the Lord" [Zech 1:3; cf. Mal 3:7]. And again, "I am the Lord. I do not remember evils, only that a person turn himself from his wicked way and from all the iniquities that he has done, in order that he might live" [see Ezek 18:22, 23, 28, 32]. Thus we understand that there exists much hope for salvation in the confession of sins. We recognize that

this should not be neglected even by the example of the blessed Job, who was not even silent about his sins of ignorance, saying, "And if I sinned without knowing it and I hid my sin, for I did not stand in awe of a great multitude, so as not to confess before them" [Job 31:33–34].

2. Now John pressed the Pharisees and Sadducees who had come to his baptism, saying, "Brood of vipers! Who has shown you how to flee from the wrath to come? Therefore, produce fruit worthy of repentance" [Matt 3:7–8]. Those who for a long time were called God's children are now due to their wickedness called a "brood of vipers," because by doing the will of the devil, who from the beginning was called a serpent, they made themselves the devil's children. This agrees with what he says in the gospel: "You are from your father the devil, and it is your will to fulfill your father's desires" [John 8:44]. For Scripture is accustomed to reckon sinners to the race they are worthy of, on the basis of the resemblance of those who are sinning, when it says, "Hear this, ye rulers of the Sodomites, pay heed to the law of God, O people of Gomorrah" [Isa 1:10]. And again, "Your father was an Amorite and your mother a Hittite, and your generation was from the land of Canaan" [Ezek 16:3]. Surely this rebuke is directed at the Jewish people, who, it is clear, were neither rulers of the Sodomites nor the people of Gomorrah nor progeny of an Amorite father and Hittite mother. Rather, they are attributed the name of these wicked races on the basis of the similarity of their sin. Hence it is not unfitting that John convicted them with a judgment like this, when he said, "Brood of vipers, who warned you to flee from the coming wrath? Therefore produce fruit worthy of repentance." The goal of this is that they could escape the punishment of the future judgment by means of a just repentance, by coming to their senses with respect to their evils. Likewise the blessed apostle shows that wrath indicates eternal punishment, when he says, "For if when we were enemies we were reconciled with God, how much more shall we be saved from wrath through him?" [Rom 5:8–9]. And again, "You are storing up for yourselves wrath on the day of wrath" [Rom 2:5].

3. And therefore, to blunt their pride, which they had based on their presumption of stemming from a holy race, he went on to say, "And do not presume to say to yourselves, We have Abraham as our father. For I tell you that God can raise up children of Abraham from these stones" [Matt 3:9]. According to the flesh, they were indeed children of Abraham, but they are estranged from Abraham's faith and works, so that they flattered themselves undeservedly with the

privilege of belonging to his race, as we read in another passage: "They said to the Lord, We have Abraham as father" [John 8:39]. But the Lord answered and said to them, "If you were children of Abraham, you would do the works of Abraham" [John 8:39]. Hence it is without doubt that the one who has followed the faith and works of Abraham deserves to hear that he is Abraham's son. This agrees with what the apostle says: "For not all who are from Israel are Israelites, nor are the seed of Abraham all sons, but in Isaac shall your seed be called" [Rom 9:6–7]. That is to say, it is not those who are children of the flesh who are children of God, but the children of promise are reputed as seed. For those who do not respond to the sanctity of their race lose the honor of belonging to that race. And that is why John went on to say, "I tell you that God can raise up children of Abraham from these stones." Let us consider, then, who these stones are of whom saint John promises Abraham's children shall consist. Doubtless the Gentiles (*gentes*) are signified in the stones from whom believers in Christ are raised up as worthy children of Abraham by the merit of their faith, after the faithlessness of the Jews has been rejected. This accords with what was said to him: "For I have appointed you father of many nations (*gentium*)" [Gen 17:5]. Likewise indeed the Lord in the gospel showed that after the Jewish unbelief these stones come together in God's praise through the outcry of faith, when he says, "If these are silent, the stones shall cry out" [Luke 19:40].[42] We notice then that the Gentiles have been compared with these stones, either that the stones were worshiping, or that they hardened their hearts with a stony and obtuse mind, which through the prophet the Lord had predicted would be removed, when he said, "I shall remove from them their stony hearts and I shall give them a heart of flesh, and I will write my laws on their hearts and I shall write them on their mind" [Ezek 11:19; 36:26; Jer 31:33]. He is Christ Jesus, our Lord and Savior, to whom is the praise and the glory in the ages of ages. Amen [see 1 Pet 4:11].

Tractate 11 on Matthew 3:10–12

1. There follows next, "But already the ax is laid at the roots of the trees. Every tree that does not produce good fruit will be cut down and cast into the fire" [Matt 3:10]. Doubtless this ax signifies

the power of the divine word, for the Lord says through Jeremiah the prophet, "Are not my words like fire, says the Lord, and like an ax that cuts rocks?" [Jer 23:29]. Therefore this ax that has been laid at the very roots of interior faith, in this forest of the human race, always threatens with the severity of divine judgment. By it's unfruitful trees, that is, barren people, bearing no fruit of fecund faith, it will be cut down and consigned to perpetual fire [see John 15:6]. It is likewise confirmed by a testimony of Ezekiel that this ax represents the power of divine judgment. For angels are appointed by the Lord to take up axes and lay waste to unbelievers. For it is written as follows: "And each shall have axes in their hands" [Ezek 9:1]. And it is said to them, "Go, run about and strike, and do not spare them, from the greater to the lesser. But do not touch anyone on whom you find my sign, and begin with my very holy ones" [Ezek 9:5–6].[43] And so, unbelievers are indeed cut down with a gospel ax of this sort, but believers are purged, so that they may be able to bring forth better fruit [see John 15:2].

2. And he says to them, "I baptize you in repentance" [and the rest up to] "he shall burn with inextinguishable fire" [Matt 3:11–12]. John therefore in accordance with the counsel of divine mercy baptized the people in repentance, as the Lord himself declared in the Gospel, when he said to the Jews, "Prostitutes and tax collectors are preceding you into the kingdom of God" [Matt 21:31]. For they accepted being baptized with John's baptism [see Luke 7:29]. In this therefore it is shown that it had been the counsel of God that each one be purged of sin in John's baptism by the confession of sin, and should by this means be deemed worthy of the gift of heavenly grace, lest the Holy Spirit should refuse to enter into bodies that had been defiled by sins. This agrees with what is written: "The Holy Spirit of discipline will flee deceit" [Wis 1:5]. And again: "For into a malevolent soul wisdom shall not enter; nor dwell in the body that is subject to sins" [Wis 1:4]. Thus it is not without cause that saint John baptized with a baptism of repentance, so that when the hearts of human beings had been wiped clean of the filth of sins, he could prepare the way for the Lord and a habitation for the Holy Spirit, the very thing that the Lord also shows through Isaiah, when he says, "Wash yourselves and be clean, remove wickedness from your souls" [Isa 1:16].

3. So then, John says, "I baptize you in repentance, but one who is stronger is coming after me whose sandals I am not worthy to carry. He shall baptize you in the Holy Spirit and fire" [Matt 3:11]. Saint John did indeed baptize with a baptism of repentance, but he announced

another more powerful baptism coming in the future, in fire and the Holy Spirit. But since he said that this was to be granted after himself, by him who would be even stronger than he, and whose sandals he was not worthy to carry; and since saint John is the greatest[44] among the prophets [see Luke 7:26–28], first among the apostles, filled with the Holy Spirit in his mother's womb [see Luke 1:41], given preference by the Lord's words over all who have been born of women [see Matt 11:11], even called an angel [see Matt 11:10; Mark 1:2]; and since he professes that he is unworthy to carry the Lord's sandals; how is it that impious heretics have dared to deny that Christ is Lord, when such a great prophet without any doubt declares him to be God, by means of this confession of his divine honor?

4. But now we give consideration to what is meant by these sandals according to the spiritual understanding. We know that a long time ago it was said to Moses, "Put off your sandals from your feet. For the place on which you are standing is holy ground" [Exod 3:5]. We also read that it was said to Jesus the son of Nun likewise: "Loose the latchet from your sandal" [Josh 5:16]. But in their being ordered by the Lord to remove the sandals from their feet, we understand this to be a type of a future truth. For in the law it was said that if a man was unwilling to take the wife of his brother after his brother's death, he should take off his sandals, so that another groom could marry her and succeed by right of law [see Deut 25:7–9]. We find that this commandment prefigured in law has been fulfilled in Christ, who is the true bridegroom of the church. Therefore, because neither Moses the lawgiver nor Joshua the leader of the people could be the bridegroom of the church, not unfittingly was it said to them that they should remove the sandals from their feet, because the true future bridegroom of the church, Christ, was expected. John says concerning him, "He who has the bride is the bridegroom" [John 3:29]. To carry or loosen his sandals, John professed himself to be unworthy. The Lord himself through David reveals that these sandals signify the tracks of gospel proclamation, when he says, "Into Idumea I shall stretch out my sandal" [Ps 60:9; 108:10];[45] that is, through his apostles he would show the steps of gospel teaching everywhere.

5. "He therefore baptizes in the Holy Spirit and fire" [Matt 3:11]. John's baptism was one thing, the Lord's something else. The former pertained to repentance, the latter to grace and sanctification, in which the Holy Spirit is at work in each believer to boil out sins like a fire, to burn up transgressions, to purge off the filth of the flesh

and the soul, in accordance with what Isaiah has related: "The Lord will wash away the filth of the sons and daughters of Zion, and he will purge the blood from their midst by a spirit of judgment and a spirit of burning" [Isa 4:4]. This therefore is what John is testifying to in the present passage, when he says, "He will baptize you in the Holy Spirit and fire." Also, the Lord desires to cast this fire of the Holy Spirit onto the earth and set it aflame, as he says, "I have come to cast a fire on the earth, and what do I wish but that it be kindled?" [Luke 12:49]. That is, he wants the earth of our body to catch on fire, so that the filth of our sins would be burned out by the action of the Holy Spirit. Isaiah also knew this fire of the Holy Spirit by whose heat he boasts that his own sins had been purged away. For this is what he says: "Behold, one of the seraphs took a coal off the altar with the tongs, and he touched my lips and said to me, Behold, I have taken away your iniquities, and I have purged off your sins" [Isa 6:6–7]. Jeremiah likewise testified that a fire was in him in a prophecy of the Holy Spirit [Jer 20:9]. David too is not unaware that bodies of believers are purged like silver by this fire, when he says, "Silver tested in the fire, purged on earth seven times" [Ps 12:6]. For just as fire immediately converts the silver that is cast into it to the color of its own nature, once the impurities are boiled off, so the Holy Spirit brings someone who has been purged of the vices of sins to the glory of the spiritual nature. This is also why in the Acts of the Apostles the Holy Spirit appeared like fire upon the disciples and believers. For this is what it reports: "And he sat upon each one of them, and there appeared to them tongues distributed like fire" [Acts 2:3]. There is likewise that true avenger of the future judgment, eternal fire, in which sinners will be purged with a penal burning, as it were by a kind of baptism, after they have lost the grace of the Holy Spirit. Whence it is that the Lord says in the gospel, "You will not come out of there until you pay back the last penny" [Matt 5:26]. He is showing that one cannot be released from the fire's punishment until you pay in full, even for the smallest sin, by means of a penal cleansing. The apostle is known to indicate this when he says, "Fire will test the quality of each one's work. If his work remains, he will receive a wage, if his work burns, he will suffer loss. But he himself will be saved, but as through fire" [1 Cor 3:13–15].

6. Whence it is not unbefitting that it follow, "He has his winnowing shovel in his hand and will purge his threshing floor. He will store up the wheat in barns, but the chaff he will burn with unquenchable fire" [Matt 3:12]. He speaks of a winnowing shovel of divine judgment

with which he will separate sinners from the just, like chaff from wheat, by a judgment of divine fairness. Therefore with such a winnowing shovel he will purify the threshing floor of the church in the future judgment, when he lays up his own just ones, like unscathed grains of wheat, into barns, that is, into the heavenly mansion [see John 14:2]. But he who is a judge of fairness and justice hands sinners over to the unquenchable fire to be burned like chaff. To him is the praise and glory in the ages of ages. Amen [see 1 Pet 4:11].

Tractate 12 on Matthew 3:13–15

I.1.[46] There follows next, "Then Jesus came from Galilee into the Jordan" [and the rest up to] "to fulfill all justice" [Matt 3:13–15].[47] To accomplish all the mysteries of the law, therefore, Jesus descended from Galilee into the Jordan to be baptized by John. But John, recognizing his Lord and God through the Holy Spirit, declared that he was not even worthy to carry his sandals [see Matt 3:11]. He excuses himself from fulfilling what he was commanded because he could not believe that baptism was necessary for the one whom he knew had come to blot out the sins of the world by his own baptism [see John 1:29]. And therefore he testifies that he himself ought rather to be baptized by him, saying, "It is I who should be baptized by you, and do you come to me?" [Matt 3:14]. **2.** It is as if he were saying, "I am a man, you are God. I am a sinner because I am a man; you are without sin because you are God. Why do you want to be baptized by me? I do not refuse to obey, but I am ignorant of the mystery. I baptize sinners in repentance. But you have no taint of sin. So why do you want to be baptized? Or rather, why do you want to be baptized as a sinner, who came to forgive sins?" This then is what John is saying to the Lord: "I ought to be baptized by you, and you come to me?" But the Lord is indeed testing the faithful obedience of service on the part of his servant, but he reveals the mystery of his dispensation by saying, "Let it be so now; for thus it is fitting for us to fulfill all justice." He is showing that true justice is for the Lord and Teacher to fulfill in himself the entire mystery of our salvation. **3.** Therefore the Lord did not want to be baptized for his own sake, but for ours, to fulfill all justice. Indeed, it is just that whatever someone instructs another to do, he should first begin. Since then the Lord had come as the Teacher of the human race, he wanted to teach by his own example what must be done in order for disciples to follow their Teacher, servants their Lord. **4.** Since, therefore, a new baptism had to be given for the salvation of the human race and the remission of sin, first he himself deemed it fitting to be baptized, not to lay aside sins, who alone had not committed sin, but to sanctify the waters of baptism for the washing away of the sins of believers.[48] For the waters of baptism would never have been able to purge the sins of believers, if they had not been sanctified by the touch of the Lord's body. **5.** Therefore he was baptized, that we might be washed of our sins. He was dipped in water, that we would be purged of the filth of our transgressions. He received the bath of regeneration, that we might be reborn from water and the Holy Spirit, since, as he himself says in another passage, "Unless one is reborn from water and the Holy Spirit, he will not enter the kingdom of heaven" [John 3:5].

II.1. Therefore the baptism of Christ is a washing away of our sins and a renewal of saving life. Listen to the apostle demonstrating the same thing when he says, "As many of you who have been baptized in Christ have put on Christ" [Gal 3:27]. And he added, "Therefore, you were buried together with him through baptism into death; so that just as Christ rose from the dead, so you too might walk in the newness of life" [Rom 6:4]. **2.** And so through baptism we die to sin, but we live together with Christ; we are buried with respect to our former life, but we rise again to a new life; we are stripped of the error of the old man, but we take up the garments of the new man [see Col 3:10]. Therefore the Lord likewise fulfilled all justice in baptism, since he willed to be baptized that we might be baptized; he willed to receive the bath of regeneration, that we might be reborn unto life.

III.1. Granted, John baptized our Lord and Savior, but really he was baptized by Christ, since the latter sanctified the waters, whereas the former was sanctified by the waters; the latter gave the grace, the former received it; the former laid aside his sins, the latter remitted them. For the former was a man, the latter God. For to forgive sins pertains to God, as it is written: "Who can forgive sins but God alone?" [Mark 2:7; Luke 5:21]. And that is why John says to Christ, "I ought to be baptized by you, and you come to me?" For John needed baptism, since he was unable to be without sin; but Christ who had committed no sin could not have needed baptism. **2.** Thus in this baptism our Lord and Savior first purged John's sins, then those of the whole world [see John 1:29]. And that is why he says, "Let it be so for now; for thus it is fitting for us to fulfill all justice." A long time ago the grace of his baptism was shown in advance mystically, when the people were led into the promised land through the Jordan River [see Josh 3]. **3.** Just as back then, there was a way through the Jordan for the people going to the promised land, with the Lord going in front, so now through the same waters of the Jordan River, first the journey of the heavenly way has been opened, by which we are brought to that blessed promised land, that is, the inheritance of the heavenly kingdom. For them Jesus son of Nun was the guide in the Jordan; for us, on the other hand, through baptism Jesus Christ the Lord stands forth as guide of eternal salvation, the only begotten Son of God, who is blessed in the ages of ages. Amen [see Rom 1:25; 2 Cor 11:31].

Tractate 13 on Matthew 3:16–17

I.1. It then follows, "And when Jesus was baptized, immediately he ascended from the water. And behold, the heavens were opened to him, and he saw the Spirit of God descending as a dove. And behold, there was a voice speaking from heaven: This is my beloved Son, in whom I am well pleased" [Matt 3:16–17]. As in the Lord's bodily birth, so too in his baptism, all things worthy of admiration and befitting his majesty were clearly seen. **2.** The heavens opened, therefore, when the Lord ascended from the waters after his baptism; the Holy Spirit, arrayed in bodily form and outward appearance as a dove [see Luke 3:22], came down bearing testimony about the Son; the voice of the Father too at once is heard from heaven, saying, "This is my Son, in whom I am well pleased." David too had earlier predicted the sound of his sacred voice over the waters, when he said, "The voice of the Lord [is] over the waters, the God of majesty has thundered" [Ps 29:3]. Surely it was in this voice of the Father's majesty bearing witness to the Son that he has caused a thunder of sorts to resound.

II.1. What room do the heretics have here, those who oppose the faith? What occasion is left to them to blaspheme in this declaration of the Father, seeing that the mystery of the perfect Trinity is shown, with their unique characteristics explicitly expressed in the words? For in the mystery of the baptism, the Son is seen abiding in his body, the Holy Spirit descends in the outward form of a dove, and the Father's voice is heard from heaven. Thus the unity of the Trinity is declared, since the Father cannot be understood without the Son, nor can the Son be known without the Holy Spirit. **2.** Consider therefore the kind of testimony the Father gives to the Son, when he says, "This is my Son." His, assuredly, not by a gracious adoption, nor by the choice of the creature, as the heretics think it means, but his own, by the unique property of the class, and by the truth of nature. For many saints are called sons of God, and they are; but this one is without comparison, the only begotten Son of God the Father, both true and unique, born from no other source than from the Father. For the Father is both a true Father and he is also true God; just as the Son is both a true Son and he is also true Lord. **3.** Therefore the perfect faith of the Trinity is shown, since the Father testifies that Christ our Lord and God is his own Son, and the Holy Spirit, that is, the Paraclete [see John 16:7], is united with the Father and the Son in such a great mystery of faith, so that we believe in the true Father, the true Son, and likewise the true Holy Spirit, three persons, but one divinity and one substance of the Trinity. These things have been said in passing about the mystery of the Trinity.

III.**1.** But since we know that everything that the Lord did for us has been exhibited as a mystery of our salvation, then in the heavens being opened at the Lord's baptism, it was shown that when we are reborn in baptism, the kingdom of heaven is opened.[49] The Son of God first opened it for us when he ascended to heaven with his body. **2.** Whence also in the Holy Spirit's immediately coming down in the outward form of a dove, and in the voice of the Father being heard from heaven saying, "This is my Son," in these things the arrangement of the heavenly mystery and of our salvation is revealed.[50] For through saving baptism in water we became and we shall be children of God, and by the giving of the gift of the Holy Spirit, through whom there is praise and glory to the Father and the Son in the ages of ages. Amen.

Tractate 14 on Matthew 4:1–11

1. It then follows, "Then he was led by the Spirit" [and the rest up to] "afterward he was hungry" [Matt 4:1–2]. O the incomparable endurance of the Lord and the example of admirable humility! The Lord endures temptation from the devil, he who a long time ago in the desert struck those who tested him with the deadly bites of

serpents [see Num 21:6]. Likewise, the one who fasted for us in the desert and who grew hungry is he who a long time ago over a period of forty years refreshed with heavenly food his own hungering people in the wilderness [see Exod 16:14]. And though God cannot become hungry according to the incorruptible and blessed eternal nature, as it is written, "The eternal God shall not hunger nor be weary" [Isa 40:28], nevertheless for the sake of our salvation, in accordance with his taking on a body, he deems it fitting both to be tempted and to grow hungry, in order to demonstrate in himself the reality of the flesh he assumed.[51]

2. Therefore the devil incites in order to tempt, and the Lord follows in order to conquer. Now the enemy accosted him with the combat of this sort of temptation by saying to the Lord, "If you are the Son of God, tell these stones to become loaves of bread" [Matt 4:3]. Unaware of the mystery of the divine dispensation, then, he asks about what he does not know. For this is the voice of one who is in doubt about what he is investigating, and he says, "*If* you are the Son of God." Now let us see why he seeks, if he is wavering, and why he questions, if he does not know. He had already heard what the angel had announced to the virgin, that she would give birth to the Son of God [see Luke 2:32]. He had also seen that the Magi, who had laid aside the error of their worthless knowledge, humbly adored the child that was born [see Matt 2:11]. He had also seen the Holy Spirit descending like a dove after the baptism. And he had heard the Father's voice from heaven saying, "This is my Son" [see Matt 3:16–17; Mark 1:10–11; Luke 3:22]. And he had heard John testifying publicly, "This is he who takes away the sin of the world" [John 1:29]. Disturbed by so much testimony, therefore, and now troubled by this voice, this is what he feared most of all the things he had heard: that after he had filled the world with sins, he hears there would now come someone to take away the sin of the world. He was terrified indeed by all these utterances, but he did not yet fully believe that the Son of God, whom he had heard, whom he now beheld as a man and saw in the flesh, would take away the sins of the world.[52] In a terrible state of fear he seeks to find out whether these things he had heard were true. He sees indeed the Lord fasting forty days and nights, but the ruined one was not immediately willing to believe that this was the Son of God. For he recalled that both Moses and Elijah also fasted for forty days [see Exod 34:28; 1 Kgs 19:8]. And so he asks to be given some sign of the miracle proposed to show that this was truly the Son of God. He therefore proposes, "If

you are the Son of God, tell these stones to become bread." It was not indeed impossible for the Son of God to convert stones into bread, who in like manner raised up sons of Abraham from stones [see Matt 3:9], but it would not have been right for the Lord to comply with the devil's will. And therefore the Lord does not grant him what he was seeking to know. For he does not deem it fitting to respond to him, that he himself was the Son of God, but concealing his divinity, he struck him with an arrow, as it were, solely with a response from the law, saying, "It is written: Man does not live by bread alone but by every word of God" [Matt 4:4]. By this response he nullified the devil's temptation. Now the Lord was hungry not by necessity but willingly, in order to provoke the devil to this temptation, so that since a long time ago the devil himself had conquered Adam in paradise, now he would be conquered by the Lord in the wilderness. And he conquered Adam when Adam was not even hungry, but now he is conquered by the Lord who is hungry. For the second Adam wanted to conquer in those ways in which the first Adam had been overcome.

3. Having been struck already by one wound, the enemy again thinks up another subject of temptation. For it is written as follows: "Then the devil took him to the holy city" [and the rest up to] "lest you strike your foot against a stone" [Matt 4:5–6]. Well then, having been defeated once already in the wilderness, he now engages in another combat. The adversary ascends to the "pinnacle of the temple" for the challenge, and the Lord follows for the triumph. And he climbs to the top of the temple in order to cast down from the height the one who was trying to cast him down. For the Lord submitted himself to all this humiliation in order to leave behind an example for us of patient endurance in temptation, and to triumph over the adversary in all things. Therefore the devil says to the Lord, "If you are the Son of God, cast yourself down. For it is written that he has commanded his angels concerning you, to take you up in their hands, lest you strike your foot against a stone" [Matt 4:6]. O the cunning skillful wickedness and the audacity of doomed temerity! He who had seen himself struck by the Lord with a response from the law no longer uses weapons of wickedness in which he had been found incompetent, but he himself borrows a testimony from the law. And from that source from which he was pained to have been defeated already, he tries to conquer. For he himself even dares to say, "It is written," but not on his own behalf, but rather against himself. Indeed it had been written, "For he commanded his angels concerning you," but what he

added on his own had not been written there: "Cast yourself down." In this we recognize his old usual cunning in that he is always capable of deceiving, mixing in good things with the bad, and tempering his poison with sweet honey. For in this way long ago in order to deceive Adam about himself, he prefaced as it were God's previously spoken words: "Exactly why did God say to you, You shall not eat of every tree of paradise?" [Gen 3:1], and the rest. This was in order to deceive the unwary man by the command proposed by God, and by a false interpretation, and by the addition of some words. For there too he added on his own what he says: "Exactly why did God say, You shall not eat from every tree of paradise," though the Lord had [actually] said, "You shall eat from every tree of the paradise. But from the tree of knowledge, which is in the middle of the paradise, you shall not eat" [Gen 2:16–17]. Thus he altered the divine words, and he joined his own words to certain of the Lord's statements, that he might more easily persuade and deceive by persuasion. He intermingled words of his own wickedness with the divine words, that he might inject deadly venom by means of sweet honey.

When therefore the enemy had cited an example from the law, to be sure, but one that was opposed to himself, the Lord despised his incompetent temptation and again struck him with another arrow from the law, saying, "It is written, You shall not tempt the Lord your God." By this response the devil received another wound once again, and yet he did not leave off attacking the Lord again with another temptation, though he had been struck by two blows already. And the Lord could have laid him low at once with the first temptation, but he held on to patience in order that the enemy might become more prideful in the face of his own ruin, and be wounded by multiple blows before his own destruction.

4. Finally, when he engages the Lord twice and is defeated, still a third time he attempts to arm the audacity of his wickedness. For the evangelist reports this: "And he took him to a very high mountain" [and the rest up to] "you shall worship the Lord your God and him alone shall you serve" [Matt 4:8–10]. The Lord's patient endurance is marvelous and worthy of imitation, whereas the devil's audacity is one of a kind! The enemy therefore challenges him now for a third time and ascends a very high mountain in order to tempt him, and the Lord does not refuse to follow in order to conquer. But he conquered not for himself but for us.[53] For it would not have been a great thing if

the Son of God conquered the devil, but the great thing was in the fact that he conquered as a man and he conquered for us.

It says, "Then he showed him all the kingdoms of the world and their glory and he said to him, All these things I shall give to you if you fall down and worship me" [Matt 4:8–9]. He promises the kingdoms of the world to him who prepared the kingdom of heaven for believers. He promises the glory of the age to him who is Lord of heavenly glory. He who has nothing pledges to give the universe to him who possesses all things. He wants to be worshiped on earth by him whom angels and archangels worship in heaven.

Whence the Lord again lays low the audacity of his insolent adversary by another testimony from the law, saying, "Begone, Satan, it is written, You shall worship the Lord your God and him alone shall you serve." Now therefore as victor and Lord he threatens the devil with his divine authority and commands him to depart. Whence not without cause, since their own prince had been defeated, the demons cry out later on, "What have you to do with us, Son of the Most High God? Why have you come to torment us before the time?" [Matt 8:29]. For they could no longer have been ignorant that he was the Son of God, whom they had recognized to be God in the condemnation of their own forefather.

5. Now in Zechariah as well we read about the battle of this temptation to come. It is shown in the passage where it is said, "Jesus was clothed with filthy garments and the devil stood there to speak against him" [Zech 3:1]. Surely this can be understood not inappropriately about that Jesus, son of Joseph, since he received the filthy garments of the priests, that is, a body from the race of sinners. With good reason too Solomon testified that the tracks of a serpent could not be found upon the rock [see Prov 30:19], since in this temptation the serpent devil did not leave behind traces of sin in the Lord, who is called the rock [see 1 Cor 10:4]. David also shows this when he speaks the following of the Lord, saying, "And the scourge did not approach his tabernacle" [Ps 91:10]. For no sin of a diabolical scourge could come close to the body of the Lord. Therefore the Lord withstood the temptations of the enemy, that he might carry back a victory to humankind. He thereby made sport of the devil, according to what David also predicted when he said, "That dragon whom you formed to sport with him" [Ps 104:26]. And again, "He will lay low the false accuser" [Ps 72:4]. And again, "You crushed the head of the dragon on the water" [Ps 74:14, 13]. In the Book of Job, the Lord testified

beforehand that this dragon would be made sport of and caught in this temptation. He says, "But you will draw out the dragon on a hook" [Job 40:20]. And let us see why he is said to be drawn up on a hook. Just as we sport with and deceive fish with the prey of a meal that is set on a hook, fish that see the meal but not the hook, and they are caught by the hook, while eagerly wishing to seize the prey of a meal, so too it happened to the devil. While he was looking only at the human body in the Son of God and does not recognize God in the body, he hurries after the prey prepared for himself with his usual rapine. But while eagerly wanting to seize the prey, the dragon himself is drawn up on the hook like a fish, and is captured as the Lord's prey. In what follows, the same Job declared not only that this devil is drawn up on a hook as a dragon, but is sported with as a sparrow by a child. He says, "And you will net him as a bird and play with him as children with a sparrow" [Job 40:24]. In these things both the power of the Son of God and the weakness of the devil is shown, since just as it is easy for a bird to be caught in a net and for children to play with sparrows, so it was easy for the Son of God to nullify the powerful devil, who was indeed always powerful in his opposition to men, but against the Lord he was found to be weak and pitiful.

6. But in this temptation the Lord has given especially to us an example of combat and conquest against the adversary. And although there may be many different temptations of the devil all around us, yet in these three temptations he conducted against the Lord, he has been accustomed to tempt even his elect [see Matt 24:24].[54] For in the fact that the Lord allowed himself to be tempted by the enemy after his baptism and his fast, it is shown that the tempter devil approaches each one of us immediately after the bath of regeneration, after the resolution for a holy life, after the religious effort of fasting, in order to turn us aside from our religious resolution, either by a desire for food or by bodily lust. But the Lord has shown us how we ought to conquer temptation of this sort, that is, how not to comply with his desire. We should immediately set forth examples for ourselves from the divine law in opposition to the temptation, so that we would always desire to be satiated instead by the food of the divine word, overcoming the hunger of the body and the desires of the flesh. For this is what the Lord answered to the devil when he said, "It is written, Not by bread alone does man live, but by every word of God" [Matt 4:4].

This first cause of the devil's temptation has been shown to us. When he is overcome in it, he attacks with another stronger temptation. After all, the devil's challenge of the Lord on the pinnacle of the temple with a second temptation shows that when he is unable to deceive someone by the lust of the body, he tries to tempt. After the first victory of the body, he strives by means of spiritual causes to cast each one of us down headlong, even one already stationed on the height. "Throw yourself down" [Matt 4:6]. He does not say, "I throw," lest he seem to use force, but he says, "Throw yourself down." This shows that each of us by freedom of choice falls into death by the fault of his own will. It belongs indeed to him to suggest, but it is up to us to overcome his suggestions through the observance of the law.[55] Whence even in the fact that he interprets the prophetic statement as if speaking with approval of the matter, afterward he says, "Throw yourself down; for it is written that he has commanded his angels concerning you" [Matt 4:6]. The enemy's cunning is shown, since he was about to interpret the divine Scriptures in a depraved sense and with underhanded deceit.[56] And instead of faith, he would assert faithlessness, in order that by means of testimonies from the divine law, as it were by the outward appearance of a good confession, he might cast the simple and incautious from the height headlong down to their deaths. Ultimately, in this way he has cast down many heretics from the height of the Catholic faith into the depths; in this way he casts many headlong by some works of justice, as from a tower, when he severs them from the Lord's humility, and exalts them with arrogance of mind.

But in the third temptation he sets forth the glory of the age and the world's wealth [see Matt 4:8] by means of which, as the apostle relates, he has caused many to shipwreck their faith [see 1 Tim 6:10; 1:19] and to pass from heavenly to earthly glory. He suggests to a man earthly honors, in order to rob him of heavenly honors; he encourages worldly wealth, in order to deprive him of spiritual riches. Whence not without reason the following is said of him in the Book of Job: "All the gold of the sea is under him" [Job 41:21]. For the enemy's custom is to entice and deceive many on the occasion of gold and desire for wealth. And by this means he must be scorned and silenced in these respects as well, in order for a complete victory to be carried back from the tempter.

7. But in the fact that when every temptation was completed, the evangelist reports that angels ministered to the Lord [see Matt 4:11], we recognize clearly that the Son of God is God and the Creator of the universe. For angels could only have ministered to their Lord

and Creator, the only begotten Son of God, to whom is the praise and glory in the ages of ages. Amen [see 1 Pet 4:11].

Tractate 15 on Matthew 4:12–17

1. Then it follows, "But when Jesus heard that John was handed over, he withdrew into Galilee" [and the rest up to] "those who sat in the shadow of death a light has risen for them" [Matt 4:12–16]. And so, our Lord and Savior left Nazareth and illumined various locales of Judea with a visitation of his honor. He went "into the borders of Zebulun and Naphtali" [Matt 4:13] in order to fulfill the prophetic preaching, to drive out the error of darkness, and to pour the light of the knowledge of himself into those who believe in him, not only among the Jews but also among the Gentiles. For this is what the evangelist recorded in the present passage out of the prophet's words: "Beyond the Jordan of the Galilee of the Gentiles, the people who sat in darkness have seen a great light" [Matt 4:15–16]. In what darkness? Surely in the profound error of ignorance. What great light did they see? Surely the light concerning which it is written, "He was the true light that illumines every man who comes into this world" [John 1:9]. In the gospel, the just man Simeon testified of him and said, "A light you have prepared for revelation to the Gentiles and the glory for your people Israel" [Luke 2:31–32]. And David had predicted that this light in the darkness would arise at some time, when he said, "A light has arisen in the darkness to the upright of heart" [Ps 112:4]. Also, Isaiah makes clear that this light will come for the illumination of the church, when he says, "Shine, shine, Jerusalem; for your light is near, and the majesty of the Lord has risen in you" [Isa 60:1]. Concerning that light also Daniel related the following: "He reveals the profound and hidden things, knowing those things that are in darkness and the light is with him" [Dan 2:22], that is, the Son with the Father, for even as the Father is light, so too is the Son light. Hence David also says in the psalm, "In your light shall we see light" [Ps 36:9], for the Father is seen in the Son, as the Lord himself says in the gospel: "He who sees me, sees also the Father" [John 14:9]. For from the true light, the true light proceeded, and from the invisible the visible. For "he is the image of the invisible God" [Col 1:15], as the apostle has related.

2. Concerning this light, then, it is related in the present passage, "The people who sat in darkness have seen a great light" [Matt 4:16]. They see not with bodily observation—for the light is invisible—but with the eyes of faith and with the mind's vision. This then is what he is saying: "The people who sat in darkness have seen a great light, and for those who sat in the region of the shadow of death, light has dawned" [Matt 4:16]. Therefore not only to those who were in darkness did this light appear, but he says that a light has arisen for those sitting in the region of the shadow of death. This shows that there are some who were sitting in darkness, others who sit established in the region of the shadow of death. And what is this region of the shadow of death, if not the region of the infernal abode? David speaks of it and says, "For even if I walk in the midst of the shadow of death, I shall fear no evils, for you are with me" [Ps 23:4]. Surely he shall not fear evils, that is, the punishments of hell. Therefore a saving light is arising even for those who are sitting in the region of the shadow of death, that is, Christ the Son of God, who says in the gospel, "I am the true light. He who follows me shall not walk in darkness" [John 8:12]. After that venerable passion that saves all, he penetrates the region of the infernal abode. Suddenly he introduced the light of his majesty to those stunned souls of the lower world, to free those who were being held among the dead in expectation of his arrival, just as the Lord himself in the person of Wisdom says through Solomon: "I will penetrate all the way to the lower parts of the earth and gaze upon all those who are asleep, and I shall enlighten those who hope in God" [Sir 24:45].

3. After that it follows, "Then Jesus began to preach and say, Repent, for the kingdom of heaven has come near" [Matt 4:17]. Likewise through David the Holy Spirit earlier forewarned these words of the Lord, by which he urged the people to repentance, that they might take heed, saying, "Today, if you hear his voice, harden not your hearts, as in the preparation in the day of temptation in the desert" [Ps 95:7–8]. Higher up in the same psalm, in order to invite the sinful people to repentance and to show the feelings of one who was grieving, he testified and said the following: "Come, let us fall down before him and cry aloud before the Lord who made us, for he is our God" [Ps 95:6–7]. Now the Lord exhorts to repentance, he who promises to pardon sin, that one surely who says through Isaiah, "I am. I am the one who wipes out your iniquities and I will not be mindful of your sins. But you be mindful, declare first your iniquities that you may be

justified" [Isa 43:25–26]. Rightly then does the Lord urge the people to repentance when he says, "Repent, for the kingdom of heaven has come near," so that through this confession of sin they may already be made worthy to come near to the kingdom of heaven. For no one can receive the grace of the heavenly God, unless he has been cleansed of every stain of sin by the confession of repentance, by the gift of the saving baptism of our Lord and Savior, who is blessed in the ages of ages. Amen [see Rom 1:25; 2 Cor 11:31].

Tractate 16 on Matthew 4:18–25

1. It then follows, "But passing by the sea, he saw two brothers" [and the rest up to] "but they immediately left their boat and their own father and followed him" [Matt 4:18–22]. O blessed are those fishermen whom the Lord chose as the first for the task of divine preaching and the grace of the apostolate, from among so many doctors of the law and scribes, from among so many wise men of the world! Such a selection was clearly worthy of our Lord and appropriate for his preaching, that in the preaching of his name the wonder of praise might be all the greater as the humblest men and the lowliest ones of the age preached it. They did not capture the world through the wisdom of their words, but delivered the human race from the error of death through the simple preaching of the faith. This is what the apostle says: "That your faith may not be in the wisdom of men but in the power of God" [1 Cor 2:5]. And again: "God chose the foolish things of the world to confound the wise, and God chose the weak things of the world to confound the strong, and God chose the ignoble and contemptible things of the world, and the things that are not, to destroy the things that are" [1 Cor 1:27–28].[57] Therefore he has not chosen the noble of the world, or the rich, lest their preaching be suspect; not the wise of the world, lest people believe that they persuaded the human race by the wisdom of the world; but he chose illiterate, unskilled, and uneducated fishermen to disclose the Savior's grace. To be sure, they were humble in respect to the world, even in the very task of the art; but they were lofty in faith and in the devoted obedience of their mind. They were looked down upon on earth, but most pleasing in the sight of heaven, ignoble in the world, but noble in Christ; not inscribed on the roster of the world's senate, but written down on the

roster of the angels in heaven; poor in the world, but rich to God. For the Lord who knows the secrets of the heart knows those whom he has chosen [see 1 Cor 14:25], those assuredly who were not seeking after the wisdom of the age, but who desired God's wisdom; they did not long for worldly riches, but they desired heavenly treasures.

2. Finally, when they heard the Lord saying, "Come after me" [see Matt 4:19, 22], immediately they left their nets, their father, and all their material resources, and followed him. Here they proved to be true sons of Abraham because by a similar pattern they followed the Savior on hearing God's voice [see Gen 12:1–4]. For they immediately left behind their physical livelihood in order to seek eternal rewards. They left behind their earthly father that they might have a heavenly Father. Hence it was not without reason that they merited to be chosen. So the Lord chose fishermen, who in a better way of plying their fishing trade were converted from earthly to heavenly fishing, that they might catch the human race for salvation, like fish from the deep waters of error. This agrees with what the Lord himself said to them: "Come after me, and I will make you fishers of men" [Matt 4:19]. It was the very same thing he had promised earlier through Jeremiah the prophet when he said, "Behold, I shall send many fishermen, says the Lord, and they shall fish for them. And after this I will send out hunters and they shall hunt them" [Jer 16:16]. So we recognize that the apostles are called not only fishermen but also hunters: fishermen, for in the nets of the gospel preaching they catch all believers like fish out of the world; hunters, for by heavenly hunting they catch for salvation those people who are roving about in the error of this world, as though in the woods, and who are living like wild animals. And long ago through David the Holy Spirit had shown the grace of these fishermen when he said, "They that go down to the sea in ships do business in many waters. They have seen the works of the Lord and his wonders in the deep" [Ps 107:23–24]. Isaiah too reports of them in a similar fashion: "And they shall fly in the ships of foreigners, at the same time despoiling the sea from the rising of the sun, and they shall lay their hands first on Idumea and Moab; but the children of Ammon shall first obey. And God shall make desolate the sea of Egypt" [Isa 11:14–15]. The "ships of foreigners" then signify the churches gathered from the nations through which the apostles "despoil the sea of Egypt," that is, this world, by faith in the divine preaching. Whence he said that the "children of Ammon obeyed first," namely Cornelius the centurion, and those who first believed with him from the Gentiles,

when the apostle Peter preached [see Acts 10]. But to "make desolate the sea of Egypt" properly means to overthrow the error of the world and the worship of idols, which happens daily through the apostolic preaching.

3. And so, by the preaching of these men, believers are caught daily leading to life. And consider how different this heavenly fishing of the apostles is from earthly fishing. For fish, when caught, die. People are caught in order to live, according to what the Lord says to Peter when he caught a huge multitude of fish: "Do not be afraid: from now on you will be giving life to men" [Luke 5:10].[58] Ezekiel too clearly shows that these gospel fishermen catch fish in order that they may live: "And there shall be there very many fish, for this water goes there, and it shall save [them], and everything on which the river shall come shall live. And fishermen shall sit there; and there shall be a place to dry out their nets upon; and the fishes thereof [shall be] as the fishes of the great sea, a very great multitude" [Ezek 47:9–10]. And so this is a wonderful form of fishing and these are wonderful fisherman who do not fish for the death of those they catch but for life. In the earthly example it is the fish who are not caught that live; in this other form of fishing, those who do not deserve to be caught die. The prophet shows clearly in the passage recorded above how this fishing of fish catches those it catches for life, when he says, "For this water goes thither, and it shall heal[59] [them], and every fish[60] on which the river shall come shall live" [Ezek 47:9]. Here the prophet surely is not speaking of that water that is common to everyone, nor of some earthly river, but he is speaking of the water of saving baptism and of the river of the gospel preaching, by which believers are restored unto life. Do you want to know which water this is that heals, cures, and gives life? Listen to the Lord speaking in the gospel: "Whoever drinks from the water that I give him, will not thirst forever, but it will become in him a font of water welling up to eternal life" [John 4:13–14]. Again, do you want to recognize what this river is in which one is made to live? Hear the prophet saying, "The force of the river gladdens the city of God" [Ps 46:4]. So then, we are caught by these fishermen from the sea of the world, thus are we drawn out from the deep waters of error, in order that we may be reborn in the water of baptism, and having been cleansed by the gospel river, let us abide unto life.

4. Then it follows, "And Jesus went around all of Galilee" [and the rest up to] "and across the Jordan" [Matt 4:23–25]. Earlier Isaiah predicted this would happen when he said, "He himself took

our infirmities and cured our sickness" [Isa 53:4; cf. Matt 8:17]. For it was for this purpose that the doctor of life and heavenly physician Christ the Lord had come, in order that by his authoritative teaching he might educate people to life and with his heavenly medicine cure the sickness of body and soul; that he might free bodies possessed by the devil, and call back those persons afflicted by various infirmities to true and complete health. For by the word of divine power he cured the ailments of bodies, but by the medicine of heavenly teaching he healed the wounds of souls.[61] David clearly showed that the wounds of the soul are healed by God alone, when he said, "Bless the Lord, O my soul, and forget not all his repayments" [Ps 103:2].[62] And he added, "Who forgives your iniquities, who heals all your diseases" [Ps 103:3]. He is the true and perfect physician, therefore, who gives healing to the body and restores the soul to health, our Lord and Savior, who is blessed in the ages of ages. Amen [see Rom 1:25; 2 Cor 11:31].

Tractate 17 on Matthew 5:1–12[63]

I.**1.** It then follows, "Seeing the crowds, he went up on a mountain and sat down. His disciples came to him, and opening his mouth, he taught them, saying, Blessed are the poor in spirit, for theirs is the kingdom of heaven" [Matt 5:1–3], and the rest that follows. Ready to lead his disciples from earthly and humble things to those that are high and lofty, the Lord climbed up a mountain—specifically the Mount of Olives[64]—in order to show the gift of his divine mercy by the very significance of this name. **2.** The Lord went up the mountain, therefore, that he might give the precepts of the heavenly commandments to his disciples, who are to leave behind earthly things and seek the things high up [see Col 3:1], as though already placed on high. He went up that he might now give the divine gift of the long foreseen blessings, according to what David had earlier declared when he said, "For indeed he who gave the law will give blessings" [Ps 84:7]. **3.** And that he might more openly show the grace of the apostles and the author of this very great blessing, he went on to say, "They shall walk from strength to strength; the God of gods shall be seen in Zion" [Ps 84:7], that is to say, the Son of God, who gave blessings to the apostles on Zion. For on this mountain he gave his apostles a blessing, he who had once given the law of Moses on Mount Sinai, proving that he was the author of both laws. This agrees with what the Lord himself makes clear through Jeremiah when he says, "And I will give them a new covenant, not like the one I gave long ago to their fathers, when I led them from the land of Egypt, but this is the covenant that I will give them: I will write my laws on their hearts and I will write them on their minds" [Jer 31:31–33]. **4.** And indeed when the law was given long ago on the mountain, the people were forbidden to draw close [see Exod 19:12]. But now, as the Lord was teaching on the mountain, no one is forbidden. Rather, all are invited to listen, because there is severity in the law and grace in the gospel [see John 1:17]. In the former, terror is instilled in the unbelievers; in the latter, a gift of blessings is poured out on the believers. **5.** If therefore you too want to receive blessings from the Lord, forsake an earthly way of life, seek a higher life; ascend to the height of faith like a mountain, that you may deserve to be rightly blessed by the Lord. But let us see what now these words of blessings are.[65]

II.**1.** "Blessed are the poor in spirit, for theirs is the kingdom of heaven" [Matt 5:3]. We know many poor people, indeed, but they are not blessed merely because they are poor. For the distress of poverty does not make each of us blessed, but faith from poverty accompanied by devotion. For we know many indeed who lack worldly resources, yet they do not cease sinning and are estranged from faith in God. Clearly we cannot call these people blessed. **2.** And therefore we ought to inquire just who these blessed are of whom the Lord says, "Blessed are the poor in spirit, for theirs is the kingdom of heaven." Surely he means that those poor persons are blessed who have willed to be poor in the world, by showing contempt for the riches of the world and by having spurned the material resources of the age, in order to become rich in God. Indeed, such people seem to be poor in the sight of the world, but they are rich in God, needy in the world, but wealthy in Christ. **3.** The apostles were the first to offer us an example of this blessed poverty in themselves. They deserved to be his disciples by their showing contempt for all their worldly resources and by immediately following the Lord's voice [see Mark 1:16–18]. Even in the times of the apostles we find this kind of poor people, who as the first believers sold all their possessions and obtained riches by this form of poverty of being devoted to the Lord [see Acts 2:45]. **4.** And this is why the apostle shows that heavenly wealth consists in this kind of poverty, when he says, "As having nothing, and possessing everything" [2 Cor 6:10]. After all, this is why Peter, when he went up to the temple and was asked for alms by the lame man, said, "Silver and gold I do not have; but what I have I give you: In the name of the Lord Jesus Christ rise and walk" [Acts 3:6]. **5.** O truly blessed poverty, which, though it has none of the resources of the world, gives generously only from heaven! To be sure, he does not give silver and gold, but he restores health to the body, which is more than all riches. He did not have the image of Caesar on the coin he could give [see Matt 22:20–21]; but he refashioned the image of Christ in the man. The Lord is speaking of poor people like this in the present passage. David also testifies about them in many passages, when he says, "The poor are needy and shall be satisfied; and their heart will live in the age of the age" [Ps 22:26]. And again, "He will judge the poor of the people and save the children of the poor" [Ps 72:4]. And again, "This poor man cried, and the Lord heard him" [Ps 34:6]. **6.** The Lord is showing that the kingdom of heaven belongs to those who are poor like this, who for the sake of religion and faith have made themselves poor, in order to possess the riches of the Holy Spirit [see Matt 7:11; Luke 11:13]. Or certainly he calls the poor blessed who are not puffed up by any of the devil's pride [see 1 Tim 3:6], they are not extolled by any ambition of the world, but they preserve the humility of the Spirit with the devotion of faith.[66] Hence David says in the psalm, "A sacrifice to God is an afflicted spirit; God does not spurn a contrite and humble heart" [Ps 51:17]. Those who are poor in spirit like this then are blessed before God.

III.**1.** Then he says, "Blessed are those who mourn, for they shall be consoled" [Matt 5:5].[67] He speaks here of those who mourn as he had done of the poor higher up. The blessed of whom he speaks are not those deeply mourning over the death of a spouse or the loss of dear children.[68] Rather, he is indicating those blessed persons who either strive to atone for the sins they have committed by a constant tearful weeping, or who with a pious, duty-bound sentiment do not cease to mourn over the iniquity of the world and the transgressions of sinners. **2.** To those who mourn in a holy way like this, therefore, not without reason the Lord promises the consolation of eternal rejoicing. After all, after his sin saint David even drenched his own couch with a constant tearful weeping, saying, "I will wash my bed every night, I will drench my couch with tears" [Ps 6:6]. And again, "My tears were my bread day and night, when it is said to me daily, Where is your God?" [Ps 42:3]. **3.** And again, "I ate ashes like bread, and I mingled my drink with weeping" [Ps 102:9]. And again, "You will feed us with bread of tears, and will cause us to drink tears by measure" [Ps 80:5]. Do you want to know the pious mourning of the saints? Listen to the statement of the prophet Samuel, that he will mourn for King Saul until the day of his own death [see 1 Sam 15:35]. Jeremiah, too, while weeping bitterly for the sins of the people, says the following: "My eyes shall pour down rivers of water, for the contrition of my people" [Lam 3:48]. And again: "Who will give water to my head, and a fountain of tears to my eyes? Then I would weep for this people day and night" [Jer 9:1]. **4.** Daniel too is afflicted with deep mourning for the sins of the people, as he himself attests when he says, "And I was mourning for three weeks of days, eating no bread and drinking no wine" [Dan 10:2–3]. The holy apostle too weeps bitterly for some of the Corinthians with a similar grief, saying, "And I shall come to you to mourn many of them that sinned before and have not done penance for the uncleanness and fornication and lasciviousness that they have committed" [2 Cor 12:21]. **5.** The Lord compensates mourning of this sort, then, with the consolation of everlasting joy. This agrees with what Isaiah related when he said, "To give to them that mourn in Zion glory instead of ashes, the oil of gladness to the mourners, the garment of glory for the spirit of sadness" [Isa 61:3]. This is also why David says, "You have turned my mourning into joy for me, you have torn up my sackcloth, and girded me with gladness" [Ps 30:11].

IV.**1.** Then it says, "Blessed are the meek, for they shall possess the earth as an inheritance" [Matt 5:4]. The graces of the divine promises differ because the degrees of merits differ. Thus he says, "Blessed are the meek, for they shall possess the earth." The meek are gentle people, humble and modest, simple in faith and patient of every injury, who have been instructed by the precepts of the gospel to imitate the example of the Lord's gentleness, who says in the gospel, "Learn from me, for I am meek and humble in heart" [Matt 11:29]. **2.** Finally, Moses long ago found the greatest favor before God because he was meek. For that is what is written of him: "And Moses was meek beyond all men who were on the earth" [Num 12:3]. This is why David says in the psalm, "Lord, remember David, and all his meekness" [Ps 132:1]. **3.** He shows that meek people like this are blessed, to whom not in the present life but in the future he has promised the possession of this blessed land, of which we read the statement in the psalm: "But the meek shall possess the land, and they shall delight in a multitude of peace" [Ps 37:11]. And again: "Those who wait for the Lord shall possess the land as an inheritance" [Ps 37:9]. And the Holy

Spirit testifies to this through Solomon when he says, "For the upright shall dwell in the earth, and the holy shall dwell in it" [Prov 2:21]. **4.** The Lord is pointing to these as the meek who are blessed, who follow the Lord's mildness and gentleness. They will enjoy the everlasting inheritance of this blessed land as their possession. But he is speaking in particular of the land of our body in which [land] the transfigured saints, according to the apostle's statement, will reign in glory with eternal happiness [see Phil 3:21; Rev 5:10; 20:4, 6].[69]

V.**1.** Then he says, "Blessed are those who hunger and thirst for justice, for they shall be satisfied" [Matt 5:6]. He taught that we must seek after justice, but not with a desire that is unserious and not with passionate ardor that is fleeting. Indeed, he calls those persons blessed who in their search for justice burn with passionate longing internally, in their hunger and thirst. For if each one of us hungers and thirsts for justice with desire, we can do nothing else but think and seek after justice. For one who is hungry and thirsty necessarily eagerly longs for that for which he hungers and thirsts. **2.** Rightly, then, the one who is the heavenly bread and the fountain of living water [see John 6:41, 51; 4:10, 14] promises in return to those who thus hunger and thirst in such a manner the satisfaction of this perpetual refreshment: "Blessed are those who hunger and thirst for justice, for they shall be satisfied." This surely is that justice of faith that comes from God and Christ, of which the apostle says, "The justice of God through faith in Jesus Christ to all and upon all who believe in him" [Rom 3:22]. **3.** And surely it is our Lord and Savior himself, who according to the apostle "became for us justice and sanctification and redemption" [1 Cor 1:30]. The blessed always burn with a longing for him, as for food and drink, in accordance with what the Lord himself attests through Solomon, speaking under the persona of Wisdom: "They who eat me will yet be hungry, and they who drink me will yet be thirsty" [Sir 24:21]. **4.** We likewise should always hunger and thirst for this justice, then, that we may deserve to be satiated with the food of perpetual refreshment. But he spoke well when he added in the present passage, "Blessed are those who hunger for justice," for there are others who hunger not for justice but for injustice, namely those who long for gold and silver, who yearn for wealth and secular honors and who are never satisfied by earthly resources and the desires of the flesh. But those who are like this are not blessed, but are wretched, since to them is owed not the hope of the promised glory but the punishment of damnation.

VI.**1.** Then he says, "Blessed are the merciful, for God will be merciful to them" [Matt 5:7]. The Lord challenges us to practice mercy in a great number of testimonies indeed, both in the Old Testament and in the New. But as a summary of the faith, we deem it enough and more than enough what the Lord himself in the present passage brings forth with his own voice, when he says, "Blessed are the merciful, for God will be merciful to them." **2.** The Lord of mercies says that the merciful are blessed, showing that no one can earn God's mercy unless he is merciful himself. This is why he also says in another passage, "Be merciful, just as your Father who is in heaven is merciful" [Luke 6:36]. **3.** Then he says, "Blessed are the pure of heart, for they shall see God" [Matt 5:8]. The pure of heart are those who have gotten rid of sin's filth, have cleansed themselves of all the pollution of the flesh, and have pleased God through works of faith and justice. This agrees with what David testifies in a psalm when he says, "Who will climb up the Lord's mountain, or who will stand in his holy place? The one with innocent hands and a pure heart, who has not lifted up his soul in vain" [Ps 24:3–4]. **4.** And David, rightly knowing that God can be seen only with a pure heart, prays as follows in the psalm: "Create in me a clean heart, O God, and renew a right spirit within me" [Ps 51:10]. So the Lord shows that it is pure-hearted people like this who are blessed. They are the ones who, living by faith in the Lord with a pure mind and unstained conscience, will win the right to see the God of glory in the heavenly kingdom to come, "no longer in a mirror and in a riddle, but face to face" [1 Cor 13:12], as the apostle related. **5.** For although now we contemplate God with the eyes of faith, yet we cannot see his brightness in view of the weakness of the flesh; but then we will see him, when we have received immortality and have been transformed into heavenly glory, and we will begin to look upon the immortal God with immortal eyes.[70] And at that time, the following Scripture will be truly fulfilled in us: "As we have heard, so too we have seen in the city of the Lord of powers" [Ps 48:8]. **6.** When the same David showed the glory of the time to come in which [glory] the saints will dwell with God, not without cause did he relate the following: "And yet the just shall acknowledge you, and the upright shall dwell with your face" [Ps 140:13].

VII.**1.** Then he says, "Blessed are the peacemakers, for they shall be called children of God" [Matt 5:9]. The peacemakers are those who, standing apart from the stumbling block of disagreement and discord, guard the love of fraternal charity and the peace of the church under the unity of the Catholic faith. In the gospel the Lord particularly urges his disciples to guard this peace, saying, "I give you my peace; I leave you peace" [John 14:27]. **2.** David earlier testified that the Lord would give this peace to his church, saying, "I will listen to what the Lord speaks in me, for he will speak peace to his people and over his holy ones and to those who turn to him" [Ps 85:8]. The apostle also warns about guarding this peace when he says, "Preserving the unity of the Spirit with the bond of peace" [Eph 4:3; cf. Rom 12:18]. **3.** And again, "May the peace of God that surpasses all understanding guard your hearts and bodies from evil" [Phil 4:7; cf. 2 Thess 3:3; 1 Pet 3:10–11]. For the apostle shows the Hebrews that nothing is so critical to the servants of God, so salutary for the church, as the preservation of charity, as the esteeming of peace, without which one cannot see God. He says, "Above all esteem peace, without which none of us will be able to see God" [Heb 12:14[71]]. **4.** Thus it is fitting for us to preserve peace in the church with all zeal and devotion and to summon back with zeal for peace and faith those who are estranged from peace to the church's charity, as far as it lies within us.[72] This agrees with the example of the prophet who says, "I was peaceable with those who hated peace; when I spoke with them, they fought against me for no reason" [Ps 120:7]. It is fitting that in the gospel as well, in the exultation of the angels who were proclaiming the Lord's nativity, this voice came that is reported: "Glory to God in the highest, and peace on earth to people of good will" [Luke 2:14]. **5.** Of this peace David related, "Those who love you have great peace, and they have no stumbling block" [Ps 119:165]. And Isaiah likewise says, "And I shall set your children in great peace and you will be built in justice" [Isa 54:13–14]. For if the Son of God deemed it fitting to receive flesh and suffer in order to make us at peace with God through the blood of his cross [see Col 1:20], surely, in accordance with what the apostle has related, we ought to be peaceable in all things.[73] Then we would truly deserve to have the God of peace himself in us [see Phil 4:9]. **6.** For this is written: "His place has been in peace, and his dwelling place in Zion" [Ps 76:2]. And so, not only will we be children of God, but "heirs of God, and coheirs of Christ" [Rom 8:17]. For the apostle said this: "If sons of God, also heirs of God, and coheirs of Christ" [Rom 8:17].

VIII.**1.** Then he says, "Blessed are those who suffer persecution for the sake of justice, for theirs is the kingdom of heaven" [Matt 5:10]. Not without cause did the Lord mention higher up hungering and thirsting for justice [see Matt 5:6]. He instructs us so to thirst in our desire for justice that for its sake we should despise the world's persecutions, the punishments of the body, and death itself. **2.** He is proclaiming the martyrs above all, those who for the justice of faith and the name of Christ endure persecutions in this world. To them a great hope is promised, namely, the possession of the kingdom of heaven. The apostles were chief examples of this blessedness, and all the just people who for the sake of the justice of the law were afflicted with various forms of persecution. By the merit of their faith they have reached the heavenly kingdom.

IX.**1.** Then he says, "Blessed shall you be when men persecute you and reproach you and shall speak every evil against you. Rejoice on that day and exult; for I tell you that your reward in heaven is great; for thus their fathers treated even the prophets" [Matt 5:11–12]. **2.** Not only should we patiently endure all the criminal treachery of the persecutors that can be contrived in a time of persecution for Christ's name against the just, and the various reproaches that can be heaped upon us, and the punishments that can be applied to the body, but we should even welcome them with the joy of exultation in view of the coming glory. **3.** For he says this: "Rejoice in that day and exult; I tell you that your reward in heaven is great." How glorious is the endurance of this persecution, the reward for which the Lord says is laid up in heaven! And so, taking into consideration the reward of the proposed glory, we should be ready with devout faith for every endurance of suffering, so that we may deserve to be made sharers in the glory of the prophets and apostles, through Christ our Lord, who is blessed in the ages of ages. Amen [see Rom 1:25; 2 Cor 11:31].

Tractate 18 on Matthew 5:13

I.**1.** Then he says, "You are the salt of the earth; but if the salt of the earth loses its savor, it is good for nothing except to be thrown out and trampled by people" [Matt 5:13]. The Lord names his disciples the "salt of the earth." And let us see what the Lord wants to be understood about his apostles under the comparison with this term. In order to be able to observe this in more detail, we should first ask carefully what this salt is, and whose earth, and then under what conditions and use does it help. **2.** We need now to discuss the nature and use of this salt as well, so that when this is known, we may more easily arrive at the force of the Lord's statement by means of a spiritual understanding. The nature of salt then is that it comes into being from water, the sun's heat, and the blowing of the wind; and from that which was, a new species of thing is produced. So, too, the apostles and all believers have been reborn unto God through the water of baptism, by faith in Christ, who metaphorically is called the sun of justice [see Mal 4:2], and through the inspiration of the Holy Spirit. They have transitioned from an earthly to a heavenly birth. **3.** Whence not without cause does the Lord call the holy apostles the salt of the earth. And whose earth? It is easy to know this, namely the earth of our body, which they seasoned with the wisdom of the gospel preaching, since long ago it was insipid and unsalted by the mind-set of vanity. For they themselves became the salt of our earth, since through them we received the word of wisdom, and by a heavenly birth we were changed into a spiritual nature. **4.** Therefore just as this salt, that is, the salt of the earth, is indiscriminately necessary to everyone, that is, to kings and potentates, to rich and poor, to slaves and masters; so too is the word of heavenly wisdom, which was preached by the apostles: it is necessary to everyone for life. "For all need the grace of God" [Rom 3:23], according to the apostle. For just as we do not conduct this present life without the use of salt, so too we cannot arrive at that eternal life without the gift of divine wisdom.

II.**1.** But since we have already spoken about the nature and grace of salt according to the spiritual understanding, now we should treat of salt's virtue as well. Thus he says, "You are the salt of the earth." And so, just as salt, when it goes to work on some meat, does not allow it to decay, removes the stench, purges out impurities, and prevents maggots from being born; so too the heavenly grace and faith that is given through the apostles works in the same manner in us. **2.** For it removes the corrupting decay of fleshly lust, it purges away the impurities of sins, it banishes the odor of an evil manner of life, it prevents the maggots of transgressions from being born, that is, libidinous and deadly pleasures from arising from the body. It preserves our bodies likewise from that immortal maggot who torments sinners with constant punishment, of which it is written, "Their worm shall not die and their fire shall not be quenched" [Isa 66:24; Mark 9:43, 45, 47]. **3.** And just as salt is put on the outside but works to the inside through the virtue of its nature, so too heavenly grace penetrates thoroughly both the outer and interior parts of the human being, and it preserves the whole person unscathed by sin and uncorrupted. But by a prefiguration of the law it was likewise shown long ago that these people who are seasoned with the salt of heavenly wisdom are worthy of God, namely in that every sacrifice offered to God was seasoned with salt. **4.** This is precisely what the evangelist recorded when he said, "Every sacrifice shall be seasoned with salt" [Mark 9:48; Lev 2:13]. He was showing that a person who has been infused with the virtue of heavenly wisdom truly becomes a sacrifice that is worthy of God. **5.** Whence not without cause when the Lord rebuked Jerusalem, or rather, the synagogue, through the prophet Ezekiel, among other things he says, "You were not washed in water, nor salted with salt" [Ezek 16:4]. He was declaring that they would not receive the grace of saving baptism for the washing away of their sins, nor would they receive faith in the heavenly wisdom. And so, if someone uses this heavenly salt, he will be seasoned; but the one who refuses will lose his savor. And not without cause the apostle has issued the warning that our speech should always be seasoned in grace with salt [see Col 4:6].

III.**1.** Still, we find a foreshadowing of the grace and virtue of this salt also in the Books of Kingdoms. When there were harmful waters in Jericho that caused sterility, saint Elisha the prophet was sought to provide a saving cure for these same waters [see 2 Kgs 2:19–22]. Then saint Elisha, not unaware of the heavenly mystery, said to bring him a clay pot and to put salt in it. And he went and threw the salt into the outlet of the waters; and thus the sterile nature of the waters was cured and was changed to fecundity. We recognize by the plain account that this was carried out as a sign pointing to the coming truth. **2.** For Revelation has clearly related that waters signify nations, when it says, "The waters you have seen are the peoples and Gentiles and crowds and nations" [Rev 17:15]. They were unable to be healed or to receive a wholesome remedy in any other way but that salt be cast into a clay pot, that is, that God's wisdom should receive a human body [see 1 Cor 1:24]. When it reached the outlet of the waters, that is, the outlet of human death, for the sake of our salvation, then the nature of all believers, which had been sterile in respect to the fruit of seed, was changed into the fecundity of faith and justice. **3.** Whence not without reason the Lord calls his apostles the salt of the earth, whom he filled with divine and heavenly wisdom springing from himself. But as he testified that they are the salt of the earth, so too they are the light of the world [see Matt 5:14]. For although he confessed that he himself is the light of the world [see John 8:12], nevertheless, likewise he willed to name his disciples with this name, not taking away from himself what was his own, but freely bestowing what was his own upon them as well. For the true and eternal light freely gives what is his own without any detriment to his own proper nature. **4.** We know, of course, that some salts are produced from the earth, but even this point of similarity matches the persona of the apostles.[74] For although they seemed to be born from the earth of a human body, yet they already had begun to be something else through faith in Christ, so that they were no longer deemed earth but salt of the earth; for out of flesh they became spiritual, that is, in order that they could season the unsalted hearts of believers by faith.

IV.**1.** He says, "You are the salt of the earth; but if the salt loses its savor, how will it be seasoned? It is good for nothing but to be thrown out and trampled by men" [Matt 5:13]. He shows that those who have once been instructed by the faith and heavenly wisdom ought to remain faithful and steadfast. They "lose their savor" if they forsake the faith and divine wisdom, or if they plunge headlong into heresy, or return to the folly of pagans. And so he says, "But if the salt loses its savor, with what will it be seasoned?" For people of this sort who have lost their savor by the devil's deceit and have lost the grace of faith are "good for nothing." **2.** Though they could have seasoned other non-believers, who were still foreign to the faith, with the word of divine preaching, they instead showed themselves to be useless. After all, Judas Iscariot (*Scariothes*) was made of salt of this sort; but later on he rejected the divine wisdom and turned from being an apostle into an apostate [see Matt 27:3–5]. Not only did he become of no use to others, but he became wretched and useless even to himself. **3.** And that is why the Lord went on to say, "It is good for nothing except to be thrown out and trampled by men." For those who are like this must be deemed no longer to be faithful members of the household, but people who are cast out of the church, foreigners, and enemies of the faith. Whence, too, Judas became an enemy of the truth, having once been a member of the household of faith. And so, since those who are like this have been cast outside of the church, it is inevitable that they be trampled by the various vices of the flesh and by various pleasures of the world; and that is what he says: "It is good for nothing but to be cast out and trampled by men." **4.** Even Solomon has spoken about what it means to be trampled by men in his own book, when he said of the harlot woman, "An immoral woman is trampled on by men who pass by like dung on the road" [Sir 9:10 Vlg]. Since therefore we have already been seasoned by the apostolic salt, let us persevere with such fine seasoning of spiritual grace that we too may deserve to be called the salt of the earth by Christ Jesus our Lord, who is blessed in the ages of ages. Amen [see Rom 1:25; 2 Cor 11:31].

Tractate 19 on Matthew 5:14–16

I.1. Then he says, "You are the light of the world. A city set on a mountain cannot be hidden, nor do they light a lamp and place it under a bushel, but upon a lampstand, so that it may give light to all who are in the house" [Matt 5:14–15]. The Lord has called his disciples the "salt of the earth" because they seasoned with heavenly wisdom the hearts of the human race that had lost its savor due to the devil. Now he also calls them the "light of the world." For, illumined by his very own self who is the true and eternal light, they too become light in the darkness. **2.** For since he is the "sun of justice" [Mal 4:2], he fittingly also names his disciples "light of the world." For through them, as if through shining rays, he has poured the light of his knowledge on the entire world. For by showing the light of truth, they scattered the darkness of error from people's hearts. Indeed, we ourselves have been illumined by them and have become light from being darkness, as the apostle says: "For you were once darkness, but now light in the Lord; walk as children of the light" [Eph 5:8]. **3.** And again: "You are not sons of night and of darkness, but you are sons of light and sons of God" [1 Thess 5:5]. Fittingly, too, saint John has borne witness in his epistle and said, "God is light" [1 John 1:5], and he who abides in God is in the light [see 1 John 4:16; 2:10], "just as he is in the light" [1 John 1:7]. Therefore, since we rejoice that we have been liberated from the darkness of error, we ought always to walk in the light as sons of light.

II.1. And he added, "A city set on a mountain cannot be hidden." Here he is signifying the church as the city. In many places the divine Scriptures testify about it, and David in particular speaks of it when he says, "Glorious things are said of you, O city of God" [Ps 87:2]. And again, "The force of the river gladdens the city of God" [Ps 46:4]. And again, "As we have heard, so have we also seen, in the city of the Lord of virtues, in the city of our God; God has founded it forever" [Ps 48:8]. **2.** And in order for the Holy Spirit to show clearly that he was speaking about this city, he made mention of the very mountain as well, saying, "In the city of our God, on his holy mountain" [Ps 48:1]. The Lord speaks of this through Isaiah when he says, "Behold, I will prepare carbuncle stone for you, and sapphire for your foundations; and I will make your buttresses jasper, and your gates crystal stone, and your circumference chosen stones, and [I will cause] all your sons [to be] taught of God" [Isa 54:11–13]. **3.** And we have passed over many similar things, lest we become tedious to the readers, especially since the things that have been said suffice quite abundantly as attestation of this city. Therefore he shows the church as the city set on the mountain, established in heavenly glory upon its faith in our Lord and Savior. In its spiritual activity it rises above all the lowliness of its earthly weakness and has become conspicuous and glorious in the whole world. It is no longer obscured by the proclamation of the law, but through the doctrine of the gospel is seen in its open preaching.

III.1. And he added, "For neither do they light a lamp and place it under a bushel, but upon a lampstand so that it may give light to all who are in the house" [Matt 5:15]. And so, let us consider the rationale for this statement of the Lord. We know that a lamp is not lit in order to be placed under a bushel or to be concealed by any covering. If that happens, it will be of no use. But the reason it is lit on a lampstand is so that when it is set in an exposed location, it may expel the blind darkness of night and bring the benefit of its light to those who are in the house. **2.** The reason the Lord mentions this is for us to know that the reason we have been lit by the grace of faith and illumined by the light of the Spirit is so that we may shine spiritually like lamps through the works of faith and justice. And we are to illumine those who are found to be in the darkness of error, driving out the night of ignorance by the light of truth itself. This is why the apostle says, "Among whom you shine like lights in this world, holding on to the words of life" [Phil 2:15–16]. **3.** But if we do not do this, by our unbelief, to our own loss and that of others, we shall seem to be covering over and darkening with a kind of veil as it were the benefits that come from such a necessary light. We know and read that it was on this account that the one who wanted to cover up the talent he had received in order to make a profit in heavenly business, rather than give it to the bankers, incurred the punishment that was owed him [see Matt 25:25–30].

IV.**1.** And, therefore, this spiritual lamp that was set alight for the benefit of our salvation should always shine in us. For we have the lamp of the heavenly commandment and of spiritual grace of which David has spoken: "Your commandment is a lamp to my feet and a light to my paths" [Ps 119:105]. And Solomon says of it, "For the precept of the law is a lamp" [Prov 6:23]. The Lord testifies to it through Zephaniah the prophet as well: "And I will search Jerusalem with a lamp" [Zeph 1:12]. **2.** For he shows in this lamp the inextinguishable light of the law and of his grace, which must not be covered over or darkened by any veil of a blind mind, as the Jews and the heretics do, who strive to cover and conceal the clear light of the divine proclamation with perverse interpretations. They preach faithlessness instead of faith, and they veil over the light of truth with the darkness of error. **3.** Whence we must not conceal this lamp of the law and of faith, but it should always be set in the church as on the lampstand for the salvation of many, in order that both we may enjoy the light of its truth and all believers may be illumined. The Holy Spirit exhorts us to view its light through Isaiah as well when he says, "Come, let us walk in the light of the Lord. For he has forsaken his own people, the house of Israel" [Isa 2:5–6]. Of this light the blessed Peter also testified in his epistle and said, "Who rescued you from darkness and called you into his wonderful light" [Col 1:13; 1 Pet 2:9]. **4.** Whence also Zechariah the prophet, in order to clarify among the other mysteries of this spiritual light and of the heavenly lampstand, which was shown as a figure of the church, testified that he saw a golden lampstand as well, together with its lamps [see Zech 4:2]. These were shown to him in view of the merit of his prophecy. For the lampstand together with its lamps shined with constant light even in the tabernacle of testimony, as a witness to the coming truth [see Exod 25:31 (?)]. **5.** The rationale for this matter was hidden from the Jews to be sure, as were all the mysteries of the law, but it has now been manifested to us. For we know that in the lampstand a type of the true and eternal light was shown, that is, of the Holy Spirit who always illumines the whole body of the church by his manifold grace. Whence, too, the Lord exhorts his disciples in the gospel among other things that they should keep their lamps burning in their hands. He says, "Let your loins be girded and your lamps burning" [Luke 12:35]. **6.** Surely one is to understand that the Lord commanded this not in a physical sense but by the spiritual reckoning. For since in the lamp God's commandment or the light of the law is signified, therefore we are commanded to carry a lamp in our hands, in order that when illumined by the grace of the Holy Spirit, we may shine with works of faith and justice. This agrees with what Solomon has related: "The ways of the just will shine like light; for they go on and shine until the day rises" [Prov 4:18].

V.**1.** Fittingly, then, when the Lord mentioned a lamp in the present passage and said, "They do not light a lamp and place it under a bushel, but upon a lampstand, so that it may give light to all who are in the house" [Matt 5:15], he went on to say, "So let your light shine before others, that they may see your good works and glorify your Father who is in heaven" [Matt 5:16]. For God is glorified in us among unbelievers and the unfaithful, if we live according to the divine precepts, if we shine with good works. **2.** And this is why the holy apostle says, "Glorify and carry God in your body" [1 Cor 6:20; cf. Phil 1:20]. And blessed Peter gives a similar warning in his epistle: "So that when they speak against you as evildoers, they may, by the works of justice that they shall behold in you, glorify our God" [1 Pet 2:12]. But this can be understood in another way, since the spiritual understanding is manifold. Thus in the lamp we may recognize the Lord himself being signified, owing to the humility of the body he assumed. **3.** He is indeed according to the glory of his divinity called the sun of justice [see Mal 4:2], but according to the mystery of the body he assumed he is likewise shown as a lamp; for though he was the God of glory and of eternal majesty, he appeared in humble form in this world as a lamp. And not without reason as a lamp, since a lamp is accustomed to shine through the night. And so, for that reason he appeared humble in this world, as a lamp, so that he could drive out the darkness of error and the night of ignorance from our hearts, we who spent our time while placed in this world as in a night. **4.** A lamp of this sort then, that is, the incarnation of Christ, is shown from the law and the prophets, no longer darkened by the preaching of the law, as though covered by a bushel, nor by the unbelief of the scribes and Pharisees, as if covered by some vessel of faithlessness.[75] But set on the cross, as on a lampstand, it gives light to the entire house of the church. **5.** And so, according to the mystery of the incarnation, he is a lamp; but according to the glory of his divinity he is sun of justice [see Mal 4:2]. Finally, in the very lampstand of the cross he shined like the sun, when through the preaching of the apostles, as with certain sunbeams, our Lord and Savior brought the most brilliant light of the knowledge of himself to the whole world, he who is blessed in the ages. Amen.

Tractate 20 on Matthew 5:17–20

I.1. Then he says, "Do not think that I have come to destroy the law or the prophets; I did not come to destroy but to fulfill" [Matt 5:17]. The Son of God, who is the author of the law and the prophets, did not come to completely destroy the law or the prophets. For he himself through Moses gave the people the law that was to be handed down, and he inspired the prophets with the Holy Spirit for the preaching of the things to come. Therefore he says, "I have come not to destroy the law or the prophets but to fulfill." **2.** Now he fulfilled the law and the prophets in this way: He brings to pass those things that had been written about him in the law and the prophets. Hence, when he drank the vinegar offered him on the cross, he said, "It is fulfilled" [John 19:30]. This shows clearly that everything written about him in the law and the prophets had been completed, even including the drinking of vinegar. He fulfills the law in every manner when he completed by the sign of his passion the mystery of the Passover and of the lamb, once shown in a figure. This is why the apostle says, "For Christ our Passover has been sacrificed" [1 Cor 5:7]. **3.** By receiving a body he fulfills the law, as he completed in the reckoning of the truth the sacrifices of the law and all the examples that prefigured him. Or certainly he fulfills the law when he confirms with the supplement of evangelical grace the precepts of the law he had given.[76] In what follows he proceeds to demonstrate that he had come to fulfill the law: "Until heaven and earth pass away, not one iota, and not a dot, shall be lost from the law until all is accomplished" [Matt 5:18]. **4.** Therefore we know how true and divine is the preaching of the law from the fact that the Lord reveals that not even one iota and one dot will be able to be lost from it. Although the mystery of the cross likewise could be understood in this iota and dot of the law, since the iota and dot show in themselves a kind of image of the cross, it could have been overlooked when preached by the law and the prophets with no explanation.[77]

II.1. Then he says, "Whoever breaks one of the least of these commandments and teaches this to men will be called least in the kingdom of heaven" [Matt 5:19]. While it is impious to break the least of the commandments, all the more so the great and most important ones. Hence the Holy Spirit affirms the same thing through Solomon, saying, "Whoever despises small things falls little by little" [Sir 19:1]. **2.** Consequently, nothing in the divine commandments should be broken, nothing altered, but everything must be preserved and taught with a faithful and devoted mind, that the glory of the heavenly kingdom may not be lost. For those things considered least important and insignificant in the judgment of unfaithful and worldly people are not small before God but essential. But the Lord shows that "he who teaches and does them" [Matt 5:19] will be great in the kingdom of heaven. **3.** For this reason, not only words but also deeds are to be carried out; and you should not only teach, but you should practice what you preach. And let us hear the Lord himself in the gospel rebuking such teachers who say and do not do: "Woe to you, scribes and Pharisees, hypocrites, for you load men with burdens, which they are unable to carry, but you yourselves do not touch these burdens with your finger" [Luke 11:46]. Whence the apostle also says, "It is not the hearers of the law who are just before God, but the doers of the law shall be justified" [Rom 2:13]. **4.** If he says this even of the hearers, what must be understood of the teachers? Whence Solomon says as well, "Be not hasty in your tongue, and in your deeds slack and remiss" [Sir 4:34]. And therefore it is proper that he who teaches offer himself as an example of faith and of an upright manner of life, as the apostle writes to Timothy: "Be a model to the faithful" [1 Tim 4:12]. **5.** And again: "Offering yourself as an example of good works, in justice, in chastity, in sobriety, in sound teaching" [Titus 2:7–8]. Hence even the very Son of God, who is the teacher and Lord of the law, as an example to us, willed to fulfill in reality all that he taught.

III.**1.** And he added, "Unless your justice surpasses that of the scribes and Pharisees, you will not enter the kingdom of heaven" [Matt 5:20]. He finds fault with the justice of the scribes and Pharisees, for they were not seeking the faith of the divine promise but human praise and worldly glory [see Matt 6:2; John 12:43]. We have an example of this in the arrogant and puffed up Pharisee, who, as it seemed to himself, preferred the merits of his own justice and shamelessly vaunted himself in God's sight with an elated mind and with arrogant words [see Luke 18:10–14]. **2.** Thus the scribes and Pharisees retained the outward form of justice, not in order to please God, but in order to seek the reputation of human glory, in order to acquire earthly gain and material comforts. And therefore the Lord exhorts us to go beyond that infamous justice of human praise, by means of works of heavenly justice and the merits of faith, through Christ our Lord, who is blessed in the ages. Amen.

TRACTATE 21 ON MATTHEW 5:21–24

I.**1.** It then follows, "You have heard that it was said to them of old, You shall not kill. But he who kills shall be liable to the judgment. But I say to you, If anyone is angry with his brother, he shall be liable to the judgment" [Matt 5:21–22]. This is what the Lord said: "I have not come to destroy the law but to fulfill" [Matt 5:17], that is, to add what was less, namely, to reform the precepts of the law for the better. **2.** And for this reason the holy apostle says, "Do we, then, destroy the law through faith? By no means! On the contrary, we establish the law" [Rom 3:31]. The law's commandments of justice were delivered to a people who were uncultivated and hardened, but the gospel precepts of consummated faith and heavenly justice are delivered to a perfect and faithful people. The law commands us not to kill. But the gospel commands us not to get angry without reason,[78] in order to remove every root of sin from our hearts, because anger can even lead to homicide. **3.** Whence not without reason blessed Job testified in his book to the following, saying, "Wrath kills the foolish one, and envy kills the one that has gone astray" [Job 5:2]. David too says the following: "Be angry, and do not sin, speak in your hearts, and feel compunction upon your beds" [Ps 4:4]. The holy apostle interpreted this testimony and said, "Let not the sun go down upon your anger, nor give room to the devil" [Eph 4:26–27]. **4.** Since therefore it is not allowed to be angry without reason, how much more so is the crime of murder forbidden! And since anger is held liable at the future judgment, what penalty do we think he will have who commits the crime itself?

II.**1.** "But he who says to his brother or sister, Raca, shall be liable to the council. But he who says, You fool, shall be liable to the Gehenna of fire" [Matt 5:22]. Thus the Lord teaches us to be perfect in every way, lest we be held liable to the coming judgment, even for careless and vain words [see Matt 12:36–37]. For he even forbids saying to one's brother or sister, "Raca," that is, empty and useless;[79] for he or she should not be called empty and useless who is full of faith and the Holy Spirit. **2.** Nor indeed should a brother or sister be named "fool" who has obtained the grace of divine wisdom by believing in Christ. Whence also when through Solomon the Holy Spirit spoke about the man of the gospel, he testified as follows and said, "Blessed is the one who has not slipped with the word of his mouth, and is not pricked with the grief of transgression" [Sir 14:1]. **3.** And on that account in another passage the same Solomon says, "Make bolts for your mouth and make a bar for your tongue and for your words" [Sir 28:28–29]. And again: "Circumcise from yourself a depraved mouth, and put far away from you unjust lips" [Prov 4:24]. And again: "Let not your mouth grow accustomed to lacking discipline, for therein is the grief of transgression" [Sir 23:17]. Whence also David says, "Place a guard on my mouth, O Lord, and a door around my lips" [Ps 141:3]. **4.** And again in another psalm, "I said, O Lord, I will guard my ways, that I sin not with my tongue" [Ps 39:1]. For as Solomon says, "The lips of the imprudent will be telling foolish things, and the word of the prudent will be weighed in the balance" [Sir 21:28]. And therefore in the gospel the Lord attested that we will render an account even for idle speech [see Matt 12:36]. For this reason, too, the apostle gives the following exhortation: "Let no evil speech proceed from your mouth, but only what is good for the edification of the faith" [Eph 4:29]. **5.** And again: "Let your speech be always seasoned in grace with salt, that you may know how you ought to respond to each person" [Col 4:6]. On this account we need to be on guard in all things, lest we experience the loss of our salvation by our familiarity with useless words.

III.**1.** Then he says, "If you offer your gift before the altar, and there remember that your brother or sister has something against you, leave your gift there, and go first and be reconciled with your brother or sister, and then you shall offer your gift" [Matt 5:23–24].[80] We know how much the Lord esteems fraternal love from the fact that he makes clear that a gift offered to God is not acceptable unless the giver of the gift to his brother puts aside his anger and becomes reconciled to him. **2.** Finally, we find that the reason God rejected the gifts offered by Cain is because he failed to observe the laws of charity, but harbored anger in his heart against his brother or sister [see Gen 4:1–8]. Hence, not without reason does the Lord in the gospel emphasize in many places that love of fraternal charity must be preserved above all, when he says, "A new commandment I give you, that you love one another" [John 13:34]. **3.** And again, "By this all men shall know that you are my disciples, if you have love for one another" [John 13:35]. Not unfittingly, the Lord also says through Zechariah the prophet,

"Render a just and peaceable judgment, and do not retain malice in your hearts toward one another" [Zech 8:16–17]. Through David he likewise testifies similarly: "Refrain from anger and forsake wrath" [Ps 37:8]. **4.** In the same way as well the Holy Spirit speaks through Solomon and says, "As a man you harbor anger against another man, and you seek healing from God? You yourself have no mercy on a man who is like yourself, and you plead to God on behalf of your own sins? And though you yourself are but flesh, you harbor anger, and you seek reconciliation with God? And who will pray for your transgressions?" [Sir 28:3–5]. **5.** And he added further and said, "Remember the last things and let your enmity cease" [Sir 28:6]. Hence too saint David, not ignorant of the gospel precept through the Holy Spirit, testified the following about himself and said, "If I have regarded iniquity in my heart, God will not hearken" [Ps 66:18]. **6.** For what is so pleasing to God, so necessary to our salvation, than what the Lord commands, not to harbor anger, to offer our gift to God with a peaceable spirit and a sincere conscience, as Abel first offered his? And the reason his gifts were received by God, whereas Cain's were rejected, is because Abel offered his gifts to the Lord with a sincere and pure mind, whereas Cain harbored anger against his brother. And therefore, since he was pleasing in his heart, he pleased him in his gift. **7.** For this reason, if we want our gifts to please God, we ought to banish wrath from our heart, to kill the malice against one's brother or sister that has been received, but to hold on to fraternal peace, to preserve charity, to esteem unanimity, to guard concord, in order that we may deserve to please the Lord, who is blessed in the ages. Amen.

Tractate 22 on Matthew 5:25–26

I.1. After this it follows, "Be in agreement with your adversary while you are with him on the way, lest perhaps the adversary deliver you to the judge, and the judge deliver you to the officer, and you be cast into prison. Amen I say to you, you shall not go out from thence till you repay the last penny" [Matt 5:25–26]. Some think the following is to be understood of this statement of the Lord.[81] An "adversary" like this is one who became an enemy by his own or someone else's fault. He must quickly be called back to peace and friendship, while we are "with him on the way," that is, during the course of the present life, lest when he has departed from the world, each one may begin to be brought to God as judge, as those who are unmindful of love and guilty of hostilities. He may be handed over by the judge to the officer, that is, to the one in charge of the torments, so that he can pay off the penalties owed for his sin by being thrown into the prison of Gehenna. **2.** But this explanation[82] does not seem to contain a complete account. For why would this be? If someone arises as an adversary from the brothers and sisters on account of the faith, would agreement in the very treachery have to be adopted to prevent continuance in such religious discord? We have adversaries and pagans who are opposed to our faith, who compel us sometimes during times of persecution to participate in criminal sacrifices. Must this be done on account of adversaries of this sort? Are we to adopt their will in a sacrilegious agreement, so that they do not continue as enemies? In their sacrilegious persuasion not only must we not consent, but we must resist with invincible faith.

II.**1.** Some even openly conjecture that the adversary here should be understood as the devil.[83] By what reckoning they affirm this, I do not follow. For how ought one to undertake an agreement with the devil, whose task it is to persuade, suggest, and twist everything against the faith, against salvation, against the divine religion? **2.** Unless perhaps it ought to be understood in this sense, that if perhaps some hostile persecutor and devil, who is the author of persecution, should will to inflict death on a Christian for the sake of Christ's name, one should gladly accommodate oneself in agreement in order to be handed over to death for Christ's sake, lest the same devil, who is our accuser, establish us as culpable before God of violating the faith and should make us subject to punishment. For the devil, though he is the author of every crime, nevertheless is also an accuser. For we read this statement about him in Revelation: "And the dragon, the accuser of our brethren, who accuses them in the sight of God day and night, was cast headlong" [Rev 12:10]. This persuader, this accuser, persuades in order to deceive; he accuses in order to condemn.

III.**1.** But others, whose explanation (*assertio*) seems to me to be more complete, believe that the adversary here must be understood as the Holy Spirit, who opposes the vices and desires of the flesh. As the apostle points out, "The flesh lusts against the Spirit, and the Spirit against the flesh; for these are opposed to each other, so that you do not do what you would" [Gal 5:17]. **2.** For the Spirit desires heavenly things; the flesh lusts after earthly things. The Spirit rejoices over spiritual gifts; the flesh is attracted to bodily vices. And this is why the apostle says, "Do not grieve the Holy Spirit of God, with whom you have been sealed for the day of redemption" [Eph 4:30].[84] Therefore, the Lord commands us to obey this adversary of sin and human error in all things, who suggests to us things that are just and holy, while we are with him on the way, that is, in the caravan of this present life, so that we may be able to have eternal peace and perpetual fellowship with him. **3.** But if someone does not obey the unspoken will of the Holy Spirit and shows himself to be resistant, doubtless a man of this sort, after his departure from this life, must be offered to the Son of God, who is the judge of the living and the dead, by whom he is handed over to the officer, that is, to the angel of torments, to be thrown into the prison of Gehenna. From there he will not be released until he pays back even the last penny, that is, discharges the entire penalty of the debt down to the last sin. **4.** Therefore in the present passage the Lord is understood to be speaking of that adversary who longs for our salvation by his opposition to our sins, who desires that we be in agreement with him in order that we become worthy of escaping the punishments of hell and of attaining to the heavenly kingdom. **5.** Solomon also testifies of him in his book when he says, "There is one, and there is not a second; and indeed, he has neither son nor brother" [Eccl 4:8]. And, "Two are better than one, they have a good reward for their labor; for if one falls, the other will lift up his fellow. Woe to him that is alone when he falls, for he does not have anyone to raise him up" [Eccl 4:9–10]. This shows that the flesh that deserves to have concord and fellowship with the Holy Spirit, when it falls into death, is raised up by the same Spirit in life and eternal glory. **6.** And therefore, "Woe to him that is alone when he falls, for he does not have anyone to raise him up," that is, flesh that due to its infidelity does not deserve to have fellowship with the Holy Spirit, is not raised up unto eternal life, but it is raised up unto everlasting punishment, by him who is the judge of the living and the dead, to whom is the praise and the glory in the ages of ages. Amen.

Tractate 23 on Matthew 5:27–30

I.1. Then he says, "You have heard that it was said to them of old, You shall not commit adultery. But I say to you, If anyone looks at a woman to lust for her, he has already committed adultery with her in his heart" [Matt 5:27–28]. Not without reason does saint David say the following: "You have commanded your commands to be kept exceedingly" [Ps 119:4]. So "exceedingly" that not only is adultery held to be a criminal act, so is lust. The law condemns adultery, but the gospel punishes even lust, which is the root of adultery. **2.** Hence the Holy Spirit attests to the same thing in many passages in Solomon when he says, "Go not after your lusts, but keep yourself from your pleasure. For if you give your soul to lust, she will make you a laughingstock to your enemies and to those that malign you" [Sir 18:30–31]. And again, "Turn away your face from a beautiful woman, and look not upon another's beauty" [Sir 9:8]. **3.** And after this he added, "Many have been reprobated by admiring the beauty of another woman; for conversation with her kindles as a fire" [Sir 9:8]. He said well "kindles as a fire," for it is by conversation with a woman of this sort that the desire of lust is set aflame like a fire. Therefore you should avoid such women, lest the flame of desire for her consumes you. **4.** On this account too Solomon says, "Let not the desire of beauty overcome you, neither be caught by your eyes, neither be captivated with your eyelids" [Prov 6:25]. And again he says, "Remove from me the lust of the belly and let not the lust to lie down together take hold of me; and do not hand me over to a soul that is irreverent and senseless" [Sir 23:6]. **5.** Let us also hear blessed Job, who showed himself to be a man of the gospel in all things, and fulfilled the Lord's command before he heard it. He testifies to the same thing concerning himself when he says, "If my foot has turned aside out of the way, or if my heart has followed my eye, and if too I have touched gifts with my hands, then let others eat my crops and let me be uprooted on the earth. If my heart has gone after another man's wife, and if I laid wait at her doors, then let my wife also please another. For it is the rage of anger and of an unclean spirit to defile [another] man's wife. It is a fire burning" [Job 31:7–12]. **6.** Therefore, since adultery is a grave sin, as a means of blotting out the root of this sin, lest our conscience be defiled, he has forbidden even lust, which is the source of adultery. This agrees with what blessed James relates in his epistle: "Lust gives birth to sin; but the lust of sin obtains death" [Jas 1:15]. For this reason too the Holy Spirit speaks concerning this through David: "Blessed shall he be who takes your little ones and dashes them against the rock" [Ps 137:9]. **7.** He is pointing to the blessed and truly evangelical person who kills the desires and lusts of the flesh that arise from human weakness, immediately before they grow, at the very beginning of their birth, through faith in Christ, who is called the rock [see 1 Cor 10:4].

II.1. Then he says, "But if your eye scandalizes you, pluck it out and cast it from you. For it is expedient for you that one of your members should perish, rather than that your whole body go to hell. And if your hand scandalizes you, cut it off, and cast it from you; for it is expedient for you that one of your members should perish, rather than that your whole body go to hell" [Matt 5:29–30].[85] Here the eye and hand do not mean those of the human body, but the eye and hand of the heart, that is, the feeling of wicked lust and the thought of carnal desire he commands to pluck out and cut off from our hearts through heavenly faith. In the gospel the Lord himself makes clear that all evils proceed from that source, when he says, "For from the heart proceed evil thoughts, murder, adultery, blasphemy, false witness, and other things that defile a man" [Matt 15:19–20]. **2.** But to maim one's body does not lead to the correction of a wicked mind, in which exists an entire raging abyss of vices. After all, we see many lame people deprived of the use of their eyes and body who nevertheless do not cease from the vices. This is why the Lord commands us instead for the sake of the kingdom of heaven to cut off those members of the vices that come from a wicked mind and a twisted way of thinking. Otherwise, if the vices gain control, both body and soul, that is, the whole self, may become liable to the eternal fire. **3.** But some conjecture that this should be understood of children and close relatives, who are as dear and esteemed by us as the eyes of our head.[86] Thus if perchance some of these stand in opposition to us and become a stumbling block with respect to our faith and hope of this sort, we should cast them away and regard them as enemies of salvation. Otherwise, those of us who have been associated with faithless and blasphemous people of this sort would be condemned with the same punishment.

III.1. But since the body has been mentioned, this can be understood more correctly of the body of the church.[87] In it as the eye, as a precious member, the bishop is recognized as being signified. He enlightens the entire body by the light of a divine commandment. The statement properly applies here: "If your eye scandalizes you, pluck it out and cast it from you; for it is better for you that one of your members should perish than your whole body should go to hell." Hence, if this type of eye, that is, bishop, through his depraved faith and disgraceful manner of life becomes a scandal to the church, he commands him to be plucked out, that is, cast out of the body, lest the people be held guilty for his sin. **2.** For it is written that "a little leaven corrupts the whole lump" [1 Cor 5:6]. And again, "Remove the evil man from your midst" [1 Cor 5:13]. The hand is understood to signify a priest who, if he holds to a depraved faith or does not live uprightly, creates a scandal to God's people. The Lord commands that he be cut off, that is, cast out, lest the church become defiled by his sin. For the church, according to the apostle, ought to be "holy and spotless" [Eph 5:27], through Christ our Lord, who is blessed in the ages. Amen.

Tractate 24 on Matthew 5:31–37

I.**1.** Then it follows, "You have heard that it was said to them of old, Whoever divorces his wife should give her a bill of divorce. But I say to you, Whoever divorces his wife except in the case of fornication causes her to commit adultery" [Matt 5:31–32]. In all things our Lord and Savior reforms for the better the justice of the old law. Indeed, it seemed that long ago a license for divorce was granted by Moses on tenuous grounds to the Jewish people who were living unlawfully and serving their own pleasures [see Deut 24:1]. This was due not to the system of law but to the unbridled pleasure of carnal people unable to uphold the justice of the law according to rigorous standards. **2.** Therefore, this possibility is allowed, according to what the Lord himself makes clear in another place in his reply to the inquiring Sadducees. For when they asked why Moses had allowed a bill of divorce to be given, the Lord answered and said, "In view of the hardness of your heart Moses wrote this, that a bill of divorce is given, but it was not so from the beginning" [Matt 19:8, 7]. And now, not undeservedly does our Lord and Savior restore the precepts of the old constitution, removing that allowance. For he orders that the wedlock of chaste marriage be preserved by indissoluble law, showing that the law of wedlock was first instituted by himself. **3.** For he says, "What therefore God has joined together, let no one put asunder" [Matt 19:6; Mark 10:9]. By this statement he has condemned both the permitted license of the Jews and the foolish and wretched presumption of the Manichees, who deny that marriage is from God.[88] He shows that it is not lawful to divorce one's wife by the pronouncement of this sentence, saying, "Except in the case of fornication." He shows plainly that he acts against the will of God who presumes to profane a marriage joined by God by means of an unlawful separation of divorce. **4.** Hence they are not unaware of how serious a damnable crime they fall into who, after divorcing their wives, want to move on to other marriages through the unbridled will of lust, apart from the case of fornication. The reason they think that they can do this without penalty is because it seems to be allowed by human and secular laws. They do not realize that they are committing a graver transgression in this, because they are placing human laws above divine laws. Thus what God has laid down as unlawful they believe is lawful because it is freely permitted by human beings. **5.** But just as it is not right to divorce a wife who is living chastely and purely, so too it is permitted to divorce an adulterous woman, since she has made herself unworthy of being associated with the husband, she who dared to outrage the temple of God by sinning against her own body [see 1 Cor 3:17].

II.**1.** Then he says, "You have heard that it was said to them of old, You shall not swear falsely; but you shall pay back your oaths to the Lord. But I say to you not to swear at all, neither by heaven, since it is God's throne, nor by earth, since it is his footstool, nor by Jerusalem, since it is the city of the great King, nor shall you swear by your head, since you cannot make one hair white or black. But let your speech be yes, yes; no, no; but what is beyond that is from the evil one" [Matt 5:33–37].

2. By the grace of gospel teaching, the law given by Moses acquired an advantage. The law prescribed that one must not swear falsely; but according to the gospel, one must not swear. Long ago the Holy Spirit deliberated in advance through Solomon to command this when he said, "Do not accustom your mouth to oaths" [Sir 23:9]. And again, "But just as a servant who is constantly beaten will not be without a bruise, so whoever swears and does business will not be purged from sin" [Sir 23:11]. Therefore it is absolutely inappropriate for us to swear. **3.** For what need is there for us to swear, when we are not allowed to lie at all, and our words must always be as true as they are completely trustworthy, so much so that they may be taken as an oath? And this is why the Lord not only forbids us to swear falsely, but even to swear, lest we appear to tell the truth only when we swear; and lest while we should be truthful in our every word we think it is all right to lie when we do not take an oath.[89] For this is the purpose of an oath: everyone who swears, swears to the fact that what he is saying is true. **4.** And the reason the Lord does not want any distance between our oath and our ordinary speech is because just as there must be no faithlessness in an oath, so too in our words there must be no falsehood. For both false swearing and lying are condemned by the punishment of divine judgment, as the divine Scripture says: "The mouth that lies kills the soul" [Wis 1:11]. So whoever speaks the truth swears, for it is written, "A faithful witness does not lie" [Prov 14:5]. **5.** Hence not without cause divine scripture often records that our God swears, for whatever is said by God, who is truthful and does not know how to lie, is taken as an oath, for all that he speaks is true. Indeed we find God swearing a few times, but because of human unbelief and especially because of the faithlessness of Jewish infidelity, those who think that truth depends solely upon fidelity to an oath; on that account, then, even God wanted to swear, so that those who would not believe in the God who spoke would indeed believe him when he swears.

III.**1.** Therefore the Lord says, "You have heard that it was said to them of old, You shall not swear falsely. But I say to you not to swear at all, neither by heaven, since it is God's throne, nor by earth, since it is his footstool, nor by Jerusalem, since it is the city of the great King" [Matt 5:33–35]. These statements of the Lord whereby he forbids us to swear by these different elements have a twofold understanding. **2.** For, first, he wanted to remove from us the use of oaths and the habit of human error, lest each of us through swearing by these elements accord a creature the honor of divine veneration, or believe one has impunity in swearing falsely if one swears by the elements of the world. For it is written, "Nor has he sworn deceitfully to his neighbor" [Ps 24:4]. **3.** In this he condemns both the error of Jewish unbelief and likewise that of the human race, those who have forsaken the Creator and regarded the creation with divine veneration, in accordance with what the apostle has said: "And they worshiped and served the creation rather than the Creator" [Rom 1:25]. Moreover, it can also be understood in this way: when one swears by heaven and earth, one swears by him who made heaven and earth, as the Lord himself made clear elsewhere when he said, "He who swears by the altar swears by it and by all things that are on it; and he who swears by the throne of God swears by it and by him who dwells in it" [Matt 23:20, 22]. **4.** He says, "Nor by Jerusalem, for it is the city of the great King," that is, a type of Christ's body, which is the spiritual and heavenly church. "Neither shall you swear by your head," for according to the apostle, "the head of a man is Christ" [1 Cor 11:3].[90] Therefore the one who swears by these things swears by him who is the author of these things.

5. He says, "But let your speech be yes, yes; no, no; but what is beyond that is from the evil one" [Matt 5:37]. He is teaching that all speech that comes forth from us ought to contain nothing but the truth, since all falsehood, that is, "what is beyond that," traces back to the devil as its author, who is ever a liar from the beginning, as the Lord says in the gospel: "He who speaks falsehood speaks from his own, since he is false, as also his father" [John 8:44]. Therefore we ought always to speak and deliberate upon what is true, that we may show ourselves to be disciples of him who is the truth, who is blessed in the ages. Amen.

Tractate 25 on Matthew 5:38–42

I.1. Then it follows, "You have heard that it has been said to them of old, An eye for an eye, a tooth for a tooth [see Exod 21:24; Lev 24:20; Deut 19:21]. But I say to you not to resist one who is evil, but if any one strikes you on the right cheek, turn to him also the left. And if a man wants to contend with you in judgment, and to take away your tunic, let go your cloak also unto him" [Matt 5:38–40]. By the gospel precepts, the Lord conforms us to every example of patience and humility. **2.** Long ago it had been commanded in the law that if someone incited by an outburst of rage rips out someone's eye or tooth, he too would be subjected to a like punishment and to the same bodily damage [see Lev 24:19–20]. With this precept, both the justice of the law is shown and the temerity of the insolent people is kept under the restraint of this threat, as he kept back from criminal wickedness, at least by the penalty of a present vengeance, those who did not fear the future judgment. **3.** But those who live according to the gospel faith do not look for the retribution of this vengeance. For them all hope of retribution and vengeance is reserved for the future. And that is why the Lord in the gospel not only commands us not to pay each other back for an injury, but he even commands those who have been struck on the right cheek to turn the other also, if the wrath of the striker demands it. **4.** For this is what he says: "He who strikes you on the right cheek, turn to him the left as well." For this is what it means truly to live by faith, not to expect vengeance in the present but in the future from him who says, "Vengeance is mine, I shall repay, says the Lord" [Rom 12:19]. Jeremiah clearly shows a man of the gospel of this sort, who when struck on the cheek freely offers the other, when he says, "It is good for a man when he bears a heavy yoke in his youth. He will sit alone, and be silent, because he has borne a heavy yoke. He will give his cheek to be struck, he will be filled full with reproaches" [Lam 3:27–30]. **5.** Surely in this he clearly shows the blessed man, who while living under this yoke of the law of the gospel, does not turn himself away from any injustice of a persecutor. For meditation on patient endurance like this leads to the passion for martyrdom. For he would easily be able to endure even punishments of the body during times of persecution, if having been trained earlier during times of peace, he receives injuries of this sort with equanimity and gladness. **6.** Nor of course does it befit the Christian to pay back recompense for an injury, lest he be judged like him to whom he rendered the recompense. For if it is wrong to inflict an injury, he is not estranged from blame who pays out recompense for a wrong, and through this he cannot be deemed a good man who imitates a bad one.

II.**1.** But not only does the Lord command us to offer the cheek to the one who strikes us, but also to undergo losses. For he adds the following: "And to him who wants to contend with you in judgment and to take away your tunic, let go your cloak also unto him." After the patient endurance of bodily injury, the Lord wants us also to have contempt for things of this world, and to be so far removed from every lawsuit or court trial, that if by chance a slanderer or tempter comes forward to initiate a lawsuit for the sake of testing our faith, and desires to rob us of the things that are ours, the Lord orders us to offer willingly not only the things that the person unjustly demands, but even those he does not seek. **2.** For if each one is trained by practice of this sort to despise things that are of little worth on account of the slander of a litigant, he will easily be able to show contempt for all things that pertain to this world in persecution as well. For this is perfect faith and perfect victory against the one inflicting injury, if we offer him even those things he does not demand.

III.**1.** Then he says, "And whosoever will force you one mile, go with him still another two" [Matt 5:41]. The Lord commands us to be active and ready for every dutiful task. For he wants our good to be not so much from compulsion as from our own will, so that when we do more than what is asked of us by others, we may attain the glory of a greater reward. For it is the duty of complete love and perfect devotion of one's own accord to offer more than you are asked. **2.** Some have thought that the meaning of this section, that he who is forced one mile should go with him still another two, is to be understood spiritually in this fashion: if a nonbeliever, one who has not yet attained to the knowledge of the truth, makes mention of the one God the Father, the Creator of all things, as if coming by the road of the law, you should go with him still another two. That is, that after his profession of God the Father, you should lead this same person, by the way of truth, to the knowledge of the Son and the Holy Spirit, showing him that he must believe not only in the Father but also in the Son and the Holy Spirit.

IV.1. Finally it follows, "And give to the one who asks of you" [Matt 5:42]. That is, we should bestow the gift of heavenly grace to an eager spirit, after the knowledge of the Trinity. Or certainly we should grant mercy to those who ask for it, as we are able, so that we can more easily procure what we ask for from God, if we have previously merited this, from him who says, "Ask and it will be given to you" [Matt 7:7]. But if we despise those who ask us, with what confidence do we believe God will grant us what we ask for, since the Scripture says, "See to it that you do not turn your face away from any poor man; thus it will happen that the face of God shall not be turned away from you" [Tob 4:7]? "And do not turn away anyone who wants to borrow from you" [Matt 5:42]. We are commanded to guard the religious duty of piety and faith in all things, so that we would reckon the distress of another's tribulation as our own, and we should not have more material resources than our brothers and sisters. And therefore we ought to share both with brothers and sisters who ask and mutually with those who make requests when in need, with a religious spirit and pious feeling, awaiting the reward of eternal repayment, in accordance with what David says: "The agreeable man who pities and lends will distribute his words in the judgment" [Ps 112:5]. **2.** And again: "He has dispersed; he has given to the poor; his justice endures for evermore" [Ps 112:9]. Whence also saint Job, whose example it befits us to follow, fulfilled these very evangelical precepts and mentions himself when he says, "But if I permitted a poor man to go out of my door with an empty bosom, but if I had someone's bond and did not tear it up; and if I believed, I took nothing from the debtor; or if for my sake the land ever groaned, and if its furrows mourned together; or if I ate its fruit alone without price, or if I too grieved the heart of the owner of the land, by deceiving him" [Job 31:34–39]. Therefore Job faithfully carried out all these things, since he was expecting a reward from him who is the redistributor of eternal goods, to whom is the praise and glory in the ages. Amen.

TRACTATE 26 ON MATTHEW 5:43—6:4

I.1. Then it follows, "You have heard that it has been said to them of old, You shall love your neighbor, and hate your enemy. But I say to you, Love your enemies, do good to them that hate you, and pray for them that persecute and slander you, that you may be the children of your Father, who commands his sun to rise upon the good and the bad, and rains upon the just and the unjust. For if you love them that love you, what reward shall you have? Do not even the tax collectors do this? And if you greet your brethren only, what do you more? Do not also the heathens do this? Be ye therefore perfect, as also your Father who is in heaven is perfect" [Matt 5:43–48]. In all things the Lord wants us to be perfect in his commandments. **2.** Indeed long ago it was commanded in the law, "You shall love your friends and hate your enemies" [see Lev 19:18], but these commands were given to a people who were earthly and carnal at the time, just as the following: "An eye for an eye, a tooth for a tooth" [Matt 5:38; Lev 24:20]. But now to the people of the gospel the commands of heavenly and perfect justice are given, that we should love our enemies, love those who hate us, pray for those who slander and persecute us, so that we may deserve to be children of God, who in view of his own mercy indiscriminately gives the benefits of the present life from his heavenly gift to the good and the bad, the just and the unjust. **3.** The Holy Spirit exhorts us through Isaiah as well to keep such gospel precepts, when he says, "Hear the word of the Lord, you who fear his name; say, you are our brethren, to them that hate you and abominate you; let the name of the Lord be glorified, and appear to them in their joy; and they shall be ashamed" [Isa 66:5]. Whence not without reason does David testify in the psalm and say the following: "O Lord my God, if I have done this, if I have requited with evil those who requited me, may I then fall down deservedly empty by means of my enemies" [Ps 7:3–4]. **4.** Blessed Job, too, calls to mind the same thing when he says, "But if I was glad at the fall of my enemy, if I said in my heart, Well done! let my ear hear [my] curse" [Job 31:29–30]. But we have found these precepts of gospel grace, which have now been given for the salvation of human beings, composed for animals in the commandments of the law, when it is said, "If you see your enemy's oxen fallen under its burden, you shall not pass by it, but shall raise it with him" [Exod 23:5]. Thus even then in the law of Moses, everyone learned in respect to animals what he would do toward man at one time under the gospel.

II.1. And fittingly it follows, "If you love them that love you, what reward shall you have? Do not even the tax collectors do this? And if you salute your brethren only, what do you more? Do not also the heathens do this? Be you therefore perfect, as also your Father who is in heaven is perfect" [Matt 5:46–48]. The Lord has shown that we cannot have the merit of perfect love, if we love only those from whom in turn we know the return of mutual love will be paid in kind. For we know that love of this sort is common even to Gentiles and sinners. Hence the Lord wants us to rise above the common law of human love by the law of gospel love, so that we may show the affection of our love not only toward those who love us but even toward our enemies and those who hate us. Thus we would imitate in this the example of true godliness and of our Father's goodness.

III.1. And he added, "Take heed that you do not your justice before people; otherwise, you shall not have a reward from your Father who is in heaven" [Matt 6:1]. The Lord wants us to be estranged from all boasting of vain glory and of human desire, that we do the duty of our justice not with that zeal by which we want to please others, but for God alone, from whom we await a meritorious wage. **2.** For one loses the merit of his justice before God, who wants to live justly in order to obtain the glory of human praise. This is why the apostle says, "If I were still pleasing people, I would not be a servant of Christ" [Gal 1:10].

IV.1. Then he says, "But when you give alms, sound not a trumpet before you, as the hypocrites do, who love to stand in the synagogues and in the streets, that they may be honored by men. Amen I say to you, they have received their reward. But when you give alms, let not your left hand know what your right hand is doing, that your alms may be in secret, and your Father who sees in secret will repay you" [Matt 6:2–4]. **2.** In all things the Lord configures us to the glory of perfect faith by means of heavenly doctrine. Earlier he taught that the work of justice is to be done not for the sake of humans but for the sake of God. Now we are also commanded not to sound the trumpet when we give alms. That is, we should not broadcast what we do because it is not the mark of a devout mind to do any of the works of God in order to anticipate the glory of human praise. **3.** For many people make a donation for the use of the poor in order to be rewarded from the gesture with human praise and worldly renown. The Lord shows that they have received the reward of their work in this age. For as long as they seek the glory of this age, they lose the promised future reward.

V.**1.** And that is why the Lord went on to say, "So that your alms may be in secret; and your Father who sees in secret will repay you" [Matt 6:4]. He wanted the work of mercy to be hidden, not public, that is, we should work not for the sake of human praise but for the sake of God alone, from whom we await heavenly glory and the reward of future repayment. While warmly praising the church, Solomon once bore witness to alms of this faithful work under the silence of religious taciturnity, saying, "Your cheeks are beautiful behind your taciturnity" [Song 6:6]. **2.** He is referring namely to that taciturnity of which the Lord speaks: "Do not let your left hand know what your right hand is doing." But the Lord is not speaking of the hands of the human body, which have no sense of sight or speech. Rather by the "right and left hand" he means either works or people. After all, we read it written in the Book of Kingdoms that "hand" means people, when it says, "Do I not have ten hands in Israel?" [2 Sam 19:43]—that is, the ten tribes of Israel. **3.** Therefore, there is no doubt that the "right hand" means "just men" and "left hand" means "sinners." This agrees with what Solomon has said: "The Lord acknowledges the division on the right; the perverse are those who are on the left" [Prov 4:27]. The Lord makes very plain the meaning of this "right" and "left" in the gospel when he declares that the just are to be placed on the right, the sinners on the left [see Matt 25:33]. **4.** This right hand of just men, therefore, if it does some work according to the precept of the Lord, is commanded to be ignorant of the left hand; that is, in order for us to labor religiously and faithfully, we should not boast in the sight of sinners and unfaithful people. But if we do anything faithfully, not pursuing human praise, even before religious brothers, a work of devotion and faith cannot be judged by the boasting of brothers before our Lord and Savior, who is blessed in the ages. Amen.

Tractate 27 on Matthew 6:5–8

I.**1.** Then he says, "And when you pray, you shall not be as the hypocrites, who love to stand in the synagogues and corners of the streets, standing to pray, that they may be seen by people. Amen I say to you, they have received their reward. But you when you shall pray, go into your room, and having shut the door, pray to your Father, and your Father who sees in secret will repay you" [Matt 6:5–6]. **2.** The Lord is instructing us in every perfection of heavenly justice and faith. For he wants us to carry out every work of divine religion without hypocrisy, without any pursuit of human praise. For we are forbidden boastfully like hypocrites to show off our prayers to everyone, lest we lose the merit of grace. For the Lord demands simple and faith-filled prayer, not prayer that is feigned and boastful.[91] **3.** And therefore, the Lord commands us to pray with the door shut, that is, to go into the secret place of the heart and conscience, in order that we may receive the reward for secret prayer from him who knows what is secret and concealed. For it is characteristic of a religious mind to pray to God not with the clamor and sound of the voice, but with devotion of mind and faithfulness of heart, according to what David attests in the psalm when he says, "Speak in your hearts and feel compunction on your beds" [Ps 4:4].[92] **4.** Finally, we find in the Books of Kingdoms that the very holy woman Hannah (*Annam*) fulfilled the precepts of this gospel teaching. For while praying faithfully without uttering a sound, in the secret place of her heart, in the sight of the Lord, she poured out her desire in her prayers. She was immediately found worthy to be heard by the Lord [see 1 Sam 1:13–17].[93] In the same way, the Lord granted to Daniel, who always prayed in secret with the three youths, to understand the interpretations of the dream and the secrets of the revelations [see Dan 1:17]. Cornelius, too, not yet instructed by the precepts of the gospel, prays secretly and faithfully while in his room, and he was found worthy to hear the voice of a holy angel speaking [see Acts 10:1–4]. What shall we say of Jonah, who, not only in his room, but enclosed in the belly of the whale, deserved so greatly to be heard through his prayers, that from the depth of the sea and from the stomach of so great a beast he escaped unharmed and alive [see Jonah 2:1–11]?[94] **6.** But he was heard by God, not because he cried out with his voice but with his faith. And therefore the task of prayer to God, who we know looks at the secrets of the heart, is not the cry of the voice but the cry of faith and the devotion of a religious mind.

II.**1.** And thus, not without cause does the Lord say in what follows, "And when you are praying, speak not much, as the heathens do. For they think that in their much speaking they may be heard. Do not then be like to them, for your Father knows what is needful for you, before you ask him" [Matt 6:7–8]. For heathen people think that they can more easily obtain from the Lord what they require by the loquacity of using many words, but the Lord does not expect this from us. **2.** Rather, he wants us to offer our prayers not with wordy speech but with faith that comes from the heart and with the merits of justice. He surely knows better all the things of which we have need, and before we speak he is aware of everything that we are going to request. Finally, we have an example of just how great a distance there is between the wordy and the humble and simple prayer in the story of the Pharisee and the tax collector. **3.** For the prayer of the Pharisee vaunting himself in his abundance of the words is rejected. But the humble and submissive tax collector, asking forgiveness for his sins, went down more justified than the self-boasting Pharisee [see Luke 18:10–14].[95] In this we find fulfilled what was written: "The prayer of the humble penetrates the clouds" [Sir 35:17], reaching God, who is accustomed to hearing the request of the one who prays. He is blessed in the ages. Amen.

Tractate 28 on Matthew 6:9–15

I.1. Then he says, "In this way then shall you pray" [Matt 6:9].[96] Our Lord, who is accustomed to hearing those who pray to him, shows us with what words we ought to pray. O what a reliable and blessed prayer this is to us, the arrangement of which the doctor of life and heavenly teacher has established for us! Likewise, how blessed can we be if we preserve these words of the Lord's Prayer not only by the function of the mouth but in the action of a completely faithful manner of life! And so, for the hope of human salvation the Lord laid down for his disciples this form for praying, saying, "Our Father who art in heaven" [Matt 6:9].[97] **2.** How great is the Lord's love for us![98] How great is his mercy and piety, which has bestowed upon us the gift of such great grace that we slaves boldly dare to call our Lord and God Father! By this name he shows that we are no longer merely slaves, but also children of God. And though it would be more than sufficiently gracious for us to deserve to be called merely his slaves, the love of God superabounded to the point that we are called not merely slaves but even God's children by adoption. **3.** In his Gospel, John has shown that the grace of this name has been given to those who believe in Christ through faith, when he said, "As many as believed in him, he gave them the power to become children of God, to those who believe in his name, who were born not from blood nor from the will of the flesh nor from the will of a man, but from God" [John 1:12–13].[99] **4.** Whence too the apostle says, "But since you are children of God, God sent the Spirit of his Son into our hearts, crying out, Abba, Father" [Gal 4:6]. Since therefore we have attained such a great gift of grace, that we have not only become slaves but even children of God, we ought to act and live as children of God, so that by spiritual action we may prove to be that which we are called.[100] This would agree with what John says in his epistle: "He who is born of God does not commit sin, for the birth of God guards him and the devil does not touch him" [1 John 3:9; 5:18]. **5.** "But he who commits sins," is not from God, but "is of the devil, since the devil sins from the beginning" [1 John 3:8]. And therefore, by guarding the mystery of our heavenly birth, we ought to be estranged from all sin, so that we may truly deserve to be called and to be God's children. The holy prophets also know the grace of this divine mercy, in which it is granted to call God Father. For Isaiah says, "For you are our Father; for [though] Abraham knew us not, and Israel did not acknowledge us, yet you, O Lord, our Father, your name is upon us from the beginning" [Isa 63:16]. **6.** In a similar way Jeremiah also testifies in his book and says, "For there is one Father of us all" [Mal 2:10].[101] How great is the Lord's mercy! We who long ago had adopted the devil as our father by our own will [see John 8:44], now reborn through water and the Holy Spirit [see John 3:5], have now begun to have God as Father. **7.** For God himself is one Father to us who regenerates by his Spirit those whom he makes his children for an eternal inheritance. And therefore we ought to walk as children of God, lest by acting differently from what is fitting for children of God, we might be held guilty of using unlawfully such a great name.

II.**1.** Therefore he says, "Our Father who art in heaven. Hallowed be (*Sanctificetur*) thy name" [Matt 6:9]. It is not that anyone can sanctify God's name, since he is the one who sanctifies everyone, who says through the prophet, "Be holy (*sancti*), just as I too am holy, says the Lord" [Lev 11:44; 19:2; 20:7].[102] **2.** But the reason we ask that his name be sanctified is so that it may be sanctified in us through the works of justice, through the merit of faith, through the grace of the Holy Spirit.[103] The help of his mercy is necessary for us to be able to receive this sanctification through the gifts of this sort. But he who is the fount of eternal sanctity is not in need of any sanctification.

III.1. Then he says, "Thy kingdom come" [Matt 6:10].[104] Similarly, here as well we are not asking God to reign, who is the king of the eternal ages, whose kingdom has neither beginning nor end; but that that kingdom, that is, the heavenly one that he promised us, may arrive. **2.** But to ask boldly that this kingdom of the Lord may arrive is a matter of great confidence and of a sincere conscience. And that is why, because we always pray that God's kingdom may come, we ought to show ourselves to be the kind of people who could be worthy of the future kingdom, in our faith in the Lord and in respect to his commandments.[105]

IV.1. Then he says, "Thy will be done on earth as it is in heaven" [Matt 6:10].[106] The account of the interpretation is the same here as well. For there is no one who could resist or contradict God, to keep him from doing what he wants, since all things in heaven and on earth maintain their existence by his will. Rather, we pray that his will be done in us. Now it is the will of God that we carry out those things that he commands to be done, by believing in him with all our heart. The apostle bears witness to this will of God when he says, "The will of God is your sanctification: that you keep yourselves from fleshly desires" [1 Thess 4:3–4; 1 Pet 2:11]. The Lord too spoke of it in the gospel when he said, "But this is the will of my Father who sent me, that everyone who sees the Son and believes in him may have eternal life" [John 6:40]. **3.** Therefore, when we say, "Thy will be done on earth as it is in heaven," we are praying namely for this, that just as the will of God is kept faithfully by angels in heaven, so too it may be preserved always by us on earth with religious and faithful devotion. For us to be able to carry out this will properly, the aid of the divine regard must be sought without interruption. **4.** Or surely, "Thy will be done on earth as it is in heaven," so that as the will of God is carried out in heaven, that is, in holy and heavenly human beings, so too we pray that the will of God be done "on earth," that is, in those who have not yet believed, by means of ready belief in the faith and the knowledge of the truth.[107]

V.1. Then he says, "Give us this day our daily bread" [Matt 6:11]. We understand this statement of the Lord in two ways. First, that we should ask for food on a daily basis only; for we are not commanded to seek wealth and affluence in worldly things, but daily bread, because for the present life this is all that is necessary to Christians, who live by faith and await the future glory.[108] For the apostle says, "Having food and clothing, let us be content with that" [1 Tim 6:8]. **2.** Solomon clearly points to the same thing as well, when he says, "A person's need: bread, water, and clothing" [Sir 29:21]. But when we say, "this day," we are being taught to think about the present day only, not about the entire period of life, lest our mind become occupied with secular concerns, as the Lord himself shows clearly in another passage when he says, "Do not think about tomorrow, for tomorrow will worry about itself" [Matt 6:34]. **3.** But we ought to pay attention to the fact that this is commanded to us spiritually as well, that we should seek daily bread, that is, that heavenly and spiritual bread, which we receive daily for the healing of our soul and the hope of eternal salvation.[109] The Lord speaks of it in the gospel: "The heavenly bread is my flesh, which I shall give for the life of this world" [John 6:52]. **4.** And we are commanded to ask for this bread daily, that is, to be worthy of receiving daily the bread of the Lord's body, as the Lord's mercy offers it. For the holy apostle says, "Let a man examine himself and then eat of the Lord's bread and drink of his cup" [1 Cor 11:28]. **5.** And again, "He who eats the bread of the Lord and drinks the cup unworthily will be guilty of the body and blood of the Lord" [1 Cor 11:27].[110] Therefore not without reason should we always pray that we may be worthy of receiving this heavenly bread daily, lest some sin intervene and separate us from the body of the Lord.

VI.**1.** "And forgive us our debts as we also forgive our debtors" [Matt 6:12]. This utterance obviously is just and necessary for all.[111] First, that we should admit that we are sinners; second, that we should pray to be forgiven of our sins by God, just as we ourselves forgive those who sin against us.[112] But if we do not do that, we ourselves become accountable before God for our words, since the Scripture says, "For a man's own lips are a strong snare" [Prov 6:2]. **2.** Hence not without reason Solomon, too, who was not unaware of this form of the Lord's prayer through the Holy Spirit, gave the following warning in advance and said, "Do not speak a lying word in your prayer" [Sir 7:13–14]. For who would dare, or how could one lie to God in prayer? **3.** Except perhaps the one who while asking for pardon for his sins from God in accordance with the Lord's Prayer, he himself does not forgive those who have sinned against him, failing to maintain the divine statement: "One man harbors anger against another, and do you seek reconciliation from God? And he shows no mercy to a man who is like himself, and do you plead to God for your own sins?" [Sir 28:3–4]. **4.** The Lord clarifies this very plainly in another passage, when he sets forth the example of that slave who has a debt, to whom the Lord had forgiven the entire debt when asked to, which was very great. But after the cancellation of the debt, he was unwilling to forgive a fellow slave who owed him something, and he was handed over to a prison and was condemned to be punished [see Matt 18:23–25].[113]

VII.**1.** Then he says, "And lead us not into temptation, but deliver us from evil" [Matt 6:13].[114] The understanding of temptation here is twofold, and its causes are diverse. For upon some people temptation is brought in by sin, for their correction; on others it is brought in for the testing of the faith leading to glory. This agrees with what blessed James has testified in his epistle when he says, "Blessed is he who endures temptation, for having become blessed he will receive the crown of life, which God promises those who love him" [Jas 1:12]. **2.** For we do not pray to completely recuse ourselves from temptation, which we know to be useful, since saint David says, "Test me O Lord and tempt me, set fire to my reins and my heart" [Ps 26:2]. For we likewise know that it was by means of temptation that saint Abraham attained to the glory of perfect faith [see Gen 22:1; Heb 11:17–19].[115] We also read that the blessed apostle was handed over to temptations for the advancement of his faith. **3.** When he requested of the Lord to drive off from him the author of the temptation, he answered him, "My grace is sufficient for you, for virtue is perfected in weakness" [2 Cor 12:9]. Therefore we do not pray to be completely free of temptation, but not to be handed over to temptation beyond the limits of the strength of our faith to endure. This exact thing is clearly shown in another book of the gospel. For it is written as follows: "And lead us not into a temptation that we cannot endure" [Luke 11:4]. **4.** In order to show this same thing, the apostle also testified and said, "God is faithful, who will not allow you to be tempted beyond what you are able, but with the temptation he will provide a way of escape, that you may be able to endure it" [1 Cor 10:13]. And therefore we do not plead that a temptation that could be useful to us be removed from us, but the one that surpasses the measure of our weakness, which would lead to the overthrow of our faith. **5.** And therefore, fittingly and necessarily at the end of the prayer, we ask as well to be "delivered from evil." This refers to him who does not cease to fight against our faith daily by means of diverse temptations. We pray not unfittingly to be delivered from him by means of daily prayer, lest we should be unable to carry out the divine commands, having been hindered by his suggestions.

6. Everything therefore that is necessary to our faith and salvation is contained in this brief prayer of the Lord, as we confess and declare the Father's name, as we ask that the sanctification of his name be in us, as we request that the kingdom of God comes, as we pray that his will be done in us, as we plead daily for bread, whether earthly or heavenly, in the hope of our salvation, as we implore pardon of our sins, as we pray that heavy temptation be removed from us; finally, as we ask of the Lord without ceasing to be delivered from the evil one, who is the author of all sin.[116] **7.** Long ago through Isaiah, the Holy Spirit had predicted this very thing, saying, "For the Lord will make his word brief throughout the whole earth" [Isa 10:23]. Whence not unfittingly it follows, "If you forgive people their sins, your Father who is in heaven will forgive you; but if you do not forgive people, neither will your Father forgive you your sins" [Matt 6:14–15]. In what we pray, "Forgive us our debts just as we forgive our debtors," the just sentence of the Lord follows whereby he says, "If you do not forgive people their sins, neither will your Father who is in heaven forgive you." And therefore in order for us to be able to pray confidently to the Lord for the forgiveness of our sins, we ourselves should first forgive those who sin against us. **9.** And this is why Solomon says, "Forgive your neighbor his sin and then your sins will be absolved" [Sir 28:2]. But if we hold fast to the sins of those who transgress against us, with an unfaithful spirit and a hardened mind, the Lord makes perfectly clear that we too will not be worthy of receiving pardon for our sins. To him be the honor, praise, and glory together with the Holy Spirit, before all ages both now and always and in the ages of ages. Amen.

Tractate 29 on Matthew 6:16–18

I.**1.** Then he says, "When you fast, do not be sad like the hypocrites. For they disfigure their faces that they may appear unto people to fast. Amen I say to you, they have received their reward. But you when you fast, anoint your head and wash your face, lest you appear unto people to be fasting, but to your Father who is in secret; and your Father who is in secret will repay you" [Matt 6:16–18]. **2.** As in the precepts given previously, so too concerning the observance of fasting, the Lord has established for us the merit of perfect faith by the commands of his teaching. Thus we should fast not for the sake of human glory, as the hypocrites do, but for the sake of the future hope, for the Lord alone, from whom we await the reward for this devoted act of humility. **3.** But those who fast in this way, to please people more than God, indeed have the effort of the affliction of their body, but they cannot have a reward for the labor from God due to their vain glory. For although they should do it solely for the sake of religion and faith, they prefer to seek the glory of human praise instead. And therefore the Lord says, "Amen I say to you, they have received their reward." **4.** To be sure, there appears to be a single purpose for the fasting of the one who fasts only for God with a devout mind, and of the one who longs to please other people by his fasting. But the grace of the ones fasting is far apart, since although the purpose of each seems to be the same, and the effort involved in the fasting appears identical, yet the fruit is not the same, nor is the repayment of merits the same. For he who fasts for God's sake is far different from him who purposes to fast for the sake of people, since the compensation of human praise comes to the latter as a wage for his effort, but to the former, in view of the devotion of his humility, the merit of glory is reserved for the future. **5.** So, too, the state of those who pray does not seem to be different in terms of their purpose; but in terms of the faith of the heart and the affections of the mind there is a great distinction in the merits. For it is one thing, as was said earlier, to pray with the expectation of receiving human praise, something else to pray with this end alone in view, that one awaits reward for one's prayer from God who is the rewarder. The situation is similar with respect to all observances of the divine religion.[117]

II.1. Whence it is not without cause that the Lord wants all pursuit of human praise and boasting to be far removed from us. He shows us how we may please him with a religious spirit and a devout mind when he says, "But you when you fast, anoint your head and wash your face, lest you appear unto people to be fasting." Thus, if possible, we should conceal by a cheerful countenance the work of religious fasting and the affliction of body and spirit. **2.** We read examples of this matter, even according to history, prefigured in saints of past times. For the most holy Judith, when she was afflicted with great grief on behalf of the people, after the solemnity of a three-day fast, so covered up the sadness of her internal affliction by anointing her head and washing her face, that she seemed to delight her enemies by her feigned joy [see Jdt 12—13]. And what is more, when she covered up her fasting by her glad countenance, she brought back a triumph of victory over the enemy. **3.** In a similar way most holy Esther also, when she could [not] be understood by the king after she had washed her face and anointed her head after a three-day fast, destroyed Haman, that most vile enemy of her people [see Esth 4:16; 5:1; 7:10]. What shall we say about Daniel and the three youths, who were found to be more pleasing than the others by their faces alone, in the midst of such great abstinence, among so many young men who fed on the royal food [see Dan 1:12–15]?

III.**1.** But since we have said this according to the letter, we ought to consider what is to be thought also according to the spiritual understanding. In the anointing of the head we recognize mercy being signified. Hence to show mercy to a neighbor is to anoint the head, mercy that when done to the poor is referred to the Lord, who is understood as the head of the human being according to the apostle [see 1 Cor 11:3], since the Lord himself says, "As long as you did it to one of the least of these, you did it unto me" [Matt 25:40].[118] **2.** At the divine retribution we are drenched with a certain heavenly oil, as it were, in compensation for this mercy, by him who says, "Blessed are the merciful, for God will be merciful to them" [Matt 5:7]. Saint David also knows of this anointing on the head with heavenly oil, when he says, "As ointment on the head that runs down to the beard" [Ps 133:2].[119] But in the washing of the face is signified and recognized the purity of a cleansed body and of a sincere conscience. Thus to wash the face means to display a clear conscience and the face of our heart that is cleansed of every filth of sins and of the squalor of transgression. Thus would we truly be able to possess the gladness of heavenly joy and the good cheer of the Holy Spirit within us. And what is more, it is done in such a way that while we fast with faith out of devotion to God rather than for people, we may receive the reward of eternal repayment from God, who knows secrets. **4.** For this is what the Lord says: "Lest you appear unto people fasting, but to your Father who is in secret; and your Father who is in secret will repay you." If then you want always to bear an anointed head and to have a clean face of your heart, in accordance with the Lord's statement, be persistent in the faithful performance of works of mercy, be persistent in your devotion to fasting, that you may become worthy of pleasing the Lord, to whom is the praise and glory in the ages of ages. Amen.

Tractate 30 on Matthew 6:19–21

I.**1.** Then he says, "Do not treasure up for yourselves treasures on earth, where rust and moth destroy and where thieves dig up and rush upon. But treasure up for yourselves treasures in heaven, where neither rust nor moth destroy and where thieves do not dig up and steal; for where your treasure is, there shall be also your heart" [Matt 6:19–21]. The Lord forbids us to treasure up on earth, where everything is unstable and fleeting. For to seek these earthly treasures is contrary to faith and salvation—to seek after worldly wealth, to pursue riches of the world, which even moths can ruin, and rust consume and thieves seize. **2.** For whoever wants to treasure up on earth, rather than in heaven, cannot have those treasures of eternal and heavenly life, since the Lord himself says, "For a rich man will enter the kingdom of heaven with difficulty" [Matt 19:23]. Similarly the apostle says, "For those who want to become rich fall into temptation and the trap of the devil" [1 Tim 6:9]. Let us call to mind that rich man who set all this glory in the treasures of the world and in the abundance of their returns [see Luke 12:16–21]. Owing to the abundance of his crops, he gave thought to making bigger barns, and he promised his soul the delights of wealth and the security of a long life. I shall not say that he lost these things that he had collected by the sneaking in of a thief, but he forfeited his very soul, for which he was treasuring them up, on the very same night. **3.** Whence not without cause David himself has testified and said, "He lays up treasures, and knows not for whom he is collecting them" [Ps 39:6]. Let us also consider that young man who, though he had carried out nearly all the commandments of the law, since he regarded earthly treasures more than heavenly, was unable to attain the treasures of eternal life [see Matt 19:20–22]. And that is why David spoke well when he said, "If wealth should flow in, do not set your heart upon it" [Ps 62:10].

II.**1.** For this reason the Lord wants us to store up our treasures not on earth, where they can perish, but in heaven, where no adversities lord over them, where thieves do not dig them up, that is, the devil and his angels, and where no rust or moth destroy, that is, sins that lord over this world. But in the gospel the Lord shows us how we ought to lay up this treasure in heaven, when he says to the young man, "Go, sell all that you have, and give it to the poor, and you will have treasure in heaven" [Matt 19:21]. **2.** We are commanded to lay up in heaven treasures of this sort, then, which are eternal and incorruptible, which cannot perish, by means of works of justice, through merits of piety and mercy. For according to the reliability of Scripture, whatever is stored up in heaven is expended for the use of the poor, since Scripture says, "He that gives to the poor lends to God" [Prov 19:17]. Hence, too, we have found that those who believed during the time of the apostles were mindful of this command of the Lord and laid up treasures for themselves in heaven. They sold all their possessions and transferred their earthly treasures to the heavenly kingdom [see Acts 2:45; 4:34].

III.**1.** And that is why the Lord went on to say, "Where your treasure is, there shall your heart be also." For if we always lay up treasure in heaven by means of good works, where all our hope and salvation is, where eternal life is laid up for us, though we are still on earth, yet we always have our heart in heaven. But one's heart cannot be in heaven, who has been taken captive by worldly greed and who prefers to lay up treasure for himself on earth instead. **2.** Justly, too, the holy apostle exhorts the wealthy of this world on how they can attain to this heavenly treasure. He says, "Instruct the rich of this world not to be high-minded, nor to set their hope in the uncertainty of riches, but in the living God, who gives us abundantly all things to enjoy; to do good, to be rich in good works, to give readily, to share, to lay up treasure for themselves for the future, that they may lay hold on the true life" [1 Tim 6:17–19], from him who is the author of life and of eternal immortality, to whom is the praise and glory in the ages of ages. Amen.

Tractate 31 on Matthew 6:22–24

I.**1.** Then he says, "The lamp of your body is your eye; if your eye is simple, your whole body is bright; but if your eye is evil, your whole body is darkened. If then the light that is in you is darkness, the darkness itself how great is it?" [Matt 6:22–23].[120] The lamp of the body is understood to refer to the thought of the mind and the faith of the heart, which, if it is pure and bright within us, doubtless illumines our whole body. **2.** But the reason the lamp is put in comparison with faith is because just as a lamp illumines the steps of those who travel at night, to keep them from either walking into pitfalls or striking against little stumbling blocks [see Matt 15:14], so in the night of this world, the brightness of faith illumines all the steps of our life, as the light of truth goes ahead of us. It keeps us from falling into the pitfalls of sins, or striking against the little stumbling blocks of the devil. **3.** This then is what the Lord says: "The lamp of your body is your eye; if your eye will be simple, your whole body is bright; but if your eye is evil, your whole body is darkened." He is showing that if this faith of ours, which is signified as a lamp and eye of the body, is blinded within us either by the obscurity of sins or by the darkness of faithlessness, doubtless our whole body is rendered obscure and darkened.

4. Saint John shows this same thing when he says, "God is light" [1 John 1:5]. And, "Whoever loves a brother or sister abides in the light, just as he himself is in the light; but whoever hates another is in darkness and walks in darkness, and does not know the way to go, since the darkness has blinded his eyes" [see 1 John 2:10; 1:7; 2:11]. Although according to the statement of John this is understood about those who hate their brother or sister, we ought to apply it to the darkness in which the heretic lingers. He has lost the light of the Catholic truth, and stands forth as a treacherous blasphemer. And that is why the Lord says, "If the light that is in you is darkness, the darkness itself how great is it?" Namely, in the one who has exchanged truth for a lie and faith for faithlessness.

II.**1.** But in another sense we observe that the bishop is being signified as the eye of the body, which is more beautiful and precious than all the members.[121] As a sort of eye, he illumines the body of the church with the brightness of his preaching of faith and doctrine. If he stands forth as a faithful Catholic teacher through his simple faith and holy manner of life, the people over whom he presides can abide always in the light of truth by the example of his teaching and pattern. **2.** But if he who appears to offer light to others stands forth as an evil and faithless teacher by his perverse faith or by a disgraceful manner of life, doubtless the entire body can be darkened by the example of his life and faithlessness. Therefore it is not without reason that the Lord says of such an eye, "If the light that is in you is darkness, the darkness itself how great is it?" That is, if a teacher of this type, who ought to radiate from himself the light of faith to others, becomes blinded by heresy and stands forth as darkened, we ought to consider how great among that people would the darkness of sins be!

III.**1.** And he added, "No one can serve two masters; for either he will hate the one and love the other, or he will endure the one and despise the other. You cannot serve God and mammon" [Matt 6:24]. The Lord plainly declares that none of us can serve two masters (*dominis*), that is, God and the devil. And God indeed, though he is Lord (*Dominus*) of all [see Gal 4:1], since all things were created by him and he himself lords over all things by his authority, power, and nature, nevertheless he deems it fitting chiefly to be Lord of those who know him as their Lord and God, the Creator of the universe, and who keep his commands by faithful service. **2.** But the devil is understood to be the lord of those only whom he subjugates to his very evil service, seducing them away from their Lord and parent by means of sin. And by an illicit law he lords over them through the action of his iniquity. For this reason then he himself is called lord in his own place, since through sin he lords over foolish men of this sort. And that is why it is written, "Whoever commits sin is a servant of sin" [John 8:34]. **3.** But since we have already been visited by the mercy of God and liberated from the devil's dominion, and we have come to know the Lord, by whom we were created and redeemed, we are forbidden to serve our former master, that is, the devil, who lorded over us like a tyrant; or rather, we are not to serve avaricious desire, which he calls mammon, which sometimes has been accustomed to entice even religious minds. Therefore let us flee from and avoid the desire for money and worldly greed, lest we subjugate ourselves to its unworthy service and to the devil, who is the author of greed.

IV.**1.** And this is what the Lord says: "No one can serve two masters; for either he will hate the one and love the other, or he will endure the one and despise the other" [Matt 6:24]. For whoever loves his Lord and God with his whole heart necessarily hates the devil, together with his actions, since in his love it is manifest that the devil is always held in execration. But he who loves mammon and the devil through his unjust works of sins, by doing his will, cannot love God whose commands he is despising [see John 14:15; 1 John 2:4]. **2.** And therefore, he who loves God cannot be called a servant of the devil, whom he already lords over through the faith of heavenly grace. Likewise, too, he who is enslaved to sins and who submits himself to a diabolical domination of this sort does not deserve to have God as his Lord. And therefore the Lord says, "You cannot serve both God and mammon," showing that we cannot serve both God and the devil, that is, God, the author of mercy, and the devil, the lord of mammon and avarice. **3.** The apostle also shows this when he says, "What fellowship is there between light and darkness? Or what do justice and iniquity have in common? Or what share is there between the faithful and an unbeliever? Or what consensus between the temple of God and idols? Or what agreement between Christ and Belial?" [2 Cor 6:14–16]. Thus there are two masters set before us: God and mammon, that is, the devil, who is the author of mammon. The former invites us to mercy, the latter to greed; the former to life, the latter to death; the former to salvation, the latter to perdition. Which of the two should we obey? Surely the one who invites us to life, not him who drags us off to death. For this reason let us love God, who is the true Lord and who is the author of life, but despise the devil, who is the author of death and who lays claim to an unjust lordship for himself. Then we will be able to become worthy of God's mercy, to whom is the praise and the glory in the ages of ages. Amen.

Tractate 32 on Matthew 6:25–34

1. Then it follows, "Therefore I tell you, do not think in your hearts about what you will eat" [and the rest up to] "clothing" [Matt 6:25]. The Lord wants all the actions of our life to be heavenly; he forbids us from thinking at all about the things of this world and the needs of this present life, since through worry of this sort, the spirit called by God and away from heavenly desires is called back to worry and care about that world. Let us recall that our father Adam, through the desire for a little food, did not keep the Lord's commands and lost the grace of immortality. And that is also why after the food of his belly he began to be anxious about clothing as well, since indeed by transgressing the commandment, he lost the covering of heavenly grace and saw that he was naked [see Gen 3:10]. Therefore it is not without reason that the Lord forbids us from thinking at all about food and clothing, since it pertains to perfect faith not to have concern about the things of this world. For there is no doubt that those things that are necessary for the present life, namely food and clothing, cannot be lacking us when the Lord is our provider, since we know that we daily receive from him also the spiritual food for salvation, and have been clothed with the covering of heavenly grace, especially since God has always been accustomed to providing for his servants, even apart from our being anxiously concerned about it. For that is what he himself says: "Seek first the kingdom of God and his justice, and all these

things shall be added unto you" [Matt 6:33]. Let us consider the way saint Elijah did not think at all about the food of the world during a time of famine. At the Lord's command he was fed spontaneously by a widow, who together with her children had only a small amount of meal [see 1 Kgs 17:8–16]. And that same widow thought nothing of tomorrow and hence stayed alive together with her children during the entire time of the famine. And we read that Elijah was indeed at first fed by the widow, but also after the same holy man stayed in the wilderness, he was fed by ravens administering food to him [1 Kgs 17:4–6]. We also find that by means of a prophet the Lord brought dinner from Judea to Babylon in an instant to saint Daniel as well, who was living by this gospel faith in a lion's den amidst the ravenous mouths of huge beasts [see Dan 6; 14:31–42]. By these examples we recognize very clearly that God's servants who were living in accordance with the precepts of the gospel could not have lacked these things, since the prophet says, "I was young and now am old and I have not seen the just man forsaken nor his seed begging bread" [Ps 37:25]. And again, "God will not kill a just soul by famine" [Prov 10:3]. And again, "The merciful and compassionate Lord gave food to those who fear him" [Ps 111:4–5]. And again, "The rich were lacking and hungry, but those who seek the Lord will not want any good thing" [Ps 34:10]. And again, "The eyes of the Lord [are] upon those who fear him" [and the rest up to] "in famine" [Ps 33:18–19]. Through Isaiah, too, the Lord says the following to the stubborn and unbelieving concerning his saints: "Behold, those who serve me shall eat, but you shall be hungry. Behold, those who serve me shall drink, but you shall be thirsty" [Isa 65:13].

2. Whence it is not unfitting that the Lord says in the present passage, "Do not think in your hearts" [and the rest up to] "clothing" [Matt 6:25]. In this he has taught us not to be anxiously concerned about the soul's sustenance and the body's clothes, but to think instead about the very salvation of the soul and body. For "the soul is more than food." For this food perishes, but the soul abides forever. "And the body is more than clothing" [Matt 6:25], for this corruptible clothing will wear out and perish, but the body is covered with the garment of immortality through the resurrection. And therefore one must not give thought to these things, since the Lord who gives generously to human beings that which is more, namely eternal life and immortality, doubtless shall also deign to provide as well these things that are temporal.

3. Finally, the Lord immediately sets forth in what follows the example of the birds as well and says, “Look at the birds of the sky” [and the rest up to] “you are [worth] more than they” [Matt 6:26]. The Lord has set this forth to instruct us in the faith. For if the necessary nourishment is not lacking the birds, which do not labor or think about their sustenance, as God daily provides for them, how much more can these things not be lacking God’s servants and the faithful. But since it is plain that not only birds but also cattle, beasts, all the wild animals of the forests and all living things live and feed by the disposition of God, one should ask why the Lord mentions only the birds. We ought to observe that this example has been applied not without a spiritual understanding. And first of all their nature comes from water.[122] Second, among all the living creatures of the world, they alone fly to the heights and high places. In the comparison with them, we recognize holy and faithful people being signified, who in a similar way are born to God through the water of baptism, daily are fed on heavenly food apart from worldly concern, are weighed down by no burden of sin, through their spiritual and immortal nature like birds fly from the earthly things to the heavenly kingdom, in order that what is written may be truly fulfilled in them: “Who are these that fly as clouds, and as doves with young ones come to me?” [Isa 60:8]. Not without reason are the apostles preferred to them in what is said: “Are you not more than these?” [Matt 6:26], since even though the saints are people of this sort, yet the apostles are the princes of the saints.

4. And he added, “But which of you can add to his stature a single cubit? And why are you anxious about clothing?” [Matt 6:27–28]. It does not pertain to human power nor to our virtue either to give increases to the body or to add anything beyond the measure of our state, but this belongs to God alone, who deigns to give to each of us what he wants and how much he wants, in view of the choice of his own will. If these things therefore that lead to natural increase with us are provided by God’s disposition without our anxious concern, how much more will those things that are necessary to the body be provided by the condescension of him who is the author of our life! But according to the spiritual understanding, “to add a cubit” signifies the future hope in which the Lord will cause us to arrive at perfection, having been changed through the glory of his resurrection, in accordance with what the apostle has related: “Until we all attain to the perfect man in the measure of the age of the fullness of Christ” [Eph 4:13].[123]

5. Then follows, "Consider the lilies of the field" [and the rest up to] "of little faith" [Matt 6:28–30]. Higher up, a comparison with birds was made in order to ward off from us anxiety over daily food. Now there is another comparison that concerns the body's clothing, to keep us from having worldly concerns. <But since we see> not only lilies, but also diverse seeds and all things that sprout from the earth, according to the nature of their kind, are clothed by the divine disposition, one must ask why he only mentions lilies. And indeed we see that these lilies give off a wonderful fragrance, they blossom, they are clothed, they grow; but we think that this was said not about these lilies only, although it is religious to understand this also about them. Hence we also observe in the lilies, on account of the grace of their whiteness and the sweetness of their smell, the saints, that is, the patriarchs and others like them, who while living without the labor and the burden of the law, pleased God by faith alone (*sola fide*) and natural justice, and were clothed white in the garment of light. In the name of the church, the Holy Spirit likewise bears witness through Solomon to these lilies, when he says, "Let my kinsman (*frater*) go down to his garden, to the beds of spice, to feed [his flock] in the gardens, and to gather lilies" [Song 6:1]. And again, "I am my kinsman's (*fratri meo*), and my kinsman is mine, who feeds among the lilies" [Song 6:2]. Isaiah too indicates holy people in the lilies when he says, "Be glad, O desert; let the wilderness exult, and flower as the lily. And let the desert places of Jordan rejoice" [Isa 35:1–2]. Thus it is not without cause that the Lord himself, in order both to show that he is the prince of all the saints, and to point out that he would receive the flower of human flesh, has thought it fitting to identify himself with this same designation, when he says through Solomon, "I am a flower of the plain and a lily of the valleys" [Song 2:1]. For this reason in what follows he has compared his own church to a lily, owing to the whiteness of her faith and the very sweet fragrance of her holy life, when he says, "As a lily among thorns, so is my sister among the daughters" [Song 2:2]. He is showing that just as the Lord himself, who called himself a lily, endured various persecutions from the thorny people, so too his church would suffer various persecutions from the same people, in accordance with what he himself says in the gospel: "If they persecuted me, they will also persecute you" [John 15:20]. In the gospel, the Lord exhorts us then to resemble lilies like this, that is, as an example of life for the saints, so that by living by the same example of faith and holiness, we may be able to possess

the glory of the immortality that is promised. But according to some interpreters,[124] we can also see the angels signified in these lilies, who live without any worldly anxiety or labor and bloom clothed with the bright light of immortality. Not unfittingly are we invited to emulate them, so that by living in this world in imitation of angelic sanctity, we may merit to attain to the blessedness of angelical glory, as the Lord himself in the gospel deemed it fitting to promise when he said, "But in the resurrection they will neither marry nor be married, but they shall be as the angels in heaven" [Matt 22:30]. And that we might recognize more clearly that this was spoken spiritually, the Lord went on to say: "But I tell you that not even Solomon in all his glory was clothed as one of these" [Matt 6:29]. For no clothing, however precious, even of that royal quality in which Solomon flourished, can be compared with that heavenly and angelic clothing.

6. Now in the grass of the field that he said is here today, and tomorrow is thrown into the furnace [see Matt 6:30], we recognize the signification of nations estranged from the knowledge of God and all sinners, of which it is written, "All flesh is grass and all human glory is like the flower of grass; the grass has withered, the flower has fallen" [1 Pet 1:24].[125] That is, those who rejoice when the flower of the present life falls, and in worldly glory—people of that sort are destined like dry grass for perpetual fire. Saint David testifies about them as well when he says, "Do not be envious of them that do iniquity, for they shall soon be withered as the grass, and shall soon fall away as the green herbs" [Ps 37:1–2]. And again, "[As for] the human being, his days are as grass and as a flower of the field, so has he flourished" [Ps 103:15]. And again, "Let them be as the grass of the housetops" [Ps 129:6], that is, the bodies of sinners, which, having no fruit in themselves of the heavenly hope, had only the flower of the world that will soon perish. But he shows the time of the present life in his words: "today is" [Matt 6:30]. But "tomorrow" [Matt 6:30] points to the judgement of the future day. If then "God clothes" this, "how much more you of little faith" [Matt 6:30], that is, if God cares for the unbelieving nations, and freely gives them earthly clothing from his goodness, how much more will he deem it fitting to provide these things for his saints and the faithful.

7. And this is why he has gone on to say, "Do not think about what you shall eat or what you shall drink. For the nations of this world seek after all these things. For your Father knows that you need all these things. Therefore seek first the kingdom of God, and his justice,

and all these things shall be provided unto you" [Matt 6:31–33]. Therefore, we are forbidden from thinking at all about food, drink, and the things of this world. For to seek these things pertains to the nations that are ignorant of God, who live like cattle in this world and think only about sustaining their present lives, and think that there is nothing after death. For this reason it is not right for us to become like people of that sort, who set their entire hope in the present life; instead we ought to think of the things that pertain to the heavenly kingdom and future glory, since if we always think of those things that are heavenly and eternal, it will not be possible for us to be lacking even these things that are temporal. For that is what he says, "Seek first the kingdom of God, and his justice, and all these things shall be provided unto you." Earlier the Lord declared this very thing through Isaiah as well, when he said, "Hearken to me, and you shall eat that which is good, and your soul shall delight in good things" [Isa 55:2].

8. For this reason he added more and said, "Therefore, do not think about tomorrow. For tomorrow will think about itself. The day's own evil suffices" [Matt 6:34]. By forbidding us from thinking about tomorrow, doubtless the Lord has removed all worldly concern from us. But we ought to inquire about the following: since he says that one must not think about tomorrow, why did he go on to say, "The day's own evil suffices"? What exactly do we understand is being signified by the "day's evil"? For we know that at the beginning of the world, the Lord blessed all the days, and we see light provided daily to human beings, and all the days preserve the course appointed for them by God and maintain the laws of creation. The Lord therefore has not spoken about the evil of that day, which is free from the blame of sin, but rather about our evil we commit every day. And since on a daily basis we cannot be without sin, however trivial, the Lord warns us of this, to purge ourselves with constant solicitude of faith and with just reparation for daily transgressions, however small. That is why the holy apostle teaches us to let go of anger before the setting of the sun [see Eph 4:26], lest a whole day enclose us within its space in the guilt of sin. Whence saint David, who indeed lived before the gospel yet in accordance with the gospel, lest he should be held liable of some sin of the day, blotted out his daily transgressions every night by means of the reparation of tears. He says, "I shall wash my bed every night; I shall water my couch with tears" [Ps 6:6]. Blessed Job, too, who was not unaware of the virtue of this gospel command through the Holy Spirit, in order to purge the daily transgressions of his children, offered daily

sacrifices to God not only for transgressions but even for ignorance of sin [see Job 1:5]. The holy apostle likewise wants us to redeem the transgressions of the day by heavenly faith. He gave the following warning about this in his epistle: "Walk with wisdom among those who are without, desiring nothing from anyone, redeeming the time, since the days are evil" [Col 4:5; cf. 1 Thess 4:12; Eph 5:16]. Surely he does not mean the arrangement and cycle of the days, but the sins of evil people, who daily live in this world in iniquities and crimes. And therefore by good works we ought to redeem days of this sort and this time of the present life, so that we may become worthy of attaining to that blessed day of future glory, at the coming of our Lord and Savior, who is blessed in the ages. Amen.

Tractate 33 on Matthew 7:1–12

1. Then it follows, "Judge not that you may not be judged" [and the rest up to] "it shall be measured to you" [Matt 7:1–2]. Here the Lord is not forbidding judging, but he is saying that one must not judge hastily. After all, he added, "For with what judgment" [and the rest up to] "it shall be measured back to you" [Matt 7:2]. What the Lord is instructing, then, is that no one should stand forth as an insolent and rash judge against their own brother or sister. For there are many who readily believe, quickly condemn, even those who commit certain faults and light transgressions of crimes. Whence the Lord well added, "For with what judgment you judge, you shall be judged, and by what measure you measure, it shall be measured to you." At the future judgment we shall receive repayment from the Lord, the just judge, for the things that pertain to our judgment, just or unjust.

2. Finally, in order to show this clearly, he went on to say, "Why do you see the speck in your neighbor's eye, but do not notice the plank in your own eye?" [and the rest up to] "from your neighbor's eye" [Matt 7:3–5]. What the Lord had said previously he has now shown clearly and openly, namely, that he was not forbidding the saints and the faithful from judging people, but he was rebuking impious and unworthy judges, who are themselves burdened down with serious sins, who think that others deserve condemnation for trivial reasons. For this is what he says: "But why do you see the speck in your neighbor's eye, and the plank that is in your own eye, you do not see?" In

this surely he is rebuking people of this sort, who think that judgment of others is to be hastily conducted, though they themselves are guilty of serious wickedness and sins. And this is why the Lord added, "Hypocrites, first cast out the plank from your eye and then you will see clearly to remove the speck from your neighbor's eye" [Matt 7:5]. He is showing that each one of us ought not to so hastily judge the other for a transgression, unless he first explains the weight of his own sin. For in the speck he is indicating a transgression that is indeed small in view of its scantiness. But in the plank he is showing a serious sin and a weighty crime in view of its magnitude with which the eye of the inner mind is weighed down. On this account, too, David shows abhorrence for the chastisement and judgment of such people, when he says in the psalm, "The just shall chasten me with mercy, and reprove me, but let not the oil of the sinner anoint my head" [Ps 141:5]. For the chastisement of the just person is done with mercy and is faithful. It reproves in order to correct, it rebukes in order to invite to salvation. But the rebuke of an iniquitous person and a sinner is abhorrent. It does not heal but inflicts a wound.

3. Then he says, "Do not give what is holy to dogs" [and the rest up to] "tear you to pieces" [Matt 7:6]. In the administration of the faith and in the mysteries of heavenly grace, the Lord wants us to exhibit careful concern and diligent caution, lest we randomly deliver the mysteries of the divine service to blasphemous men and to adversaries of the faith, and indeed to filthy minds and those filled with the dirt of sins. For dogs here signify the enemies of the truth and those who insult Christ's name. The apostle says of them, "Beware of the dogs, beware of evil workmen, beware of the mutilation" [Phil 3:2]. The Lord himself had testified about them through David when he said, "Many dogs have surrounded me, fat bulls have besieged me" [Ps 22:16]. Thus we clearly recognize that the dogs here signify blasphemous people who have made it their custom to bark against God with a rabid mouth, or surely heretics who do not cease to disturb the Lord's flock by their impious discussions, as it were with a kind of verbal barking. But in the pigs he is showing people who are unclean and defiled by much filth of sins. For indeed we know that pigs are unclean by nature. They bury themselves in the earth and in all muddy holes, and with open mouths they ever seek nothing else but fodder for satisfying the stomach. As long as they live they provide no usefulness from themselves, no wool like sheep, no milk like other animals, nor do they provide transportation, but they only seek food for their bellies

and they are fed until they die. Doubtless under their persona, we observe, as we mentioned earlier, unclean and filthy people are being signified. Like pigs they roll about in the mud, in the filth of their sins. They think only of their gullet and belly. Without a single work of mercy or of religious effort to their credit, they have no hope of future salvation. And the apostle seems to testify of them when he says, "Whose god is their belly and their glory is in their shame, who think earthly things" [Phil 3:19]. And so, we are forbidden from entrusting our pearls, that is, the mysteries of the divine faith and heavenly grace, to people of this sort, lest <when> we reveal the divine mysteries randomly and undeservedly to such people, they may by their infidelity begin to repudiate and trample upon our good and tear to pieces the hope of our faith and indeed of the church. Whence not unfittingly the former law had instructed that this animal, being unclean as a figure of the future truth, not be possessed for use as food [see Lev 11:7]. In this surely the following is being indicated, that an unclean man like this who displays a filthy life should not be joined to the body of the church. Rightly, too, David, when he reproached the unclean life and serious sins of the people, testified the following about this and said, "They have been satisfied with swine's flesh, and have left the remnants to their babes" [Ps 17:14]. Likewise, Solomon is known to have given an advance warning about this very thing, when he says, "Give to the just man, and help not a sinner. Do well unto him that is lowly, but give not to the ungodly" [Sir 12:5–6]. Surely we recognize clearly that this is not being commanded about alms, which we are ordered to give to everyone, but it concerns the transmission of the Lord's grace.

4. And he added, "Ask and it shall be given to you" [and the rest up to] "to the one who knocks, it shall be opened" [Matt 7:7–8]. The Lord commands us to ask, that we may receive, but to ask not for the glory of the age or the riches of the world, which are contrary to the faith, but to ask for the things that coincide with our hope and salvation, that is, the heavenly gifts, faith, justice, mercy, modesty, patience, understanding of the Scriptures. For God is accustomed to be generous in granting this request to the faithful who ask him and who believe with their whole heart. He does so through the Lord himself, who says in the gospel, "You shall receive whatever you ask the Father for in my name with faith" [see Mark 11:24; Matt 11:22; John 14:13–14; 16:23]. Similarly, he exhorts us also to seek that we may find [see Matt 7:7]. Now the Lord made clear previously what we are to

seek, when he said, "Seek first the kingdom of God and his justice and all these things will be added unto you" [Matt 6:33]. Therefore we ought to seek not the goods of this world, but those heavenly and eternal goods of which the apostle says, "What things eye has not seen nor ear heard, nor ascended the heart of man, which things God prepared for those who love him" [1 Cor 2:9]. Therefore we ought to seek these goods and the giver of all these good things, of whom David testifies in the psalm and says, "With my whole heart I have sought you" [Ps 119:10]. Isaiah too refers to this: "Seek God and you will find [him]. But as soon as he draws nigh to you, let the ungodly leave his ways, and the unjust man his crimes, and mercy shall be offered him" [Isa 55:6–7]. And it fittingly follows, "Knock and it will be opened to you" [Matt 7:7]. In a similar way, the Lord commands us here also to knock not on the doors of strangers but on the gate of life and the entrance to the kingdom of heaven. Therefore he will deem it fitting to open this gate of life to us, if we knock with faith in our heart and with works of justice. He has thrown open the heavenly kingdom to those who believe in him. Finally, saint John has testified that a gate of life of this sort and a door to the kingdom of heaven was opened to him as he knocked with the merits of his faith [see Rev 3:20]; for that is what he says in Revelation: "And I came in the spirit and a door was opened to me in heaven" [Rev 4:2, 1].

5. Hence it is not unfitting that it follows, "Everyone that asks receives, and he who seeks finds, and to the one who knocks, it shall be opened" [Matt 7:8]. For if those who ask for things that are holy receive, and those who seek after heavenly things find, it will be easy, if the merits of faith pave the way, for the door of the kingdom of heaven to be opened to those of us who likewise knock. For it is not opened to everyone, but only to those who are commended by their just merits and a holy manner of life. For we read that those foolish and negligent virgins indeed knocked in order to enter; for they said, "Lord, Lord, open to us" [Matt 25:11]. But he answered them, "Depart from me, for I do not know you" [Matt 25:12]. But in order that the Lord may deem it fitting to open to us as we knock, we ought first to open our heart to the knocking Lord. For that is what the Lord himself says in Revelation: "Behold, I stand at the door and knock. If anyone opens to me, I will enter unto him and dine with him" [Rev 3:20]. Therefore if we faithfully open our hearts to the knocking Lord, doubtless he too will deem it appropriate to open the doors of the kingdom of heaven to those of us who knock.

6. But to show us that we need to ask, seek, and knock with persistence, that nocturnal knocker provides us an example.[126] Even at night he demanded, impertinently indeed but repeatedly and out of necessity, and he received what he was asking for and seeking [see Luke 11:5–8]. For this reason, to instruct us in our faith the Lord shows us the fleshly example of our father and says, "What person is there among you, whose son, if he shall ask him for bread, will he offer him a stone? Or if he shall ask him for a fish, will he offer him a serpent? If you then, being evil, know how to give good gifts to your children, how much more will your Father who is in heaven give good things to them that ask him?" [Matt 7:9–11]. From this comparison to earthly and fleshly parents, therefore, he shows the feeling of the heavenly mercy toward us and of his divine and paternal devotion. For in view of his paternal devotion, no father, even though he be an earthly and temporary one, can deny food to live on to his children who ask only for this. Nor can he offer anything useless and contrary to those who desire good things, since although everyone is capable of being mean to others, yet toward his children he can exhibit nothing but <a heart> of goodness and devotion. If then fleshly parents, who are incapable of being without some sort of evil, retain this love and affectionate devotion for their children, with how much mercy does that heavenly and eternal Father who alone is devoted, good, and merciful, freely impart heavenly goods on those who desire and seek them!

7. But to some interpreters,[127] it seems that the same thing can be observed by the spiritual understanding as well in the following way. If any of us is asked for the bread of saving food and of eternal life by one who longs to be our son through heavenly grace, let us gladly and joyfully share even the food of life with those who desire it. But we can harden our hearts <in> the manner of stones, or set in opposition to them some lack of hope and hardness of unbelief, so that we with a ready and willing soul do not provide those things that they faithfully ask for. The method of interpreting the request for the fish is similar as well. For the fish is understood as the grace of life-giving water and of heavenly baptism, in which we are born to God like fish and by remaining in it, we may possess everlasting life. To those asking for a fish of this sort, then, that is, to those who long for the grace and faith of baptism, we cannot offer serpents, that is, supply the venom of serpentine wickedness and diabolical cunning, so that rather than saving them we should want to trip them up and deceive them, in the manner of the serpent devil.

8. "And whatever you want" [and the rest up to] "for this is the law and the prophets" [Matt 7:12]. In a few words the Lord has summarized everything that was necessary for our faith and salvation, so that we ourselves should also do likewise to others, what we want them to do to us. The Lord has openly shown that all the precepts of the law and the prophets consist in these commands, when he says, "For this is the law and the prophets." We therefore who want nothing but what is good and useful to be done to us by others should pay out in turn grace and love, so that by carrying out the precepts of the law and the prophet, we may attain from the Lord a retribution for our faith, who is blessed in the ages. Amen.

Tractate 34 on Matthew 7:13–14

1. It then follows, "Enter by the narrow gate" [and the rest up to] "who find it" [Matt 7:13–14]. Broad then is the way to perdition and death in which the devil reigns and has prepared plenty of room to perish. Many are the entrances to this broad and spacious road of perdition, namely greed, desire, luxury, lust, drunkenness, immodesty, rage, impatience, and all iniquity [see Gal 5:19–21]. By this way all travel who are led to their deaths with the devil as their guide, those who are enslaved to sins and vices of the world's pleasures without the narrowness of any hardship. But the narrow and constricted way pertains to faith, justice, and holiness, by which one reaches heaven with great effort and unlimited narrowness of hardship. Of this way the Lord testified earlier through Isaiah, saying, "I am the Lord who has shown you the way on which you should walk" [Isa 48:17]. Blessed David also indicates that we are to walk on this way, when he says, "Blessed are those who are spotless on the way, who walk in the law of the Lord" [Ps 119:1]. But many are the paths to this way to heaven, namely faith, justice, chastity, wisdom, holiness, goodness, patience, gentleness, godliness, mercy [see Gal 5:22–23], and the other good things by which the Holy Spirit through Jeremiah exhorts each of us to travel, when he says, "Stand in the ways of the Lord, look for the eternal paths of God, and see what is the good way, and walk in it" [Jer 6:16]. One must stand in the ways of the Lord, then, one must look for the eternal paths of God, so that we may be able to walk by this good way, that is, the way of the gospel. Saint David also boasts that the

Lord led him along the paths of this life, when he says, "You led me on paths of justice for your name's sake" [Ps 23:3]. In another psalm as well he bears testimony to these paths when he says, "Make known to me, O Lord, your ways and show me your paths" [Ps 25:4]. Therefore it is not without reason that the Lord, too, in order to show that he is the guide on this heavenly way, testified the following in the gospel, and said, "I am the way, the truth, and the life. No one comes to the Father except through me" [John 14:6]. This narrow and constricted way that leads to heaven, then, which guides one to paradise, is the one by which the few, all who are just and chosen, are led to life, with the Lord as their guide. This takes place by the various distresses and tribulations of the world, namely those of whom it was said, "Many are called but few are chosen" [Matt 20:16; 22:14].

2. And so the Lord has set before our eyes two ways, one of life and the other of death, one of salvation, the other of perdition. Christ is the guide on the way of life and salvation; but the devil is the guide for the way of perdition and death. And so the former invites us to life, the latter drags us off to death; the former to salvation, the latter to perdition.[128] Which guide should we follow and whose will should we obey? Surely his who invites us to life, not his who drags us off to death; for Christ has redeemed us from death and has called us back to everlasting salvation, having condemned death. He is blessed in the ages of ages. Amen.

Tractate 35 on Matthew 7:15–20

1. Then he says, "Beware of false prophets who come to you in sheep's clothing but inwardly they are ravenous wolves. By their fruits you shall know them" [Matt 7:15–16]. The Lord knows in advance that there will be many false prophets and false apostles. By his prescient majesty he warned us in advance not to be caught unawares. For he shows that all heretics are false prophets, who are enemies of the faith and adversaries of the truth, who lurk as wolves in sheep's clothing, that is, they conceal the deadly teaching of their treacherous minds underneath the outward form of faith and holiness.[129] They cover over the darkness of their error with a veil of light. Saint Paul also testified about them in the Acts of the Apostles when he said, "I know that after my departure savage wolves will come in and not

spare the flock, and from you yourselves men will arise speaking perverse things" [Acts 20:29–30]. And he says of them in his epistle, "And with sweet sounding words they seduce the hearts of those who are without malice" [Rom 16:18]. And again, "Their speech spreads like cancer" [2 Tim 2:17]. Saint John calls them not merely false prophets but even antichrists, when he says, "You have heard that the antichrist is coming, even now many antichrists have come. They went out from us, but they were not of us. For if they had been of us, they would no doubt have remained with us" [1 John 2:18–19]. The same John, in accordance with the Lord's statement, shows that one must not hastily believe them, when he says, "Dearly beloved, believe not every spirit, but test the spirits, if they be of God, because many false witnesses have gone out into this world. Every spirit that confesses that Jesus Christ has come in the flesh is of God, and every spirit that dissolves Christ Jesus, is not of God. And this is the antichrist, of whom you have heard that he is already coming, and he is now already in the world" [1 John 4:1–3].

2. We read that false prophets were designated with this term *wolves* even in past times. For the Lord says the following about them through Ezekiel: "Her princes are as wolves ravening after rapine to shed blood" [Ezek 22:27]. In a similar way the Holy Spirit warned in advance through Jeremiah that they must not be listened to, when he said, "Do not listen to the words of the false prophets who deceive, for they speak of vain visions for themselves from their own heart and not from the mouth of the Lord" [Jer 23:16]. Similarly, in another passage as well the Lord says of them, "I did not send the prophets, and they themselves ran. I did not speak to them, and they themselves prophesied" [Jer 23:21]. The Lord warned ahead of time therefore that false prophets like this, that is, heretics, must be guarded against beforehand. In order to conceal the impiety of their faithlessness they display veils of godliness under the outward appearance of Christ's name, and by means of their pretended faith they take away the truth of the faith. The Lord makes clear however that they can be known by the fruit of iniquity and their works, when he says, "By their fruits you shall know them."

3. Let us see how this in fact is the case. Long ago Photinus[130] came in the clothing of a sheep, that is, proclaiming the name of Christ, and to such an extent did his sheep's clothing deceive that he was even ordained a bishop by Catholic men; but inside he was a wolf, who held treacherousness in his heart instead of faith. This he revealed later on.

Finally, he entered among God's flock in Sirmium[131] as shepherd, but with his sacrilegious mouth he devastated Christ's flock like a ravenous wolf. In sheep's clothing came Arius,[132] preaching Christ the Lord, but inwardly he was found to be a wolf. He claimed that the Creator of all things is a creature, and he even laid waste to Christ's flock like a ravenous wolf in many churches in the east. Even today his disciples try to beguile and deceive God's sheep in a considerable number of churches, but since the master of treachery was exposed long ago, the disciples cannot conceal themselves.

4. And therefore the Lord says, "By their fruits you shall know them," since by the preaching of their faith they are shown to be wolves. For indeed Photinus claimed that our Lord and Savior Christ was only a man. Arius, on the other hand, professes him to be a creature, but the faith of the church does not recognize the kind of Christ they preach. For we do not believe in a man, like Photinus, but in God; nor in a creature, like Arius, but in the Creator. He who believes in man is accursed. For that is what is written: "Cursed is the man who places his hope in man" [Jer 17:5]. He who believes in a creature, too, is condemned. For we read this statement about the impious from the apostle: "And they worshiped and served the creature rather than the Creator" [Rom 1:25]. Therefore although men of this sort come in the clothing of sheep, as if proclaiming Christ, yet within they are shown to be wolves, who carry about a deadly conscience within themselves to harm Christ's sheep. And so, Photinus is a wolf, Arius is a wolf, Sabellius[133] is a wolf, who reduced the unity of the Father and the Son into a union, claiming that he who is the Son is the very Father to his own self. For with a sacrilegious mind he professes that the Father himself was born of the virgin, and that the Son began to exist. Likewise, all heretics are wolves, who by their perverse doctrine tear apart the helpless body of Christ with their deadly mouths. But let wolves like this rage against the flock of God as much as they like; the sheep are safe who are kept by their guardian Christ.

5. Likewise, Jews and Gentile persecutors of the church are indeed called wolves, of whom the Lord himself says in another passage, "Behold, I am sending you like sheep in the midst of wolves" [Matt 10:16]. But after they believe in Christ, they become sheep from being wolves, having been changed not in the outward appearance of their bodies but in their minds. After all, when the apostle Paul was a Jew and persecuted the church, he was held to be a wolf. For it had been said of him, "Benjamin is a ravenous wolf" [Gen 49:27]. But after

he believed in Christ, from being a wolf he became a sheep. For he laid aside the ferocity of a persecutor and adopted the innocence of a sheep. For he who previously persecuted God's sheep like a wolf later on as a sheep himself endured persecution from wolves. Hence the case of the Jews and pagans is better than that of heretics. For if they become believers in Christ, they become sheep from being wolves. But the heretics, on the other hand, are made into wolves from being sheep. They have made a transition from faith to faithlessness. They are the ones whom Isaiah is known to have signified when he says, "They have hatched asps' eggs, and weaved a spider's web" [Isa 59:5]. Thus the deceit and subtlety of heretical doctrine is revealed to be like that of a spider. For as we know by a kind of natural instinct of their own cunning, spiders weave webs for this purpose, to catch by deceit flying bugs for use as their own food. They use snares of this sort—as it were a kind of net that is spread out. So do heretics, by an instinct of diabolical cunning in the manner of spiders, spread out nets as it were for their fraudulent doctrine in order to deceive unstable people and those who are mentally wandering by their fallacious deceit. We read of each of these things under a different signification in the writings of Solomon when it is said, "For nets are not without cause spread for birds" [Prov 1:17]. And again, "Pestilent flies corrupt the sweetness of oil" [Eccl 10:1].

6. It then follows, "Do men gather grapes from thorns, or figs from thistles? Even so every good tree brings forth good fruit. A good tree cannot bring forth evil fruit, neither can an evil tree bring forth good fruit. Every tree that does not bring forth good fruit shall be cut down, and cast into the fire. By their fruits you shall know them" [Matt 7:16–20]. Nature does not allow grapes and figs to be gathered from thorns and thistles, or an evil tree to bring forth good fruit. Whence by a comparison of this sort the Lord reveals that faithless and wicked men who abide in evil cannot bear the fruit of good works. Similarly, he shows in the comparison with a good tree that just and faithful people bring forth nothing but justice and piety. And therefore he is bearing witness that every tree that does not produce good fruit is cut down and thrown into the fire. This shows that each person who does not produce the fruit of good works is destined for the punishment of perpetual fire.

7. But according to the allegorical reckoning, we recognize that the Jews have been signified in the thorns. We read that it is written of them, "I waited [for it] to bring forth grapes, but it brought forth

thorns" [Isa 5:2]. And so it was not possible for grapes to be gathered from thorns like this, since instead of the fruit of justice they inflicted the spines of persecutions. But in the thistles we understand that the heretics have been shown, who are unable to generate the sweetness of faith by their thorny disputations, since in the fig that is sweet by nature the sweetness of faith is signified. But in the good tree the church is signified, which can only bear good fruit, since through baptism it was born unto God for this purpose, it was planted in faith for this purpose: that it produce nothing but the fruit of faith and of every good work. But in the evil tree the synagogue is understood, which can produce no good fruits of faith and godliness, since it has shown contempt for the author of goodness and piety itself and has followed the devil, the prince of evil.

8. But since we read that many have been converted from the synagogue, and we see them converting daily to the knowledge of Christ, from the church too we see many transferring to life in the world and deviating from the faith to faithlessness, it seems more advanced to me to understand Christ as the good tree, who is the font of goodness; but in the evil tree one should consider the devil, who is the origin of evil and the cause of sin. But in the good tree the Lord himself is signified because of the sign of the flesh and the mystery of the cross, the exact thing that Solomon shows clearly when he speaks of the wisdom of God, which is Christ [see 1 Cor 1:30], and says, "She is a tree of life to all that lay hold upon her" [Prov 3:18].[134] And so, a tree of this nature truly was unable to bring forth bad fruit, since Christ alone committed no sin in the flesh [see 1 Pet 2:22]. The nature of human beings likewise can be changed into just people and move from justice toward sin. The nature of Christ alone remained unchangeable even according to the flesh, since no sin was able to exercise dominion over him. Therefore it is more fitting to understand this statement of the person of the Lord, that "a good tree cannot bring forth evil fruit" [Matt 7:18]. And not only does that tree not bring forth evil fruit, but it likewise eradicated all fruit of diabolical iniquity in us, in order to generate the very abundant fruit of faith and justice throughout the whole world in the body of our flesh. For after he was nailed to the cross, he spread forth branches of his wisdom into the whole world, in order to satisfy the entire human race with the fruit of his goodness. This is why it is said by the church in the Song of Songs, "I desired [to be] under his shadow and sat down, and his fruit was sweet in my throat" [Song 2:3]. And so the statement is understood more

completely and perfectly of a tree of this sort, that "a good tree cannot bring forth evil fruits." Whence in the evil tree too we understood rather that the devil is signified, who is truly the root of all evil and the fruit of all iniquity. An evil tree like that can never bring forth good fruit, since he labors daily for this purpose, he goes about the whole world for this purpose, not only to avoid bringing forth any fruit of goodness, but even to stockpile the fruits of his iniquity and the works of his malice by increasing sins. He is to be damned shortly to eternal punishment by our Lord and Savior, who is blessed in the ages. Amen.

Tractate 36 on Matthew 7:21–23

It then follows, "Not everyone who says to me, Lord, Lord, shall enter into the kingdom of heaven" [Matt 7:21]. The Lord is showing that there is no profit if we merely confess his name and do not carry out his commands, since the kingdom of heaven is not only in words but in fruit, as the apostle says, "For it is not the hearers of the law who are just before God, but the doers of the law shall be justified" [Rom 2:13]. Whence saint James says well in his epistle, "Be doers of the word and not hearers only..." [Jas 1:22].

[The CCSL critical edition skips from 36 to 38]

Tractate 38 on Matthew 8:2–4

1. Great is the faith of this leper and perfect his confession![135] For first he worshiped, then he says, "Lord, if you are willing, you can cleanse me" [Matt 8:2]. In the fact that he worshiped, he showed that he believed that the one he was worshiping was God, for the law had commanded that God alone was to be worshiped [see Exod 20:3–6; Deut 6:4–5]. Then, when he says, "Lord, if you are willing, you can cleanse me," he prevails upon the Lord his omnipotence and the nature of the divine power, under the effect of his will, that he may only will his healing, knowing that the power of his virtue is subject to his divine will. Hence since he believed that it pertained only to the

Son of God to be able to will and to will to be able, therefore he says, "Lord, if you are willing, you can cleanse me."[136]

Not without cause the Lord, knowing that the leper believed in him with a devoted and faithful mind, in order to strengthen his faith, immediately repays him with the gift of healing, saying, "I am willing, be cleansed." Finally, "stretching forth his hand he touched him. And at once his leprosy was cleansed" [Matt 8:3]. Here he has manifestly declared himself Lord of all power in accordance with what the leper had believed. For as soon as he willed it, the power of his unique authority effected his will. For this is what he said, "I will, be clean. And at once his leprosy was cleansed. And Jesus said to him, See to it that you tell no one, but go, show yourself to the priest and offer the gift that Moses commanded as a testimony to them" [Matt 8:3–4]. The Lord commands the one whom he had cleansed from leprosy to show himself to the priest, and offer the sacrifices prescribed in the law for himself [see Lev 14:2]. In this he wanted to show that he himself carried out the sacraments of the law and to expose the unbelief of the priests, so that upon seeing that the leper was cleansed, whom neither the law nor the priests had been able to cleanse, they might indeed thus believe he was God's Son and acknowledge him as Lord of the law; or at least, if they are unwilling to believe, by the justice and faith of the leper and by the testimony of the work itself, they would receive condemnation for their unbelief.[137] For who could have cured a leper, whom the law was not able to cleanse, by the authority of his own power, except the one who is the Lord of the law, and who is the God of all virtues, of whom we read it written, "The Lord of virtues [is] with us, our protector, the God of Jacob" [Ps 46:7,11]? And even before he was cured, that leper indeed believed that the Son of God was God, with a religious confession of faith; but the priests refused to believe even after the miracle of the divine operation.

2. But since in these very sacrifices that the law had commanded to be offered for lepers we recognize a figure of the future truth shown in advance, we need to examine what these sacrifices are and what meaning in respect to the heavenly mystery they contain in themselves. For indeed we understand that the reason the Lord even commanded the one whom he had cleansed of leprosy to offer the sacrifices prescribed for him in the law was to show both that he was the author of the precept given and that the mysteries themselves were fulfilled through himself in truth, which had been shown earlier as types. And indeed in the law different sacrifices were commanded

to be offered for leprosy [see Lev 14:1–7]. But the greatest sacrifice was commanded for the cleansing of leprosy itself. For the following was stated in the law, that if someone should be cleansed of leprosy, he should go to the priest and offer for himself the sacrifice of two birds, or two live chicks, and cedar wood, and spun scarlet, and hyssop [see Lev 14:4]. And it was commanded that the priest should take one bird and one chick and kill them over an earthen vessel over living water [see Lev 14:5]. And as for the living bird and the cedar wood, and the spun scarlet, and the hyssop, he shall dip them into the blood of the bird that was slain over living water and sprinkle it upon the one cleansed of leprosy seven times and he would be clean, and he would release the live bird in a field and it would fly away [see Lev 14:6–7], and the other things that are too long to tell. <If> we consider this sacrifice prescribed in the law according to its spiritual sense and mystical account, we find no small mysteries.

3. For in the leprosy, a figure of sin is shown by whose defilement the entire human race had been stained as it were with a kind of leprosy. This agrees with what the apostle has said: "A little leaven corrupts the entire lump" [1 Cor 5:6]. Long ago the law showed in types that this cleansing from sin could not happen in any other way than through the previously mentioned sacrifice. For in the two chicks is shown the mystery of the Lord's incarnation, for he who is an eternal priest [see Heb 7:24] received both body and soul <from> a holy virgin for the cleansing of our sins. But in the cedar wood the mystery of the cross is clearly shown;[138] but in the scarlet-colored shrub is the redemption by his precious blood; in the hyssop, however, is the apostolic preaching by which we are <sprinkled> with the blood of the Lord and purified from sins. This is why Moses was commanded to dip a small bundle of hyssop branches in blood and thus cleanse the people [see Exod 24:8]. This is also the reason David testified in the Psalm and said, "O Lord, you will sprinkle me with hyssop and I will be cleansed; you will wash me and I will be whiter than snow" [Ps 51:7]. But in the living water is shown the grace of baptism that gives us birth to eternal life.

4. But it is not without reason that one of the two chicks is reported to be killed, since only his body undertook the suffering of death. But the soul and Word remained as God with an immortal nature. But because a living chick was dipped in the blood of the slain chick, this showed that the suffering of his body should be attributed even to the soul and divinity of Christ. And this is why the holy apostle

attested that the Lord of majesty was crucified [see 1 Cor 2:8]. But the reference to the living chick being dipped in the blood of the slain chick and released in a field to fly away, surely this showed that the Son of God through his worshipful resurrection, once he had taken up his body again, would fly from the field of this world to heaven, in accordance with what is written: "And he ascended upon the cherubim and flew upon the wings of the winds" [Ps 18:10]. And so, long ago the law had shown figuratively that our Lord and Savior, who is a true and everlasting priest [see Heb 6:20], would offer this kind of sacrifice for the leprosy of our sins, or rather for those of the whole world [see 1 John 2:2]. Whence too it is commanded to the one who was cleansed from leprosy to be sprinkled seven times with the blood of the slain chick because through the blood of Christ by which we are redeemed [see 1 Pet 1:18–19] and through the sevenfold grace of the Holy Spirit [see Isa 11:2; Rev 3:1] by which we are illumined, a complete cleansing of our sins takes place. Whence in this leper who met the Lord as he was coming down from the mountain in order to be cured, a figure of all sins and of the entire human race has been shown, because we were all being held, sprinkled by the iniquity of Adam's sins, as it were by a kind of leprosy. But when our Lord and Savior came down from the summit of the heavens, as from a mountaintop for the sake of our salvation, we received the remission of sin and sensed the cure of eternal healing. Whence not without cause was it commanded that this kind of man return to the camp on the eighth day [see Lev 14:8], to show that by means of the Lord's resurrection, which is on the eighth day, once the cleansing of sin had taken place, we would be presented back in the heavenly encampments by our Lord and Savior <who is blessed in the ages of ages. Amen.>

Tractate 39 on Matthew 8:5–13

1. It follows, "After these things, when he had entered into Capernaum, there came to him a certain centurion, beseeching him, and saying, My servant (*puer*) lies at home a paralytic, and is grievously tormented. And Jesus said to him, I will come and heal him. The centurion, making an answer, said to him, Lord, I am not worthy that you should enter under my roof, but only say the word, and my servant shall be healed" [Matt 8:5–8], and the other things that follow in the

reading. How glorious is the faith of the centurion and how wonderful his devotion, which believed in the Son of God with such perfect faith with no instruction from the law! The centurion beseeches the Lord to deign to cure his paralyzed servant. The Lord is disposed to go to the place where the paralytic was lying, but the centurion, full of faith and very aware of his own lowliness, professes that he is unworthy of such a great act of condescension on the Lord's part, and excuses such a great burden of divine condescension. For this is what he says: "I am not worthy that you should enter under my roof, but only say the word, and my servant shall be healed." This is a confession of very advanced faith and perfect knowledge, to confess the omnipotence in such a way that one believes that all things are possible for him. Whence this centurion, although he saw our Lord and Savior as a man according to the body, yet recognized him to be God with the vision of his mind and faith. After all, he says this: "Only say the word, and my servant shall be healed," for he believed that he was present everywhere through the power of his divine nature, and that if he only willed it, he could cure everything with a word. He knew that he was the one of whom it had been written, "He sent his word and healed them" [Ps 107:20]. And again, "For it was not a mollifying plaster that cured them but your word, O Lord, which heals all things" [Wis 16:12]. Although the centurion was still ignorant and unaware of this writing of the law, nevertheless he confessed with believing faith. Whence not unfittingly he even adduced an example of this necessary earthly authority when he said, "For I also am a man subject to authority, having under me soldiers. And I say to this one, Go, and he goes, and to another, Come, and he comes. And to my servant, Do this, and he does it" [Matt 8:9]. Through this and by believing in this way he confessed that he was the Lord and the prince of the heavenly army, and that all things were subject to his authority. For he believed that he was the one to whom angels and archangels and all the powers of heaven were subject to the obedience of service. And so through faith like this the centurion succeeded in obtaining what he had requested, and he became worthy of the testimony of divine praise, that he was preferred to all the Israelites. For thus did the Lord testify about him, saying, "Amen I say to you, I have never found such great faith in Israel" [Matt 8:10]. Indeed in no one. For higher up when the leper was cleansed the priests of the law refused to acknowledge the Lord of such great power. The centurion, a man of the Gentiles, uneducated in the law, uninstructed by the prophets, acknowledged the Son of God before his servant was healed. And indeed the priests refused to believe even after the sign of a divine miracle had been recognized in the leper. But the centurion obtained eternal salvation not only for himself but also for his household, by believing with complete faith. Therefore from this man we know how much a religious confession of devout faith achieves before God for each one. It benefits not merely oneself but one's own people. The centurion believes and his servant obtains healing.

2. We have said these things then according to the history of the letter. Now we need to give attention to what should be thought in the same operation by way of the spiritual understanding. In this centurion, who believed in the Son of God with complete faith, is shown a figure of those saints who pleased God apart from the law of the letter.[139] But in the centurion's servant who lay at home paralyzed, a type of the Gentile people is shown, those who lie in the home of this world out of joint in soul and body, burdened down with serious transgressions. The Lord comes for this purpose, then, when he is prayed to by the prayers of the saints to grant the healing of the divine Word for the salvation of the Gentiles, whereby those who have been liberated from such a malady of sins may receive the perfect healing of faith and salvation. Whence also in what he has said, "I am not worthy that you should enter under my roof, but only say the word, and my servant shall be healed," it is recognized that his house signifies this world, which he attests is unworthy of God, defiled by the sacrileges of the Gentiles and by the superstitions of idols and by all sins. Finally, although the Lord had come down to this world where there was a dwelling place of the nations, yet he was found to be completely estranged from the vices and sins of the world. And although he had come into this world to give salvation to the nations, yet the Lord delivered the precepts of life, which would benefit the people of the Gentiles not in the temples of idols but in the temple of God, which had been built for a time in Jerusalem. And therefore it is said by the centurion, "I am not worthy that you should enter under my roof," to show that the polluted dwelling place of the Gentiles was still unworthy of the Son of God. But he added, "Only say the word and my servant shall be healed." In this it is recognized to be indicated that the Lord would appoint through the apostles the word of the divine preaching for the salvation of the Gentiles after his passion, not before it. Whence too there is this statement of Paul to the Jews: "It was necessary first to announce the word of God to you. But since you have judged yourselves unworthy of eternal life, behold we are

turning to the nations. For thus has the Lord commanded us" [Acts 13:46–47]. For this reason, too, the Lord praised the faith of the centurion and declared this future hope for the Gentiles, when he said, "Amen I say to you that many shall come from the east and the west, and shall recline with Abraham, and Isaac, and Jacob in the kingdom of heaven. But the children of this kingdom shall be cast out into the outer darkness" [Matt 8:11–12]. By this statement he has declared openly that once the unfaithful people of the Jews were rejected, there would be a noble gathering of the church from all nations, which by their faith and devotion would be considered worthy of feasting with the saints in the heavenly kingdom, through the coming of our Lord and Savior, who is blessed before all ages both now and always in the ages of ages. Amen.

Tractate 40 on Matthew 8:14–17

1. Then it says, "And when he came to Peter's house" [and the rest up to] "and she ministered to him" [Matt 8:14–15]. Our Lord and Savior entered Peter's home and healed his mother-in-law, who was sick with a serious fever, solely by the touch of his hand. In this he shows himself to be the Lord of all healing, the author of heavenly medicine, who long ago had spoken to Moses and said, "I am the Lord who heals you" [Isa 60:16; cf. Exod 15:26]. But in the fact that he bestowed the healing with the touch of his hand, it was not a question of impotency but of grace. But he who had cured the paralytic earlier by a word alone surely could easily likewise have expelled the present fever with a word, but he showed the gift of his condescension through the touch of his hand and made manifest that he was the one of whom it had been written, "He quickly offers his healing through the touch of his hand" [see Mark 5:23, var.], which we understand was carried out in this work. After all, the fever is put to flight at once through the touch of the Lord's hand, healing is given to the one with believing faith; he who examines the inner heart gives the gifts of healing and she who was in need of the other's ministry herself began to minister to the Lord, since she had been restored to her original soundness. Surely Christ's divinity is manifestly proven by these miraculous works.

2. But according to the figurative account, Peter's mother-in-law contains a type of the synagogue, which was lying ill and oppressed

with serious transgressions as with a kind of fever. Now the reason Peter's mother-in-law is understood as the synagogue is because when this same man preached after the Lord's resurrection, as we read in the Acts of the Apostles, the first calling of the church came from the synagogue, which saint Peter is known to have joined to her faith [see Acts 2:14–42]. Thus Peter's mother-in-law was freed from her fever through the touch of the Lord's hand and began to minister. This shows that whoever believed in the Son of God from the synagogue has been liberated from the fever of sin through the grace of divine power and will be the Lord's ministers through works of justice. There is no difference, since the synagogue is recognized to be signified in the portion of believers. For it is customary in many passages in the divine Scriptures for the whole to be reckoned in the portion.

3. But in another sense Peter's mother-in-law and the law can be understood. Her daughter, that is, that people of believers that had been born through the law, Peter took in his faith through the preaching of the gospel. For it was said to him, "You are Peter, and upon this rock I shall build my church" [Matt 16:18]. This law, then, of which Peter's mother-in-law is a figure in person, until the time when the Lord would come in the flesh for the salvation of the human race, was weak as it were with a kind of malady, due to the transgressions of the Jewish people. This agrees with what the apostle reported: "For since the law was weak through the flesh, God sent his own Son in the likeness of the flesh of sin, in order that concerning sin he might condemn sin in the flesh" [Rom 8:3]. But when the Lord of the law came, the entire weakness of the law was removed, in that the law was not able to give salvation. Through the grace of the Lord this very law was reformed for the better and grew strong through the faith of the gospel, and thus the same law, which previously had been an occasion of death through human weakness, later on through faith and the grace of Christ became a minister of salvation.

4. Then it says, "But when evening came they brought to him many" [and the rest up to] "and he cured our troubles" [Matt 8:16–17]. The Lord of powers and the author of human salvation, as a pious and merciful God of heavenly medicine, generously healed everyone, he freed those who were oppressed by the devil, he put unclean spirits to flight, all diseases and maladies of the body too he removed by the word of his divine power, so that he could both show that he had come for the salvation of the human race and manifest clearly that he was God through the working of such great miracles. For only God

could perform such great miraculous signs. Not without cause the Lord exposed the faithlessness of Jewish unbelief when he says, "If you do not want to believe in me, at least believe the works and know that the Father is in me and I in him" [John 10:38].

"In order to fulfill what was spoken through Isaiah the prophet: For he took up our infirmities and bore our troubles" [Matt 8:17; cf. Isa 53:4]. For the Son of God took up the infirmity of the human race for this purpose, to make those of us who were once infirm strong and robust by faith in him. For this purpose he assumed a body from the race of the sinner, to blot out our sins by the mystery of his flesh. But according to the spiritual understanding, the mystery of the Lord's passion is shown in the words "in the evening." That is when the Son of God himself, who is called the "sun of justice" [Mal 4:2], received the setting of death for our salvation.[140] After his passion all who have been offered to the Lord and are being offered, <having been set free> from various infirmities of sins and from the chains of the devil, attain to the healing of everlasting salvation from our Lord and Savior and the eternal physician, to whom is the praise and glory in the ages of ages. Amen.

Tractate 41 on Matthew 8:18–22

1. Then it says, "But seeing great multitudes about him" [and the rest up to] "the Son of man has nowhere to lay his head" [Matt 8:18–20]. The Lord not only does not refuse any of us from coming to him with faith, but of his own accord even invites us to his grace by his divine condescension, in accordance with what he says: "Come to me, all you who labor and are heavy laden and I shall give you rest" [Matt 11:28]. It needs to be asked, therefore, why he refused this scribe using these opposing examples, a man who had offered himself of his own accord and who said that he wanted to follow the Lord. He says to him, "Foxes have holes and the birds of the sky have nests where they may rest" [Matt 8:20]. Consequently, this scribe, as the sense of the reading shows, approached the Lord not with believing faith but with a mind characterized by hypocrisy. He failed to retain the earlier prophecy of Solomon: "My son, do not approach God with a double heart" [Sir 1:28]. Indeed, in the first place, how arrogant and unfaithful is the boast of this scribe, to say to the Lord, "I will

follow you wherever you go!" [Matt 8:19]. For he does not say merely, "I will follow you," but "I will follow you wherever you go." From this it is understood that he neither had reverence for God nor did he believe faithfully in the Son of God. For who that believes the Son of God is God would dare to say, "I shall follow you wherever you go," the one whom he knew would soon return to heaven and dwell with the Father along with the angels in unapproachable light, in accordance with what the apostle has said: "Who dwells in unapproachable light" [1 Tim 6:16].

2. Whence God, the examiner of hearts and the knower of secrets, not without cause refused the one who was tempting him rather than truly and faithfully wanting to follow him, by saying, "Foxes have holes and birds of the sky nests where they may rest." Foxes here signify the false prophets who were among the people of Israel at that time, and now are the heretics. The Holy Spirit testifies about them through Ezekiel the prophet when he says, "Your prophets, O Israel, are like foxes in the desert" [Ezek 13:4]. Through Solomon he related of them, "Take us the little foxes that spoil the vineyard, and our vines flourish" [Song 2:15]. That is, by foxes he means the false prophets and all heretics, who attempt to spoil the Lord's vineyard like foxes. Whence too in the gospel the Lord said the following concerning Herod, who was a Sadducee, that is, a heretic of the Jews: "Go tell that fox" [Luke 13:32]. Foxes like this have holes, then, that is, impious and dark gatherings buried in the depths of earthly infidelity. By their doctrine they live in their hearts as it were in certain holes. The Lord says the following concerning this hole in another passage: "But when a blind man guides a blind man, they both fall into the hole" [Matt 15:14]. Solomon also refers to it: "But he who does not know the Lord will fall into it" [Prov 22:14; cf. Sir 28:26]. David plainly shows that impious and unfaithful assemblies like this are handed over to punishment, when he says, "They will be handed over to the hand of the sword, the portions for foxes" [Ps 63:10]. Samson likewise in the foxes he found has warned in a figure that their punishment is coming, along with the preceding example. When he caught thirty foxes and tied them tail to tail, he set fire to them and burned the Philistines' crops [see Judg 15:4–6]. In this it is shown that all heretics are to be handed over to the punishment of the fires of Gehenna, bound together under one verdict, namely those who are found estranged from the faith and from the knowledge of the truth. During the preaching of the cross of Christ, they were in possession of a perverted faith. This will

happen at the consummation of the world, since the harvest, as the Lord interprets it [see Matt 13:39], is shown to be the consummation of the world. Now the natural inclinations of cunning in the fox are diverse. These are justly and rightly compared to the false prophets and heretics. They lie in wait for domestic birds to catch them by some deceit, then in the very holes they dig they make many different exits, to keep themselves from being easily captured. So, too, the heretics lie in wait for Christ's domestic birds, in whom are the wings of virtues and the feathers of good works, to seize them out of the church by some deceptive doctrine and to entice them to their holes of faithlessness to devour them. Then also, if they recognize that they can be captured by some Catholic man and powerful teacher, they have different escape routes prepared for their impious assertions by which they endeavor to flee for the time being. Whence we rightly observe that false apostles and false prophets are signified in the foxes.[141] But in the birds of the sky we understand that unclean spirits are indicated, in accordance with what the Lord himself makes clear in another passage when he says the following about the devil and his angels: "The birds came and devoured it" [Matt 13:4; Mark 4:4].[142] Now the reason unclean spirits are called birds is because by their spiritual natures they fly about like birds in a moment of time, just as the devil himself admitted to the Lord in the Book of Job when he said, "In a moment of time I have gone around the whole world and have come" [Job 1:7; 2:2]. But the nest signifies the hearts of unbelieving and unfaithful men in which birds of this sort, namely unclean spirits, rest as it were in their own homes.

3. "But the Son of man has nowhere to lay his head" [Matt 8:20].[143] For the Lord was unable to find a place to lay his head both in the false prophets, owing to their false preaching, and in the unclean spirits that possessed the entire people of Israel, owing to their worship of idols, that is, a place to set the knowledge of his Father's name, who is Christ's head [see 1 Cor 11:3], or at least who would have recognized through the Father himself by faith that Christ is God's Son, since according to the apostle, God is Christ's head. For among the Jewish people everything was possessed by a spirit of unbelief. Whence not unjustly the Lord had testified earlier through Isaiah to this same thing when he said, "For I came, and there was no man. I called, and there was none to hearken" [Isa 50:2]. But these are all found outside the boat in which the Lord crossed with his disciples [see Matt 8:23], since none of them deserve to be in Christ's church. And therefore it

was not in those who were in the boat with the Savior that he was not able to lay his head, that is, in the apostles and believers, but in those who scarcely deserved to be received by the Lord.

4. It then follows, "But another disciple said to him, Lord, permit me first to go and bury my father" [and the rest up to] "their own dead" [Matt 8:21–22]. This disciple believed with a religious spirit and faithful mind to be sure, but still he did not have the knowledge of perfect faith. For he had not yet heard from the Lord, "Whoever does not leave his father and mother and children and brothers and sisters and follow me cannot be my disciple" [see Luke 14:26]. And therefore since he does not know the perfection of faith, he did not know what he was talking about. For that reason the Lord, who tested the heart rather than the words of his disciples who believed, showed him his ignorance. Whence wanting him to be perfect in all things, he orders that no cure of the world be held onto when he says, "Let the dead bury their own dead."[144] For it would have been inappropriate that one who, by once believing in the Son of God had already begun to have the living and heavenly God as Father, should give thought to his dead father. And therefore the Lord exhorts only that he follow him. For he says to him, "Follow me."

5. Higher up, the infidelity of a scribe who freely offers himself is rejected [see Matt 8:19]; but here the faith of one who only believes is chosen. For surely it is manifest that the Lord passed this sentence not by acceptance of persons but by the judgment of divine knowledge. For he who knows the secrets of the heart knew whom he had chosen. This accords with what Solomon says in the persona of wisdom: "She goes about seeking such as are worthy of her, showing herself cheerfully unto them in the paths" [Wis 6:17]. And again: "She chose him at the first, wisdom lays up treasure upon him" [Sir 4:18, 21]. Therefore the one who had approached with a hypocritical mind is rejected, but he who sought with a simple mind and a pure heart is chosen, in accordance with what is written: "Seek him with simplicity of heart" [Wis 1:1]. And therefore, here the one who believed with faith is received by the Lord into the boat, that is, into the church, where the choir of apostles is. But the scribe did not deserve to be received by the Lord, or rather, he was rejected, because he did not believe with faith. Blessed therefore is that disciple who has merited to be received by the Lord while the scribe was rejected! Whence not unfittingly long ago through Solomon he exhorts this man as it were to follow him with the following words: "Prepare your works for [your]

going forth, and prepare [yourself] for the field; and come after me, and you shall rebuild your house" [Prov 24:27], that is, that the one who has been prepared in his soul through works of faith and justice may follow the Lord of life as his guide, because he had received the house of his body restored through the glory of the resurrection. This accords with what the apostle has said: "We have a house not made by hands, but eternal in the heavens" [2 Cor 5:1].

6. Since therefore the Lord desired that this disciple of his who was still thinking somewhat about the world arrive at the perfection of faith, he said to him, "Follow me, and let the dead bury their own dead."[145] He is showing that the faith and knowledge of Christ is to be placed before the duties of piety like this, and the burial of a deceased unbelieving father ought to be scorned for the sake of God, for the sake of him for whom we are ordered to abandon even living parents [see Matt 4:22].[146] For it is right to do more for God than for human beings, more for the father of nature than of the body, more for the author of life than the burial of a dead man, especially since duties of the same sort are usually exhibited to the dead even by unbelievers, who are themselves called "dead" here, since all unbelievers and unfaithful people are considered to be truly dead before God, according to the reliability of the Scriptures, since they do not live for God but for the world.[147]

7. And this statement of the Lord is indeed so understood according to the letter. But let us discuss in still greater detail why the Lord said that the dead are buried by the dead.[148] To be sure we know that there is no obligation for dead human beings to bury dead people, nor does the law of nature itself permit this. But let us see whether perhaps this can be understood in another way. We said earlier that all unbelievers and unfaithful people, though they live in this world, yet they are accounted as being dead to God. We read that it is written of them, "The dead shall not praise you, O Lord, nor do all who go down to the lower world. But we who are alive bless the Lord" [Ps 115:17–18]. And again, "Will you work wonders for the dead?" [Ps 88:12]. And Isaiah testifies of them and says, "O Lord, we know not any other God besides you. But the dead do not have life" [Isa 26:13–14]. And again, "For they that are in the lower world shall not praise you, neither shall the dead bless you" [Isa 38:18]. And the holy apostle knows that all unbelievers are dead to God when he says, "And when you were dead in your transgressions and sins" [Eph 2:1]. For this reason, too, he testified that the unfaithful widow is a living

dead woman [see 1 Tim 5:6]. Here then the Lord is speaking of dead people of this sort, who are dead in respect to God, who are understood to bury their own dead in this manner, because they live by an earthly manner of life, and by means of mortal deeds of the flesh they bury themselves in eternal death. For indeed the holy apostle shows that there is a twofold nature in us, namely of the soul and of the body. Yet he called both of them "man" when he said, "For if he who is our outer man is being corrupted," that is, the flesh, "but he who is within is being renewed" [2 Cor 4:16], namely the soul. Whence clearly we recognize that the dead who bury their own dead signify all the impious and the sinners who are dead in the inner man through the unbelief of their mind. Through their vices and sins they bury their own dead, that is, their mortal bodies in everlasting death. For just as saints and all who believe are alive to God through the works of life and justice, but they are dead and buried to this world (in accordance with what the apostle makes clear when he says, "Therefore we have been buried together with him through baptism unto death" [Rom 6:4]), so, too, all the ungodly and sinners are dead and buried to God, since they are living for this world through the desires of the flesh and through works of iniquity.

8. Similar to this statement is the apostle's statement as well where he says, "What are those who are baptized for the dead doing, if the dead do not rise at all?" [1 Cor 15:29]. Some indeed claim that at the time of the apostle, certain people with religious feelings to be sure but also superfluous presumption, were baptized by certain ones on behalf of their close relatives, in case they had departed without baptism, so that that baptism they themselves received would bring the benefit of salvation for the dead. But this claim seems superfluous and irrational, that some are believed to have been baptized for others, or the living for the dead. But since the resurrection of the flesh was being denied by certain unbelievers [see 1 Cor 15:12], the blessed apostle, in order to convict minds of this sort who did not believe in the future resurrection of bodies, brought this testimony: "What are those who are baptized for the dead doing, if the dead do not rise at all?" This was to show clearly that each of us is baptized in this mortal body for this purpose, that he may believe that he will rise to eternal life with the same body. This agrees with what we profess in the faith of the creed (*symboli*), in which we receive baptism by saying, "the resurrection of this flesh for eternal life."[149] Therefore, to be baptized for the dead means [to be baptized] for our bodies, which seem to

be subject to death. For souls are immortal by nature, and are not destroyed in that common death with the bodies but separated. Since, then, in baptism we are baptized not only for the salvation of the soul but for the future resurrection of the body, therefore the apostle says, "What are they who are baptized for the dead doing if the dead do not rise at all?" {Finally, that we should know that the holy apostle said this in this way, he makes clear with the examples he sets forth from the entire context of the reading itself and from the heavenly doctrine, which speaks of nothing else than the true future resurrection of the body. For this reason, too, he started with the Lord [see 1 Cor 15:3–4, 13–19] who deigned to rise in the same body he had taken on for the sake of salvation}.[150]

9. Here, then, in the words that the Lord speaks, "Let the dead bury their own dead" [Matt 8:22], he has not inhibited the obligations of religious piety, by which we know that many saints have pleased God [see Tob 1:17; 12:12–13], but he has forbidden mortal works of the flesh through which a person would become subject to eternal death.[151] Whence long ago the law had shown the same thing figuratively, that anyone who had touched a dead body is defiled [see Num 9:6; Bar 3:10]. Surely we notice that this was said not about the burial of a body but about works of the flesh, dead in transgressions. If someone is associated with those, doubtless he is made unclean and defiled. For which reason as well the holy apostle said, "We should not share in the unfruitful works of darkness" [Eph 5:11]. But if we think that a person can be defiled by touching a dead body, how is it that holy Moses carried the bones of Joseph with him [see Exod 13:19], from which he was not only not defiled but heaped up all the more merits for his faith in this by exhibiting devoted service and religious feelings of piety toward such an ancestor? Or how is it that that man who had been killed by thieves, as we read in the Books of Kingdoms, came back to life by touching the body of the deceased Elisha [see 2 Kgs 13:21], if someone who touches a dead body becomes unclean and defiled? Contact with a dead body could do so much that not only did it not defile the one who touched it, but it summoned back from death to life the man who had been killed.

10. And to be sure, saint Matthew mentioned only these two, but Luke recorded in the same passage, the one who says to the Lord, "I will follow you, but allow me to report back to those who are at home. And the Lord said to him, No one who looks behind after setting his hand to the plow is suitable for the kingdom of God" [Luke 9:61–62].

This shows that the one who desires to follow the Lord, who sets his hand to the plow, that is, the one who has been established in the hope of the cross of Christ with evangelical faith and who renounces the world, ought not look back, that is, return again to the things that belong to the world. Otherwise, he becomes unworthy of the kingdom of God through vain worldly concerns of this sort and through empty desire. Whence not without cause does the holy apostle warn us not to return to the weak and impoverished things of the world [see Gal 4:9]. In these three young men who approached the Lord, then, both the rejection of unbelievers and the diverse graces of believers are shown. For the first man is rejected as an unfaithful unbeliever; the second, as a believer, is in fact chosen to follow the Lord and to preach the kingdom of God; but the third is warned not to look back in order to be worthy of the kingdom of God. And in the first indeed, the one who was a scribe, a type of the Pharisees and teachers of the law was shown, those who are puffed up by the teaching of the law, since they approach the Lord as tempters rather than believers [see Matt 16:1; 19:3; 22:18, 35]. They are rejected by reason of their unbelief. But in the second there is shown a figure of the apostles, who believe faithfully and are commanded to follow the Lord and are known to be destined to preach the kingdom of God throughout the whole world. Now in the third man there is shown a figure of the people who believe from the Gentiles, who have been delivered from the error of the age and established at the plow of heavenly hope and gospel faith. They are warned not to return again to the world in order to be able to be deemed worthy of God's kingdom. The Holy Spirit also exhorts us through Isaiah to the grace of this gospel plow when he says, "They will shatter their swords into plows and spears into pruning hooks" [Isa 2:4]. In this it is shown that when the weapons of our iniquity and evil have been broken, we would live in the gospel faith and the peace of the church, through Christ our Lord, to whom is the praise and the glory together with the Father and with the Holy Spirit in the ages of ages. Amen.

Tractate 42 on Matthew 8:23–27[152]

1. It then follows, "And when he got into the boat" [and the rest up to] "that the winds and the sea obey him" [Matt 8:23–27]. While the Lord was sailing with his disciples, a great storm arose so that the

rising waves of the violent sea covered the boat. "But he was asleep" [Matt 8:24]. A marvelous account![153] He entered the little boat to sail, when it is he who steers the whole world with his divine power. He slumbers in sleep, when it is he who guards his people with eternal vigilance. But the Lord slept, not by the necessity of human weakness but of his own free will. For although it is not in the eternal nature of God to sleep (as we read in that which is said about him: "Behold he who guards Israel has neither slumbered nor will he sleep" [Ps 121:4]) nonetheless our Lord and Savior thought it proper to fulfill all things pertaining to human nature, even to the point of sleep, in order to prove the truth of the body he had taken on himself, so that he could plainly show the truth of the body he had assumed for himself.

2. But while the Lord was sleeping, a storm was raging, and violent waves swamped the boat and endangered it. The disciples were struck with fear and roused the Lord, saying, "Lord, deliver us; we are perishing" [Matt 8:25]. Long ago David seems to have signified this very thing under the persona of the apostles rousing the Lord, when he says, "Rise up! Why do you sleep, O Lord? Rise up, help us and deliver us for the sake of your name!" [Ps 44:23, 26].

3. So then, "the Lord rising up says to them, Why are you afraid, you of little faith? And he commanded the wind and the sea and there came a great calm" [Matt 8:26]. Thereby the Lord clearly declared the power of his divinity as he checked the violent waves of the sea by the word of divine power. The winds and the sea could not have obeyed anyone other than their Lord and Creator. David had foretold what would happen when he said, "The waters saw you, O God, the waters saw you and were afraid, and the depths were troubled. [There was] an abundant sound of waters; the clouds uttered a voice" [Ps 77:16–17]. And what are those clouds that uttered a voice to the frightened waters if not the disciples, who on seeing this sign of divine power exclaimed, "Truly this man was the Son of God!"? [see Matt 14:33; Mark 15:39]. But the reason the apostles are understood as clouds is because they arise from the earth like the clouds and are carried to heaven without any burden of sin by the spiritual lightness of their nature, and they pour forth the rain of divine preaching to water the hearts of believers.[154]

In another passage, too, David likewise attests that the violence of the sea must be calmed down by the Lord giving a word of command: "You rule the power of the sea; and you still the motion of its waves" [Ps 89:9]. And again: "He spoke, and the stormy wind stood, and its waves grew calm" [Ps 107:25, 29]. And again: "You trouble the bottom of the sea, and you calm the sounds of its waves" [Ps 65:7]. And again: "Behold, he will utter his voice, the voice of power" [Ps 68:33]. Surely this refers to that voice by which the tranquility of the sea was restored by virtue of his divine power, as he commanded the winds. Also blessed Job through the Holy Spirit was not ignorant that this would take place, when he spoke of the Lord and said the following: "With power he calmed the sea" [Job 26:12].

4. When therefore the stormy sea had been calmed and tranquility had been established at the command of his word, it says, "Those who were in the boat marveled, saying, What sort of man is this, that the winds and sea obey him?" [Matt 8:27]. Long ago saint David had predicted this power of the Lord's word and the astonishment of those who were in the boat, when he said in the psalm, "They go down to the sea in ships, doing business on the great waters; they saw the works of the Lord and his wonders in the deep. For he spoke and the stormy wind arose" [Ps 107:23–24]. And again, "He stayed the storm into a breeze, and calmed its waves and they rejoiced because they had become still" [Ps 107:29–30].

5. Therefore we first recognize that according to the simple account of the history these things took place in this way by the power of the Lord. But we ought to diligently pay attention to what figure is shown in all these matters according to an allegorical account.[155] For one must ask how this ship ought to be understood according to a spiritual reckoning, and what the sea refers to, and the rising waves and the winds that stirred up these waves. And what does the Lord's sleep mean and his rebuke of the winds and the restoration of tranquility and the fitting admiration of the sailors? There is no doubt that the ship is a figure of the church. This agrees with what the Holy Spirit says through Solomon about it when he says, "She became like a merchant ship from afar" [Prov 31:14]. That is, it is the church that runs everywhere by the word of preaching, as the apostles sail, the Lord steers, and the Holy Spirit fills her sails.[156] She carries with her a great and priceless cargo, by which she has purchased the whole human race, or rather the whole world, by the blood of Christ. In another passage, too, Solomon referred to this, saying, among other things, "But the trace of a ship sailing in the open sea cannot be found" [Wis 5:10]. This shows that the church's way of life is not earthly or of this age, but heavenly, as the holy apostle reports and says, "Our manner of life is in heaven" [Phil 3:20].

But the sea is understood to be this age, which swells with different sins and various temptations as with types of waves. We read that it has been written about this, "[So is] this great and wide sea, there are things creeping innumerable, small animals and great, and this dragon whom you have made to play in it" [Ps 104:25–26]. And again, "I have come into the depths of the sea, and a storm has overwhelmed me" [Ps 69:2].

Now the winds are understood as the spiritual forces of wickedness [see Eph 6:12] and unclean spirits who rage furiously to shipwreck the church by various temptation of this world, as by waves of the sea.[157]

That the Lord is sleeping in this boat is therefore understood to mean that he allows his church to be tested by the oppressions and persecutions of this world in order to test her faith.

As for the prayer of the disciples who roused the Lord and implored his help to be delivered, these are shown to be the prayers of all the saints, who with devout faith and constant prayer rouse the patience of the Lord as from sleep whenever the storm of persecution has arisen and the devil and his angels rage violently.[158] They pray that he might deem it fitting to help, by the aid of his mercy, those who are in danger owing to their fear of human weakness. When the winds, that is, the unclean spirits who are the authors of persecution, have been rebuked by him, and every storm of the world has calmed down, he restores his church to peace and tranquility.

But the marvel of those who were in the boat, who confess him to be the Son of God after tranquility had come, shows the character and faith of all who believe, who are in the church. They had earlier roused the Lord with their prayers, and when peace was restored to them, they confess that the Son of God is truly the Lord and defender of their church. We recognize that this was done immediately by the saints on behalf of the church in the Acts of the Apostles, after the persecution of Herod and of the Jews [see Acts 12:1–5].

6. Therefore, although the church labors under the harassment of the enemy and the storm of this world, and though it is struck by some floods of testing, it cannot suffer shipwreck because it has the Son of God as its helmsman. Amid the very hurricanes of the world, amid the very persecutions of the age, the church obtains more glory and power, while she remains firm and indestructible in faith.[159] Fitted with the rudder of faith, she sails a fair course through the sea of this age, having God as her helmsman, the angels as her rowers,

and carrying the choirs of all the saints, with the saving tree of the cross erected as a mast in the middle, on which hang the sails of evangelical faith, while the Holy Spirit blows.[160] She sails into the harbor of paradise and into the safety of eternal calm. And although this ship sails through this time of life and through these testings of the world, nonetheless it is not a ship of this world but God's. For there is also another ship of the world that is not God's, namely the gathering of the heretics, which lays claim to the name of this church for itself. Isaiah clearly shows that there will be a day of judgment against it when he says, "The day of the Lord Sabaoth against all that is proud and insolent" [Isa 2:12]. And after a little bit he says, "And against every ship of the sea" [Isa 2:16], that is, every church of the heretics. Elsewhere the same Isaiah said of it, "Your ropes are broken, for your mast (*arbor*) had no strength, your sails were bent down and your sails shall not loosen" [Isa 33:23]. He said that this is a ship "of the sea" because a church of this kind does not belong to God but to the world. Although it seems to have in it the preaching of the Lord's cross, it nonetheless shows a mast that is weak, because the proclamation of the cross is weak wherever there is not the truth of faith. Whence its sails are shown to be bent down and <not> loosened, because they are not guided by any breeze of the Holy Spirit. And so a ship of this kind, that is, a church of heretics, which has lost the rudder of the true faith and is lorded over by hostile spirits, sinks down in a shipwreck of eternal death. It does not deserve to have Christ the Lord at its helm, who is God blessed in the ages of ages. Amen [see Rom 9:5].

Tractate 43 on Matthew 8:28–34

1. Then it follows, "Now when he had come across the channel to the country of the Gerasenes, there met him two men who had demons" [and the rest up to] "into a herd of swine" [Matt 8:28–31], and the other things that follow. After the calming of the storm then and the return of tranquility to the sea [see Matt 8:23–28], the Lord arrived at the country of the Gerasenes to deliver men from demons. And this sequence of events befits the Lord, of course, that after the winds are rebuked, unclean spirits as well should be driven out. There the winds that were rebuked recognize the Creator and Lord of such

great power; here the terrified demons profess the Son of God with their shouts and say, "What have we to do with you, Son of God? Have you come to torment us before the time?" [Matt 8:29]. Thus the virtue of his divine authority exacted from the demons the words of a true confession. For they confess the day of the divine judgment carried out in punishment, and that Christ our Lord and the Son of God is the judge. But one must ask, since higher up the prince of demons approached the Lord to tempt him, as though ignorant when he said, "If you are the Son of God" [Matt 4:3], why is there now such an open profession by these demons concerning the Son of God? For they do not say, as that one formerly had said, "*If* you are the Son of God." But what do they say, or rather, proclaim? "What have we to do with you, Jesus, Son of God? Have you come to torment us before the time?" But this was not without cause, for they had already seen that their ruler had been conquered at the Lord's temptation; they had also seen different signs of divine power carried out by the Lord, through which they had learned that he was the Son of God, and they could no longer ignore this. And justly they proclaim and say, "What have we to do with you, Jesus, Son of God? Have you come to torment us before the time?"

2. Since they say they are being tormented before the time, clearly they admit both that a judgment is coming and that he is the judge, by whom they know that they are to be condemned to the everlasting punishment of Gehenna. And seeing that this profession of the demons concerning the Son of God is so clear, what impiety belongs to the Jews and what great insanity belongs to the heretics, to want to deny the Son of God, whom the demons cannot deny. Will not all deniers of the divine name be condemned by a just judgment at the future judgment, no longer by the words of the prophets and the Gospels, but by the very confession of the demons? For by denying the Son of God, whom the authors of denial itself did not deny, they will no longer deserve pardon due to ignorance. And it is clearly fitting that the authors of such great impiety no longer be convicted by the divine miracles, but by the mouth of the demons saying, "What have we to do with you, Jesus, Son of God? Have you come to torment us before the time?"

3. But in a psalm, David had shown this punishment of demons in which they admit to their being tormented before the time of judgment, when he says, "Lord, bend the heaven and come down, touch the mountains and they shall smoke" [Ps 144:5]. He meant these very

mountains, that is, the demons who, owing to the greatness of their wickedness and the enormity of their sins, are very frequently called mountains. He has testified then that mountains like this do not burn but smoke, indicating the same thing, that they first needed to be burned by such great heat of that eternal fire through the coming of the Lord's humility.[161] For at that time the Lord is known to have bent the heaven and come down; for the sake of human salvation he came down from heaven and took up a body from the holy virgin. But these words need to be taken into consideration: "Bend the heaven and come down." For he did not say, "Come down from heaven," but "Bend the heaven and come down." Thus he has clearly shown the immensity of his divinity, who although the Lord comes down from heaven to take up the flesh of human weakness, nonetheless heaven was within him, even when he comes down. For although he stayed on earth, he had not left heaven, according to what the Lord himself made clear in the gospel when he said, "No one ascends into heaven except he who came down from heaven, the Son of Man who is in heaven" [John 3:13].

4. Therefore these things must first be understood according to the letter. But according to the allegorical account, these two demoniacs who met the Lord in the land of the Gerasenes, that is, in the land of the Gentiles, are a figure of two peoples, either of those who had descended from Ham and Japheth, that is, from Noah's two sons, since the Jewish people trace their origin from Shem, the first-born son of Noah; or surely of the Jews and all Gentiles who were being held captive by the devil in the error of idolatry, burdened down by the chains of their offenses and the fetters of their sins.[162] They were not living in the city, that is, in the manner of life where law and the divine precepts were in force, but they dwell among the tombs, that is, worshiping idols and venerating the memories of kings or the images of dead men [see Luke 8:29, 27]. Therefore from Judea to the country of the Gerasenes, he came down to save them, that is, by the assumption of a body from the Virgin Mary. He deemed it fitting to illumine the land of the Gerasenes, that is, this world, in order to deliver these demoniacs, that is, peoples, from the chains of diabolical captivity, namely he of whom David had testified in the psalm when he said, "The Lord looked from heaven to hear the groaning of those in chains, to loosen the sons of the slain" [Ps 102:19–20]. But before the Lord liberated these demoniacs, as was mentioned earlier, he went by sea and experienced a storm and

endured sleep and the disciples were in danger. In that it is shown that salvation cannot be given to these two peoples in any other way than that the Lord first comes by this sea of the world, experienced the storm of Jewish persecution, and endured the sleep of death while the disciples were in danger, who arrived at such a great state of terror at the sleep of the Lord's passion that even saint Peter, the first of the apostles, was compelled to deny the Lord three times [see Matt 26:75].

5. But the swine into which the demons fled symbolize the unfaithful and unclean people who, feeding near the sea, that is, living according to the sins of the world, show themselves to be a worthy residence for the demons [see Matt 8:30–32]. Enveloped in the sea of this world, that is, in the depths of its error, they are drowned by the demons through the various desires of sins. But the herdsmen of the swine fled at the sign of the divine power and reported to the town what had happened, so that they entreated the Lord to depart from their district [see Matt 8:33–34]. In this a type has been shown of the leaders of the Jews and the priests of idols, who, dispensing the food of their error and unbelief to unclean and unfaithful people, are feeding them like swine to perpetual death. When they see believing men convert to the Son of God, having forsaken the faithlessness of the synagogue and the superstition of idols, they not only refuse to believe the divine signs, but moreover the terrible wretches are stirred up with a wicked zeal to drive away from themselves the saving advent of the Lord's humility. That is when we understand the fulfillment of what is said in the psalm: "Shall your wonders be known in darkness or your justice in a forgotten land?" [Ps 88:12]. Clearly it is a forgotten land that was not only unwilling to receive the author of salvation after the divine signs, but even forced him to depart from the district.

6. But this can be understood in another way, for there are multiple spiritual meanings. Thus we can understand these two [demoniacs] as two peoples, as we mentioned earlier, who by the faith and grace of Christ were freed from the bond of the demons. But we may take the swine as heretics who, when they were driven from the people of believers, are known to have migrated to them. But the herdsmen of the swine could be viewed as the authors of heresies and teachers of faithlessness who offer these same heretics, as if swine, the foul and unclean food of their completely perverse teachings, fattening them up not for life but for death. For such people are fed by

their teachers, not the heavenly bread nor the food of saving life, but the most foul and unclean teachings of faithlessness. And that is why that prodigal son, who had squandered by luxurious living among prostitutes that money he had received as his portion from his father, later on feeds not on bread but longs to fill his belly with the pods of swine, not his soul but his belly, since the soul is not refreshed by the food of faithlessness unto salvation but the body is nourished leading to punishment [see Luke 15:11–16].

7. The city from which they came to meet the Lord, asking him to leave their district, represents the synagogue, which did not want to receive the Lord and Savior of the human race, even after seeing his divine miracles [see Matt 8:34].[163] He therefore returned to [his own] city [see Matt 9:1]. Because he was rejected by the synagogue, he came to his church, which is properly called the city of Christ. And then indeed, the Gerasenes asked the Lord to depart from their district. But let us see whether perhaps such a person may also be found among us, who with an unbelieving mind compels the Lord and Savior of the world to depart from the district of their hearts. For according to Scripture, "The Holy Spirit of discipline will flee deceit and does not dwell in a body that is subject to sin" [Wis 1:5, 4].

8. But since saints Matthew and Mark reported that there were two demoniacs in this country of the Gerasenes, one must ask why the most saintly Luke mentioned only one, whom he remembers as not wearing any clothing and that he was bound with chains and fetters [see Mark 5:1–20; Luke 8:26–39]. But "having shattered his chains, he was driven by the demon into deserted places" [Luke 8:29]. Matthew and Mark then mention two, since in these two demoniacs a type of each believing people was shown. But Luke is known to have mentioned only one for the reason that the same Luke was recording a figure of the one people according to the law, namely he showed a figure of the people who lived under the law, who shatters the chains of the law and the fetters of doctrine, to which Solomon referred: "Doctrine unto fools is as fetters on the feet, and like chains on the right hand" [Sir 21:19]. It was driven by demons into the desert of error. Matthew has reported then that both these demoniacs were delivered through the grace of the Lord. For by believing in Christ from each people, they were saved and are daily being saved. To him is the praise and glory in the ages of ages. Amen.

TRACTATE 44 ON MATTHEW 9:1–8

1. Then it follows, "And getting into a boat, he crossed over and came to his own town. And behold, they brought to him a paralytic lying on a pallet. Then Jesus, seeing their faith, said to the paralytic, "Take courage, son; your sins are forgiven you." But some of the scribes said within themselves, "This man is blaspheming." And when Jesus saw their thoughts, he said, "Why do you think evil things in your hearts? Which is easier to say: Your sins are forgiven you, or to say, Arise and walk?" [Matt 9:1–5]. And the rest that follows. A paralytic lying on a pallet is brought, therefore, to the Lord, as he is returning from the land of the Gerasenes and coming to his own town. He is cured by the Lord in accordance with the faith of the men carrying him. For it is said to him, "Take courage, son; your sins are forgiven you." In the healing of this paralytic, our Lord and Savior shows that he is God, both by his doing a work of salvation and by forgiving sins. For not only does he grant healing of body to his paralytic, but over and above this he says, "Your sins are forgiven you." When some of the scribes heard this, they murmured within themselves and said, "Who can forgive sins but God alone?" [Mark 2:7; Luke 5:21]. Then the Lord, in order to expose their unbelief, shows the power of his divine nature whereby he saw the secrets of their hearts, and he said to them, "Why do you think evil things in your hearts?" Assuredly in this the faithless scribes should have understood that no one else could see the secret thoughts of the hearts, except him who had previously said to Samuel, "Not as man shall God see. For man looks at the appearance, but God looks at the heart" [1 Sam 16:7]. It is also written of this in the psalm: "God searches the hearts and reins" [Ps 7:9]. And Isaiah testifies of this and says, "By reason of the great glory and power of his might, nothing escapes you" [Isa 40:26]. And Jeremiah speaks of it: "Lord, you who test just things and understand the reins and hearts" [Jer 11:20]. Thus it is not without reason that the Lord in order to show that he is the one of whom these things had been written testified the following in Revelation and said, "And all the churches shall know that I am he who examines the reins and hearts" [Rev 2:23]. And so, since in what the Lord had said to the paralytic, "Your sins are forgiven you," the unbelieving scribes try to blaspheme the Lord, saying, "Who can forgive sins but God alone?" To refute their unbelief the Lord wanted to clarify to the same people which is greater, saying, "Why do

you think evil things in your hearts?" Thus he showed the power of his divine nature, not only by forgiving sins but also by telling the secrets of the hearts, since to know the thoughts of the heart is proper and unique to God alone.

2. But in order to refute the unbelieving and impious scribes more completely, the Lord says to the paralytic, "Arise, take your pallet and go to your home. And he got up and went to his home" [Matt 9:6–7]. Thus no one could doubt any longer that he forgave the paralytic's sins, who by the word of divine authority commanded the same paralytic to walk, when his mattress had been taken away. Whence the unbelief of the scribes, while it is opposed by the Lord, gave testimony to the truth, and it professes that the Son of God is God even while it denies him. For they say, "Who can forgive sins but God alone?" [Mark 2:7; Luke 5:21]. And on that account the Lord shows the sign of his divine power in order to show that he forgave the paralytic's sins, likewise by granting the healing of his body, so that the impious scribes would be convicted even by this sign and would believe that the paralytic's sins were forgiven, and would recognize that Christ was Lord and God, whom they were denying. And although the scribes indeed did not know the Son of God, nevertheless they are not unaware that God is the one who is able to forgive sins. Therefore we ought to pay attention to what impiety the heretic is held, who indeed admits that the Son of God forgives sins, yet dares to deny that he is God, since they themselves who deny this admit that God is the one who forgives sins.

3. Therefore the Lord says to the paralytic, "Arise, take your pallet and go to your home. And he got up and went to his home" [Matt 9:6–7]. Here we understand that the testimony that Isaiah gave earlier concerning the future advent of the Lord was partially fulfilled, when he said, "Be strong, you relaxed hands, and be strong, you palsied knees. Fear not; behold, our God shall render judgement. He will come and save us" [Isa 35:3–4]. David also testified about this in the psalm when he said, "The voice of the Lord is mighty; the voice of the Lord is full of majesty. The voice of the Lord who breaks the cedars" [Ps 29:4–5]. Surely this voice of the Lord is understood as mighty and full of majesty because by restoring the already collapsed body of the paralytic to its original health, he broke cedars, that is, the scribes and Pharisees, who were puffed up with an arrogant mind and are broken by the sign of the Lord's power.

4. But since these very deeds of the Lord contain an account of spiritual things in themselves, a type of which this paralytic bears, we should consider this. For we recognize that a figure of the people of the Gentiles has been shown in advance in him, who had collapsed in spirit under the heavy weight of their sins.[164] Bound up as it were with a certain incurable weakness, they were lying as it were on a pallet [see Mark 2:3], suspended by the four corners of this world. Therefore for the sake of the salvation of this paralytic, that is, of the Gentile people, or at least of Adam, who is known to be the author of the human race, after the rejection of unfaithful Israel, the angels and all the holy suppliants stood forth before God, by whom they are offered to our Lord and Savior to heal from the four directions of the earth, as from a mattress. The Lord who had come for the salvation of the human race considers their faith, and deemed it fitting to grant a heavenly healing to Adam and to the people of all nations.[165] Whence also in what was said to the paralytic: "Your sins are forgiven you" [Matt 9:2], it is shown that the people of the Gentiles, who labored under the heavy malady of sins, when forgiveness was given to them through the heavenly medicine, they received the whole and perfect healing of eternal salvation in body and soul. It is now said to them not unfittingly after the remission of sins, when salvation is given, "Go back to your home" [Matt 9:6], that is, to the home of paradise, from which Adam had long ago been expelled, who has stood forth as the author of this infirmity.

5. And fittingly it follows, "When the crowds saw this, they were afraid and glorified God who had given such power to humans" [Matt 9:8]. For God is glorified who gave even to his apostles the power to forgive sins, and he granted such great grace to humans that after the forgiveness of sins through the merit of faith and justice, they receive power to return to paradise, through the power and grace of our Lord and Savior, who is God blessed in the ages. Amen [see Rom 9:5].

Tractate 45 on Matthew 9:9–13

1. It then follows, "Now as Jesus passed on from there, he saw Matthew sitting at the tax booth" [and the rest up to] "for I came not to call the just but sinners" [Matt 9:9–13]. The Lord, who is about to give salvation to all sinners who believe in him, of his own accord

deems it fitting to choose first Matthew the tax collector. In him the gift of his condescension and the example for our salvation excelled, so that we would know that every sinner must be chosen by God and can arrive at the grace of eternal salvation, if a religious spirit and a devout mind are not lacking. After all, Matthew is freely chosen by God, even though he was tangled up in worldly obligations and secular activities, yet because of the religious devotion of his mind, he merits <being appointed> by the Lord: "Follow me," surely by him who by virtue of his divine nature knows the hidden recesses of the heart. From what follows, ultimately, we know that this Matthew was chosen by the Lord not by the Lord's partiality [see Eph 6:9; Col 3:25] but by the merit of his faith and devotion.[166] For as soon as the Lord said to him, "Follow me," he does not linger or delay, but directly "he arose and followed him" [Matt 9:9]. Higher up, the scribes and teachers of the law not only did not believe in the marvel of such a great work, but over and above this, in the midst of the very divine works, they accused the Lord of being guilty of blasphemy, saying, "This man is blaspheming" [Matt 9:3]. This Matthew, on the other hand, upon hearing only the Lord's voice, at once "followed him." By following the voice of the Lord he proved himself in this to be faithful to God and a son of Abraham by a similar example. Whence he received the Lord immediately, by the example and hospitality of Abraham, and he lays out a banquet for him, in order that the son worthy of Abraham would truly be recognized through all these things.

2. After Matthew's faith was proven worthy, therefore, who was one of the tax collectors, it is now fitting that sinners and tax collectors recline at a banquet with the Lord. For that is what follows: "And it came about while he was reclining in the house, behold many tax collectors and sinners were reclining with Jesus and with his disciples" [Matt 9:10]. But the Pharisees were jealous and said, "Why does the Lord eat with tax collectors?" The Lord said, "It is not the healthy who need a physician but the sick" [Matt 9:12]. In this he shows himself to be the true heavenly physician, who had come to heal the wounds of the human race, and he exposes the unbelief of the scribes, who though they were lying there with a serious infirmity of sin, were puffed up with an arrogant mind and considered themselves to be healthy. They did not retain the statement of Solomon: "Who will boast that he has a chaste heart and that he is clean of sins?" [Prov 20:9]; and the statement of blessed Job, who said, "Who

will be clean of filth, not even if his life will last a single day?" [Job 14:4–5 LXX]. On account of this they were unwilling to receive and acknowledge the author of heavenly medicine, of whom David had testified when he said, among other things, "Who forgives your iniquities, who heals all your diseases" [Ps 103:3]. The Holy Spirit exhorts through Solomon as well that this physician must be honored, when he says, "Honor the physician before the day of need" [Sir 38:1]. And though Solomon had instructed that this physician must be honored before the day of need, the unbelieving scribes and Pharisees were unwilling to honor and recognize the giver of heavenly medicine at the present time, though they had seen such great signs. For that reason they did not deserve to receive the cure of salvation. And therefore the Lord says, "It is not the healthy who need a physician but the sick." He is showing that they who think that they are healthy, that is, just, do not deserve to attain heavenly healing, since they have rejected the Lord's medicine. Rather, it is those who by recognizing their own infirmities, that is, their own sins, and by believing with complete faith, have sought for the healing of heavenly grace.

3. Saint Jeremiah knows that this physician is not being sought by the Jewish people and he exposes their infidelity, giving them the following warning in advance and saying, "And is there no balm in Gilead, or is there no physician there? Why has not the healing gone up for my people?" [Jer 8:22]. By this statement he rebukes the people who despise the author of heavenly medicine. They have been wounded by sins, but are unwilling to receive the healing of salvation. But since we have found that there are many necessary kinds of heavenly medicine as well, it must be asked why he mentioned only "balm" for the healing of the whole people, when he said, "And is there no balm in Gilead, or is there no physician there? Why has not the healing gone up for my people?"[167] Whence we need to consider what this balm is, which all by itself could offer healing to the people. According to the earthly example, we recognize that balm comes from no other source but wood. In its signification we clearly understand that the medicine of the cross is shown, through which the healing of eternal salvation has truly been given to the human race. Since the Jewish people were unwilling to receive the medicine of this balm, they remained in the perpetual infirmity of sin. And therefore it is not hasty for them to be told by the Lord through the prophet, "And is there no balm in Gilead, or is there no physician

there? Why has not the healing gone up for my people?" For that physician who came down from heaven healed the wounds of the human race by the medicine of his cross. Finally, the prophetic word reported that this balm was in Gilead, that is, in the land of Judea, since there the Lord took up his saving cross for the salvation of the world.

4. For this reason the Lord rebukes them and says, "Go and learn what this means: I want mercy rather than sacrifice" [Matt 9:13]. The scribes and Pharisees thought that all their sins could be blotted out by the sacrifices of the law. And therefore the Lord placed mercy ahead of sacrifice, to show clearly that the transgressions of sins could be purged not through the sacrifices of the law but through works of mercy. This agrees with what the same Lord made clear elsewhere when he rebuked the Pharisees and said, "But give alms and behold all things are clean for you" [Luke 11:41]. This then is what the Lord is saying to them: "Learn what this means: I want mercy rather than sacrifice." And he followed up and said, "I have not come to call the just but sinners" [Matt 9:13]. Could the Lord have rejected the just, he who had come to make just people out of sinners? Assuredly not, but he is speaking against the Pharisees and scribes, who showed contempt for works of mercy, or rather, for the author of mercy itself, since they were observing certain unnecessary burdens of the law and were offering the sacrifices of cattle, to such an extent that they thought they were just, so that they opposed the very Lord and author of heavenly justice. Rejecting their feigned and false justice, the Lord, not without cause, has called sinners who believe in him to grace.

5. According to the allegorical and mystical account, Matthew's house is understood as his mind, which Christ entered through faith in his grace.[168] He is known to have truly "reclined" there, for this same Matthew deserved to be the writer of this Gospel, in which he lays out a heavenly feast of the Lord's deeds and power, not only for the Lord and his disciples, but also for all believers who, coming as tax collectors and sinners to the knowledge of Christ, have deserved to be included in so great a feast. Or surely, Matthew's house can be understood as the church that is gathered from tax collectors and sinners, in which the same Matthew lays out the feast of his faith and preaching for all believers, with the Lord reclining there with his disciples, who is blessed in the ages of ages. Amen.

Tractate 46 on Matthew 9:14–17

1. It then follows, "At that time the disciples of John came to him saying, Why do we and the Pharisees fast?" [and the rest up to] "and then they shall fast in those days" [Matt 9:14–15]. The disciples of John had followed a good teacher, to be sure, who was the Lord's precursor and way preparer, but since they were unaware of the mystery of the Lord's incarnation, they were not able to know why it was not fitting for the apostles to fast. And the solemnity of fasting is religious indeed, but it cannot benefit a person for salvation without the knowledge of the truth, that is, without faith in Christ's name. For this reason the disciples of John and the Pharisees fasted not only in body but also in soul, since they did not know the heavenly bread who had come to feed the hearts of believers. Finally, this very question of theirs came more from boasting than from faith, wherein they say, "Why do we and the Pharisees fast frequently, but your disciples do not fast?" [Matt 9:14].

2. But the Lord, either to restrain their boasting or instruct their ignorance, answers them and says that the sons of the bridegroom are not able to fast as long as the bridegroom is with them [see Matt 9:15]. By this he both showed a plain account of the case that it was not fitting for his disciples to fast in the meantime, and he declared that he was the bridegroom of the church. We can observe the rationale for this matter even from the example of the earthly comparison. For we know that in the feast days of a marriage, when a bridegroom is united to a bride, those who are in attendance when the vows are prayed cannot fast. For this reason the Lord shows that it is inappropriate for the sons of the bridegroom, that is, the apostles, to fast at that time when the Lord himself, the bridegroom, had united the church to himself as his bride, when he took on a human body. He therefore is the heavenly and eternal bridegroom of the church, who long ago, when he spoke to the same church as follows through the prophet, had testified and said, "I shall betroth you to myself in truth and in judgment and in mercy, and you shall know that I am the Lord" [Hos 2:19–20]. David also foretold this in a psalm when he said, "And he comes forth as a bridegroom out of his chamber" [Ps 19:5]. And Isaiah relates of him, "As a bridegroom rejoices over his bride, so shall the Lord rejoice over you" [Isa 62:5]. But in the Canticles, frequent mention is made of this bridegroom and bride when it is said under the persona of the Lord,

"I entered my garden, my sister, my bride, my dove, my perfect one" [Song 5:1]. Whence it is not without reason that saint John, upon recognizing that this bridegroom had come to betroth the church to himself, testified as follows in the Gospel and said, "He who has the bride is the bridegroom. But the friend of the bridegroom stands and hears him and rejoices with joy because of the voice of the bridegroom" [John 3:29]. And in Revelation, John reported of this, "And I saw the new Jerusalem coming down from heaven, a bride and one adorned for her husband" [Rev 21:2]. Whence even in what the Lord says, "The days shall come when the bridegroom will be taken from them and then they shall fast in those days" [Matt 9:15], he shows clearly that it was not fitting for his disciples to fast until after the mystery of his resurrection. For the Lord rose again from the underworld with the bride of his flesh united with himself. The apostle makes clear that in that flesh is signified the body of the church [see Eph 5:31–32; Col 1:24]. Then he went back to heaven, which we read of as fulfilled in the Acts of the Apostles [see Acts 1:9]. After the Lord's ascension to heaven and when the Holy Spirit was sent on the fiftieth day [see Acts 1—2], at once the apostles and all the believers began to undergo fasts and prayers [see Acts 13:2–3; 14:23]. But this was not according to the oldness of the letter like the scribes and Pharisees, but according to the newness of spiritual grace and gospel tradition.

3. And it rightly follows, "And nobody puts a piece of raw cloth onto an old garment. For it will take away the firmness (*fortitudinem*) thereof from the garment, and the tear becomes worse. Neither do they put new wine into old wineskins. Otherwise the wineskins will break, and the wine will run out, and the wineskins perish. But new wine they put into new wineskins, and both are preserved" [Matt 9:16–17]. The account is clear, that a piece of raw cloth cannot be matched to an old garment. By the metaphor of this comparison the Lord is speaking against those who refused to be renewed through the Lord's passion and who boasted in the oldness of the law. For in the raw cloth is understood the gathering of the people of the gospel, which has been renewed through faith in Christ and through the grace of baptism, and is woven by the Holy Spirit. But in the old garment we observe a signification of the people of the synagogue, who have become an old garment as it were by the corruption of the oldness of sin. The Lord shows this very thing clearly through Isaiah when he rebukes the people of the same synagogue and says, "Behold, all of you are growing old as a garment, and a moth shall devour you" [Isa

50:9]. It was not fitting, therefore, to join a piece of raw cloth, namely the congregation of the new people, to this old garment, that is, to the synagogue, which was abiding in the oldness of the letter and had been corrupted by the oldness of sin. For the faith of the church and the faithlessness of the synagogue did not match with each other.

4. And for that reason he went on to say, "For it will take away the firmness (*fortitudinem*) thereof from the garment, and the tear becomes worse" [Matt 9:16]. Doubtless if raw cloth is attached to an old garment, its firmness is taken away and it causes a greater tear. By this example, too, it was not fitting for the people of the church, who have been renewed through the grace of Christ and through the Holy Spirit, to observe according to the oldness of the letter either circumcision or the Sabbaths or the various burdens of the law, according to Jewish tradition. Otherwise the tear would become worse, that is, no small scandal to the faith would arise, not only among those who believed from the Gentiles, but also among those who had come to faith from the synagogue. After all, as we read in the Acts of the Apostles, when some of the believing Jews wanted to burden those who came from the Gentiles with the superfluous burdens of the law, and when no small dissension had arisen, the apostles decided through the Holy Spirit that these burdens of the law were not to be imposed upon the necks of believers [see Acts 15]. This then is what the Lord is saying: "No one puts a piece of raw cloth onto an old garment. For it takes away the firmness (*fortitudinem*) thereof from the garment, and the tear becomes worse." Whence not without cause long ago, when the Holy Spirit exhorted the people through Isaiah to the newness of this evangelical law and future grace, he gave the following advance warning: "Remember not the former things, and consider not the ancient things. Behold, I [will] do new things, which shall presently spring forth, and you shall know [them], and I will make a way in the wilderness, and rivers in the dry land" [Isa 43:18–19]. And again: "Behold, I [will] do new things, which I will tell [you], and after I told [them], they were made known to you" [Isa 42:9]. And again: "Be renewed to me, you islands, for your princes shall exult with strength" [Isa 41:1]. Hence through Jeremiah the Lord says the following: "Renew for yourselves the newness and do not sow among thorns" [Jer 4:3]. And justly the apostle says, "Old things have passed away, behold, all things have become new" [2 Cor 5:17].

5. He cited a similar example likewise about wineskins when he said, "Nor do people pour new wine into old wineskins, else the skins

burst and the wine is spilled, but they put new wine into fresh skins and both are preserved" [Matt 9:17]. It is clear according to the statement of the Lord, if new wine is put in old wineskins, both perish, since due to their oldness the old skins cannot hold the fervent heat of the new wine. By this metaphor he is showing in the old skins unbelieving people who are living according to the old way of life. But the new wine signifies the new grace of the Holy Spirit. And this is why when the apostles were filled with the Holy Spirit, they were said to be drunk with unfermented wine [see Acts 2:13]. Therefore in what the Lord says, "Nor do people put new wine into old wineskins, else the wine is spilled and the skins perish," he shows clearly that those who continue as unfaithful unbelievers in accordance with their old doings cannot attain to this new grace of the Holy Spirit. We observe this as fulfilled among the Jews especially, who live according to the oldness of the letter and according to former sins. They were unable to receive the grace of the new birth and the gift of the Holy Spirit. But in the new skins, in which he says that new wine must be put in order that both be preserved, he is pointing to the faithful, who have been renewed by the heavenly birth and by the grace of Christ.[169] They have accepted the new wine into themselves, that is, the gift of the Holy Spirit. They keep the grace that has been handed down to them intact and undiminished.

6. Since therefore the disciples of John followed the example of the Pharisees more than that of the Lord's disciples, the Lord necessarily reminded them of this, in order to show John's disciples that it was not the example of the Pharisees that was to be followed, who were remaining corrupted in their minds like an old garment or old wineskins, but rather that of his own disciples, so that they too would equally be renewed by the Lord's grace and become new wineskins, as it were, and be deemed worthy of the gift of the Holy Spirit. Thus by believing in the Son of God, they could recognize both the definition of true fasting and the sons of the bridegroom and Christ the Lord, the bridegroom of the church, who is blessed in the ages of ages. Amen.

Tractate 47 on Matthew 9:18–26

1. It then follows, "As he was speaking these things unto them, behold a certain ruler came up and adored him" <...> "Then Jesus

rising up followed him, with his disciples. And behold, a woman who had a flow of blood twelve years came behind him and touched his garment" [Matt 9:18–20]. And the rest that follows. When the Lord was asked by Jairus, the ruler of the synagogue, to come raise his daughter who had recently died, he did not delay but arose at once and followed him. By this example he taught us not to be lazy in respect to any work of God. But when the Lord was going to raise the dead girl, it says, "Behold, a woman who had a flow of blood for twelve years came behind him and touched his garment, saying, If I touch his garment, I will be saved. But he, turning and seeing her, said, Take courage, daughter, your faith has saved you. And the woman was saved from that hour" [Matt 9:20–22]. How blessed is this woman who believed in the Son of God with such perfect faith! For she did not approach from the front but from behind. And she did not embrace the Lord's feet, for she judged herself to be unworthy; nor was she willing to touch the upper part of his garment, only the hem, as Luke reports [see Luke 8:44]. For she believed that that would suffice for her salvation, if she would have merited to touch the Lord's hem.[170] She was not unaware that he was the one of whom the Holy Spirit had testified earlier through the prophet Zechariah saying, "Thus says the Lord Almighty: In those days, if ten men[171] should take hold of the hem of one Jewish man, saying, We will go with you, for we have heard that God is with you" [Zech 8:23]. Although this statement could be understood of every holy man, yet we apply it particularly to the person of the Lord, who for the sake of our salvation received a body from the race of the Jews, "for salvation is from the Jews" [John 4:22]. With trusting faith those who came "from all languages" took hold of his hem, that is, his advent in bodily humility. For the hem is the very last part of a tunic. It shows and signifies the end-time, when the Son of God took up a human body and deemed it fitting to come for the world's salvation.

2. This most saintly woman, then, who had paid out all her money and, as the evangelist Luke reported [see Luke 8:43], was unable to be cured by any doctor, acknowledges that the Savior of the human race had come and that he was the source of heavenly medicine. In order to receive healing, she approaches from behind and touches the Lord's hem. But the woman not only touched the Lord's hem with the touch of the body but also with faith. After all, as the evangelist Luke testifies, after the woman's touch we read that the Lord said, "Who is it that touched me? For I know that power went forth from me" [Luke 8:45–46]. For the Lord's power was always ready to heal, if

only the faith of believers is not lacking. For that is why this woman who believed with her whole heart touched the Lord not only with the bodily touch but also with faith.[172] And therefore she received at once the healing that <she sought>. For it was said to her, "Take courage, daughter, your faith has saved you" [Matt 9:22]. How great is the potency of divine power! After twelve years a flow of blood is checked solely by a touch of the hem of the Lord's garment; the woman's faith is paid back; complete health is restored to her body. Indeed, a certain law had said that sacrifices are offered for those who suffered from a flow of blood [see Lev 15:29–30]. But by no reckoning could this woman be cured, not through doctors of the world, not through sacrifices of the law. They were not able to offer in person medicine to those laboring under this malady, but this showed the mystery of the truth to come. For this reason the woman approaches from behind and touches the Lord's hem. She acknowledges the Lord of the law and the author of heavenly medicine, and immediately believes with the full power of faith. For at last she had found the true heavenly physician by whom alone she knew her malady could be healed. Solomon had said of him, "For it was neither a poultice that cured them, but your word, O Lord, which heals all things" [Wis 16:12]. Therefore to this good physician who grants healing to everyone by his word, this woman offered only the wage of her faith, not her money that she had paid out to the doctors. For that is the only wage this physician requires of us in order to bestow upon us the grace of his medicine. We are shown by this example that we cannot be delivered from a physical malady and from any malady of sin if we do not believe in the Lord with our whole heart and with a perfect mind.

3. Therefore after healing was given to the woman who suffered from the flow of blood, "he came to the house of the ruler," whose daughter he had been asked to raise. "And he saw the flute players and the crowd making an uproar, and he said, Depart from here. For the girl is not dead, but sleeps. And they laughed him to scorn. And when the crowd was cast out, he went in, and took her by the hand. And the little girl arose. And the report of this went forth into all that land" [Matt 9:23–26]. In this sign, too, of his divine power in which he takes hold of the little girl's hand and calls her soul back to her body and says, "Little girl, arise" [Luke 8:54], we recognize the fulfillment of what David testified when he said, "The right hand of the Lord has wrought power" [Ps 118:16]. And again, "The voice of the Lord is with power, the voice of the Lord is full of majesty" [Ps 29:4].[173] And again, "Behold,

he will utter his own voice, the voice of power" [Ps 68:33]. Assuredly this is the voice of power by which he raised the dead girl, by which he also called Lazarus from the tomb and said, "Lazarus, come out" [John 11:43]. And to be sure, this girl arose when she heard the Lord's voice; but Lazarus, though his hands and feet were wrapped up, could not thus be hindered from immediately emerging from the tomb at the Lord's bidding. But we ought to consider why Lazarus comes forth from the tomb bound hand and foot. Could the Lord, who had broken the bonds of death, not have shattered his burial bonds for him? But he wanted Lazarus to come forth from the tomb bound up for this reason, first to show clearly the power of his divine potency, [and] because Lazarus was not only raised from the dead but, what is more, was commanded to come forth from the tomb bound up. Hence, this was in order that the one bound up with bandages by the unbelieving Jews themselves would be recognized, lest perhaps it be thought that it was not Lazarus himself who had been buried by the same people. How great is the Lord's power! With greater difficulty one rouses someone from sleep than Lazarus was roused from death, from bodily decay.[174] There was still a stench in the nostrils of the Jews, and there in their sight stood the living Lazarus when he had been called. Whence the Jews cannot have an excuse for their sin, who refused to believe in such great miracles.

4. Soon, therefore, when the little girl heard the Lord's voice saying, "Arise" [see Luke 8:54–55], as soon as the statement was made, she arose. For death could no longer hold the girl's soul. It acknowledged that he who is the Lord of death and life had commanded it. Assuredly he is the one who says through Moses, "I will kill and I will make alive; I shall strike and I shall heal" [Deut 32:39]. Solomon also testified of him when he said, "For you have the power of life and death, and you lead down to the gates of death and call back" [Wis 16:13]. Therefore it is not without reason that the Lord himself had already said in the gospel, "The hour will come and now is, when the dead will hear the voice of the Son of God, and those who hear will live" [John 5:25]. For the unique and proper work of God is by his own power to call back man from death. To be sure, we read that both prophets and apostles raised the dead, but this was not by their own power, nor by their own authority, but through the power of his name, who has the power of life and death. After all, in order for the prophets and apostles to be able to do this, they first prayed and then, when they had called upon the name of the Lord, they merited being heard. But the Son of God,

as the Lord of all power and the God of the universe, commands souls to be called back to their bodies by his own power. For it was the same one who worked these signs of divine power both earlier through the prophets and later through the apostles. This is why as soon as the Lord said, "Little girl, arise" [Luke 8:54], death obeyed its Lord and Creator and her soul was restored to her body. And the girl who had been dead rises again alive. For death could not hold the one whom Life was calling back.[175]

But in what the Lord says, "The girl is not dead but sleeps" [Matt 9:24], first, this is so that we might know that with God the dead are considered to be like those asleep, since it pertains to God's power that a man rises from death as from sleep; second, this is so that we might understand in what was said, "The girl is not dead but sleeps," that the hope of the future resurrection has been shown, that we might observe that the death of the faithful is not to be called death but sleep instead, in which the saints rest in slumber as those sleeping. Hence concerning the death of Lazarus, we read likewise that the Lord said, "Lazarus our friend sleeps" [John 11:11]. And blessed Paul makes the same thing clear about the death of the faithful when he says, "But I do not want you to be ignorant about those who are sleeping, brothers and sisters, that you not be grieved as the rest who have no hope" [1 Thess 4:13].

5. Now we are identifying these actions first in accordance with the simplicity of the letter. But according to the spiritual understanding, this woman who suffered from the flow of blood <...>[176] by killing the just and the prophets, lastly it shed the sacred blood of our Lord and Savior himself. Not unjustly do we read that it was faulted by the Lord through the prophet with the charge of such a great sacrilege, when the following is said to it: "And I passed by to you, and saw you bespattered with your blood" [Ezek 16:6]. Hence, too, the following words of the Lord are spoken by Isaiah to the Jews: "If you make many supplications, I will not hearken to you; for your hands are full of blood" [Isa 1:15]. Fittingly, too, the Lord in the gospel, when he was reproaching the same people for such serious sins, says among other things the following: "That upon you may come all the blood that has been shed, from the blood of Abel the just, even unto the blood of Zachariah the prophet. Amen I say to you, it shall be demanded from this generation" [Matt 23:35–36]. Therefore the people of the synagogue suffered from this flow of blood. Now in the number of years, twelve, the same people of Israel <is shown who> had been

assembled <in the twelve tribes.> But in the doctors to whom she had paid out all her money and was unable to be cured by any of them, we recognize that the elders of the people and the priests of the law are signified. Although they receive tithes and many gifts from the people and offer sacrifices according to the law, yet they were unable to grant the health of salvation to the same people. For the guilt of such a great sacrilege could not be restrained by the sacrifices of the law, but solely through the passion of the Lord.

Hence it is not without cause that this woman approached from behind and touched the hem of his garment, and thus was saved by believing with faith. In this it is shown that that people from the synagogue who believed in the Son of God through Peter's preaching would approach from behind, that is, after the passion of the Lord, and touch the hem of his garment, that is, believe in the mystery of his incarnation, which he undertook for the sake of our salvation, and thus through faith like that, having been delivered from the guilt of blood as from a kind of flow, they received the gift of eternal salvation [see Acts 2:41]. We also understand that this was fulfilled in those who believed from the same synagogue during the time of the apostles, and it will be fulfilled in those who will believe at the consummation of the world from the same Jewish people, when Elijah appears, of whom Revelation has related that 144,000 will believe from each of the tribes [see Rev 7:4; 11:3].[177]

6. But in the daughter of the synagogue ruler, we recognize a prefiguration of the church that believed from the Gentiles. In the synagogue ruler we understand a type of the prophets and apostles being shown, especially of saint Peter, by whom the calling of the Gentiles first came about [see Acts 10], therefore of all those saints who pleased God not by works of the law but by the justice of faith. This people who believed from the Gentiles is reckoned as a daughter, who pleased the Son of God by believing with faith in a similar manner. Yet at one time, before the Lord came in the flesh, she was considered to be dead, as it were, through her infidelity, since the apostle says, "And though you were dead in your transgressions and in the uncircumcision of your flesh, he made you alive in Christ" [Col 2:13]. For the sake of this church of the Gentiles, therefore, which merited to be a daughter through the faith of the apostles, this is the prayer of the synagogue ruler, concerning which long ago the Lord had spoken to Moses and said, "Allow me to destroy them, and I will make of you a nation great and better than this one is" [Deut 9:14]. It was also said

of her through the prophet, "I shall call not my people my people" [Hos 2:24; Rom 9:25]. Hence the apostles have been prefigured in the persona of the little girl's father. They beg the Lord on behalf of the people of the Gentiles, after the unbelief of the Jews was rejected, that the salvation of life that had been promised to it long ago would be given through Christ's grace, namely that she would rise again unto eternal life from the error of the world, as one who had been raised from death.

7. Finally, the Lord directs her to eat as well in order that we might understand that the entire mystery of our salvation is prefigured in this girl, after she was raised from death, as Luke reports [see Luke 8:55]. Clearly the sequence of our faith and salvation is here shown. For when each believer among us is set free in baptism from perpetual death and comes back to life, upon acceptance of the gift of the Holy Spirit, it is necessary that one be commanded to eat as well, namely that heavenly bread, about which the Lord says, "Unless you eat my flesh and drink my blood, you shall have no life in you" [John 6:54].[178]

Now in the flute players and crowd making an uproar who laughed to scorn the Lord, who said, "The girl is not dead but asleep" [Matt 9:24], we understand an example of the synagogue rulers and the crowd of the Jewish people.[179] When they heard that the hope of eternal life had been promised by the Son of God to the Gentiles, they held up to ridicule and contempt this great grace of the Lord. Not unjustly did the Lord order them to be cast out in order to show that incredulous and unbelieving people of this kind are to be completely excluded from the promise of eternal life and from God's kingdom, by him who is the author of life and the Lord of the heavenly kingdom, to whom is the praise and glory in the ages of ages. Amen.

Tractate 48 on Matthew 9:27–31

1. <...> Although these blind men did not have bodily sight, yet they had clear vision of faith and of the heart with which they could see the true and eternal light, the Son of God, assuredly that light of which it is written, "He was the true light that enlightens every man coming into this world" [John 1:9]. Through Isaiah he had predicted that he would come to illumine the blind, when he said, "The Spirit

of the Lord is upon me, because he has anointed me; he has sent me to preach glad tidings to the poor, and to restore sight to the blind" [Isa 61:1]. The same Isaiah testifies about it in another passage as follows: "Behold, our God will render judgment; and he will come and save us. Then shall the eyes of the blind be opened, and the ears of the deaf shall hear" [Isa 35:4–5]. David had testified of it through the Holy Spirit as well when he said, "The Lord sets up the broken down, the Lord will release the fettered ones, the Lord illumines the blind" [Ps 146:7–8]. Since, therefore, these blind men recognized by the sight of their minds that this Savior of the human race had come in the flesh, in accordance with the prophetic proclamation, not without reason do they cry out and say, "Have mercy on us, son of David" [Matt 9:27].[180] Now the reason they said "son of David" is because he received his body from David's seed. But these blind men not only believed that Christ the Lord was the son of David, but what is the principal thing, the Son of God, and for that reason they were saved. For they would not have presumed to have been able to receive the sight of their eyes from him unless they had believed that he was the Son of God. And fittingly when the Lord said to them, "Do you believe that I am able to do this?" they say, "Surely, Lord" [Matt 9:28]. In this they clearly confessed him to be both God and man, Son of God and son of man; Son of God our Lord according to the spirit, son of David according to the assumption of the body. But also in this we observe the wonderful grace of the Lord, that he said to these blind men, "Do you believe that I am able to do this?" It is not that the Lord would have been unable to do this if they had not believed, but he wanted to establish the work of his power in the gift of faith and in the reward for believers. Hence not unjustly he pays back their faith with the reward of the divine miracle. It says, "He touched their eyes and said to them, Let it be done to you according to your faith. And their eyes were opened" [Matt 9:29–30]. Assuredly by this faith these blind men deserved to be illumined, since they faithfully believed that Christ the Lord was not only man but also God. But in what the Lord asked them when he said, "Do you believe that I am able to do this?" he who knew the secrets of the heart was not unaware of their faith, but the reason he wanted to question them was so that by confessing with the mouth what they believed in the heart they would receive the salvation they asked for. This agrees with what is written: "With the heart one believes unto justice, with the mouth confession is made unto salvation" [Rom 10:10]. And again: "Everyone will be justified by his words, or by his words will be condemned" [Matt 12:37].

2. But according to the allegorical account, these two blind men prefigure the two peoples who were split into two kingdoms after the death of Solomon by Rehoboam, the son of Solomon, and by Jeroboam, servant of the same Solomon [see 1 Kgs 12]. For if we want the people of the Jews and the people of the Gentiles to be prefigured in these two blind men, it does not match. For how would it be possible for the people of the Gentiles to confess Christ to be the Son of David before their illumination? For they had not heard of the law or the prophets. For that reason, it is understood more correctly concerning the two peoples just mentioned. They were capable of knowing from the law and the prophets that Christ is the Son of David. Both were blind, therefore, through the unfaithfulness of their mind, for they were not yet able to see the true light, the only begotten Son of God, who was foretold in the law and the prophets. Bereft of the light of faith and covered by the veil of the law, they were being held in the gloom of blindness, as it were, according to what the blessed apostle relates when he says, "To this day, whenever Moses is read, a veil lies over their hearts; but when someone turns to the Lord, the veil is removed" [2 Cor 3:15–16]. And again, "When they read the Old Testament, that same veil remains, while it is not revealed, because in Christ it is taken away" [2 Cor 3:14]. Therefore, in the fact that sight was restored immediately to these blind men after their faith by which they believed in the Son of God, it is shown that anyone from these two peoples who should believe with faith that the Son of God came for the salvation of the human race, he would receive knowledge of the true light, as soon as all the blindness of error is removed. Nevertheless, it is shown that the gift of his divine grace can exist at no other time and place than this, when the only begotten Son of God took up a human body, he dwelled in his own house [see Matt 9:28], that is, in the church, in which all believers are delivered from the blindness of former error and gaze upon the glory of eternal light. But in the fact that these blind men spread abroad the Lord's power everywhere, once they had received their eyesight, this shows that the grace of this divine gift had to be proclaimed everywhere by those who had believed, since the grace of such a great gift cannot be concealed or kept silent, which the Lord worked and works daily. He is blessed in the ages. Amen.

Tractate 49 on Matthew 12:22–28

1. "There was brought to him a man, blind and mute, who had a demon, and he healed him, so that he spoke and saw" [Matt 12:22], and the rest that follows. After health was restored to the man who had the withered hand in the synagogue [see Matt 12:9–14], and heavenly medicine was given to many who had followed him [see Matt 12:15–21], it says, "There was brought to him a man, blind and mute, who had a demon, and he healed him, so that he spoke and saw." In the healing of this man, too, he showed the potency of the Lord's own power. For who could have shown so many miraculous signs in a single man who had a demon, one who was both blind and mute, so that the man was delivered from the demon and spoke and saw, except he who is the Lord of all virtues and the God of universal power, assuredly he of whom David has attested in the psalm and says, "The Lord of virtues is with us, our helper the God of Jacob" [Ps 46:7]? And again, "Lord, God of powers convert us and show your face and we will be saved" [Ps 80:3]. This Lord of all powers, then, by the power of his divine potency healed the man brought to him, who both had a demon and was blind and mute. He showed clearly through all these things that he was the one in whose coming the prophets predicted that these signs were coming, as Isaiah clearly declares of him when he says, "Behold, our God will pay back judgment. He will come and save us. Then will the eyes of the blind be opened and the ears of the deaf shall hear" [Isa 35:4–5]. And again under the persona of Christ, "The Spirit of the Lord is upon me, because of which he anointed you, he sent me to preach good news to the poor, to heal the contrite of heart, to preach remission to the captives and to restore sight to the blind" [Isa 61:1; Luke 4:18–19]. And again under the persona of the Father to the Son, "I the Lord God have called you by name in justice, and I will take hold of your hand, and I have given you for the covenant of my race, for a light of the Gentiles, to open the eyes of the blind" [Isa 42:6–7]. David also speaks of this in the psalm: "The Lord sets up the broken down, the Lord releases the fettered ones, the Lord illumines the blind" [Ps 146:7–8]. Indeed Solomon in the Book of Wisdom has clearly declared that the Lord would loose the mouths of the mute when he said, "Wisdom opened the mouth of the mute, and made the tongues of them that cannot speak eloquent" [Wis 10:21]. Surely this

Wisdom, namely Christ the Son of God [see 1 Cor 1:24], is he who loosed the mouth of that mute man into eloquent speech.

2. Therefore the Lord showed such a great work for the purpose of manifesting the power of his own divinity in this man who was blind and mute and had a demon. Thus the man immediately was delivered from the demon and saw and spoke, while all were amazed and all were struck with astonishment over such a great work. For he who was believed to be merely David's son according to the assumption of the body had carried out such splendid signs of divine power. But "when the Pharisees heard this they said, He does not expel demons except by Beelzebub prince of demons" [Matt 12:24]. How great was the blindness, how great was the unbelief, or rather, how great was the insanity of the Pharisees! Not only did they not believe in the divine miracles, but over and above this they slanderously accused them! By the foreknowledge of the Holy Spirit, David had predicted that they would do this when he said, "The strange children lied to me, strange children grew old" [Ps 18:44–45]. And again, "Through the abundance of your power your enemies shall lie to you" [Ps 66:3], surely this means that through this abundance of power in the presence of which they said in response to seeing the manifest signs of power being done by the Lord, "He does not expel demons except by Beelzebub prince of demons." Where had those who were doctors of the law read this? By what scriptural authority were they able to fabricate such a criminal assertion, that he could deservedly be deemed [so] at that time?[181] But the insanity of a poisonous mind is always inaccessible, so that it does not consider what it is saying. Hence the Pharisees were so blinded in their malice and iniquity that they did not consider what they were saying. Not without cause does the Holy Spirit proclaim against them through David, "Let the unjust lips become dumb, which speak wickedness against the just man with pride and scorn" [Ps 31:18]. For what pride is greater, and what scorn so serious as to blaspheme the author of divine miracles with the name of the adversary? Not unfittingly, the same person likewise testified of them in the psalm when he said, "They turned back to a crooked bow" [Ps 78:57], because by taking up the weapons of their godlessness and iniquity against the Son of God, they dared to attribute divine miracles to diabolical power.

3. "But Jesus, knowing their thoughts, said to them" [Matt 12:25]. When our Lord and Savior exposes the thoughts of their heart, he shows clearly to these same people that he is God, which they refused

to believe. For it belongs to God alone to know the thoughts of the heart. We read of this in the Scripture: "God searches the hearts and reins" [Ps 7:9]. And again: "Humans look at the appearance, but God at the heart" [1 Sam 16:7]. Therefore the Lord convicts the iniquities of the Pharisees and says that they have distorted the divine miracles by the use of a false term. He says, "Every kingdom divided against itself will be laid waste, and every city divided against itself will not stand. And if Satan drives out Satan, he is divided against himself. How then shall his kingdom stand?" [Matt 12:25–26]. Using a comparison with earthly things, the Lord silences and confounds the insanity of the Pharisees. For if a kingdom divided against itself is doubtless laid waste, and a city or house cannot stand in opposition to itself, how could Satan expel Satan, so that he himself would be destroying his own kingdom, when assuredly conspiring wickedness would not be able to fight against one demon in opposition to itself, unless they were losing the kingdom of sin and death that were reigning in accord with themselves? Thus it is not without reason that in order to silence the injustice of the Pharisees in all ways, the Lord says to them, "But if I cast out by Beelzebub, by whom do your sons cast out?" [Matt 12:27]. He is referring to the apostles, who, although they seemed to have been born from the race of the Jews, whence they too are said to be their "sons," nevertheless they drove out unclean spirits from bodies by no other name than that of Christ, having received authority from the Lord. Therefore he says, "They shall be your judges" [Matt 12:27], when they condemn their wickedness at the future judgment, since they were unwilling to believe in the Son of God, who worked divine miracles through himself, nor in the same apostles, who did many signs in the name of the Lord. "But if I expel demons by the Spirit of God, surely the kingdom of God will draw near among you" [Matt 12:28]. For if the apostles drove out demons by no other name than the name of Christ, how much more the Lord himself, who deemed it fitting to give this grace, power, and virtue to his disciples [see Matt 9:8; 10:1]. Through this he was proving that he expelled demons not by Beelzebub, as the Pharisees thought with their sacrilegious mind and spoke in blasphemy with their impious mouth, but he was working by the Spirit of God, that is, by the potency of his own divine power.

4. But since these very powers of the Lord contain an account of spiritual matters in them, we ought to consider what is being signified here according to the figurative understanding, as far as we are able

to understand it. In that man who had the demon and was blind and mute, we recognize a figure of the Gentile people being shown. At one time, namely before the coming of the Lord, through the error of idolatry, they were subjected to a demon and were mute and blind. The reason they were mute is because they either did not confess the Son of God or because they did not give the Lord the thanks they owed him. For every unbelieving and unfaithful person, even if he be eloquent, but if he does not confess the Son of God, he is considered to be mute as it were before God. But they were blind because they were blinded by the error of the world and the night of ignorance and did not yet know the true and eternal light. Therefore he is brought to be healed by the Lord, after health was restored to him who had the withered hand in the synagogue [see Matt 12:9–14]. Everyone who has been set free from the error of Satan by the Lord's mercy, who has abandoned the worship of idols, at once begins to see and speak: to see in this manner, when he gazes upon the true light he could not see before; to speak for this reason, because he confesses freely and faithfully Christ the Lord in respect to whose praise he was previously mute.[182]

5. When the unbelieving Pharisees realized that this grace of salvation was given to the people of the Gentiles by the Son of God, they were inflamed by jealousy and wicked rivalry and with malicious resentment. They not only refused to honor the author of such great power but over and above this they blasphemed him. Whence, too, in what the Lord testified, that a kingdom or city or house divided against itself cannot stand, this is understood to have been called to mind because both the kingdom the Jewish people themselves possessed, and the one that had existed under Jeroboam servant of Solomon, was divided before it was laid waste; and the Jews were going to lose completely the city of Jerusalem, against which Samaria arose in opposition, and the house of the temple, against which the golden calves and houses of idols had been set up [see 1 Kgs 12:25–33]. For this reason he shows them that that kingdom that cannot be divided must instead be followed, namely the heavenly and eternal one, and the spiritual Jerusalem, which always continued fixed and immovable, and the true house of God, which no hostile power either ever was able or will be able to fight against. For that house is sufficiently safe that is defended by the Son of God, to whom is the praise and glory in the ages of ages. Amen.

Tractate 50 on Matthew 12:29–32

1. It then follows, "Or how can anyone enter into the house of the strong [man] and plunder his goods, unless he first binds up the strong [man], and then he will plunder his goods. He that is not with me is against me. But he that does not gather with me, scatters" [Matt 12:29–30], and the rest that follows. Since he clearly showed that he expelled demons by the Spirit of God [see Matt 12:28], now the same Son of God comes to destroy the very devil himself. He mentioned him when he said, "Or how can anyone enter into the house of the strong [man] and plunder his goods, unless he first binds up the strong [man], and then he will plunder his house." He is showing that the strong [man] here is Satan himself, prince of demons, who in the house of this world possessed the captive bodies of human beings as his own goods. For he had captured the whole human race, and he lorded over everyone through <the power> of sin like a tyrant. We may hear just how strong he was in past times, when the Lord speaks to blessed Job about this same devil: "His tail goes down deep like a cypress; and his nerves are wrapped together like ropes. His sides are rocks of brass; and his backbone is as cast iron. This one was made as the beginning of the creation of the Lord; to be played with by his angels" [Job 40:17–19], and the rest that follows. We understand from these very statements of the Lord therefore that long ago the devil was strong. In these words is shown the devil's power, pride, and malice, under the figure of an allegorical comparison. Isaiah likewise reported of his arrogance, "But you said, I will ascend on high and set my seat above the stars of heaven and I will be like the Most High" [Isa 14:13–14]. A stronger one comes to bind this strong one, therefore, namely the only begotten Son of God, so that when the strong one is tied up, he could snatch from his power all of us who once were the devil's goods and spoils. For both David and the apostle make clear that he is the one "who by ascending on high took captivity captive and gave gifts to humanity" [Eph 4:8; Ps 68:18]. And in another place David related of him, "Who leads forth prisoners mightily, also them that act provokingly in anger, that dwell in tombs" [Ps 68:6]. Isaiah likewise has testified clearly about him when he said, "In that day God shall bring [his] holy and great and strong sword upon the dragon, the crooked serpent; he shall destroy the dragon on that day" [Isa 27:1]. Long ago David justly prayed through the Holy Spirit that the

Lord would deign to assume a body and come to bind this strong one, saying, "Take up arms and shield, and arise for my help. Bring forth a sword, and stop [the way] against them that persecute me" [Ps 35:2–3]. What arms was the prophet asking the Lord to take up to help the human race and to destroy the persecutors if not his taking on a human body, by which he offered the help of his divine mercy to humanity, and waged war against the enemy of the human race, the devil who persecutes? This agrees with what the apostle makes clear when he says, "For what the law could not do, in that it was weak through the flesh, God sending his own Son, in the likeness of the flesh of sin, from sin has condemned sin in the flesh" [Rom 8:3]. For by his assumption of a body he destroyed the devil, who a long time ago stood forth as the author of sin. Whence not unfittingly, in order to show the combat of this kind of Lord, who waged war against the enemy devil, the same David has testified under his own persona in the psalm as follows and says, "Blessed [be] the Lord, who trains my hands for war, [and] my fingers for combat" [Ps 144:1]. Surely he shows these hands of his trained for war, which he raised up on the cross against the devil for the sake of the salvation of the human race, and his fingers for combat, which he allowed to be pierced by nails in order to triumph over the devil.[183]

2. And rightly he went on to say, "He who is not with me is against me. And he who does not gather with me scatters." By this he showed that his own work is very much one thing, the devil's is something else. For the devil is the enemy of human salvation. It is proper for the devil to scatter to destruction; Christ's business is to gather to salvation.[184] Hence it is clear that one who is against the Lord cannot be with the Lord. Therefore, although the Lord seems by this statement to be arguing with those Pharisees who were unwilling to gather with Christ and were the Lord's enemies and adversaries, yet he is speaking also of all heretics and schismatics. By gathering impious things against the church, or rather against the Lord, by way of depraved doctrine or schismatic presumption, they aim to tear asunder and ravage the incorrupt body of the church and the unity of peace and faith. They do not retain Solomon's words: "He who splits wood will be endangered by it" [Eccl 10:9]. Clearly he is showing that those who cause schisms in the church are in danger of eternal death. For here the Holy Spirit is not speaking about the wood of trees but about all the faithful who abide in the church of the Lord, planted in paradise like trees of life.[185] As we have said, if anyone either through perverted

faith or by schism wants to split these trees, doubtless he incurs the danger of everlasting death for himself in accordance with Solomon. But we have the example even from nations of the past [to show] how serious it is before God to pervert faith, to tear asunder the peace and unity of the church, to scatter the members of Christ. Long ago, when Korah, Dathan, and Abiram usurped the authority of the priesthood for themselves in opposition to Moses and Aaron, they attempted to cause no small schism among the people.[186] Immediately the earth opened its mouth and swallowed them down alive into the underworld [see Num 16:1–35; 26:8–10].[187] The authors of the schism were plunged alive in different directions in the chaos of the earth by the divine judgment, so that henceforth there would be shown what penalty before God they would incur who would arise as authors of faithlessness and schism, for the destruction of faith and the peace of the church. Hence not unfittingly in the present passage the Lord, in order to show that whatever had been seized upon contrary to the unity of the church was being done against himself, said, "He who is not with me is against me. And he who does not gather with me scatters."

3. Finally it follows, "Therefore, I say to you that every sin and blasphemy shall be forgiven to humanity, and whosoever shall speak a word against the Son of man, it shall be forgiven him. But he that shall speak against the Holy Spirit, it shall not be forgiven him, neither in this world, nor in the future" [Matt 12:31–32]. To be sure, as we mentioned earlier, we recognize clearly in the first place that the Lord has spoken this against the Pharisees.[188] Though they had seen such great signs and miracles being done, they blasphemed with a wicked mouth and sacrilegious mind the author of this great divine power. They said that he cast out demons by prince Beelzebub [see Matt 12:24]. The Lord makes clear that on account of this they are guilty of such a wicked blasphemy and of such a great sacrilege that they will obtain no forgiveness of sin either in the present age or in the future. For to sin against someone and to blaspheme someone can be a forgivable sin, if the person turns and makes amends with his brother or sister against whom that person has transgressed. For the Lord answered Peter, who had asked the Lord how many times he ought to forgive someone who sins, that not merely seven times but even seventy-seven times he must be forgiven [see Matt 18:21–22], but only if the one who committed the transgression against his brother or sister turns back again to him or her and repents. But to sin against God as the Pharisees did,

or rather, to blaspheme so gravely, is an unforgivable and inexpiable crime. But this judgment of the Lord is not only against the Pharisees but against all the teachers of heresy who corrupt the meaning of the divine Scriptures by depraved interpretations.[189] They blaspheme the eternity and true divinity of the only begotten Son of God with a sacrilegious mouth, as they presume with a sacrilegious mind that he had his first beginning from Mary, as Ebion[190] and Photinus claim; or they impiously deny that he is God and was uniquely born from the Father, as Arius claims, though the truth of the name of Father could not exist without a true and legitimate birth of the Son, nor could one God be understood in accordance with the evangelical and apostolic faith, if the one divinity without distinction of Father and Son is not recognized.[191] For this reason the heretics are both impious in respect to the Father, when they deprive him of the truth of his paternal name; and they are sacrilegious in respect to the Son, when they attempt to take away from him that which the divine nature of God the Father has; and they are blasphemous in respect to the Holy Spirit, whom they are unwilling to understand as being from no other source than from the divine substance. Hence by dishonoring the Father by means of the Son, they do not cease to blaspheme the Holy Spirit as well. Justly the Lord shows that for their guilt of such a great blasphemy they will not receive forgiveness either in the present world or in the future. For what is more base, or what could be more criminal, than to reckon the Creator of the universe among the creatures; to take away the truth of the Father's nature, so that he is not a Father; to deprive the Son of his true and proper birth, so that he is not a Son; to dishonor the Holy Spirit, so that he cannot be understood as springing from God, though the reason the Trinity is understood as one God is because there is a single and indistinguishable divinity of the Trinity to whom is the praise and glory before all ages and in the ages of ages. Amen.

Tractate 51 on Matthew 13:36–43

1. <…> "Then having sent away the crowds, the Lord Jesus went off to the house, and his disciples came to him, saying, Explain to us the parable of the wheat and the weeds of the field. But Jesus said to them, He that sows the good seed, is the Son of man; and the field is this world; but the good seed are the sons of the kingdom" [Matt

13:36–38]. And the rest. The Lord therefore clearly points out that he is the sower of good seed. In this world, as in a field, he does not cease to sow God's word into the hearts of people, like good seed, so that each of us according to the seeds sown in us by God may bear spiritual and heavenly fruit. But he also shows that our enemy the devil on the other hand sows[192] the weeds of his wickedness and malice to choke the seed of God in us. For thus he says: "But while the men were asleep, his enemy came and sowed weeds among the wheat and went away" [Matt 13:25].[193] The Lord indicates that the devil sows weeds among sleeping people, namely, among those who through negligence are overcome by their infidelity as by a kind of lethargy and fall asleep in respect to the divine commands. The apostle says concerning them, "For they who sleep, sleep at night, and they who are drunk, are drunk at night. But let us not sleep, as do the rest, but let us be wakeful and sober" [1 Thess 5:7, 6]. Surely those foolish virgins about whom we read in the Gospel were weighed down by their lethargy and infidelity. Since they did not take oil for their vessels, they were unable to meet the bridegroom [see Matt 25:1–12]. Hence the devil, this enemy of the human race, is always extremely zealous to sow weeds among the wheat. But he who watches for the Lord constantly with a faithful mind, once the sleep of infidelity has been banished from him, will not be preoccupied by this nighttime sower.

2. "And then when the blade was sprung up, and had brought forth fruit, then appeared the weeds. And the servants of the householder came and said to him, Did you not sow good seed in your field? Whence then does it have weeds? And he said to them, An enemy did this. The servants said to him, Do you want us to go and gather it up? He said, No, lest perhaps gathering up the weeds, you root up the wheat also together with it. But let them both grow until the time, and at the time of the harvest I will say to the reapers, Gather up first the weeds, and bind them into bundles to burn, but the wheat gather into my barn" [Matt 13:26–30].

The Lord himself interpreted the good seed, then, as representing the sons of the kingdom and the weeds as the wicked sons [see Matt 13:38]. But when the servants of the householder, namely under the persona of the apostles, ask the Lord whether they should separate the weeds from the wheat, he allowed them both to grow together until the time, that is, until the consummation of the age [see Matt 13:39]. He clearly showed that he would send reapers at that time, namely angels, so that, once they have separated the wheat from the weeds, that is, once the holy ones have been selected out from the midst of the wicked, they may gather the just in the heavenly kingdom, like wheat in barns. But all the wicked and sinners will burn amid the punishment of hell, like weeds in the fire, where the Lord makes clear that they will forever weep and gnash their teeth, when he says, "There shall be weeping and gnashing of teeth" [Matt 13:42]. And when the Lord attests there will be weeping and gnashing of teeth, he is undoubtedly pointing to the future resurrection not only of the soul (as certain heretics would have it) but also of the body.[194] For to weep with the eyes and to gnash one's teeth are, strictly speaking, punishments of the body. Therefore the gravity of the error that has a hold on heretics of this type can be recognized from this statement of the Lord, for they do not believe in the future resurrection of bodies.

3. And he added, "Then the just will shine like the sun in the kingdom of the Father" [Matt 13:43], that is, in the heavenly kingdom, when according to the apostle they are transfigured in glory and become conformed to the body of the brightness of the Lord [see Phil 3:21], and when according to the same apostle they are caught up by angels to meet the Lord in the clouds [see 1 Thess 4:17]. David, too, shows that there will be this separation of the just from the unjust at the consummation of the age, when he says, "God, our God, shall come manifestly, and shall not keep silence. A fire shall be kindled before him, and round about him there shall be a very great tempest" [and the rest up to] "upon sacrifices" [Ps 50:3–5]. At that time, assuredly "he will call to heaven above" [Ps 50:4], so that the people of God may be discerned, when heavenly and spiritual people will be separated "from the earth," that is, from the earthly and sinners. Then, too, the sons of God will be gathered by angels, "who have engaged in a covenant with him upon sacrifices" [Ps 50:5], that is, the martyrs who offer themselves as a sacrifice to God, mindful of the divine covenant, by handing over their bodies for the sake of Christ's name.

4. Since therefore we know what hope and glory is laid up for God's saints, and what punishments have been prepared for the impious and the sinners, we should always stay awake in respect to the Lord's commands, lest that nighttime sower secretly steals from us. Let us fear the punishment of hell in which the Lord has testified that there is weeping and gnashing of teeth, in which the prophet shows that all sinners are burned up with everlasting flames, when he says, "Behold, the day of the Lord will come burning as an oven, and it shall consume them, and all the aliens, and all that do wickedly,

shall be as stubble and it will set them on fire as brushwood, that day that is coming, says the Lord" [Mal 4:1]. Both earlier by the prophet and later on in the gospel, the Lord likewise declared in respect to that punishment that the fire is inextinguishable and the worm not subject to death, when he said, "Where their worm will not die and the fire will not be extinguished" [Mark 9:43, 45, 47]. And fittingly at the end of the reading, the Lord says, "He who has ears to hear, let him hear" [Matt 13:43]. That is, we should hear with the ears of our heart opened, both what is the punishment of eternal fire to which all the wicked will be handed over like weeds to be burned, and what is the glory of the just, in which they shall shine like the sun in the kingdom of the Father. Thus always having these things before our eyes, meditating on them day and night, may we be able both to escape the punishment of that inextinguishable fire and to merit the promised glory of the heavenly kingdom from our Lord and Savior Jesus, who is blessed in the ages of ages. Amen.

Tractate 52 on Matthew 14:22–23

1. After the display of his divine power was shown whereby from five loves and two fish he satisfied five thousand men apart from the women and children [see Matt 14:13–21], "immediately he commanded his disciples to get into a boat and cross the channel ahead of him while he dismissed the crowds. And when the crowd was dismissed, he went up on a mountain alone to pray" [Matt 14:22–23].[195] Our Lord and Savior prayed in order to show to all of us an example, as our teacher and Lord [see John 13:13]. He prayed in order to demonstrate that he was not the Father but the Son. He prayed, but not for himself. For why would he pray for himself, he who not only committed no sin but who blotted out the sins of all? Hence he prayed not for himself but for us, in accordance with what David previously foretold through the Holy Spirit when he said, "Return, O Lord, a little, and pray for your servants" [Ps 90:13]. John the evangelist declares openly that this was carried out. He revealed plainly the very words of the Lord by which he prayed for us to the Father, when he said, "Father, I want that where I am they too may be with me and may see my glory" [John 17:24]. And again, "Not for these alone do I ask, but also for those who will believe in me through their word" [John 17:20].

This then was the Lord's prayer for us to the Father, that we all be one and be considered worthy of seeing his glory in the heavenly kingdom [see John 17:21].

2. "But when evening came he was there alone. But the boat was now in the midst of the sea, buffeted by the waves. For the wind was against them. But in the fourth watch of the night he came to them, walking upon the sea" [Matt 14:23–24]. Therefore when the Lord as teacher of the human race offered the example to us of praying, and the boat was being buffeted by waves in the midst of the sea, since the wind was contrary, "the Lord came to them, walking upon the sea." Here he showed openly the power of his divinity. For who could have walked on the sea except one who is the Creator of the universe? He, surely, about whom the Holy Spirit had foretold long ago through blessed Job: "Who alone stretches out the heavens and walks on the sea as on the earth" [Job 9:8]. And who speaks about this same thing similarly through Solomon under the persona of Wisdom, when he says, "I dwelled in the highest places and my throne was in a pillar of cloud. I orbited the heavenly sphere alone and walked on the waves of the sea" [Sir 24:7–8]. David also testified about this in a psalm and said, "God, your way was through the sea, your paths through the great waters" [Ps 77:19]. Similarly, Habakkuk reported about this and said, "Scattering the waters in the crossings; the deep uttered its voice" [Hab 3:10]. What could be plainer than these testimonies, what clearer? By them he is shown clearly to walk on the sea as upon the ground, that is, God's only begotten Son, who long ago according to the will of the Father stretched out the heavens and at the time of Moses in a pillar of cloud showed the people a way to follow. Hence in what faithless impiety are the heretics being held fast who have dared to deny that Christ is God. They ought to recognize this based on these very testimonies. Therefore the Lord walked upon the sea, he who is both Creator and founder of the universe. For he who had made both the nature of humanity and the sea itself and all things heavenly and earthly could not be weighed down with respect to his body, to prevent him from walking by the waves of the sea. That is why the very waters were made serviceable to their Lord and Creator, while the waves of the sea were raging, rejoicing in the obedient duty of service.

3. Thus when the disciples saw the Lord walking upon the sea, they did not know that it was him. Struck by the wonder of fresh admiration, they thought that it was a ghost. For they knew that the nature of a human birth does not allow this earthly body to be held up by

waves carrying the burden. But in order to strengthen the trepidation of his fearful disciples, the Lord says, "Take courage, do not be afraid; I am" [Matt 14:27]. This shows that he is the one who long ago had spoken to Moses, "I am who I am" [Exod 3:14]. Thus the disciples, upon recognizing their Lord and God by hearing his voice, would cease being amazed either that the Creator lords over his creation or that the creation serves its Creator. After all, as soon as they heard the Lord saying, "I am," that which they knew was impossible for human beings, they immediately believed was possible for the Son of God.

4. Fittingly, too, Peter was strengthened by this response from the Lord and said in faith, "Lord, if it is you, command me to come to you upon the water. But he said, Come. And Peter got down out of the boat and was walking upon the water in order to come to Jesus. Upon seeing the strong wind Peter became afraid. And when he began to sink, he shouted, Lord, save me. And the Lord stretched out his hand and grabbed him and said to him, You of little faith, why did you doubt?" [Matt 14:28–31]. When Peter recognized his Lord and God, he was strengthened and asked with faith to descend and walk upon the water. In order to show the power of his divine nature and to demonstrate that all things are possible to him who believes, the Lord granted the request of his disciple who had asked with faithfulness. For he commands him to walk upon the water, he for whom nothing could be impossible by the power of his divine potency. But when Peter goes down from the boat, he begins to walk upon the waters of the sea, as long as he is safe, as long as he has courage and remained dauntless in faith. But when indeed a powerful wind increases, he lets go of the rudder of his faith, disturbed by human alarm; at once he begins to sink. Hence the Lord said to him, "You of little faith, why did you doubt?" Consider here, too, the difference between Master and slave, between God and man. The Lord was walking upon the waves of the sea. No wonder: for the Creator had lordship over his creation. For even the very waves of the sea rejoiced that they lay underneath the feet of Christ. But Peter wanted to procure by faith what he could not by nature, as he himself walked upon the waves of the sea. Finally, he, too, walked, but in order to recognize that he was a man, he began to sink in the waves. For the power of Christ was one thing, the condition of Peter something else, since the former was God, the latter a man; the former walked by his own power; the latter was held up by Christ's power. After all, Peter did not say to the Lord, "I am not able to come to you walking on the sea." The one who awaits a command professes

his weakness. For he knew that he could not walk upon the sea contrary to nature, unless he were commanded by Christ, who is the Lord of the things of nature. Therefore the fact that Peter was able to walk upon the sea was not the power of Peter but the authority of the one who commanded it. Nevertheless, Peter's faith demanded the authority of the commander. He believed that he could walk upon the waves of the sea if he were commanded by Christ. But afterward he became afraid when the strong wind increased. While walking upon the sea he also began to sink. At once he takes refuge in Christ and said, "Lord, save me." Peter was ruled in part by his own rudder of faith, to be sure, while he was walking on the sea; but when he became disturbed at the rising waves, soon he required <another> rudder, namely Christ's help, where he found the true port of salvation. It pertained to human weakness, then, that he became afraid when he sank into the waves; but it pertained to a powerful and admirable faith that he implored the help of Christ. Not of course that it would have been fitting even for saint Peter himself to walk dauntlessly upon the waves of the sea in accordance with the Lord's example, lest he become puffed up in faith and judge himself equal or similar to the Lord. Therefore when he began to sink, he shouted to the Lord, who is accustomed to deliver from shipwreck and from mortal danger those who call upon him, saying, "Lord, deliver me." And at once the Lord hears the faithful cry of his disciple, stretches out his hand and grabs him. This shows that it was he who long ago said through the prophet, "Call upon me on the day of affliction and I will rescue you and you will glorify me" [Ps 50:15]. Here in saint Peter we indeed observe this being fulfilled. When he was found to be in the affliction of a storm and faithfully cried out to the Lord, saying, "Lord, deliver me," at once he merited to be delivered by the Lord's outstretched hand. It is no wonder if the Lord delivered his own disciple who called to him faithfully from the waves of the sea. Long ago he summoned back Jonah unscathed after three days not merely from waves, but from the depths of the sea and from the belly of the whale [see Jonah 2].

5. But according to the mystical account, this boat in which the Lord commanded his disciples to cross, when he himself went up on the mountain [see Matt 14:22–23], contains a figure of the church, which the Son of God, when he was about to ascend to heaven to the Father, commended to the apostles [see John 17:9–11].[196] Therefore, it was being tossed about here and there, as it were in the midst of the sea, and struck by the various waves of temptations, with the

wind opposing it, that is, the unclean spirit in this world. In the fourth watch of the night, the Lord came to visit this boat and deliver it from the danger of the storm, that is, from the shipwreck of this world. We can identify the meaning of this fourth watch even from the worldly pattern. We know that four nightly watches were arranged when soldiers and guards were accustomed to stay awake and stand guard in turn in order to protect the encampments and the walls against ambushes from the enemy. But we find that these four watches have been arranged by the Lord also for the heavenly encampment to protect the saints. And we read of these guards in the Book of Job: "Look up to the sky and see; consider the clouds, how high they are <...>, who appoints the night-watches" [Job 35:5, 10]. Hence we ought to consider the meaning of this fourth watch in which the Lord comes to his disciples who were suffering in the storm. The first watch of this night, that is, of the present world, is understood to be from Adam to Noah. The second watch is from Noah up to Moses, by whom the law was given. But the third watch is from Moses up to the coming of the Lord and Savior. In these three watches the Lord, even before coming in the flesh, with the vigilance of the angels, defends the encampments of his saints from the ambushes of the enemy, namely, the devil and his angels, who from the beginning of the world have always plotted against the salvation of the just. For indeed in the first watch, protection is given to Abel, Seth, Enosh, Enoch, Methuselah, and Noah. But in the second watch, to Abraham, Melchizedek, Isaac, Jacob, and Joseph. In the third, to Moses, Aaron, Joshua the son of Nun, and, after that, to the other just men and prophets. But the fourth watch marks the time when the Son of God deemed it fitting to be born according to the flesh and to suffer. In it he promises his disciples and his church that he will be eternally watchful after his resurrection, saying, "I will be with you even to the consummation of the world" [Matt 28:20]. David is also familiar with this eternal protection of the Lord when he says, "Behold, he that protects Israel shall not slumber nor sleep" [Ps 121:4]. In this fourth watch of the night, then, that is, after the just ones, after the law, after the prophets, our Lord and Savior assumed a human body and came, walking upon the sea, that is, treading upon the sins of the world, with the result that he put to flight the storm of opposing winds of the unclean spirit and delivered from the shipwreck of this world his boat, that is, the church. Because of her he suffered through the storm, since he endured persecution for the sake of his own church.

6. For in the fact that Peter asks to come to the Lord by walking upon the sea, when he says, "Lord, if it is you, command me to come to you," it is shown that saint Peter was held by an enormous love for the Lord.[197] He wanted to suffer with him at that time when the Lord said that all would be scandalized over him. Peter said, "Even if I must die, I will not deny you" [Matt 26:35]. But when he saw the strong wind, at once he feared and began to sink. How is Peter understood to have become afraid at the sight of the strong wind, unless it was when he saw the violence of persecution, which the Jewish people inflicted against the Son of God? For at that time he truly became afraid and nearly began to be in danger, when he was asked by the maidservant, and said a first, second, and third time that he did not know Jesus of Nazareth [see Mark 14:66–72], that is, Christ the Lord. In this manner, then, Peter began to sink, since he later denied that he knew the one whom earlier he had confessed to be the Son of God [see Matt 16:16], for whose sake he said he would even die [see Matt 26:35].

7. Therefore when Peter began to sink in this manner, he cried out to the Lord and said, "Save me. And extending his hand he grabbed him."[198] What is understood by this outcry of Peter after he began to sink, if not that one with which he cried out and wept very bitterly with his faith and heart toward the Lord, after his denial? Hence not without cause is he grabbed by the extended hand of Jesus. After all, as we read in the gospel, immediately after his denial Jesus looked at him and then Peter wept very bitterly [see Matt 26:75; Luke 22:62]. Therefore the fact that Peter wanted to reach the Lord through the waves of the sea signified that before the passion, Peter wanted to suffer with the Lord and for the Lord.[199] But since he had not yet been strengthened by the passion of Christ, he was terrified by the fear of death and instead of the constancy of faith, experienced the danger of denial. Nor was it right, obviously, that Peter should have suffered with Christ as well, since the passion of Christ alone was required for the salvation of the world, he who alone deemed it fitting to die both for the whole world and for Peter himself.

8. Now in the fact that during the storm the Lord got into the boat and the wind ceased, and those who were in the boat came and worshiped him, this is understood to signify that our Lord and Savior, once the storm of persecution had been put to flight, would come again to his disciples continually, and to his church, in which he established saint Peter as the first of the apostles and uniquely commended his sheep to him, saying, "Feed my sheep" [John 21:17]. When the

apostles in the church of believers, set in a boat as it were, beheld the glory of the Lord's resurrection, they worshiped our Lord and Savior and declared to the human race that he was the true Son of God, to whom is the praise and glory in the ages of ages. Amen.

Tractate 53 on Matthew 15:1–16

1. When the Lord came into the land of Gennesaret with his disciples and healed with heavenly medicine many there who were afflicted by various maladies [see Matt 14:34–36], "the scribes and Pharisees came to him from[200] Jerusalem, saying, Why do your disciples transgress the traditions of the elders? For they do not wash their hands when they eat bread" [Matt 15:1–2]. Since the scribes and Pharisees did not dare to speak against the manifest miracles of the Lord, they sought different opportunities and arguments by which they could criticize and find fault with the Lord or his disciples. Thus in the present passage they also accused the Lord's disciples of being transgressors of the law. Why did they not eat bread in accordance with the tradition of the elders with washed hands? They say, "Why do your disciples transgress the traditions of the elders? For they do not wash their hands when they eat bread." Indeed among other observations, the Jewish elders ruled that a person should not take or eat food unless he first washed his hands. This observance, however, is more of a human practice and custom. No progress toward salvation comes from it. Therefore, this tradition of the elders is practically useless, for it does not advance a person's salvation. For no justification is gained from this tradition if it is observed, and no transgression is committed if it is disregarded. For God does not ask a person to wash his hands before eating, but whether he has kept his heart washed and his conscience clean from the filth of sins. Truly, what good is it to wash your hands and to have a defiled conscience? Hence because the Lord's disciples were washed in their heart and had a clean and undefiled conscience, they were not overly concerned with washing their hands. They had washed them once in baptism with their whole body, as the Lord said to Peter: "He who has bathed once does not need to wash again, but he is clean all over, as you are" [John 13:10]. But long ago through the prophet, the Lord had showed that this washing was necessary for the Jewish people, when he said, "Wash yourselves, be

clean; remove your iniquities from your souls" [Isa 1:16]. In this washing, then, the command is not to wash the hands but to remove iniquities from their hearts. Hence the scribes and Pharisees, had they wanted to understand or receive this heavenly washing, never would have asked about unwashed hands. And O how foolish and blind they are![201] They convict the Lord's disciples of unwashed hands, when they themselves had a defiled conscience and hands that were stained from the blood of the prophets! [see Luke 11:50]. For this reason the daily washing of hands could bring no benefit to the scribes and Pharisees. They were filthy with various sins and lived with a polluted mind. Yet the Lord convicted them with the opposite proposition: "Why do you also transgress the commandment of God for your tradition? For God said, Honor your father and mother. And he that shall curse father or mother shall die the death. But you say, Whosoever shall say to father and mother, Whatever gift is from me shall profit you. And he has not honored his father or his mother; and you have made void the word of God for your tradition" [Matt 15:3–6]. The scribes and Pharisees reproached the Lord's disciples on the question of eating with unwashed hands to the neglect of the tradition of the elders, though they themselves were found to be transgressors of the law in all things, having neglected the divine commandments that were given for the salvation of the people. For although in the law there is a command that parents must be honored with all honor and obedience [see Exod 20:12; Deut 5:16], and punishment is established for the one who curses father or mother [see Exod 21:17], yet the scribes and Pharisees had instructed that the gift must be offered in view of the pronouncement of condemnation, nullifying the fear of the established judgment. By this presumption they are known both to have changed the statute of the divine commandment and to have offered children an occasion of impiety, who would not have been able to be held to the lawful obedience to parents, if not by natural piety and the terror at the punishment set forth.

2. And justly the Lord followed up and said, "Hypocrites, well has Isaiah prophesied of you, saying, This people honors me with their lips, but their heart is far from me. And in vain do they worship me, teaching human doctrines and commandments" [Matt 15:7–9]. For it is truly in vain that they pretend to worship God, whom they honor with their lips rather than with their heart, and to whose divine precepts and saving doctrines they prefer human commandments. It says, "And having called together the crowds unto him, he said, Hear

and understand. Not that which goes into the mouth defiles a person, but what comes out of the mouth, this defiles a person. Then came his disciples, and said to him, Do you know that the Pharisees, when they heard this word, were scandalized? But Jesus, answering [them], said, Every plant that my heavenly Father has not planted shall be rooted up. Let them alone; they are blind, guides of the blind. And if the blind lead the blind, both will fall into the pit. And Peter answering said to him, Expound to us this parable. But he said, Are you also yet without understanding?" [Matt 15:10–16]. And the rest. In order to show in more detail that the reproach of the scribes and Pharisees concerning unwashed hands was superfluous, the Lord called together the crowds and said, "Not that which goes into the mouth defiles a person, but what comes out of the mouth defiles a person." He is showing that a person is defiled not from the food that enters his mouth but rather from the perverse thoughts of his mind, which proceed from his heart. For the food we receive for eating was created and blessed by God for use in human life, and therefore it cannot defile someone. But adverse and perverse thoughts that proceed from the heart, as the Lord himself has interpreted—"murder, adultery, fornication, theft, false witness, blasphemy," and the other things that originate from the devil—these are the things that really defile a man.

3. But as Peter makes clear, not without a stumbling block did the Pharisees receive the Lord's statement, which says, "It is not what enters the mouth that defiles a person." Indeed, long ago God had commanded through Moses that not all foods are to be used. For he declares that certain foods were clean and others were truly unclean [see Lev 11; Deut 14]. But now we must ask why God prohibited the people long ago to eat these things. For since all things created by God to be used as human food were blessed right at the very beginning, and they remain no less so by their very created nature, why is it that divine law later prescribed to the Jewish people certain things as lawful to eat because they were clean, and certain things as unlawful because they were unclean? First, precepts of this type were given by the Lord because of the extravagant and immoderate gluttony of the Jewish people. For since in their devotion to throat and belly this people became unmindful of God's precepts, they made for themselves a calf at Horeb [see Exod 32], about which it was written, "The people sat down to eat and drink and rose up to play" [Exod 32:6; 1 Cor 10:7]. Those necessary things were forbidden by the Lord, so

that with the best food having been denied and the immoderation of their gullets held in check, the people might be able to be held more easily to the discipline of divine observance. After all, it was after the prevarication of the worship of the calf that we find those things were prohibited. The Lord published this mild and moderate pronouncement concerning these things, as though to condemn a still unformed people. And that is why it was said, as we read, "They shall be unclean to you" [Lev 11:8]. He did not say, "They *are* unclean," but "They *shall be*." Nor did he say "to *all*" but "to *you*." He thus made it clear that they neither were unclean nor would they be unclean to people other than themselves. And certainly they deserved this prohibition of many foods, for this is the people that preferred the meats of Egypt, as well as cucumbers and muskmelons, to heavenly manna [see Num 11:4–6].

4. And although these things must be understood in this way in accordance with the simplicity of the letter, we nevertheless recognize in these very things, as also in the other mysteries of the law, prefiguring types of future realities. For it has been shown by sure signs what is to be regarded as clean and what as unclean among the fish and the four-footed creatures and the rest of the animals. That is, among the fish, those are shown to be clean that have scales and fins; but those that have no scales are considered unclean [see Lev 11:9–12]. But among four-footed creatures, those are identified as clean that chew the cud and have split hooves, but those that have either neither or just one are unclean [see Lev 11:26].[202] In this identification of clean and unclean things, we recognize that nothing else but a figure of believers and unbelievers is being shown. For the animal that splits the hoof and chews the cud does not slip as it goes down a path, but it always walks with a steady gait, while one hoof is strengthened by its being joined to the other. This is the person of faith who is fortified by the precepts of both testaments, that is, the New and Old Testament, as with a split hoof. He walks not on slippery tracks but very firm ones through the journey of this world. In his heart and in his mouth he always has as well the food of salutary life, that is, meditation upon the divine law.[203] He preserves it faithfully in accordance with what we read as written about the blessed person: "And on his law he shall meditate day and night" [Ps 1:2]. And again: "How sweet are your oracles to my throat, more so than honey and honeycomb to my mouth!" [Ps 119:103]. For to split the hoof means either to hold fast to the precepts of both testaments in the single root of faith, as we have said,

or surely to confess the Father and the Son in the unity of nature. To chew the cud, on the other hand, means, as we have said, always to be reflecting upon the divine words, and by constant meditation to be turning them over in one's heart and mind like heavenly food.

Hence not without reason the rest of the animals that either do not split the hoof and do not chew the cud, or that chew the cud only and do not have a split hoof, are shown to be unclean [see Lev 11:26]. Clearly we recognize all unbelievers being signified in them, that is, both Jews and Gentiles, and also heretics. For to split the hoof and not to chew the cud pertains to the heretics, who although they seem to adhere to the two testaments and to confess both Father and Son, yet they do not profess this with a pious sense in their mind, nor with a saving confession of the mouth, this very faith they claim to adhere to. And therefore they are reckoned among the unclean animals, that is, among unbelieving people. But to chew the cud and not to split the hoof pertains to the Jews, who although they have the commands of the law always in their heart, yet since they do not split the hoof, that is, since they do not receive the two testaments, nor confess Father and Son, even they are reckoned by the Lord among the unclean animals, while they hold fast to the Old Testament alone as their singular hoof, they do not walk with a firm step but on slippery paths. But neither to split the hoof nor to chew the cud pertains to the Gentiles who do not believe in God at all or receive the commands of the two testaments, or confess Father and Son. And they do not chew the cud since they do not keep any observance of divine law in their mouth and in their heart.

5. Similar distinctions are also made in the account of the fish. For those fish that have scales and fins are commanded to be used as food [see Lev 11:9]. Doubtless we recognize all faithful believers in Christ as being signified in them, who are both born unto God like fish, in the baptism in water, and they carry scales on their mouth when they confess their former sins, and they have fins when they pass through the waves of this sea, that is, the temptations of the world, by a swift and speedy course with the rudder of faith. Of them we read it written in David, "The birds of heaven and the fish of the sea who pass through the paths of the sea" [Ps 8:8]. But in those fish that have neither scales nor fins, we recognize the Jews being signified, who although they are baptized daily and like the fish never leave the water, yet since they do not have scales or fins, that is, since they

neither recognize the sins of their unbelief nor are steered by the help of faith, they cannot be used as heavenly and spiritual grace.

6. But in the birds that would be unclean, which must not to be used as food, they are even designated by their own names, that is, the eagle, the kite, the vulture, the raven, the sparrow, the swan, the falcon, the ostrich, the horned owl, the bat, the night owl, and others similar to these [see Lev 11:13–19]. But among the creeping things, there is the weasel, the lizard, the mouse, and the rest [see Lev 11:29–30]. In the signification of all these things, in a similar manner, as was said earlier, a figure is shown of wicked and unclean men. For in the eagle, the hawk, the vulture, and the kite, which live by ravaging the dead and feeding on carcasses, rapacious and profane men are signified, who seize what belongs to others and what is not their due, and who plot the death of wretched people to live on their resources. But in the raven are shown sinners and unclean people who are burdened with a blackish and dark conscience; they live impurely in the world. But in the ostrich and the swan, he signifies arrogant and puffed-up people who have a raised neck [see Jer 7:26; 17:23]. Now in the sparrow he shows those who wander about and are erratic, who, with an inconstant mind, fly about in different directions. But in the falcon, which hunts doves above all, he signifies those who are accustomed to plunder the innocent. In the horned owl, he points to those who seize the homes of foreigners and threaten death upon wretched people with a mournful voice. Now in the night owl and bat he signifies those who flee from the light of truth and linger in the darkness of their sins. One should also interpret the creeping things in a similar way. While prohibiting the eating of the weasel he convicts filthy people who bring forth unclean words from their mouths, since the weasel expels from its mouth unclean young. While avoiding the lizard, he condemns the one who leads a blemished life characterized by various pleasures. While interdicting the mouse he damns those who follow the caverns of errors and gnaw to pieces the Scriptures of the faith.[204]

7. The animals are faulted, then, in order to correct human beings, so that while what is natural in animals is rebuked, humans would understand how grave a condemnation they shall incur before God who commit sins of this sort against the law of God and against the very nature of their created state. And so if the scribes and Pharisees had understood figures of this sort, or had recognized the Lord himself who had come to lighten the burdens of the law, they would

never have experienced a stumbling block concerning the Lord's statements, in which he said, "It is not what enters the mouth that defiles a man, but what comes out of the mouth defiles the man" [Matt 15:11]. Fittingly, then, to condemn the unbelief of the scribes and Pharisees, the Lord followed up and said, "Every plant my heavenly Father has not planted shall be rooted up. Let them alone, they are blind, guides of the blind. And if the blind lead the blind, both will fall into the pit" [Matt 15:13–14]. Since therefore the scribes and Pharisees had erupted in such great presumption, and had neglected the divine law, in order to plant their own precepts but not God's, which they wanted to be observed as divine law, not without good reason did they too, with this planting of their own doctrine, deserve to be uprooted by the Lord. And so the Lord said, "Every plant that my heavenly Father has not planted will be rooted up." For that plant was not of God but of human beings. Any iniquitous plant, not only of the scribes and Pharisees but also of all heretics, shall be uprooted by the Lord. Though it may seem to extend its branches of infidelity for a time, nevertheless it cannot be firmly rooted, for such a plant is not of God but of the devil. It must forthwith be uprooted and handed over to perpetual fire, since it shows no fruit of faith and salvation from itself.

8. Finally, he followed up by saying, "Let them alone; they are blind, guides of the blind. But if the blind lead the blind, both will fall into a pit." Granted, these words may be understood as exposing the same scribes and Pharisees who were blinded by the error of their unbelief. Not only were they unable to recognize the light of truth since they did not believe in Christ, but also they dragged others along with them into the pit of death. Nevertheless the words can also be understood of the heretics. By denying that Christ is the "true light from true light, and God from God,"[205] they too were steeped in a not dissimilar blindness. Because of their perverse doctrine they also proved to be guides and leaders to wretched people. It is said of them, "They are blind, guides of the blind. But if the blind leads the blind, both will fall into the pit." For teachers of faithlessness of this sort not only are themselves not content with the error and danger of their own unbelief, but while they offer themselves as teachers of perdition to the ignorant, they seduce those as well whom they drag equally into the pit of death with themselves. For they have refused to believe faithfully in the author of life, the only begotten Son of God, who is blessed in the ages. Amen.

Tractate 54 on Matthew 16:4

1. "A wicked generation seeks after a sign; and a sign shall not be given it, except the sign of Jonah" [Matt 16:4].[206] While a wicked and adulterous generation of Jews seeks unfaithfully for a sign from heaven to be shown to them, it did not merit receiving on their forehead the sign of the cross, which alone was given for salvation to believers, that sign assuredly of which it was written in Isaiah, "Lift up a sign for the nations" [Isa 62:10]. We read that it was very clearly written about this in Ezekiel as well, when it is said, "Go through the midst of Jerusalem, and set a sign on the foreheads of the living[207] that groan over the iniquity of my people" [Ezek 9:4]. And later he goes on to say, "Go, strike every male and female, from the least to their greatest, and do not spare the elder. But leave the one upon whom you find my sign, and begin with my holy ones" [Ezek 9:5–6]. If the scribes and Pharisees, therefore, had wanted to understand or recognize this saving sign in which alone salvation and life consists, they would never have asked for another sign. Yet they accept the sign of Jonah, in which clearly the mystery of the Lord's passion and resurrection is shown. Although we have already spoken about this in a previous section at no average length,[208] nevertheless since mention has been made again of Jonah, we ought to go over again the things that were said, that we may obtain a repeat grace of faith from a second repetition.

2. When Jonah was sent to preach to the Ninevites, he suffered through a storm at sea [see Jonah 1:1–2]. The Son of God was also sent by the Father to preach salvation to the human race. By a similar example he endures a storm at sea [see Jonah 1:4], that is, the world's persecution from the Jewish people. In the former, the wind stirs up the sea against Jonah; in the latter, an unclean spirit stirs up the people against the Lord. Finally, just as that former ship in which Jonah was found was tossed about by various tempests when the hurricane arose, so too the synagogue in which the Lord was found was led by various unclean spirits to inflict mortal danger. But just as Jonah was sleeping soundly in the former danger and was snoring away in slumber [see Jonah 1:5], so too in the midst of that danger from the synagogue the Lord rested soundly in the sleep of his passion by the power of his divine nature. Jonah was cast into the depths of the sea and is received by a whale [see Jonah 1:15–17]. The Lord likewise was taken by death.

3. But just as that whale was not able to digest Jonah nor keep him alive inside itself for long, so too voracious death assuredly received the Lord, but since he was not able to keep him alive and in custody inside himself any longer, death regurgitated him on the third day, just as the whale had regurgitated Jonah [see Jonah 2:10]. For death, though accustomed always to eat and digest the dead, was nauseated and expelled the Lord alive. Truly he was not strong enough to digest him, for he was the rock—as the apostle says, "But Christ was the rock" [1 Cor 10:4]. And indeed the whale gulped and expelled only Jonah. But death in receiving the Lord vomited out not only him but many with him. For we read that many bodies of saints had risen up with the Lord [see Matt 27:52]. Just as some are accustomed to take adverse potions to expel what they have inside them, so it happened to death as well. She[209] received the Lord's body as an adverse potion in order to vomit out the other bodies that she was holding. For by gulping down the Lord's body, death did not wound his flesh, but instead she was wounded by his flesh, since that flesh was not the kind that could be swallowed by death, but was a sword of stone that cut death's throat. Hence death erred in respect to the Lord's body and was deceived. She opened her jaws to be sure; for she was thinking that just as she had received and swallowed the first Adam, so too she could receive and swallow the second Adam; but she was deluded by the Lord's flesh. For while she was longing to make room and devour, she herself was captured and devoured. For "death has been swallowed up in victory," as it is written: "Where, O death, is your sting? Where, O death, is your victory?" [1 Cor 15:54–55].

Tractate 55 on Matthew 18:1–6

1. Still unaware of the extent of the glory of his humility, the disciples were competing for the preferred place of honor and merit, and they said to the Lord, "Who do you think is greater in the kingdom of heaven?" [Matt 18:1]. The disciples had a quarrel about who was the greater in the kingdom of heaven, though doubtless that one is esteemed greater before God who is humbler, since he says, "He who exalts himself shall be humbled, and he who humbles himself shall be exalted" [Matt 23:12]. Hence not without cause in order to cut off this sort of unnecessary dispute between his disciples, it says,

"Jesus called a little child, and set him in the midst of them, and said, Amen I say to you, unless you be converted, and become as little children, you shall not enter into the kingdom of heaven. Whoever therefore shall humble himself as this little child, he is greater in the kingdom of heaven" [Matt 18:2–4]. After setting a little child in their midst as his example, the Lord exhorts his disciples and shows that unless each should become as a little child, he cannot enter into the kingdom of heaven. But the reason the Lord here brought this example of little children, and the reason he commands us to become like little children, is not that we should be like little children in our age, since old age cannot return again to childhood; but that we should imitate the simplicity and innocence of little children.

2. The blessed apostle knows the manner in which we are commanded by the Lord to be little children when he says, "Do not be little children in your minds, but be infants in respect to evil, that you may be perfect in your minds" [1 Cor 14:20]. For a little child or an infant does not know the evil of the world, he does not know how to commit sin, he does not work evil against his neighbor, he does not hold on to anger, he hates no one, he does not seek after riches, he does not stand in awe of the glory of this world, he always follows his father, he does not depart from his mother.[210] For this reason, then, the Lord wants us to become like little children, that by a similar example we may live in the present world without malice and without deceit [see 1 Pet 2:2]. Let us flee from sin, let us not work evil against our neighbor; let us not hold on to anger; let us not seek after riches nor the glory of the world; let us always follow the Father, that is God, whose children we have already begun to be by adoption; let us not depart from our mother, that is, from the church, through which we have been born spiritually unto God. Let us rest as those placed in the lap of this mother, as infants in the bosom of their mother. Let us be daily nourished by her healthful doctrine, so that we may grow in faith and in the grace of baptism, in accordance with what the apostle Peter testified in his epistle when he said, "Eagerly desire milk, infants, that you may grow in it" [1 Pet 2:2]. Saint John also shows us in his epistle what sort of little children we ought to be, when he says, "I write to you, little children, because you have known the Father" [1 John 2:14]. For this purpose, therefore, we are instructed to be little children, that we may know the Father; that we would live in this world innocently and simply like doves [see Matt 10:16]. Since therefore the Lord wants there to be this sort of resemblance

to little children in us, it is not without reason that he says in the present passage, "Unless you become converted like little children, you shall not enter into the kingdom of heaven. Therefore whoever shall humble himself as this little child, he is greater in the kingdom of heaven." The Lord makes perfectly clear therefore that that one will be greater in the kingdom of heaven who shall imitate the humility and innocence of a little child. Finally, the Lord himself, in order to show us a perfect example of humility from his own self, thought it fitting to become a little child even by assuming flesh. This agrees with what we read as being written about him: "For a child is born to us, a son is given to us, whose empire has come upon his shoulders" [Isa 9:6]. For indeed this is why even the holy patriarchs, prophets, and apostles were called little children by the Lord, in accordance with what we read as written about them: "Behold, I and the little children whom the Lord has given me" [Heb 2:13; Isa 8:17–18], for they remained as little children, without deceit, without malice. We should therefore imitate the example of little children like this, that is, of all the saints, so that we may become worthy of entering with them into the kingdom of heaven. Let us imitate the humility of the Lord himself, who deemed it fitting to become a little child for the sake of our salvation, that we might be able to reign with him.

3. And he fittingly added, "And he who receives one such little child in my name receives me" [Matt 18:5]. He is showing that whoever receives a servant who believes faithfully in Christ, one who lives in accordance with the innocence of a little child, receives him. In the reception of that one, therefore, the Lord said that he is received, so that we do not hold in contempt any servant of God like this who lives humbly. On that account he went on to say, "But he that shall scandalize one of these little ones that believe in me, it were better for him that an ass's millstone should be hanged about his neck, and that he should be drowned in the depths of the sea" [Matt 18:6]. It was necessary that after the reward for devoted faith, the condemnation for infidelity should follow, just as also a punishment is owed to unfaithful people who cause scandal. And how grave a sin it is to cause scandal, we recognize from the fact that when the Lord says that it were better for a person of that sort to have an ass's millstone hanged about his neck and he be drowned in the depths of the sea, than that he scandalize one of the little ones who believe in Christ. The aim is that having prevented a scandal of this sort of sin, if possible, by this pronouncement, he may escape the punishment of

future death. For it is better by far to live under this sentence without scandal in the present life, than to incur with scandal the penalty of that eternal death. If therefore the Lord says this about one who scandalizes one of the little ones, what penalty do we think heretics will receive, who cause scandal not to one person, but to the whole church, by their twisted and faithless doctrine?

4. And although this statement of the Lord could be understood literally of an ass's millstone, yet according to the mystical reckoning something more can be understood in the ass's millstone. Animals that are accustomed to being yoked to a millstone usually have closed eyes.[211] Hence the labor of the present life is shown by the millstone. But in the ass the pagan person is shown, who without the knowledge of God and the light of faith lives in the labor of the world like a blind animal. But the depths of the sea mean the deep error of the world. And therefore he has said well that it were better for such a one who causes scandal that an ass's millstone be hanged about his neck and he be drowned in the depths of the sea. In this he seems to signify the Jewish person in particular, who is known to suffer a scandal over the cross of Christ and over the preaching of his name [see 1 Cor 1:23]. It were better for someone of this sort, then, if he is involved in the blindness of pagan error, to be drowned in the depths of the sea, as it were, than under the preaching of the law, by which the Jew thinks that he knows the light of truth, to suffer scandal concerning Christ and his apostles, whom he calls little ones. For it is better that a pagan without law not believe in Christ than for a Jew living under the law to deny the very Lord of the law. But in the ass's millstone we can recognize also the two testaments being signified. Anyone who causes a scandal with respect to them is tied up by a just sentence and drowned in the destruction of death. We recognize that this pronouncement about the ass's millstone is fulfilled in particular in respect to the Jewish people. Though they often stirred up scandal against the Lord and against his apostles, by the judgment of the same two testaments, as a kind of remedy of salvation, they lost their own kingdom and were drowned in the depths of the sea, that is, they were dispersed into the assembly of various nations. There they live on in the error of this world, as in the depths of the sea, in ignorance of the Creator of heaven, our Lord and Savior Jesus Christ, to whom is the praise and glory in the ages of ages. Amen.

Tractate 56 on Matthew 18:8–9

1. It then follows, "But if your hand or your foot scandalizes you, cut it off and cast it from you. It is better for you to go into life maimed or lame, than having two hands and two feet, to be cast into everlasting fire" [Matt 18:8].[212] Concerning the tearing out of the eye here and the cutting off of the foot or hand, as much as we understand, the Lord is not speaking of the members of this body, but instead of the adverse thoughts of the heart and soul from which source all scandals and evils proceed, as the Lord says: "For from the heart come forth evil thoughts, murder, adultery, fornication, theft, false testimony, blasphemies" [Matt 15:19], and the rest. For how could the statement be understood literally of the hand or foot, since these members of the body cannot experience a scandal? So, too, the eye, although it sometimes seems to experience a scandal through its vision, but the scandal belongs rather to the soul, at whose suggestion and instinct the eye is scandalized. After all, we see that many people who do not have eyes of the body and who live as cripples and lame persons nevertheless do not leave off sins and vices. Thus it is clear that the Lord is not speaking here of bodily members but instead of the adverse thoughts of the soul. Therefore the Lord has instructed us to cut off not this member or these members of the body, but rather to cut off adverse thoughts of the soul and depraved desires that create scandal, as types of members of the soul, so that having amputated every wicked and scandalous thought, we might be able to enter into eternal life.

2. And although this statement of the Lord can faithfully be understood about any one of us, yet in a particular way, in the cutting off a hand or foot and in the plucking out an eye, we observe that family relations and unbelieving ministers and leaders of the church are signified.[213] For the Lord is speaking here not just to one person, but to the perfect church, of which we are all indeed one body, yet comprising many different members. This agrees with what the apostle makes clear when he speaks of the church and says, "That there might be no divisions in the body, but the members might be mutually concerned one for another; and if one member suffers, all the members suffer with it; and if one member is honored, all the members rejoice with it" [1 Cor 12:25–26]. Later he went on to say, "But you are the body of Christ and members of member" [1 Cor 12:20]. Since, therefore,

according to the apostle we are all one body, it is not unfitting that here the Lord says, as it were to the body of the church united in form, "But if your hand or your foot scandalize you, cut it off and cast it from you. It is better for you to go into life maimed or lame, than having two hands and two feet, to be cast into everlasting fire."

3. And so by "hand" we understand that priests are signified; like a hand to the body of the church, their work is necessary in every area. We find it written about them in the Canticles, "His hands," that is, of the body of the church, "are rounded gold filled with hyacinth" [Song 5:14]. By "foot" we recognize that deacons are signified. By the way they keep themselves busy with the sacred mysteries of the church, they serve the body like feet, about which it is written in the same Solomon, "His feet are like silver columns upon bases of gold" [Sir 26:18]. And so, if hands and feet of this sort, that is, any priest or deacon, either through depraved faith or through living that is not upright, has become a stumbling block to the church, the Lord orders that such a man be cut off from the body of the church, lest the whole body of the church be endangered by his scandal and infidelity. For the apostle says, "A little leaven corrupts the whole lump" [1 Cor 5:6]. And that is why he says, "It is better for you to go into life maimed or lame, than having two hands and two feet, to be cast into everlasting fire." He is showing that it is far better to enter into eternal life with people of this sort cut off from the body of the church, than to be condemned in the future judgment with them into the everlasting punishment of that fire. For according to what the apostle says, "whoever joins himself with a prostitute becomes one body" [1 Cor 6:16].

4. We also understand the statement about the eye in a similar way. For he says, "And if your eye scandalizes you, pluck it out and cast it from you. It is better for you having one eye to enter into life, than having two eyes to be cast into hell fire" [Matt 18:9]. In the eye we recognize the bishops being signified in particular.[214] They abide in the body of the church like a precious member; by their actions and heavenly teaching they illumine all the people. We read it written of them in Solomon in the Canticles, "Your eyes are like doves" [Song 5:12]. If, therefore, an eye of this sort, that is, a bishop, creates a scandal for the body of the church, either by his disgraceful life or by perverse and unfaithful teaching, the Lord has commanded to pluck out and cast away such a person from the body of the church, lest the whole body of the church, that is, all the people, be placed in danger through the

example of his life and of his unfaithful teaching, while they follow and emulate such teaching.

And so rightly did the Lord go on to say, "It is better for you having one eye to enter into life, than having two eyes to be cast into hell fire." For it is far better, as has already been said, to go into everlasting life without such a faithless and perverse teacher, than with him to be condemned in perpetual punishment. For just as the whole body of the church can be saved by a Catholic bishop, so the entire people can perish by an unfaithful and treacherous teacher. We know that this has happened at different times, that the whole people have been completely subverted in respect to their hope and heavenly faith by the perverse teaching of a single, unfaithful, treacherous priest. Thus it is not without cause that, as we have already mentioned earlier, the apostle says, "A little leaven corrupts the entire mass. Purge out the old leaven that you may be a new mixture" [1 Cor 5:6–7]. And again, "Remove the evil one from among yourselves" [1 Cor 5:13]. Therefore people of this sort must be cut off from the body of the church beforehand, they must be plucked out beforehand, before the people get infected by the poison of their treachery, as a lump is corrupted by a little leaven. For just as the Lord promises great rewards and honor to leaders and ministers of the church, but only to those who serve God faithfully, as the Lord himself says in the Gospel: "If anyone serves me, my Father who is in heaven will honor him" [John 12:26]; and "Where I am there too shall my servant be" [John 12:26]; so, too, greater punishments have been prepared for unfaithful ministers of the church, as Solomon says: "For mercy is granted to the lowly, but a very powerful examination awaits those who are more powerful; and the mighty will suffer mighty torments" [Wis 6:6].

TRACTATE 57 ON MATTHEW 18:10–11

1. "See that you despise not one of these little ones, who believe in me. For I say to you that their angels in heaven always see the face of my Father who is in heaven. For the Son of man has come to save that which was lost" [Matt 18:10–11]. For just as the Lord commands that unbelieving and treacherous people who are a stumbling block to the body of the church should be cut off and plucked out, so he also warns us not to despise any of the little ones, that is, humble people

according to the world, who simply and faithfully believe in the Son of God. For it is not right to despise anyone who believes in Christ. A believer is called not only a servant of God but also a son through the grace of adoption [see Rom 8:15], to whom the kingdom of heaven and the company of the angels is promised. And rightly the Lord went on to say, "For I tell you that their angels in heaven always see the face of my Father who is in heaven." How much grace the Lord has toward each one who believes in him, he himself declares when he shows that their angels always see the face of the Father who is in heaven. For great is the grace of the angels toward all who believe in Christ. After all, the angels carry their prayers to heaven. Hence the words of the angel Raphael to Tobit: "When you prayed along with your daughter-in-law Sarah, I offered the memory of your prayer into the presence of God" [Tob 12:12]. There is also the strong guardianship of the angels around them; by their help each of us is delivered from the ambushes of the enemy. For a human in his weakness could not be safe amid so many forceful attacks of that enemy, if he were not fortified by the help of the holy angels.

2. Now we can know that God's angels are given for the protection of the saints on account of the spiritual forces of wickedness [see Eph 6:12] not only on the basis of the present passage, but also from other testimonies, when it is said, "The Lord dispatches an angel round about them that fear him, and it will protect them" [Ps 34:7]. And again, "The mountains," that is, angels, "are round about it, and the Lord is round about his people" [Ps 125:2].[215] Hence we also read in the Acts of the Apostles concerning the blessed Peter, "Perhaps it is his angel" [Acts 12:15]. Now in Revelation we read that the angels are guardians not only of the saints but also of the ends of the earth [see Rev 7:1]. Fittingly, too, when saint Elisha long ago was under attack from enemies, when his servant boy said, "What shall we do, lord?" he responded and said to him, "Do not be afraid, for they are more who are with us than with them" [2 Kgs 6:15–16]. For he had seen that angels had come to help him on account of the enemies' ambushes. And in order that his servant boy might see them, he prayed to the Lord and said, "Lord, open the eyes of this boy that he may see. And he saw an army and chariots and a great multitude on the mountains" [2 Kgs 6:17–18]. For an army of angels had come to the defense of Elisha. In the Books of Maccabees, too, repeatedly we read that angels came to the defense of the people to fight against the enemy [see 2 Macc 3:25; 11:6; 15:23]. And so, the Lord is recognized to be speaking

about angels of this sort, who are given to saints and faithful people for grace and protection, when he says, "For I tell you that their angels in heaven always see the face of my Father who is in heaven."

3. How great is the divine condescension toward believers in Christ, then, we recognize from this, their angels always stand by in heaven in the presence of the Father. For they keep watch for them and bring the prayers and desires of the saints into the presence of God. For this reason it is right for us not to despise one of the little ones who believe in Christ, whom we also read are guarded by angels and whose angels we know always see the face of the Father in heaven. For many Christians, although they are considered despised and lowly in the world, are nevertheless great before God. Within themselves they have faith and fear of God, in accordance with what the Lord himself makes clear in Revelation when he says, "I know your tribulation and your poverty. But you are wealthy before me" [Rev 2:9]. Therefore he is showing that the one whom he said was impoverished and poor in the world is wealthy before him. "For there is no acceptance of persons before God" [Rom 2:11]. A king is not nobler before him, nor a poor man lesser, nor a rich man mightier, nor a master superior, nor a slave inferior. But to all he is a leveler, to all he is judge, to all he is God and Lord, according to what we read as written about him: "For he who is Lord over all does not stand in awe of any man's greatness, nor shall he fear any man's person, for he has made the small and great, and cares for all alike" [Wis 6:7]. Thus it is not without reason that saint Peter in the Acts of the Apostles testified to the following and said, "In truth I have discovered that God is no accepter of persons. But in every nation the one who fears him and works justice is acceptable to him" [Acts 10:34–35]. And therefore he who is Lord over all does not stand in awe of anyone's nobility or riches. He does not despise poverty, nor look down upon one's origins, but he freely bestows his heavenly grace equally to all who believe in him, to the rich and the poor, to slaves and masters, to every sex and age. For there is one Lord, the only begotten Son of God, and one mother church. Of course, the one who is holier is preferred, the one who is more pious is better. And therefore we ought to give preference not to our origins or office in the church, as though we were better based on this, or more pleasing to God based on this, and not instead by our faith and holy manner of life. Hence that one is preferred by God, as we have said, not who is commended by the nobility of his class and worldly rank, but who the devotion of his faith in God and his holy life commends.

4. In the present passage, the Lord is warning about this situation and says, "See that you do not despise one of these little ones who believe in me." For it is no small sin to despise and look down upon a believer in Christ, whom the Lord does not despise, or rather, whom the Lord honors and prefers, and whom he redeemed at the great and glorious price of his blood. The Son of God, who is Lord of the universe, does not look down upon anyone who believes in him; he despises no one. And does someone dare to despise a brother or sister who is the same, who believes in Christ, whom, as we have often said, the Lord does not despise but honors, to whom he has even promised immortality and eternal glory?

But he shows that these ones are little, not in their actions and faith, but in the simplicity of their mind and humility of heart, in accordance with what David attested in the psalm when he said, "Lord, my heart has not been exalted, nor have my eyes been lifted up. Nor have I been [exercised] in great [matters] nor in things too wonderful for me" [Ps 131:1]. And he added, "If I have not been humbly minded" [Ps 131:2]. The Lord is making clear that little ones of this sort have angels in heaven, who see the face of the Father. And rightly he warns us in advance not to despise any little one like this, with an unfaithful mind and a perverse spirit, for whom there is so much room with God, lest we incur no light sin by despising them. This is just was happened to the scribes and Pharisees and to the Jewish people who were justly rejected by the Lord for their arrogance, those who believed that the Lord's bodily humility deserved to be held in contempt as well as those who believed in him. And rightly the Lord went on to say, "The Son of man has come to save what had perished," so that he might show all the more that not one of these little ones who believe in Christ should be despised. For their sake the Son of God came from heaven and saved them by his passion. It was for this that he took on the body of human weakness, so that he might in every way save this one who had perished. For the elements of the world have kept the law given them by the Lord. The human being alone has been found a transgressor. Alone he had fallen from immortality into death. And for this reason to save him the Son of God, when the time was ripe, came down from heaven according to the will of the Father. Hence, quite rightly Solomon says, "There is a time to destroy and a time to save" [Eccl 3:6]. There was a time when the devil destroyed humanity. But again there came a time when the Son of God saved the human race for life, the only begotten [of humanity], namely Son of God, to whom is the praise and glory in the ages of ages. Amen.

Tractate 58 on Matthew 18:15–18

1. The Lord, who is the author of peace and concord, wants us to preserve the charity of fraternal love in every way, and therefore he commands us to be zealous for peace and salvation toward everyone in all things, saying, "But if your brother or sister sins against you, rebuke him or her when you are alone. If he or she shall hear you, you shall gain your brother or sister" [Matt 18:15]. He shows that the greatest gain is if you save by a spiritual rebuke the straying person and the one sinning against you. For by rebuking the sinning person, you both gain the brother or sister, if he or she is willing to hear you, and you yourself acquire no small merit, when after the honest rebuke you pardon him or her for the sin that was committed against you. The Holy Spirit reminds us of this very thing likewise through Solomon when he says, "Rebuke a friend; it may be he did not do it, and he may say, I did not do it; or if he did do it, that he do it no more. Rebuke your neighbor, it may be he did not say it, and if he did, that he say it not again. For often the accusation is vain" [Sir 19:13–15]. And again, "It is much better to reprove than to conceal anger" [Sir 20:2]. For this is truly what it means to preserve charity and peace toward others, not to lay up anger in one's spirit, but faithfully to reprove and correct the sinning person. For a brotherly correction of this sort is sweet and beneficial, which proceeds not from malice but from a pure heart and from love. In the psalm, David has testified to this rebuke when he says, "The just person shall chasten me with mercy" [Ps 141:5]. And he goes on to say, "The oil of sinners shall not anoint my head" [Ps 141:5]. The prophet desires to be reproved and rebuked not by a sinner but by a just person, for he knows that the rebuke of a just person is sweet and necessary, but that of sinners is detestable and annoying. Hence it is not without cause that the Lord has commanded that the sinning person be rebuked by a brother or sister; surely by a faithful brother or sister who rebukes their friend for the sake of the affection of love, out of the desire to gain that friend. And, of course, it is fitting for the salvation of everyone to reprove the sinning friend for the common welfare, rather than to be angry and to speak against the friend for

the offense of a sin. This agrees with the Scripture we read: "You sat and spoke against your kin, and scandalized your mother's child" [Ps 50:20]. Hence it is also not without cause that in another psalm, under the persona of the Lord, the prophetic words say the following: "I persecuted those who spoke against their neighbors in secret" [Ps 101:5]. And so, this is why the Lord commands us to preserve peace and fraternal charity, that each one may rebuke the brother or sister who sins against him in a way that leads to salvation.

2. "If he will not hear you, take with you one or two more, that in the mouth of two or three witnesses, every word may stand. But if he will not hear them, tell the church. But if he will not hear the church, let him be to you as the heathen and tax collector" [Matt 18:16–17]. How full and necessary is the affection of love that we are commanded to show toward the sinning brother, so that first he should be rebuked at once by each of us, only then, if he refuses to hear, one or two others must be summoned as well! But if he thinks that even they deserve to be despised, he instructs us to tell it to the church; if, finally, he thinks that the church must be despised, a person of this sort is to be considered as a heathen and tax collector. And so, in every way there must be great effort on our part to gain the sinning brother or sister, either by our rebuke or surely by that of the church. For if there is the benefit of no small praise to people of this world to receive back a friend into favor after correction, how much more is there greater and glorious profit for us to gain the corrected brother or sister for God and eternal salvation. He says, "But if he will not hear the church, let him be to you as the heathen and tax collector." For doubtless such a person is no longer to be considered to be a Christian, nor to be reckoned in the number of the brothers and sisters, who not only refuses to hear the two or three people who are rebuking him, but has even believed that the correction of the whole church is to be held in contempt. By showing contempt for it, doubtless he shows contempt for the Son of God, and through the Son, the Father, since the Lord himself says to his disciples, "He who spurns you, spurns me. But he who spurns me, spurns the one who sent me" [Luke 10:16]. Ultimately this happened to the Jewish people.[216] Though often rebuked, they were unwilling to hear either Moses through the law, or <the Lord> through the prophets, or his church through the apostles. Lastly, they began to be considered as heathen and tax collectors.

3. And justly he follows up and says to the apostles, "Whatever you shall bind upon earth shall be bound also in heaven. And whatever you shall loose upon earth shall be loosed also in heaven" [Matt 18:18]. Notice how great is the power of heavenly grace that the Lord has given to his disciples, and through the disciples to the church, by granting this much, that whatever things are bound by the apostles and the church on earth have been bound also in heaven, and whatever is loosed on earth has been loosed also in heaven. Likewise through David the Holy Spirit mentions this exact thing when he says, "But your friends, O God, have been greatly honored by me; their rule has been greatly strengthened" [Ps 139:17]. In fact these friends of the Son of God, the apostles, have been greatly honored. To them such great authority was granted that their earthly judgments are heavenly judgments, that is, he testifies that what his church either binds or looses on earth with respect to each one is reported to the Lord as established and accepted. Therefore the Lord has mentioned this so that we may know how serious a sin it is not to hear the church, to which we see that the Lord has granted such great authority. <Therefore> in all things we ought to hear her admonition as good children of our true and proper mother, so that by the merits of our obedience and faith, we may merit to be received into the kingdom of heaven with the same church, having been loosed from all sin. But as for the one who thinks that the church is to be despised and not heard, someone of that sort is bound in the sins of his own disobedience and stubbornness, and he will not be able to have a share in heaven. Since, therefore, the Lord has given such great grace and authority to the church, that whatever she binds or looses on earth has been <bound or> loosed in heaven, one must expend all one's strength that, even if some sin occurs, each one shall be bound by the judgment of the church. He may be absolved by satisfaction, repentance, and prayers, since the one who says, "I do not will the death of the one who dies, but rather that he turn and live" [Ezek 18:32; cf. 33:11], doubtless has absolved by the judgment of his church even sinners by a just repentance. But the one who has been bound by some serious sin, without repenting, does not deserve to be loosed by the judgment of the church in the present life. A man of that sort cannot have any hope on the day of judgment, since what the church does not forgive, the Lord does not forgive, who has gifted his church with this grace. He is blessed in the ages of ages. Amen.

TRACTATE 59 ON MATTHEW 18:19–35

1. <It then follows,> "For if two or three of you shall consent upon earth, concerning anything whatsoever they shall ask, my Father who is in heaven shall provide it to them. For where there are two or three gathered together in my name, there am I in the midst of them" [Matt 18:19–20]. How important a place the unanimity and concord of people hold with God![217] We can know this from this very fact that the Lord has made clear that when two or three pray in unanimity, the Father provides everything from heaven. For with God nothing is more pleasing than brotherly peace, nothing better than unanimity and concord, according to what is written: "Behold, how good and pleasant it is when brothers and sisters dwell in unity" [Ps 133:1]. And again: "There is great peace among those who love your name, and there is no stumbling block for them" [Ps 119:165]. And in another place: "The God who makes us live in harmony in the house" [Ps 68:6]. And this is why Isaiah also testified, "Lord, our God, give us peace. For you have given us everything" [Isa 26:12]. That this concord between brothers and sisters is pleasing to God, the Holy Spirit declared through Solomon, saying the following, "There are three things that are pleasing to God and people: concord between brothers and sisters, love between neighbors, and the man and woman who agree with each other" [Sir 25:1–2]. So quite rightly the Lord in the present passage testifies that when two or three are in agreement on earth, the Father provides all things, whatever they ask for. And he went on to say, "For where there are two or three gathered together in my name, there am I in the midst of them." How great is the merit of unanimity that when two or three are gathered in his name, he declares that he himself is in their midst! And not only do we believe this to be the case by faith, but we even learn it from examples.

Long ago there were three youths gathered together for the sake of his name in the fiery furnace;[218] but when they had gathered together in his name and were praying with united and concordant minds, the same Lord was not absent from the midst of these flames and destructive fires. For Nebuchadnezzar said, "Did we not cast three men into the blazing fiery furnace? And how is it that I see four men loose, and no harm has come to them? And the appearance of the fourth is like a son of God" [Dan 3:91–92]. Thus finally also after his passion, when Paul and Barnabas were put in prison for the sake of his name and were praying in unanimity, the Lord was so much present with them in the very prison that he delivered them from custody, having loosed the bonds of their chains [see Acts 16:23–26]. Thus it is clear that when two or three have been gathered in his name faithfully, the Lord himself likewise is present in accordance with his promise.

2. But let not schismatics flatter themselves based on this passage, those who have forsaken the peace and unity of the church and have dared to assemble all their impious gatherings against the church. They do not understand that it was said, "He who is not with me is against me, and he who does not gather with me scatters" [Luke 11:23]. Thus he is not promising to be with those two or three who come in opposition to the peace and unity of the church; but <with> those two or three who are gathered together in the Lord's name, while abiding in the church's charity and concord, united and harmonious. But if the schismatics think that this statement accords with their own understanding by some reckoning, "Wherever there will be two or three gathered in my name, there am I in their midst," let them remember that long ago during the time of Moses, Korah, Dathan, and Abiram were assuredly three.[219] And since they dared to gather themselves in opposition to the peace and unity of the people, they were not able to carry on without punishment because they had presumed to do this with a wicked and profane mindset. For at once a hole in the ground opened up on account of the unlawful assembly and they went down alive to the lower world [see Num 16; 26:8–10]. By this example it is clear that the Lord is not with two or three who are like that, who are gathered in opposition to the unity of the church and the people themselves. Not only is he not with them, but he is against those who have dared to tear apart the body of the church, to gather together impiously and faithlessly, since Solomon says, "He that splits wood shall be endangered thereby" [Eccl 10:9]. He is pointing out those very ones who cause discord and schisms in the church. Yet he shows that they are not without danger, since doubtless all authors of schism incur the danger of eternal death.

3. It says, "But Peter responded and said, Lord, if my brother sins against me, how often shall I forgive him, up to seven times? Jesus said to him, I say not to you up to seven times, but up to seventy times seven times" [Matt 18:21–22]. Saint Peter, everywhere rash with his very great love and faith, was the first to confront the Lord's admonitions. For he knew based on his Lord's teaching higher up that the merit of fraternal unanimity and concord was very great. He carefully

asks the Lord how often he should forgive his brother who sins against him, saying, "Lord, if my brother sins against me, how often shall I forgive him, up to seven times? Jesus said to him, Not up to seven times, but up to seventy times seven times."[220] Peter remembered the divine law in which long ago Cain, who had killed his brother, was avenged. In the Book of Genesis, Lamech, who was the seventh from Cain, said, "Because vengeance has been exacted seven times on Cain's behalf, on Lamech's [it shall be] seventy times seven times" [Gen 4:24]. Peter thought that this was sufficient, if he forgave the brother who sinned against him as many times as had been avenged in Cain's case. But the Lord in view of his abundant mercy wants peace and concord to be guarded among brothers and sisters completely. He responds and teaches that not only does this suffice, if one forgives seven times, but up to seventy times seven times. Here he has both dissolved the severity of the vengeance of old, and showed to what extent fraternal charity is to be esteemed. And therefore he taught that the extent of the vengeance that was carried out against Lamech, that is the extent now of the forgiveness that is to be offered to the brother or sister who sins. For if the Son of God by his divine godliness has forgiven us all our sins, has freely forgiven through his grace all the crimes that we have committed, how much more should we forgive brothers or sisters who sin against us everything, that we may be able to imitate the example of the Lord?

4. Thus it is not unfitting that the Lord offered as well a similitude to the heavenly kingdom. He said, "Therefore the condition of the heavenly kingdom is like a king man, who wanted to take an account of his servants. And when he had begun to take the account, one was brought to him who owed him ten thousand talents. And as he had not the means to pay it back, his lord commanded that he should be sold, and his wife and children and all that he had, and the debt should be paid back. But that servant, falling down, besought him, saying, Lord, have patience with me, and I will pay you back everything" [Matt 18:23–26]. And the rest that follows. Earlier, the Lord had commanded Peter, who had asked about this, that it is necessary to forgive the sinning brother not seven times but seventy times seven times. He then added the similitude of a parable, making the comparison of a king and his servant. The servant, though unworthy, had received such mercy from his master that even an infinite debt was freely forgiven him. But he himself refused to have mercy upon a fellow servant for a small debt. So, quite rightly, he was handed over

to the torturers and received the just punishment of condemnation. For what would such a wicked servant not deserve to suffer? Though he had known such piety from his master with respect to himself, he was himself impious and cruel to his fellow servant. By this example, we are clearly instructed and taught that if we do not forgive our fellow servants, that is, the brothers and sisters who sin against us, the debts of their sins, we will be condemned with like punishment. And though the comparison may seem to have been introduced for the present passage, yet the parable itself has within it an integral logic and manifest truth.

5. So we recognize that in the person of this king is signified the Son of God, who held the whole human race guilty in the infinite debt of sin, since through transgression we were all debtors of sin and death. But in the ten thousand talents the serious sins of the human race are signified. And though all men by natural law were debtors to this heavenly king and guilty, since the apostle says about the same natural law, "For when the Gentiles, who have not the law, are a law to themselves by nature, who show the work of the law written in their hearts, their conscience bearing witness to them, and their thoughts between themselves accusing, or also defending one another" [Rom 2:14–15]; yet in this debt of sin the people of the Jews were particularly held guilty. After so many great benefits, they could not keep the law received through Moses. Since they did not have the means to repay such debt, that is, how to make it good, the lord had ordered them to be divided up, along with their wives and children. That is, this same people along with their synagogue and all their offspring were to be divided in death. But in no way could either the people of the Jews, who had received the law, nor the Gentiles, that is, we ourselves, pay off such a great debt of sin. Hence the heavenly king, moved by pity and godliness, freely forgave us all our sins. And what are these debts if not those that daily in our prayers we ask to be forgiven of, when we say, "Forgive us our debts, just as we forgive our debtors" [Matt 6:12]? Therefore, since in no way, that is, by no satisfaction and by no worthy repentance, could we pay off this debt of sin and eternal death, that eternal king came from heaven and, by remitting the human race its sins, freely forgave the whole debt to everyone who believes in him. But as for how he forgave it, the holy apostle clearly shows when he says, "Having canceled the bond that stood against us, which was opposed to us, and he took it from our midst, nailing it to the cross" [Col 2:14]. For we were being held in sin guilt as if under the debt of

some creditor's note. The Son of God has annulled this note written against us by the water of baptism and the drops of his blood. Finally, in this very mystery, in order to blot out the bond, water and blood flowed from the Lord's side at the time of his passion [see John 19:34]. Nor was a sponge missing from the Lord as he hung on the cross [see Matt 26:48; Mark 15:36; John 19:29], in order to show this same thing, that the sins of the whole world were to be erased by the mystery of his passion; this was assuredly through him of whom John testified in the gospel and said, "Behold the lamb of God, behold him who takes away the sin of the world" [John 1:29].

6. Hence today each of us, when he comes to the grace of baptism, approaches as a debtor, in order that by confessing his sins, he may through these very mysteries receive pardon of the whole debt, that is, of all sins. But after such generous pardon of his lord and king, each one, if he becomes forgetful of the divine benefit and proceeds according to the example of that wicked servant, as one who is withdrawing from the faith, and if he refuses to forgive a fellow slave who sins against him, that is, to pardon the sin committed against himself, he who received a pardon from his lord for such a great debt, that is, for such serious sins; doubtless that heavenly king will be angry with such a person and will hand him over to the torturers, that is, to the angels of punishments. He will be cast into prison, that is, into hell, so that tortured by eternal punishments he may pay off the whole debt of sin down to the last penny [see Matt 5:26].

7. Finally, in order to show that this is the case, the Lord went on to say, "So also shall my Father who is in heaven do to you, if each of you do not forgive his brother or sister from your hearts" [Matt 18:35]. For one who is forgetful of such great divine mercy and godliness, who is unwilling to forgive the brother or sister who sins against him, does not deserve forgiveness and pardon of sins from God. Hence not without reason in the Lord's prayer we are all held accountable for this by the very words that we pray, when we say, "Forgive us our debts, just as also we forgive our debtors" [Matt 6:12]. Thus, if we do not forgive those who sin against us, in accordance with what we hold forth, by what effrontery, or with what confidence do we dare to ask for forgiveness of sins from the Lord? The Holy Spirit testifies as well through Solomon to this very same thing when he says, "Forgive your neighbor his sin, and then shall your sins also be forgiven" [Sir 28:2]. And he went on to say, "As a person who holds on to his anger against another, do you seek healing of the flesh from God? You have no

mercy on the one who is like yourself, and do you pray to God about your own sins? Though you who are but flesh hold on to anger, do you seek reconciliation with God? And who shall pray for your transgressions? Remember the last things, and let enmity cease" [Sir 28:3–6]. Thus God's judgment is just in every way concerning each of us, that if someone wants God to forgive their sins, they should first forgive the brother or sister who sins against them. But if they shall be hardened and pitiless toward their brother or sister, according to the Lord's pronouncement, they themselves shall not merit forgiveness of sin from our Lord and Savior, who is blessed in the ages. Amen.

NOTES

Introduction

1. Traditionally Chromatius's death has been placed in 407. This date has been recently contested by Pier Franco Beatrice, "Chromatius and Jovinus at the Synod of Diospolis: A Prosopographical Inquiry," *JECS* 22, no. 3 (Fall 2014): 437–64, who thinks he lived at least to 415, when he participated in the Synod of Diospolis, in which fourteen eastern bishops acquitted Pelagius. I will engage Beatrice's theory below. There is also debate about the year of Chromatius's birth, some scholars placing it as early as 335. Cf. R. McEachnie, "A History of Heresy Past: The Sermons of Chromatius of Aquileia, 388–407," *Church History* 83, no. 2 (June 2014): 273–96, at 275.

2. Cf. J. Lemarié, "Chromatius redivivus," in *Chromatius of Aquileia and His Age*, ed. Pier Franco Beatrice and Alessio Peršič (Turnhout: Brepols, 2011), 280.

3. M. Williams, "Chromatius and Jerome on Matthew," in Beatrice and Peršič, *Chromatius of Aquileia and His Age*, 204, says that the Latin of Chromatius's *Tractates* is "clear, elegant, and relatively simple."

4. See Pope Benedict XVI, *The Fathers of the Church: From Clement of Rome to Augustine of Hippo*, ed. and annot. Joseph T. Lienhard (Grand Rapids, MI: Eerdmans, 2009), 126–30.

5. In an appendix to his dissertation, R. McEachnie provided an English translation of the *Sermons* only: "Constructing Christian Community: The Sermons of Chromatius of Aquileia, 388–407" (PhD diss., University of Florida, 2013). I have heard that he intends to publish these in the future with Routledge. Substantial excerpts from the *Tractates* are included in English in M. Simonetti, ed., *Ancient Christian Commentary on Scripture: Matthew 1—13, Matthew 14—28*, 2 vols. (Downers Grove, IL: InterVarsity 2002). I have carefully and gratefully consulted both of these available sources.

6. See *OCD*, 133.

7. *Aquila* is the Latin word for *eagle.*

8. P. Baxa, *Roads and Ruins: The Symbolic Landscape of Fascist Rome* (Toronto: University of Toronto Press, 2010), 17, mentions an event in 1921 that restored the bond between Aquileia and Rome after centuries of

separation—the burial in Rome of an unknown fallen soldier from there: "A once-great frontier city that had been visited by emperors, Aquileia never recovered from the invasions of the Huns and later the Longobards. Its original inhabitants had either been killed or fled to the islands in the lagoon. The bond was restored in the form of the mutilated remains of a soldier who had died on the frontier in a manner similar to the Roman legionnaires. Aquileia resumed its function as a copy of Rome on the frontiers of the empire.... The city was remarkably like Rome; it was a major archaeological center; it had a forum and Via Sacra like the Eternal City. Similarly to Rome, Aquileia was always on the verge of destruction and pillage....Now in 1921, this once-frontier city of the Roman Empire was resurrected by the events of the war."

9. Cf. R. McEachnie, "Constructing Christian Community," 43.

10. Cf. Rufinus, *Apologia adversus Hieronymum* 1.4; Francis Murphy, *Rufinus of Aquileia (345–411): His Life and Works* (Washington, DC: Catholic University of America Press, 1945); E. Clark, *The Origenist Controversy: The Cultural Construction of an Early Christian Debate* (Princeton, NJ: Princeton University Press, 1992).

11. See J. N. D. Kelly, *Golden Mouth: The Story of John Chrysostom—Ascetic, Preacher, Bishop* (Ithaca, NY: Cornell University Press, 1995), 246, 278, 279, 281; Rudolf Brändle, "Chromatius und Johannes Chrysostomus: Zwei Bischöfe im Spannungsfeld zwischen Ost und West," in Beatrice and Peršič, *Chromatius of Aquileia and His Age*, 253–65.

12. Jerome, Ep 7.6 (NPNF2, 6.10).

13. Cf. R. Gryson, *Scolies Ariennes sur le concile d'Aquilée*, SC 267 (Paris: Cerf, 1980), 364, 368; D. Williams, *Ambrose of Milan and the End of the Arian-Nicene Conflicts* (New York: Oxford University Press, 1995), 181–84; N. McLynn, *Ambrose of Milan: Church and Court in a Christian Capital* (Berkeley: University of California Press, 1994), 126–37. Yves-Marie Duval, "Les Relations doctinales entre Milan et Aquilée durant la seconde moitié du IVe siècle: Chromace d'Aqulé et ambroise de Milan," in *Aquileia et Milano*, AAAd 4 (Udine: Arti grafiche friulane, 1973), 188–92, suggests that Arians were still present and active in Chromatius's city and region even after this conciliar action, even if they lacked their former vitality.

14. But on this date, see below.

15. Cf. Ambrose, Ep 50.

16. Cf. J. N. D. Kelly, *Jerome: His Life, Writings, and Controversies* (New York: Harper & Row, 1975), 168.

17. Cf. Rufinus's *Apologia adversus Hieronymum* 1.4. To my knowledge Chromatius had no links with Augustine of Hippo.

18. Cf. *Sermon* 12.7; *Tractate* 17.7; 21.3; 58.1; 59.2.

19. Ambrose's commentary on Luke is largely based on Origen's exegesis. Cf. Ambrose, *Exposition of the Holy Gospel according to Saint Luke, with Fragments on the Prophecy of Esaias*, trans. Theodosia Tomkinson (Etna, CA: Center

for Traditionalist Orthodox Studies, 2003). Unfortunately, this English edition does not bring out the connections to Origen.

20. Cf. Pier Franco Beatrice, "The Sign of Jonah: The Paschal Mystery and the Conversion of the Pagans according to Chromatius of Aquileia," in Beatrice and Peršič, *Chromatius of Aquileia and His Age*, 19–64, at 42–43.

21. Cf. Palladius, *Dialogus de vita sancti Ioannis Chrysostomi* 2.

22. Cf. Chrysostom's Ep 155 (PG 52:702–3).

23. Cf. Palladius, *Dialogus de vita sancti Ioannis Chrysostomi* 3–4.

24. Cf. Kelly, *Jerome*, 263.

25. Cf. Jerome, Ep 113; Ep 127.11.

26. Chromatius had advised Jerome to drop the quarrel with Rufinus over Origenism, but Jerome refused to comply.

27. See Jerome's comments on Matt 5:1; 5:25–26; 26:1–2; 27:33.

28. Cf. SC 154, 9–16.

29. For polemic against Arius, see *Sermon* 21.3; *Tractate* 35.3–4; 50.3.

30. "Introduction to Matthew," in Simonetti, *Ancient Christian Commentary on Scripture: Matthew 1—13*, xlix.

31. *Sermon* 19.4; *Tractate* 19.5.2; 43.6

32. Cf. *Sermon* 2, 3, 10, 14, 15, 17, 18, 18A, 34; SC 154, 60–81.

33. Cf. *Sermon* 26; SC 154, 103–7.

34. Evidence for this would be found in Chromatius's *Sermon* 26 for the dedication of the church in Concordia.

35. R. Lizzi, "Ambrose's Contemporaries and the Christianization of Northern Italy," *Journal of Roman Studies* 80 (1990): 156–73, at 159.

36. Yves-Marie Duval, "Chromace et Jérôme," in *Chromatius episcopus: 388–1988*, AAAd 34 (Udine: Arti grafiche friulane, 1989), 151–83; Duval, "Les Relations doctinales."

37. Duval, "Chromace et Jérôme," 180.

38. R. McEachnie, "A History of Heresy Past," 287.

39. Ibid., 288.

40. Ibid., 295.

41. Ibid., 296.

42. Rufinus of Aquileia: *History of the Church*, trans. P. Amidon, Fathers of the Church 133 (Washington, DC: The Catholic University of America Press, 2017), 8–9.

43. Ibid., 289.

44. Cf. I. H. Marshall, "Orthodoxy and Heresy in Earlier Christianity," *Themelios* 2, no. 1 (1976): 5–14; S. Gathercole, "E pluribus unum? Apostolic Unity and Early Christian Literature," in *The Enduring Authority of the Christian Scriptures*, ed. D. A. Carson (Grand Rapids, MI: Eerdmans, 2016), 407–55; Walther Völker, review of "Walter Bauer's Rechtgläubigkeit und Ketzerei im ältesten Christentum," introduced, trans., and annot. Thomas P. Scheck, *JECS* 14, no. 4 (2006): 399–405.

45. Beatrice and Peršič, *Chromatius of Aquileia and His Age*.

46. Augustine, *Contra Iulianum* 1.5.19 (PL 44:652) and 1.7.32 (PL 44:663); cited by Beatrice, "Chromatius and Jovinus at the Synod of Diospolis," 442.

47. Evidence for this exodus is found in the prefaces to Jerome's *Commentary on Ezekiel.*

48. C. P. Hammond, "The Last Ten Years of Rufinus' Life and the Date of His Move South from Aquileia," *JTS* n.s. 28 (1977): 372–429. Her article begins (372) with the statement, "By frequent repetition a conjectural date may acquire a false appearance of reliability. The main purpose of this note is to question one such date."

49. I have endeavored to discuss this in the introductions to my translations of St. Jerome's commentaries on Matthew, Galatians, Titus and Philemon, Isaiah, Ezekiel, and the Twelve Prophets.

50. See Chromatius, *Sermon* 3; *Tractate* 9.2; 16.2; 27.5.

51. Beatrice refers to the important work of François Bovon, *De Vocatione Gentium: Histoire de l'interpétation d'Act. 10,1–11,18 dans les six premiers siècles,* Beiträge zur Geschichte der Biblischen Exegese 8 (Tübingen: Mohr Siebeck, 1967).

52. Cf. Augustine, Ep 187.12.36 (CSEL 57:114); cited by Beatrice, "Chromatius and Jovinus at the Synod of Diospolis," 456.

53. Augustine, *De praedestinatione sanctorum* 7.12 (PL 44:969–70); cited by Beatrice, "Chromatius and Jovinus at the Synod of Diospolis," 456.

54. Beatrice, "Chromatius and Jovinus at the Synod of Diospolis," 456. See also P. Beatrice, *The Transmission of Sin: Augustine and His Sources,* trans. Adam Kamesar (New York: Oxford University Press, 2013); originally published in Italian in 1978.

55. Cf. C. Straw, "Chrysostom's Martyrs: Zealous Athletes and the Dangers of Sloth," in *Giovanni Crisostomo Oriente e Occidente tra IV e V seculo. XXXIII Incontro di studiosi dell'antichità Cristiana, Roma 6–8 maggio, 2004,* Studia Ephemeridis Augustinianum 93 (Rome: Institutum Augustinianum, 2005), 521–54.

56. Cf. Jerome, Ep 133, *Ad Ctesiphonem adversus Pelagium* 5–6 (PL 22.1154). For Chrysostom, see the passages cited in Straw, "Chrysostom's Martyrs," 523n7.

57. The most penetrating discussion of these issues known to me is Desiderius Erasmus, *Controversies: Hyperaspistes 2,* ed. C. Trinkaus, trans. and annot. C. H. Miller, C. Trinkaus (Toronto: University of Toronto Press, 2000).

58. Cf. C. Nardi, "Council of Diospolis," *EEC* 1.241.

59. Cf. Thomas P. Scheck, *Origen and the History of Justification: The Legacy of Origen's Commentary on Romans* (Notre Dame, IN: University of Notre Dame Press, 2008), 84–85; Scheck, "Pelagius's Interpretation of Romans," in *A Companion to St. Paul in the Middle Ages,* ed. Steven R. Cartwright (Leiden: Brill, 2013), 79–113.

60. For what strikes me as a balanced criticism of Augustine's theology of grace and predestination, see D. Ogliari, *Gratia et Certamen: The Relationship between Grace and Free Will in the Discussion of Augustine with the So-Called Semipelagians*, Bibliotheca Ephemeridum Theologicarum Lovaniensium 169 (Louvain: Peeters, 2003), 403–4.

61. Cf. Joseph Ratzinger, *Milestones: Memoirs 1927–1977* (San Francisco: Ignatius Press, 1998), 120–21.

62. *Tractate* 42.5; cited by Pope Benedict XVI, *The Fathers of the Church*, 129.

63. Ibid., 130.

64. R. Étaix, "Nouvelle edition des sermons XXI–XXII de saint Chromace d'Aqulée," *Revue Bénedictine* 92 (1982): 105–10; Étaix, "Un 'Tractatus in Matheum' inédit de saint Chromace d'Aquilée," *Revue Bénédictine* 91 (1981): 225–30.

65. See Jean-Marie Auwers, "Chromace d'Aquilée et le texte biblique," in Beatrice and Peršič, *Chromatius of Aquileia and His Age*, 343–59.

Sermons

1. I have translated the Latin text found in *Chromatii Aquileiensis Opera*, ed. R. Étaix and J. Lemarié, CCSL, 9A (Turnhout: Brepols, 1974). J. Lemarié alone edited the *Sermons*, while both he and R. Étaix edited the *Tractates*. For the material in the endnotes I have also consulted the SC edition. Titles of works cited are those recommended in *The SBL Handbook of Style: For Ancient Near Eastern, Biblical, and Early Christian Studies*, ed. P. Alexander et al. (Peabody, MA: Hendrickson, 1999). Exceptions are listed in the abbreviations.

2. The text surrounded in square brackets indicates an insertion of information not found in the Latin text of the critical edition. Angle brackets indicate that there is a lacuna in the manuscript for which the CCSL editors have supplied conjectural readings.

3. Cf. Cyprian, Ep 63.3.

4. Cf. Cyprian, Ep 64.4.

5. The phrase, "Your love [*dilectio vestra*] has heard," is used repeatedly in Chromatius's *Sermons*.

6. Lit. "the present."

7. The reading came from Acts 3:1–4; 4. Probably omitting 4:5–31, the lector concluded at 4:32–34, which will be commented upon at the end of the homily.

8. The cross is correlated to Jacob's ladder in Justin, *Dialogus cum Tryphone* 86.2 and Irenaeus, *Epideixis tou apostolikou kerygmatus* 45.

9. Cf. Cyprian, *De catholicae ecclesiae unitate* 25.

10. The editors of SC 154, p. 134, though not of the CCSL text, note that a portion of Scripture seems to be lacking from the manuscript, probably Acts 4:32: "All the believers possessed one heart and one soul."

11. The manuscript contains a lacuna.

12. Chromatius likes to add *sanctus*, holy or saint, before persons of the Bible, of both the Old and New Testaments.

13. Cf. Eusebius, *HE* 2.13—15.1.

14. Cf. Tertullian, *De baptismo* 8.3.

15. Notice the textual witness that differs from the RSV.

16. Cf. Ambrose, *Expositio Psalmi CXVIII*, 8.48.

17. Cf. Origen, *Homiliae in Leviticum* 7.4.

18. Cf. Hilary, *In Mt* 12.2.

19. Cf. Ambrose, *De Spiritu Sancto* 2.10.109.

20. Cf. Origen, *Homiliae in Leviticum* 7.4; 8.11; Ambrose, *De Spiritu Sancto* 2.10.105.

21. Lit. "made of broom."

22. Cf. Origen, *Homiliae in Exodum* 9.3; Ambrose, *Expositio Evangelii secundum Lucam* 10.12–13; Hilary, *In Mt* 21.4.

23. Lemarié SC 154, 165n1, says that Chromatius's opinion here about the extent of early Christian missions doubtless is too optimistic; but one must remember that at the end of the fourth century the Mediterranean world was largely Christian.

24. *A* and *R* refer to two different manuscripts of Chromatius's Sermons. According to the CCSL edition, *A* is lacunar and the word *ran* (*currebant*) seems to be a corruption. It is marked out with daggers.

25. Cf. Hilary, *In Ps* 146, 9.15–17.

26. Cf. Ambrose, *Expositio Evangelii secundum Lucam* 5.41.

27. Notice the blending of the Matthean and Lukan versions.

28. Referring to the bishop.

29. Cf. Ambrose, *Hexaemeron libri sex* 6.3.13; Ep 32.2.

30. Regrettably, the manuscript is lacunar, since no other sermon of Chromatius for the feast day of a martyr survives. Originally from Vicence, Felix and Fortunatus were put to death in Aquileia. Their cult and possibly the presence of relics led to the consecration of a suburban church in their honor in Vicence. Up through the eighteenth century, there existed in Aquileia a basilica dedicated to saint Felix. Funerary inscriptions witness to the veneration of the two martyrs.

31. Cf. Rufinus, *Commentarius in symbolum apostolorum* 29.

32. Cf. ibid.

33. Cf. Aristotle, *Hist. anim.* 5.34; Apuleius, *Apol.* 85; Pliny, *Hist. nat.* 10.62.

34. This etymology of the name of Israel is based on Gen 32:28–30. It comes from Philo, *De Abrahamo* 57; *De mutat. Nominum* 81 and is found commonly in the fathers.

35. Cf. Cyprian, Ep 58.6.

36. Cf. Ambrose, *De Spiritu Sancto* 1, Prol 7.

37. Cf. ibid.; *De virginitate* 11.64.

38. Cf. Ambrose, *De virginitate* 11.63.

39. Photinus, bishop of Sirmium, had been deacon and disciple of Marcellus of Ancyra. Westerners subscribed to the Eastern condemnation of him at Milan (345). According to M. Simonetti, EEC, II, 685–86, he affirmed a rigid Monarchianism in which the Logos was conceived as a mere impersonal power of the Father. He ascribed the OT theophanies to the Father, not to a personal Logos, and he made the Son of God be born of Mary in the sense that the Logos became Son only by being incarnate in the man Jesus and taking up his dwelling in him. He was clearer than Marcellus in affirming that the humanity assumed by the Logos was complete even in soul. Like Marcellus, he made the Son of God to be born of Mary, in the sense that the Logos became Son only by being incarnate in the man Jesus and taking up his dwelling in him. Cf. D. Williams, "Monarchianism and Photinus of Sirmium as the Persistent Heretical Face of the Fourth Century," *HThR* 99 (2006): 187–206. Cf. Rufinus, *Commentarius in symbolum apostolorum* 37.

40. Cf. Ambrose, *De Spiritu Sancto* II, Prol, 15.

41. Cf. Paulinus of Nola, Ep 23.34.

42. Cited from memory.

43. Cf. Ambrose, *Expositio Psalmi CXVIII*, 14.2.

44. Lacuna.

45. Cf. Hilary, *In Mt* 24.10.

46. The baptismal interpretation of this passage in John 5 is common in the fathers. Cf. Tertullian, *De Baptismo* 5, 6; Cyprian, *Ad Quirinum testimonia adversus Judaeos* 3.27; Ep 13.2; Ambrose, *De mysteriis* 22–23.

47. A textual variant adopted in the SC edition reads "wills."

48. Cf. Cyprian, *Ad Fortunatum*, Prol. 4.

49. Cf. Cyprian, *Ad Quirinum testimonia adversus Judaeos* 3.27.

50. Cf. Ambrose, *De Sacramentis* 1.5–6 (*De mysteriis* 2).

51. Cf. Ambrose, *Expositio Psalmi CXVIII*, 3.19.

52. Cf. Ambrose, *De Spiritu Sancto* 1, Prol 2–3.

53. Judges 6 does not record that Gideon washed the feet of the angel of the Lord, as is recorded of Abraham in Gen 18:4. Ambrose does, however, associate Gideon with Abraham in this respect (see *De Spiritu Sancto* 1, Prol 15). Possibly a rabbinic tradition is being reflected here. Chromatius likely depends on Ambrose, as there are a number of points of contact between his homily and Ambrose's discussion.

54. Cf. Ambrose, *De Spiritu Sancto* 1, Prol 5.

55. Origen, *Homiliae in Judices* 9.2, says, "For indeed the 300 are they who multiply one hundred times three and exhibit the number of the perfect Trinity, under which number census is taken of the whole army of Christ, in which army we should wish that we also may be worthy to be included."

Origen, *Sermons on Judges*, trans. E. Dively Lauro, FOTC 119 (Washington, DC: The Catholic University of America Press, 2010), 117.

56. Cf. Ambrose, *De mysteriis* 31–32.

57. Cf. Ambrose, *De Spiritu Sancto* 1, Prol 12.

58. Cf. ibid., 1, Prol 15.

59. Cf. ibid., 1, Prol 18.

60. Cf. Hippolytus of Rome, *Trad apost* 4.

61. Aquileia was exposed to incursions from "barbarians." In the winter of 401–402, an army of Goths led by Alaric crossed the Julian Alps into Italy. For the fourth time in his life, Chromatius saw a civil war at the gates of his city. Alaric bypassed the city and moved deeper into Italy. Chromatius's present sermon, delivered Easter morning 402, seems to have been given a few months after this event, while Alaric and his army were still at large in the region. Alaric eventually sacked Rome on August 24, 410, and died a few months later. Cf. J. H. W. G. Liebeschuetz, *Barbarians and Bishops: Army, Church, and State in the Age of Arcadius and Chrysostom* (New York: Oxford University Press, 1990).

62. Cf. Ambrose, *Hexaemeron libri sex* 1.4.13.

63. Jerome correctly disputes this derivation of *Pascha* from *passio*. In his *Commentary on Matthew* 26.1–2, Jerome writes, "In Hebrew the Passover is called *Phase*. The name derives not from the word passion [*passio*], as the majority think, but from passing [*transitus*], because the destroyer, upon seeing the blood on the doors of the Israelites, passed through and did not strike them [cf. Exod 12:13]." *St. Jerome: Commentary on Matthew*, trans. Thomas P. Scheck, FOTC (Washington, DC: Catholic University of America Press, 2008), 291–92.

64. *Conspersio* can mean both sprinkling and lump of dough. Cf. Tertullian, *Adversus Marcionem* 4.24.

65. Cf. Gaudentius of Brescia, Tr 7.20.

66. Chromatius here cites John 3:5–6 according to the version of saint Ambrose in *De Spiritu Sancto* 3.10, which adds "for God is spirit" to "that which is born of flesh." In the previous sermon, Chromatius had cited the biblical passage in the Aquileian version without the addition. The CCSL editors therefore have placed the added words here in angle brackets.

67. Cf. Ambrose, *De Spiritu Sancto* 2.6–7.

68. Cf. Hilary, *In Mt* 33.3; Ambrose, *Expositio Evangelii secundum Lucam* 10.104–105.

69. Cf. ibid., 10.105.

70. Cf. ibid., 10.106.

71. Cf. Origen, *In Jesu Nave homiliae xxvi* 8.3; Ambrose, *Expositio Evangelii secundum Lucam* 10.111; In Ps 118.4.

72. Cf. Rufinus, *Commentarius in symbolum apostolorum* 12.

73. Cf. Ambrose, *Expositio Evangelii secundum Lucam* 10.111, 109, 114; Cyprian, *Quod idola dii non sint* 7.

74. Origen, *Commentarium in evangelium Matthaei* 127 and the early Jerome, *Commentariorum in Epistulam ad Ephesos libri III* 5.14 also record this tradition in agreement with Chromatius. According to A. Plummer, *An Exegetical Commentary on the Gospel according to Matthew* (London: Robert Scott, 1911), 394, this tradition is not likely to have been pre-Christian, but was no doubt Jewish Christian, to bring the first Adam into contact with the Second. Jerome later rejected the tradition, *Commentary on Matthew* 27:33: "This interpretation is attractive and soothing to the ear of the people, but it is not true. For outside the city and outside the gate there are places in which the heads of the condemned are cut off. This is where they took the name 'of the skull' [*Calvariae*], that is, it refers to the skulls of the decapitated."

75. Cf. Ambrose, *Expositio Evangelii secundum Lucam* 10.95–96; *Enarrationes in XII Psalmos davidicos* 61.13; Hilary, *In Mt* 32.6.

76. A revised Latin text for this sermon was published by R. Étaix, "Nouvelle edition des sermons XXI–XXII de saint Chromace d'Aqulée," *Revue Bénedictine* 92 (1982): 105–10. I have translated the older CCSL text.

77. For a study of Chromatius's reception of John, see Francesco Pieri, "Chromatius and the Apocalypse of John," in *Chromatius of Aquileia and His Age: Proceedings of the International Conference Held in Aquileia 22–24 May 2008*, ed. Pier Beatrice and Alessio Peršič (Turnhout: Brepols, 2011), 485–501.

78. Cf. Peter Chrysologus, *Sermo* 170.

79. F. Pieri ("Chromatius and the Apocalypse of John," 492), citing Martine Dulaey, indicates that Chromatius has juxtaposed two different interpretations: one by Vitorinus of Poetovio (the word of God is both sweetness and bitterness for Victorinus because of his persecution), the other by Ambrosiaster (sweetness for the Catholics, bitterness for the heretics and for the incredulity of the synagogue).

80. Arius (260–336) was a priest from Alexandria whose doctrine was condemned at the Council of Nicaea in 325. He asserted that Christ is a creature in the proper sense of that word, and as such does not share in the divine nature. Arius believed that the Father created the Son in time, and, therefore, the Son has not always existed. The notorious Arian affirmation was this. "There was a time when he (the Son) was not (did not exist)." Cf. Arius, *Ep. ad Alex.*; cited by J. N. D. Kelly, *Early Christian Doctrines*, rev. ed. (San Francisco: Harper and Row, 1978), 228. According to M. Simonetti, "Arius," *EEC* 1.77, at first Arius stated (in his letter to Eusebius) that the Son had been created from nothing by the work of the Father; later he avoided speaking like this because of the scandal it caused, and spoke of the Son's generation from the Father. "But he continued to consider this generation as creation."

81. The report on the death of saint John is based on the *Acta Iohannis* 2.1, an apocryphal writing composed in Asia Minor in the second half of the second century. Cf. ANF 8.560–64.

82. The presence of relics of saint John is also attested in *Sermon* 26.

83. A revised Latin text for this sermon was published by R. Etaix, "Nouvelle edition des sermons XXI–XXII de saint Chromace d'Aqulée," *Revue Bénedictine* 92 (1982): 105–10. I have translated the older CCSL text.

84. Notice the freedom taken with v. 23.

85. Cf. Cyprian, *De dominica oratione* 24.

86. Cf. Virgil, *Buc ecl* 4; Cyprian, *Ad Fortunatum,* Prol 3. Pope Benedict XVI calls attention to this passage in *The Fathers of the Church: From Clement of Rome to Augustine of Hippo,* ed. and annot. Joseph T. Lienhard (Grand Rapids: Eerdmans, 2009), 128.

87. Cf. Cyprian, *Ad Fortunatum* 8.16.

88. Cf. Tertullian, *De anima* 41.4; Ambrose, *De Cain et Abel* 1.41; *De institutione virginis* 2.11.

89. Cf. Novatian, *De bono pud* 8–9.

90. Cf. Tertullian, *Adversus Marcionem* 3.18.3.

91. According to the Hebrew, Joseph was sold for twenty pieces of silver.

92. Notice the misattribution.

93. Cf. Cyprian, *De dominica oratatione* 21; Ambrose, *De Helia et Jejunio* 11.40.

94. Cf. Ambrose, Ep 63.79–80.

95. Chromatius uses an unusual word, *kapsakes,* which is normally associated with oil. The LXX of 1 Kings 17:12 uses *hydria* (jar). Gregory Nazianzen uses *kapsakes* in *Carm* 1.2.6.49 (Migne, PG 37.647).

96. Notice the stress on human cooperation and freedom.

97. Concordia was a Roman colony in the Venetian territory. This sermon concerns the consecration of a new church in Concordia, when the town was made a bishopric and was therefore in a position to start the Christianization process throughout its territory. We know from what Chromatius says below that he had begun to build a church in Aquileia earlier than that at Concordia. According to R. Lizzi, "Ambrose's Contemporaries and the Christianization of Northern Italy," *Journal of Roman Studies* 80 (1990): 165, in Aquileia there are actually three Christian buildings, one phase of whose construction can be dated toward the end of the fourth and the beginning of the fifth centuries: the basilica at the Fondo Tullio alla Beligna, S. Giovanni, and the Basilica di Monastero. Lizzi correlates Chromatius's vast construction program with that of Ambrose of Milan, who had been inspired by the famous Apostoleion in Constantinople.

98. Cf. Gaudentius of Brescia, Tr 17; Ambrose, Ep 53.2.

99. *Summus sacerdos* designates the bishop. Cf. Ambrose, *De sacramentis* 2.16; 3.4; *De mysteriis* 2.6; 3.8; Ep 4.1; 10.3; 15.9, 12; 16.3; 53.2.

100. Rufinus of Aquileia observes this in his discussion of the resurrection of this flesh; *Commentarius in symbolum apostolorum* 37; *Apologia adversus Hieronymum* 1.5.

101. Marcion of Sinope in Pontus was reputedly the son of the bishop of Sinope, who came to Rome and founded a heretical sect in the 140s. He

thought out a doctrinal system based on the irreconcilability of justice and grace, law and gospel, Judaism and Christianity, the God of the OT and the Father of Jesus. He posited two deities, a good nonjudicial God (the Father of Jesus) who is not to be feared, and a just but inferior god (the Creator of the world, who is the God of the OT and of the Jews) in whom resides the grounds of fear, anger, severity, judgment, vengeance, and condemnation. Marcion so emphasized the absolute newness of the dispensation brought by Jesus that he repudiated the OT in its entirety and denied that it predicted the coming of Jesus or spoke about the good Father proclaimed by Jesus. Moreover, he taught his followers that the received form of the NT had been corrupted by Judaizing Christians, whom he identifies as the Catholics of his day. He "edited" the Gospel of Luke and ten of Paul's letters and made these documents the canon of his church. But he removed Luke's name from the Gospel material (since Paul was the only apostle Marcion recognized) and excised texts within these writings that he found incompatible with his own preconceived theological system. In this way he endeavored to sever the link between what he regarded as the original core of his new religion and Old Testament Judaism.

102. Manicheus, or Mani/Manes (215–76), was the founder of Manichaeism, which threatened the church for many centuries. The young Augustine was one of its adherents. The originator came from Persia and is reported to have aimed to blend Christianity, Zoroastrianism, and elements of Buddhism together. He preached an extreme dualism of two independent and absolutely opposed eternal principles, that of good and evil. Like Marcion, he denied that Jesus was prophesied in the OT, and said that the good God was characterized by light while the material world was inherently dark and corrupt. Manicheus believed that Jesus and other teachers came to release souls of light from prison in material bodies. The Old Testament was the product of the forces of darkness. He also denied the free choice of the will in salvation. Manichaeism had an unusual capacity for syncretism with other religions. As it spread throughout the Roman Empire, it adapted to certain aspects of Christianity, particularly to the theology of the heretic Marcion, whose cosmology was dualistic, whereas his Christology was permeated by Gnostic elements.

103. Cf. *Acta Thomae* 2.2; ANF 8.535–52.

104. Rufinus witnesses to veneration offered to the relics of the apostle saint Thomas in Edessa. Cf. *Eusebii Historia ecclesiastica a Rufino translata et continuata* 2.5. It is also confirmed by Egeria, *Itiner.* 17.1 (SC, 296), 198 and 19.2, 202.

105. Since his soul was in the underworld.

106. Cf. Hilary, *In Ps* 119.18.

107. Cf. Ambrose, *Hexaemeron libri sex* 1.7.27.

108. Cf. Ambrose, *Expositio Evangelii secundum Lucam* 5.70.

109. Cf. Minucius Felix, *Octavius* 37.1; Cyprian, *De lapsis* 2.21–22; *De opere et eleemosynis* 26; Ep 10.2–4; 58.4, 8.

110. Cf. Beda, *Super Act Ap expos* 12.

111. Chromatius has attributed the Lord's words to the apostle.

112. Cf. Gaudentius of Brescia, Tr 5.

113. Chromatius has confused Mary, the mother of John Mark, with Mary the mother of the Lord.

114. Cf. Cyprian, *Ep* 10.5.

115. For a similar christological interpretation of the parable of the mustard seed, see Hilary, *In Mt* 13.4; Ambrose, *Expositio Evangelii secundum Lucam* 7.

116. Cf. Minucius Felix, *Octavius* 37. Pier Franco Beatrice, "The Sign of Jonah: The Paschal Mystery and the Conversion of the Pagans according to Chromatius of Aquileia," in Beatrice and Peršič, *Chromatius of Aquileia and His Age*, 19–64 (at 62), notes this passage and comments, "This observation reveals an important aspect of the pastoral personality of Chromatius. Bishop of the Catholic Church, which in that time was involved in a decisive political and military struggle against Greco-Roman paganism, and did not hesitate to take extreme repressive measures, Chromatius seems to want to confirm the superiority of faith, which springs freely from hearing the Word preached by the apostles, over adoration imposed with the force of weapons or the threat of persecution. Mindful of the recent experience of the Christian martyrs, Chromatius does not hesitate to contrast the earthly emperor who asserts his power with violence but who, being subject to death, cannot give anything after death to a soldier fallen for his cause, with the emperor Christ, sole king of all, who instead grants the reward of endless immortality to the soldiers who have died for him."

117. Chromatius is referring either to his constant instruction, or to a recently delivered homily on the passion and cross of Christ as spiritual medicine.

118. Cf. Paulinus of Nola, *Carmen* 19.352.

119. The Latin is *Cyrinus*. P. Amidon notes that Rufinus carelessly transcribed the Greek *Kurinios* or *Kurenios* as *Cyrinus* in his translation of Eusebius's *Church History*. See Rufinus of Aquileia, *History of the Church*, trans. P. Amidon (Washington, DC: The Catholic University of America Press, 2017), 39n47. It seems that Chromatius follows this transcription and associates the name with the Greek word for "lord."

120. For the same antithetical parallelisms between Christ and Augustus, see Ambrose, *Expositio Evangelii secundum Lucam* 2.37.

121. According to J. Lemarié, SC 164, 161n3, the poll tax was a fiscal system instituted by Diocletian. See W. Seston, *Dioclétien et la Tétrarchie* (Paris, 1946), 277.

122. Ambrose also mentions the martyrs in his commentary on Luke 2:1–3; see *Expositio Evangelii secundum Lucam* 2.36–37.

123. Cf. Ambrose, *Expositio Evangelii secundum Lucam* 2.41, 43, 50.

124. The CCSL text translated here reflects new manuscript discoveries and thus does not match the SC edition. The SC *Sermon* 33 is *Sermon* 36 in CCSL. Cf. Hippolytus of Rome, *Trad apost* 25.

125. Cf. Cyprian, *Ad Quirinum testimonia adversus Judaeos* 3.86.

126. Cf. Chromatius, *Tractate* 12:30.

127. Cf. Cyprian, *Ad Quirinum testimonia adversus Judaeos* 1.20.

128. Cyprian Ep 70.2; 73.4–5; 69.1; 74.11–12.

129. Cf. *Tractate* 12.

130. Cf. Novatian, *De bono pud* 9.1.

131. Cf. Cyprian, *De habitu virginum* 15.

132. Cf. ibid.

133. In the manuscript tradition, this fragment is added as an ending to *Sermons* 8, 33. With the restoration of *Sermon* 33, the paragraph has been separated and moved here.

134. The bracketed text was inserted by the manuscript compiler to substitute for the (now lost) beginning of the sermon. It comes from Epiphanius Latinus, *Interpretatio evangeliorum* 46, ed. A. Erikson (Lund, 1939), 110.

135. Cf. Pseudo-Clement, *Ep. ad Iacobum Rufino interpete* 14 (PG 2.49–50); Tertullian, *De baptismo* 12.7.

136. Cf. Ambrose, *De Helia et ieiunio* 4.9; *De excessu fratris sui Satyri* 2.37–39; *De sacramentis* 2.17; *Expositio Evangelii secundum Lucam* 7.110; *De Cain et Abel* 2.10.35.

137. Apparently cited from memory.

138. In treating death as a remedy rather than a punishment, Chromatius shows himself to be a disciple of Ambrose and Origen. Cf. H. C. Puech and P. Hadot, "L'entretien d'Origène avec Héraclide et le commentaire de saint Ambroise sur l'Évangile de saint Luc," *Vigiliae Christianae* 13 (1959): 204–5; Ambrose, *De excessu fratris sui Satyri*, 2.37–39; *De sacramentis.*, 2.17; *Expositio Evangelii secundum Lucam*, 7.110; *De Cain et Abel*, 2.10.35.

139. Cf. Cyprian, *De catholicae ecclesiae unitate* 24.580–83; Hilary, *In Mt* 4.3.

140. Cf. Cyprian, *De dominica oratione* 2–4, 12–13, 31; Hilary, *In Mt* 5.1; Tertullian, *De oratione* 1.1; 3.4, 19; 6.2; 8.1.

141. We recall that Aquileia was a wealthy and cosmopolitan port city with thriving trade.

142. Cf. Ambrose, *Expositio Evangelii secundum Lucam* 5.55.

Tractates on Matthew

1. I have translated the Latin text found in *Chromatii Aquileiensis Opera*, ed. R. Étaix and J. Lemarié, CCSL, 9A (Turnholti: Brepols, 1974). Both R. Étaix and J. Lemarié edited the *Tractates*.

2. I found a translation of Chromatius's preface by Stephen C. Carlson posted at http://www.tertullian.org/fathers/chromatius_prologue_matthew_01.htm. My new translation was greatly facilitated by consulting Carlson's excellent work.

3. Cf. Eusebius, *HE* 3.18.1.

4. Cf. Chromatius, *Sermon* 22.

5. Cf. Irenaeus, *Adversus Haereses* 3.1.1.

6. To my knowledge, no such sermon survives.

7. Cf. Victorinus Petovionensis, *In Apocalupsin* 4.4.

8. Cf. Chromatius, *Sermon* 15.

9. Cf. Jerome, *Commentarium Matthhaeum libri IV*, Prol.

10. Chromatius's treatment of the prefiguration of the four Gospels in Scripture is more detailed than any church father. As early as Irenaeus, *Adversus haereses* 3.11.8 (ANF 1.428), the creatures in Ezekiel's vision (Ezek 1.10; cf. Rev 4.7) were applied to the four evangelists. Chromatius follows Irenaeus, who understood the lion, calf, man, and eagle to refer to John, Luke, Matthew, and Mark, respectively. It is noteworthy, however, that with the exception of identifying the calf with Luke's Gospel, there was no agreement among the fathers concerning the referents. For Augustine (*Harmony of the Four Gospels* 1.9), they represent Matthew, Luke, Mark, and John, respectively. Jerome (*Commentarium in Matthaeum libri IV*, Pref) has them refer to Mark, Luke, Matthew, and John.

11. Cf. Irenaeus, *Adversus Haereses* 3.2.8; Victorinus Petovionensis, *In Apocalupsin* 4.

12. Cf. Irenaeus, *Adversus Haereses* 3.2.8; Victorinus Petovionensis, *In Apocalupsin* 4.

13. Victorinus Petovionensis, *In Apocalupsin* 4; Ambrose, *Expositio Evangelii secundum Lucam*, Prol 8.

14. Cf. Irenaeus, *Adversus Haereses* 3.2.8.

15. Cf. Pref 5.

16. Cf. Ambrose, *Expositio Evangelii secundum Lucam*, 3.7–8, 10.

17. Cf. Hilary, *In Mt* 1.2; Jerome, *Commentarium in Matthaeum libri IV*, 1.

18. Cf. Hilary, *In Mt* 1.2.

19. Cf. ibid., 1.1; Jerome *Commentarium in Matthaeum libri IV*, 1.

20. Cf. Pref 7.

21. Cf. Hilary, *In Mt* 1.1; Ambrose, *Expositio Evangelii secundum Lucam*, 3.13.

22. Cf. Hilary, *In Ps* 66.4; 118.11.1; 118.21.7.

23. Cf. ibid., 65.12.

24. Cf. Hilary, *De mysteriis* 2.5.

25. A later scribe adds to the manuscript in the bracketed space: "shall conceive and bear a son and they shall call his name Emmanuel which is interpreted God with us."

26. Cf. Ambrose, *Expositio Evangelii secundum Lucam* 4.7.

27. Cf. *Tractate* 1.6.

28. Gregory of Nyssa, in *De virginitate* 19 (NPNF2, 5.364–65), thinks that Miriam's virginity is possibly implied by the fact that she danced with the virgins and is known as the "sister of Aaron," not from her husband. It is also suggested by the timbrel she uses in Exod 15:20. He writes, "But besides other things the action of Miriam the prophetess also gives rise to these surmisings of ours. Directly the sea was crossed she took in her hand a dry and sounding timbrel and conducted the women's dance. By this timbrel the story may mean to imply virginity, as first perfected by Miriam; whom indeed I would believe to be a type of Mary the mother of God. Just as the timbrel emits a loud sound because it is devoid of all moisture and reduced to the highest degree of dryness, so has virginity a clear and ringing report amongst men because it repels from itself the vital sap of merely physical life. Thus, Miriam's timbrel being a dead thing, and virginity being a deadening of the bodily passions, it is perhaps not very far removed from the bounds of probability that Miriam was a virgin."

29. Cf. Ambrose, *Expositio Evangelii secundum Lucam*, 2.6.

30. Cf. ibid., 2.45, 48.

31. *Gentes* can be translated as "nations" or "Gentiles."

32. Cf. Ambrose, *Expositio Evangelii secundum Lucam*, 2.48.

33. Cf. ibid.

34. Cf. Chromatius, *Sermon* 32.

35. For Photinus, see n. at *Sermon* 11.4.

36. Cf. Hilary, *In Mt* 1.5; Ambrose, *Expositio Evangelii secundum Lucam* 2.44.

37. Cf. Ambrose, *Expositio Evangelii secundum Lucam* 2.46.

38. Cf. Chromatius, *Sermon* 10; 14.

39. This must refer to Photinus's doctrine.

40. Lit. "arrangement of the reading."

41. Cf. Chromatius, *Sermon* 3.

42. Cf. Ambrose, *Expositio Evangelii secundum Lucam* 2.75.

43. Or "begin with my sanctuary."

44. Lit. "greater."

45. Cf. Hilary, *In Ps* 59.12.

46. The CCSL critical edition introduces a more precise enumeration in *Tractates* 12, 13, 17–31, which I have replicated.

47. Cf. Hilary, *In Mt* 2.5.

48. Cf. Chromatius, *Sermon* 34.

49. Cf. Chromatius, *Sermon* 1.

50. Cf. Hilary, *In Mt* 2.6.

51. Cf. Origen, *Homiliae in Lucam* 19.3.

52. Cf. Ambrose, *Expositio Evangelii secundum Lucam* 4.18.

53. Cf. ibid., 4.19.

54. Cf. Hilary, *In Mt* 3.1.

55. Cf. Cyril of Jerusalem, *Catechesis* 4.21: "The soul determines its own state. Though the devil can tempt you, he can't force you against your will, for he has not power to do so. He represents to you the thought of fornication; if you choose, you consent; if you don't choose, you don't consent. For if you were a fornicator by necessity, why did God prepare hell? If you lived justly by nature and not by choice, why has God prepared indescribable rewards? A sheep is gentle, but it is never rewarded for its gentleness, for it possesses its gentleness not by choice but by nature." E. Yarnold, trans., *Cyril of Jerusalem* (London: Routledge, 2000), 104.

56. Cf. Ambrose, *Expositio Evangelii secundum Lucam* 4.26.

57. Cf. ibid., 5.44; Jerome, *Commentarium in Matthaeum libri IV*, 1.

58. Cf. Ambrose, *Hexaemeron libri sex* 5.6.16.

59. *Sanus.* The citation above read *salvus* (save).

60. The citation above omitted "fish."

61. Cf. Chromatius, *Sermon* 31.

62. Cf. ibid.

63. St. Leo the Great used this *Tractate* in his own Tr. 95 (CCL 138A, pp. 582–90). Cf. Chromatius, *Sermon* 41.

64. Surely St. Jerome is correct when, in *Commentarium in Matthaeum libri IV*, on Matt 5:1, he writes, "Some of the more simple brothers think, in accordance with the letter, that it was on the Mount of Olives that he taught the Beatitudes and the other things which follow. This is hardly the case. For from what precedes and what follows, the location is shown to be in Galilee. In my opinion it is either Tabor or some other high mountain. After all, after he finished his words, it immediately follows: 'Now when he had entered Capernaum.'" St. Jerome: Commentary on Matthew, trans. Thomas P. Scheck, FOTC (Washington, DC: Catholic University of America Press, 2008), 75. M. Williams, "Chromatius and Jerome on Matthew," in *Chromatius of Aquileia and His Age*, ed. Pier Franco Beatrice and Alessio Peršič (Turnhout: Brepols, 2011), 193–226, at 207, says that it hard to imagine Jerome writing this passage with Chromatius in mind. She thinks that this is evidence that Jerome and Chromatius wrote simultaneously in late 397 or early 398, "or, what seems to me more plausible, that Chromatius saw no need to treat Jerome's work as authoritative—indeed, that he felt free to disregard it entirely."

65. Cf. Chromatius, *Sermon* 5.

66. Cf. ibid.

67. Cf. Chromatius, *Sermon* 39.

68. Cf. Hilary, *In Mt* 4.4; Chromatius, *Sermon* 39.

69. Cf. Hilary, *In Mt* 4.3; Chromatius, *Sermon* 39.

70. Cf. Hilary, *In Mt* 4.7.

71. Notice the slight paraphrase, as is usual for Chromatius.

72. It appears to me that Chromatius applied his own principles in his (unsuccessful) effort to reconcile Jerome and Rufinus. He won over Rufinus to obedience to these principles but not Jerome.

73. Cf. Chromatius, *Sermon* 39.
74. Cf. Pliny, *Naturalis historia* 31.77.
75. Cf. Hilary, *In Mt* 4.13.
76. Cf. ibid., 4.14–15.
77. I am not certain about the meaning of this sentence.
78. "Without reason" was not found in the lemma.
79. Cf. Hilary, *In Mt* 4.17.
80. Cf. Chromatius, *Sermon* 23.
81. Cf. Hilary, *In Mt* 4.19.
82. *A ssertio.* Interestingly the first meaning of this word in *Lewis & Short's Latin Dictionary* is "a formal declaration that one is a freeman or a slave."
83. Cf. Origen, *Homiliae in Lucam* 35.5.
84. Williams, "Chromatius and Jerome on Matthew," 219, observes on this passage, "Clearly, there is considerable, if not complete overlap among the range of interpretations of this passage that were known to Chromatius and Jerome. Yet it is equally evident that each of our two commentators feels free to come to his own evaluation of those interpretive possibilities, and each of them sees his own authority as an interpreter as equal to that of his sources, whether individually or collectively."
85. Cf. Chromatius, *Tractate* 56.
86. Cf. Hilary, *In Mt* 4.21.
87. Cf. Chromatius, *Tractate* 31, 56.
88. Cf. Tertullian, *Ad uxorem* 1.2.3. On the Manichean heresy, see the note at *Sermon* 26.4.
89. Cf. Hilary, *In Mt* 4.23.
90. Cf. ibid., 4.24.
91. Cf. ibid., 5.1.
92. Cf. Cyprian, *De dominica oratione* 4.
93. Cf. ibid., 5.
94. Cf. Tertullian, *De oratione* 17.4.
95. Cf. Cyprian, *De dominica oratione* 6.
96. Cf. Chromatius, *Sermon* 40.
97. Cyprian, *De dominica oratione* 2.
98. Cf. ibid., 11.
99. Cf. Tertullian, *De oratione* 2.1.
100. Cf. Cyprian, *De dominica oratione* 11.
101. Notice the misattribution.
102. Cf. Cyprian, *De dominica oratione* 12.
103. Cf. Tertullian, *De oratione* 2.1.
104. Cf. ibid., 5.1; Cyprian, *De dominica oratione* 13.
105. Cf. Tertullian, *De oratione* 5.1.
106. Cyprian, *De dominica oration* 14–15.
107. Cf. ibid., 17.
108. Cf. Tertullian, *De oratione* 6.3; Cyprian, *De dominica oratione* 19.

109. Cf. Cyprian, *De dominica oratione* 19.
110. Ibid., 18.
111. Ibid., 22.
112. Cf. Tertullian, *De oratione* 7.1; Cyprian, *De dominica oratione* 23.
113. Cyprian, *De dominica oratione* 23.
114. Ibid., 26.
115. Cf. Tertullian, *De oratione* 8.3.
116. Cf. ibid., 9.1–2; 1.6.
117. Cf. Chromatius, *Tractate* 27.
118. Cf. Hilary, *In Mt* 5.2.
119. Cf. ibid., 5.2.
120. Cf. Chromatius, *Sermon* 6.
121. Cf. Chromatius, *Tractate* 23.
122. Due to the liquid in their shells when they are hatched?
123. Cf. Hilary, *In Mt* 5.10.
124. Cf. ibid., 5.11; Ambrose, *Expositio Evangelii secundum Lucam* 7.126–29.
125. Cf. Hilary, *In Mt* 5.12.
126. Cf. Tertullian, *De oratione* 6.3.
127. Cf. Hilary, *In Mt* 6.2.
128. Cf. Chromatius, *Sermon* 6.
129. Cf. Ambrose, *Expositio Evangelii secundum Lucam* 7.49.
130. See note on Photinus at *Sermon* 11.4.
131. An important city of lower Pannonia, now Mitrovitz.
132. See note on Arius at *Sermon* 21.3.
133. Sabellius was condemned at Rome in 220 by Callistus as an exponent of patripassian monarchianism, that is, the view that the Father suffered death on the cross. His origins are uncertain. His thought extended the original patripassian doctrine to include the Holy Spirit: one sole God is manifested as Father in the OT, as Son in the incarnation, as Holy Spirit poured out upon the apostles at Pentecost. *Patripassians* means "those who say the Father suffered." Sabellius apparently taught that "Father," "Son," and "Spirit" were successive modes or operations of God, who subsists in one person only. They were also called modalist monarchians.
134. Cf. Hilary, *In Ps* 1.14.
135. Cf. Ambrose, *Expositio Evangelii secundum Lucam* 5.2.
136. Cf. ibid., 5.3.
137. Cf. ibid., 5.8; Hilary, *In Mt* 7.2.
138. Cf. Origen, *Homiliae in Lev* 8.10.
139. Cf. Hilary, *In Mt* 7.4.
140. Cf. ibid., 7.7.
141. Cf. ibid., 7.10.
142. Cf. Ambrose, *Expositio Evangelii secundum Lucam* 7.32.
143. Cf. Hilary, *In Mt* 7.10.
144. Cf. ibid., 7.11.

145. Cf. ibid.

146. Cf. Ambrose, *Expositio Evangelii secundum Lucam* 7.41.

147. Cf. Chromatius, *Sermon* 33.

148. Cf. Hilary, *In Mt* 7.11.

149. Cf. Rufinus, *Commentarius in symbolum apostolorum* 41.

150. The CCSL editors judge the bracketed text as corrupt.

151. Cf. Hilary, *In Mt* 7.11.

152. This *Tractate* appeared as Homily 23 of the *Opus imperfectum in Math*, PG 56, 754–56, wrongly attributed to John Chrysostom [= Ps-Origenes, *Hom. in Mt* 3.1 (GCS 41, p. 257)]. I was able to consult the English translation by James A. Kellerman, *Incomplete Commentary on Matthew (Opus imperfectum)*, 2 vols., Ancient Christian Texts (Downers Grove, IL: InterVarsity 2010), 2:429–32.

153. Cf. Chromatius, *Sermon* 37.

154. Cf. Chromatius, *Sermon* 25.

155. Cf. Chromatius, *Sermon* 37.

156. Cf. Chromatius, *Sermon* 24.

157. Cf. Hilary, *In Mt* 7.9.

158. Cf. Tertullian, *De baptismo* 12.7.

159. Cf. Hippolytus, *De antichristo* 59.

160. Cf. Ambrose, *De virginitate* 18.118–19.

161. Cf. Hilary, *In Ps* 118.11.

162. Cf. Hilary, *In Mt* 8.4; Ambrose, *Expositio Evangelii secundum Lucam* 6.44.

163. Cf. Hilary, *In Mt* 8.4; Ambrose, *Expositio Evangelii secundum Lucam* 6.50, 52.

164. Cf. Hilary, *In Mt* 8.5.

165. Cf. ibid., 8.7.

166. Notice how Chromatius's understanding of election is indeed based in the free and gratuitous divine initiative and graciousness; yet it presupposes the antecedent condition of faith in the person chosen, and the meritorious disposition of recognizing one's own infirmities and unworthiness.

167. Cf. Chromatius, *Sermon* 31.

168. Cf. Hilary, *In Mt* 9.2.

169. Cf. Gaudentius of Brescia, *Tractate* 8.50–51.

170. Cf. Ambrose, *Expositio Evangelii secundum Lucam* 6.58.

171. Chromatius omits from his citation of the Old Latin "of all the languages of the nations," but he refers to these words in his exposition below.

172. Cf. Ambrose, *Expositio Evangelii secundum Lucam* 6.57.

173. Cf. Chromatius, *Sermon* 27.

174. Cf. ibid.

175. Cf. ibid.

176. Words are missing, which the CCSL editors conjecture to be the following: "is a figure of the synagogue of the Jews. It once suffered from a flow of its own blood."

177. It appears that Chromatius interprets the Book of Revelation as describing events that are still to be accomplished in the future, not as symbols that pertain to the church age.

178. Cf. Ambrose, *Expositio Evangelii secundum Lucam* 6.63.

179. Cf. Jerome, *Commentarium in Matthaeum libri IV*, 1.

180. Cf. Hilary, *In Mt* 9.9.

181. The CCSL text reads, *ut merito † his fides vel a suis † eo tempore potuisset haberi?* The editors posit that the text is corrupt here.

182. Cf. Hilary, *In Mt* 12.11.

183. Cf. Hilary, *In Ps* 143.4.

184. Cf. Chromatius, *Sermon* 33.

185. Cf. Chromatius, *Sermon* 35.48.

186. Cf. Chromatius, *Tractate* 49.

187. Cf. Cyprian, *De catholicae ecclesiae unitate* 18.

188. Cf. Ambrose, *Expositio Evangelii secundum Lucam* 7.121.

189. Cf. Hilary, *In Mt* 12.17.

190. According to Irenaeus, *Adversus haereses* 1.26.2, the Ebionites were a Judaizing heresy that used only Matthew's Gospel. They repudiated Paul as an apostate from the law, rejected the virgin birth of Christ, and insisted that the law of Moses (including circumcision) had to be kept in order to achieve salvation. See also Eusebius, *HE* 3.27. They probably were named from the Hebrew word for "poor" (*ebion*) because of their physical poverty or their attachment to the Beatitude "Blessed are the poor" (though Eusebius says that their name arose "because of the poor and mean opinions they held about Christ"). Later heresiologists (Tertullian, *De praescriptione haereticorum* 33; Epiphanius, *Panarion* 30.17; Rufinus's Origen, *Origenis Commentarius in epistulam ad Romanos* 3.11.2) adopted the apparently mistaken view that the sect was founded by a heretic named Ebion, and this view became standard.

191. Cf. Hilary, *De Trinitate* 7.13.

192. Lit. "sows over."

193. Cf. Chromatius, *Sermon* 2.

194. Valentinus, the Gnostic heretic of the second century, denied the resurrection of the flesh altogether, as did the Manichaeans. Cf. Rufinus, *Commentarius in symbolum apostolorum* 41.

195. Cf. Ambrose, *Expositio Evangelii secundum Lucam* 5.43.

196. Cf. Hilary, *In Mt* 14.14.

197. Cf. ibid., 14.15.

198. Cf. ibid.

199. Cf. ibid., 14.16.

200. The CCSL text has *ad* (to) here, which I take to be a mistake for *a* (from).

201. Cf. Tertullian, *De oratione* 14.

202. Cf. Novatian, *De cibis iudaicis* 2.11; 3.7–12.

203. Cf. Origen, *Homiliae in Lev* 7.6.

204. Tertullian describes Marcion in this way. *Adversus Marcionem Praef*, Bk. 1.

205. Cf. the Nicene Creed.

206. Pier Franco Beatrice, "The Sign of Jonah: The Paschal Mystery and the Conversion of the Pagans according to Chromatius of Aquileia;" in Beatrice and Peršič, *Chromatius of Aquileia and His Age*, 19–64, at 41, concludes from a comparison between Chromatius and his predecessors and contemporaries (Hilary, Ambrose, Rufinus, Jerome, Zeno) that Chromatius "shares the same background in exegesis, homiletics, and catechesis, but he reworks it in his own way. So it would appear that a precise relationship of literary dependence of Chromatius on one or more of these authors can be excluded."

207. *Vivorum.* Should this be *virorum,* "men," in accordance with the LXX?

208. This portion of Chromatius's *Tractate* on Matt 12:38–41 does not survive.

209. *Death* (*mors*) is feminine in Latin.

210. Cf. Hilary, *In Mt* 18:1; Jerome, *Commentarium in Matthaeum libri IV* on Matt 18:1.

211. Cf. Hilary, *In Mt* 18.2.

212. Cf. Chromatius, *Tractate* 23.

213. Cf. Hilary, *In Mt* 4.21.

214. Cf. Chromatius, *Sermon* 6; *Tractates* 23, 31.

215. Cf. Hilary, *In Ps* 124.5–6.

216. Cf. Hilary, *In Mt* 18.7.

217. Cf. ibid., 18.9.

218. Cf. Cyprian, *De catholicae ecclesiae unitate* 12.

219. Cf. ibid., 18; Chromatius, *Tractate* 50.

220. Cf. Hilary, *In Mt* 18.10.

BIBLIOGRAPHY

Primary Works

Ambrose. *Exposition of the Holy Gospel according to Saint Luke, with Fragments on the Prophecy of Esaias.* Translated by Theodosia Tomkinson. Etna, CA: Center for Traditionalist Orthodox Studies, 2003.

———. *Traité sur l Évangile de S. Luc.* Translated by Gabriel Tissot. Paris: Editions du Cerf, 1971.

Chromatius. *Chromatii Aquileiensis Opera.* Edited and translated by R. Étaix and J. Lemarié. CCSL, 9A. Turnholti: Brepols, 1974.

———. *Sermons.* Edited by Joseph Lemarié. Translated by H. Tardif. SC vols. 154 and 164. Paris: Les Editions du Cerf, 1969, 1971.

———. *Spicilegium ad Chromatii Aquileiensis Opera.* Edited and translated by R. Étaix and J. Lemarié. CCSL, 9A supplementum. Turnholti: Brepols, 1977.

Chromatius and Raymond Etaix. "Nouvelle edition des sermons XXI–XXII de saint Chromace d'Aquilée." *Revue Bénedictine* 92 (1982): 105–10.

Hilary of Poitiers. *Commentary on Matthew.* Translated by D. H. Williams. FOTC 125. Washington, DC: Catholic University of America Press, 2012.

Jerome. *Commentary on Matthew.* Translated by Thomas P. Scheck. FOTC 117. Washington, DC: Catholic University of America Press, 2008.

Origen. *Homilies on Leviticus.* Translated by Gary Wayne Barkley. FOTC 83. Washington, DC: The Catholic University of America Press, 1990.

Simonetti, M., ed. *Ancient Christian Commentary on Scripture: Matthew 1—13, Matthew 14—28.* 2 vols. Downers Grove, IL: InterVarsity 2002.

Secondary Works

Auwers, Jean-Marie. "Chromace d'Aquilée et le texte biblique." In *Chromatius of Aquileia and His Age: Proceedings of the International Conference Held in Aquileia 22–24 May 2008*, edited by Pier Beatrice and Alessio Peršič, 343–59. Turnhout: Brepols, 2011.

Basso, Patrizia. "Aquileia al crocevia di strade e di rotte maritime." In *Cromazio di Aquileia: al crocevia di genti e religioni*, edited by Sandro Piussi, 56–59. Milan: Silvana Editoriale, 2008.

Bastit-Kalinowska, Agnès. "Les *Tractatus in Matthaeum* de Chromace et leur lecture de l'évangile de Matthieu." In Beatrice and Peršič, *Chromatius of Aquileia and His Age*, 425–67.

Beatrice, Pier Franco. "Chromatius and Jovinus at the Synod of Diospolis: A Prosopographical Inquiry." *JECS* 22, no. 3 (Fall 2014): 437–64.

———. "The Sign of Jonah: The Paschal Mystery and the Conversion of the Pagans according to Chromatius of Aquileia." In Beatrice and Peršič, *Chromatius of Aquileia and His Age*, 19–64.

———. *The Transmission of Sin: Augustine and his Sources.* Translated by Adam Kamesar. New York: Oxford University Press, 2013. Originally published in Italian in 1978.

Beatrice, Pier Franco, and Alessio Peršič, eds. *Chromatius of Aquileia and His Age: Proceedings of the International Conference Held in Aquiliea, 22–24 May 2008.* Instrumenta Patristica et Mediaevalia 57. Turnhout: Brepols, 2011.

Benedict XVI, Pope. *The Fathers of the Church: From Clement of Rome to Augustine of Hippo.* Edited and annotated by Joseph T. Lienhard. Grand Rapids, MI: Eerdmans, 2009.

Bovon, Francois. *De Vocatione Gentium: Histoire de l'interpétation d'Act. 10,1–11,18 dans les six premiers siècles, Beiträge zur Geschichte der Biblicschen Exegese* 8. Tübingen: Mohr Siebeck, 1967.

Brändle, Rudolf. "Chromatius und Johannes Chrysostomus: Zwei Bischöfe im Spannungsfeld zwischen Ost und West." In Beatrice and Persic, *Chromatius of Aquileia and His Age*, 253–65.

Cain, Andrew. *The Letters of Jerome: Asceticism, Biblical Exegesis, and the Construction of Christian Authority in Late Antiquity.* New York: Oxford University Press, 2009.

Clark, Elizabeth. *The Origenist Controversy: The Cultural Construction of an Early Christian Debate.* Princeton, NJ: Princeton University Press, 1992.

De Bruyn, Theodore. *Pelagius's Commentary on St Paul's Epistle to the Romans.* Oxford: Clarendon Press, 1993.

Di Berardino, A. *Patrology.* Vol. 4, *The Golden Age of Latin Patristic Literature.* Allen, TX: Christian Classics.

Duval, Yves-Marie. "Chromace et Jérôme." In *Chromatius episcopus: 388–1988,* 151–83. AAAd 34. Udine: Arti grafiche friulane, 1989.

———. *L'extirpation de l'Arianisme en Italie du Nord et en Occident: Rimini (359/60) et Aquilée (381), Hilaire de Poitiers (367/8) et Ambroise de Milan (397).* Burlington, VT: Ashgate, 1997.

———. *Histoire et historiographie en Occident aux IVe et Ve siècles.* Burlington, VT: Ashgate, 1997.

———. "Les Relations doctinales entre Milan et Aquilée Durant la seconde moitié du IVe siècle: Chromace d'Aqulé et ambroise de Milan." In *Aquileia et Milano,* 188–92. AAAd 4. Udine: Arti grafiche friulane, 1973.

García-Sánchez, Carlos. "Was Pelagius Influenced by Chromatius of Aquileia?" In *Studia Patristica.* Vol. 17, part 3, edited by Elizabeth A. Livingstone, 1251–57. Oxford: Pergamon, 1982.

Gryson, R. *Scolies Ariennes sur le concile d'Aquilée.* SC 267. Paris: Cerf, 1980.

Hale Williams, M. *The Monk and the Book: Jerome and the Making of Christian Scholarship.* Chicago: University of Chicago Press, 2006.

Hammond, C. P. "The Last Ten Years of Rufinus's Life and the Date of His Move South from Aquileia." *JTS* n.s. 28 (1977): 372–429.

Hennecke, E., and W. Schneemelcher, eds. *New Testament Apocrypha.* Translated by R. Wilson. 2 vols. Philadelphia: Westminster, 1959.

Kelly, J. N. D. *Golden Mouth. The Story of John Chrysostom—Ascetic, Preacher, Bishop.* Ithaca, NY: Cornell University Press, 1995.

———. *Jerome: His Life, Writings, and Controversies.* New York: Harper & Row, 1975.

Kenny, A. "Was St. John Chrysostom a Semi-Pelagian?" *Irish Theological Quarterly* 27 (1960): 16–29.

Lemarié, Joseph. "Chromatius redivivus." In Beatrice and Peršič, *Chromatius of Aquileia and His Age,* 269–80.

———. "L'iconographie de Saint Chromace d'Aquilée." In *Cromazio di Aquileia: al crocevia di genti e religioni,* edited by Sandro Piussi, 20–35. Milan: Silvana Editoriale, 2008.

———. "Nouvelle edition des sermons XXI–XXII de saint Chromace d'Aqulée." *Revue Bénedictine* 92 (1982): 105–10.

———. "Un 'Tractatus in Matheum' inédit de saint Chromace d'Aquilée." *Revue Bénédictine* 91 (1981): 225–30.

Lizzi, R. "Ambrose's Contemporaries and the Christianization of Northern Italy." *Journal of Roman Studies* 80 (1990): 156–73.

McCue, J. F. "Augustine and the Strange Career of Romans 9:10–29." In *For a Later Generation: The Transformation of Tradition in Israel, Early Judaism, and Early Christianity*, edited by Randal A. Argall, Beverly A. Bow, and Rodney A. Werline, 169–82. Harrisburg, PA: Trinity Press International, 2001.

McEachnie, R. "Constructing Christian Community: The Sermons of Chromatius of Aquileia, 388–407." PhD diss., University of Florida, 2013.

———. "A History of Heresy Past: The Sermons of Chromatius of Aquileia, 388–407." *Church History* 83, no. 2 (June 2014): 273–96.

McLynn, N. *Ambrose of Milan: Church and Court in a Christian Capital.* Berkeley: University of California Press, 1994.

Murphy, Francis. *Rufinus of Aquileia (345–411): His Life and Works.* Washington, DC: Catholic University of America Press, 1945.

Naumowicz, Józef. "Les symbols des quatre Évangiles chez Chromace d'Aquilée et chez les autres auteurs patristiques." In Beatrice and Peršič, *Chromatius of Aquileia and His Age*, 469–84.

Peršič, Alessio. "Fortunaziano, il primo dei Padri Aquileiiesi: destabilis?" In *Cromazio di Aquileia: al crocevia di genti e religioni*, edited by Sandro Piussi, 286–89. Milan: Silvana Editoriale, 2008.

Pieri, Francesco. "Chromatius and the Apocalypse of John." In Beatrice and Peršič, *Chromatius of Aquileia and His Age*, 485–501.

Straw, C. "Chrysostom's Martyrs: Zealous Athletes and the Dangers of Sloth." In *Giovanni Crisostomo Oriente e Occidente tra IV e V seculo*, 521–54. XXXIII Incontro di studiosi dell'antichità Cristiana, Roma 6–8 maggio, 2004. Studia Ephemeridis Augustinianum 93. Rome: Institutum Augustinianum, 2005.

Williams, Daniel. *Ambrose of Milan and the End of the Arian-Nicene Conflicts.* New York: Oxford University Press, 1995.

Williams, Megan. "Chromatius and Jerome on Matthew." In Beatrice and Peršič, *Chromatius of Aquileia and His Age*, 193–226.

GENERAL INDEX

Abbreviations: S = Sermons; Tr = Tractates; Pref = Preface

SCRIPTURE INDEX

ABBREVIATIONS: S = SERMONS; TR = TRACTATES;
PREF = PREFACE

Leviticus

Numbers

Deuteronomy

Joshua

Judges

1 Samuel

2 Samuel

1 Kings

2 Kings

1 Chronicles

Esther

Job

Psalms

Proverbs

John

Acts of the Apostles

2 Peter

1 John

2 John

Revelation